VENTURE CAPITAL DEVELOPMENT IN CHINA 2017

中国创业风险投资发展报告 2017

主　编　胡志坚　张晓原　张志宏　副主编　房汉廷　武夷山　沈文京　郭　戎　张明喜

经济管理出版社
ECONOMY & MANAGEMENT PUBLISHING HOUSE

图书在版编目（CIP）数据

中国创业风险投资发展报告 2017/胡志坚等主编. —北京：经济管理出版社，2017.8
ISBN 978-7-5096-5306-7

Ⅰ. ①中… Ⅱ. ①胡… Ⅲ. ①风险投资—研究报告—中国—2017 Ⅳ. ①F832.48

中国版本图书馆 CIP 数据核字（2017）第 203563 号

组稿编辑：陈 力
责任编辑：陈 力 钱雨荷
责任印制：司东翔
责任校对：雨 千

出版发行：经济管理出版社
（北京市海淀区北蜂窝 8 号中雅大厦 A 座 11 层 100038）
网 址：www. E-mp. com. cn
电 话：(010) 51915602
印 刷：精美彩色印刷有限公司
经 销：新华书店
开 本：880mm×1230mm/16
印 张：15.75
字 数：529 千字
版 次：2017 年 8 月第 1 版 2017 年 8 月第 1 次印刷
书 号：ISBN 978-7-5096-5306-7
定 价：150.00 元

中国创业风险投资发展报告 2017

工作指导委员会

编委会

主编

胡志坚　张晓原　张志宏

副主编

房汉廷　武夷山　沈文京　郭　戎　张明喜

常务编委（按姓氏笔画排序）

丁飞燕	马德庆	方国银	王一军	王永胜
王守仁	王建国	王松奇	王俊艳	王树勋
王秋颖	王振伟	王润田	王朝平	王雄武
王　磊	邓天佐	韦志边	付剑峰	冯治库
卢道真	田维明	白瑞明	龙　飞	刘维华
华裕达	向　兵	孙晓芸	成　功	闫东升
何国杰	宋高堂	寿学平	张乃中	张世杰
张立新	张　华	张　帆	张自强	张建红
张明喜	张俊芳	张　洵	张浩林	张　萌
李文雷	李　庆	李希义	李　恒	李爱民
李银安	李雪婧	杨国荣	沈文京	苏岳辉
陈　千	陈工孟	陈云波	陈　伟	陈　玮
陈晓明	陈海涛	尚朝秋	房德山	罗路兵
胥和平	荆树山	赵　雯	倪振东	唐永明
贾建平	郭　戎	高　兵	崔　颖	黄慰萍
傅丽枫	董　梁	谢　岩	韩　亮	蒲毅葳
路　辉	靳晓云	熊仁章	蔡久田	黎苑楚
魏世杰				

调研分析组

组　　长：郭　戎　　　副组长：张俊芳

执笔分工：

第 1 章　张俊芳　　　第 2 章　李日强

第 3 章　张俊芳　　　第 4 章　魏世杰

第 5 章　朱欣乐　　　第 6 章　李希义

第 7 章　朱欣乐　　　第 8 章　李日强

第 9 章　李日强

附录整理　张俊芳（附录 1、2，4~7）

　　　　　朱欣乐（附录 3）

　　　　　王秋颖（附录 8）

创业风险投资调查员（按姓氏笔画排序）

王子铭	王玥瑛	王　娜	邓　凯	邓韵然
兰定成	田　园	艾　枭	刘　丽	刘　明
刘　森	华巢莘	孙　婷	巩耀亮	朱鹏程
毕朝阳	祁　阳	邢金翠	邢慧婧	宋蜀玉
张小莉	张　健	张　艳	张　捷	张雪梅
张　婷	李红玉	李国源	李昊坤	李　荟
李　哲	李晓鹏	李　根	杨继涛	杨　燕
陈文杨	陈坤鹏	陈　诚	陈　娟	陈　鑫
汪瑞民	周利平	周娴都	林维柒	武　赟
苗　红	侯　璐	姜宁鹏	姜伟琪	胡诗悦
胡　焱	赵　红	赵　婧	郝殿伦	钟家安
钟慧敏	徐东升	徐　佳	徐　茜	徐溪红
徐锦娟	郭璐璐	曹建胜	董　婷	董　键
韩巧娟	缪海波	谭艺平	潘荣翠	潘懿文
薛　润	霍利华			

参与和支持单位（排名不分先后）

科学技术部资源配置与管理司
中国科学技术发展战略研究院
科技部火炬高技术产业开发中心
科技部科技经费监督管理服务中心
国家科技风险事业开发中心
商务部外国投资管理司
国家开发银行投资业务局
中国进出口银行业务开发与创新部
中国社会科学院金融研究中心
中国科技金融促进会
中国台湾创业风险投资商业同业公会
亚洲创业基金期刊集团（中国香港）
中国风险投资研究院
《中国科技投资》杂志社
北京清科创业风险投资顾问有限公司
辽宁大学工商管理学院
北京创业投资协会
北京市科学技术委员会
北京首都科技发展集团公司
天津市创业投资协会
上海市创业投资行业协会
河北省科学技术厅
河北省科学技术情报研究院
河北石家庄高新技术产业开发区科技局
山西省科学技术厅资源配置与管理处
山西省风险投资协会
山西省科技基金发展总公司
内蒙古科技风险基金管理办公室
四川省绵阳高新技术产业开发区创业服务中心
成都生产力促进中心
重庆市科委
重庆市科技创业投资协会
贵州省科学技术厅
云南省科学技术厅
辽宁省科技创业投资协会
辽宁科技创业投资有限公司
贵阳高新区金融办
内蒙古自治区生产力促进中心
北京市科技金融促进会
贵州省科技评估中心
四川省科学技术厅条财处
辽宁省沈阳市科学技术局
辽宁省沈阳科技风险开发事业中心
辽宁省大连市生产力促进中心
大连高新技术产业园区金融工作办公室
吉林省长春市科学技术局
吉林高技术创业服务中心
黑龙江省科学技术厅科研条件与财务处
黑龙江省科力高科技产业投资有限公司
哈尔滨市创业投资协会
湖北省科学技术厅创投引导基金管理中心
湖北省创业投资同业公会
湖北省武汉市科技局
武汉市科技金融创新促进中心
湖北省襄樊高新技术创业服务中心
河南省科学技术厅条财处
湖南省科学技术厅
湖南省科技交流交易中心
山东省科学技术厅
山东省青岛市科技局
青岛生产力促进中心
江苏省创业投资协会
无锡新区科技金融投资集团
江苏省南京市科技局
浙江省科学技术厅计划财务处
浙江省风险投资协会
浙江省杭州市科技局
浙江省宁波市科学技术局
安徽省科学技术厅条财处
安徽省科技成果转化服务中心
江西省科学技术厅条财处
江西省科技金融促进会
福建省高新技术创业服务中心
福建省厦门市科技局
福建省厦门火炬高技术产业开发区管委会
福建省高新技术产权交易所有限公司
广东省风险投资促进会
山东省科技服务发展推进中心
云南省科学技术院
广州风险投资促进会
广东省珠海高新技术创业服务中心
广东省风险投资促进会

成都高新区金融办
四川省高新技术产业金融服务中心
广东省佛山高新区经济发展和科技局
珠海高新区科经局
深圳市创业投资同业公会
海南省科学技术厅
甘肃省科技风险投资有限责任公司
甘肃省兰州高科创业投资担保有限公司
宁夏回族自治区科学技术厅条财处
宁夏回族自治区科学技术厅生产力促进中心
宁波市科技金融服务中心
陕西省科学技术厅科技金融处
甘肃省科技厅条财处
陕西科技控股集团
天津市科学技术委员会
中国风投
陕西省宝鸡高新区高技术创业服务中心
陕西省杨凌农业高新技术产业示范区管委会金融办
陕西省西安高新技术产业开发区管理委员会金融服务办公室
新疆科技项目服务中心
新疆维吾尔自治区科学技术厅高新处
青海省国有科技资产经营管理有限公司
广西科技厅规划财务处
新疆新科源科技风险投资管理有限公司

万钢部长在第十九届中国风险投资论坛上的讲话（代序）

大家下午好！

众所周知，中国风险投资论坛是由前任民建中央主席成思危先生创办的。成思危先生为我国科技创新、风险投资事业发展和资本市场改革大声呼吁、建言献策，践行了“我毕生的抱负就是能为富国强民做点事”的人生追求。

今天，我国的风险投资事业已经取得了飞速的发展，形成了中国特色的发展模式，行业规模仅次于美国。创业投资已经成为中小企业融资的重要渠道，成为破除“融资难、融资贵”困局、提升直接融资水平的主要措施。新兴产业和创新创业企业已经成为创业投资机构关注的主要方向，早期投资、价值投资和创新投资已经成为主流的理念，风险投资已经成为我国民间资本的重要组成部分。

同志们，朋友们，2016 年 5 月 30 日，习近平总书记在全国科技创新大会上发表重要讲话，吹响了建设世界科技强国的号角。2017 年 5 月 14 日，习近平总书记在“一带一路”国际合作高峰论坛上提出，要将“一带一路”建成创新之路，促进科技同产业、科技同金融深度融合，优化创新环境，聚集创新资源。

近年来，我们积极聚集科技创新资源，改革配置方式，推动产业链、创新链、资金链深度融合，引导金融投资、社会资本进入科技创新领域，努力形成多元化、多层次的科技投融资体系，为建设创新型国家打下坚实基础。

2016 年，我国全社会研发支出达到了 1.54 万亿元，比 2012 年增长了 50.5%，占 GDP 的 2.1%，其中企业投入占比达到了 78%；全国技术合同成交额 1.14 万亿元；科技进步贡献率增至 56.2%，这得益于普惠性创新政策的进一步完善和落实?我国高新技术企业已经达到 10.4 万多家，2015 年减免的企业所得税 1150 亿元。研发费用加计扣除减免税收 760 多亿元。据统计，珠江三角洲九个高新区高新技术企业已经达到了 1.9 万家，在全国排名第一位。

创新政策激发了企业创新的内在动力，进一步释放民间投资的活力，将科技型中小企业研发费用加计扣除比例由 50%提高到了 75%。围绕创新创业的科技金融体系正在逐步完善，银行、证券、保险、创投、债券、担保、租赁等在促进科技型中小企业成长和科技成果转化时，不断创新金融产品和服务，共同形成了科技金融发展生态圈。

支持创新创业，还要鼓励和引导社会力量参与国家战略导向的重大研发任务，突破单一财政投入模式，形成多元化投入格局，这意味着多元化聚焦国家战略，多元化开展项目实施和监管，大幅度提高科技创新能力。目前，我们与国务院相关部门和地方政府已经就此达成高度共识。

结合本届论坛主题和近期科技创新工作的重要部署，下面谈五点意见。

1. 不断优化创业投资发展的政策环境

2016 年，国务院出台了《关于促进创业投资持续健康发展的若干意见》，提出培育多元化创业投资主体、加强政府引导和扶持等八个方面二十条具体措施和要求，为新时期的创业投资发展指明了方向，明确了要求，细化了任务，对促进创业投资与“大众创业、万众创新”、科技成果转化、中小企业发展相结合具有重要意义。

文件发布以后，各地方、各部门积极响应、加快行动。财政部、国家税务总局出台创业投资企业和天使投资个人税收优惠试点政策，极大激发了创业投资企业和天使投资者对“双创”的投资热情，引导社会资本投资方向。银监会、科技部、人民银行联合开展投贷联动试点，确定国家开发银行、中国银行等 10 家银行，在北京中关村、上海、天津、武汉等地对科创企业开展“创业投资+银行信贷”的新型融资支撑。目前国家开发银行已经组建专业创业投资公司，开展实际投资。有关部门还将继续研究完善创业投资基金的投资年限与上市后锁定期反向挂钩机制，引导具有长期投资和价值投资理念的创业投资发展，加大服务实体经济的力度。此外，有关部门正在推动成立“中国创业投资协会”，进一步加强创业投资行业规范发展。

在这些已经出台和将要出台的政策基础上，相关部门和地方要研究制定具体落实措施，形成创业投资发展的“政策包”，进一步优化政策环境：一是要体现政策制定的精准性，比如我们会同有关部门制定科技型中小企业评价办法；二是要体现可操作性，政策实施要制订完整的方案，要易于把握，快速落地，使创业投资机构和创新创业企业更好发展；三是要在实施上稳妥起步，积累经验，防范风险，逐步推动；四是希望各地有关部门为创业投资机构在工商登记、税收优惠、业务登记等方面，要加强“放管服”的改革和创新，降低门槛，便利办事，提高服务效能，净化发展环境。

2. 加强创新供给，服务和引导行业发展

近年来，我们推动科技创新资源向创业投资机构开放，开展信息共享和增值服务。科技部正在加强科技成果转化项目库建设，面向社会公布财政性资金支持形成的科技成果，吸引创业投资关注。

我们已经举办了 6 届全国创新创业大赛，参赛企业和团队 3.4 万多家，技术创新水平逐年提高，仅 2016 年的大赛就促进了 40 多亿元的创业投资和 28 亿元的银行信贷支持。科技部与深交所共同打造“中国高新技术科技金融路演平台”，为科技型中小企业与创业投资基金、上市公司开展投资对接。同时，我们组织国家高新区、科技企业孵化器、众创空间采取多种形式和创业投资合作，支持企业改革和规范运作，创业投资和天使投资入驻孵化器将成为新常态。以上工作是要将科技创新目标转化为创业投资的“风口”，将科技计划项目转化为创业投资的“跑道”，将科技园区和孵化器转化为创业投资的“集聚区”，推动创业投资融入科技创新的“大生态圈”。

3. 发挥政府引导基金作用，做合格出资人

根据中央财政科技计划管理改革的要求，在技术创新引导专项中，我们布局设立了国家科技成果转化引导基金、国家中小企业发展基金、国家新兴产业创业投资引导基金，共同践行引导社会资本投资创新创业的使命。目前，国家科技成果转化基金已经批准设立 9 家创业投资子基金，基金总规模达到 173 亿元，其中政府出资 38 亿元，财政资金放大比例为 1：4.5。国家新兴产业创业投资引导基金确定了 3 家管理公司，总规模超过 760 亿元。最近，中央企业国创投资引导基金成立，计划募集基金 1500 亿元，为创业投资基金注入新动能。各级政府科技部门、国家自主创新示范区和高新区设立的科技创业投资公司（基金）已达 550 多家，成为创业投资领域的一支重要力量。

政府引导基金要牢记使命、不忘初衷，要引导市场、不干预市场，要雪中送炭、少锦上添花：一是要体现国家对重大决策的响应与支撑，比如在科技创新 2030 重大项目实施过程中，在人工智能、新材料、量子科学、脑科学等领域，都需要政府引导基金的积极参与；二是要加强对经济欠发达地区和薄弱环节的支持，以政府引导弥补自然禀赋差异，如现代农业产业发展；三是要加强中央设立引导基金之间、中央设立基金与地方设立基金之间的协调联动，开展联合投资、信息共享和共同监管。

4. 加快推进资本市场改革，拓展退出渠道

一个活跃、规范和多层次的资本市场是发展的引擎，通过资本市场能够更加高效配置社会创新资源，加快资本、人才、技术向创新型企业流动和聚集。目前，排队等候 IPO 的企业有近 600 家。我们关注到，有一些企业为避免排队时间过长而选择到海外上市，使国内的投资失去了优质的资源，令人惋惜。

近年来，伴随着科技成果的快速涌现以及“独角兽”企业的兴起，我们也注意到，在一些热点领域已经出现了投资过热的苗头，应该引起关注，建立长期投资的理念。要通过加快创业板的改革，培养一批有专利、有技术、有团队，又符合国家科技发展战略方向的创新型企业，为资本市场注入创新资源，引导社会资本的投向。

5. 引导社会资本参与国家重大研发任务

国家重大研发任务是体现国家战略目标、集成科技资源的重要抓手。目前，国家科技重大专项、国家重点研发计划、国家科技创新 2030 重大项目工程正在加快实施。交通制造、食品、中医药、健康等“十三五”规划也将公布。我们将采取创新投融资机制和模式加快实施重大项目，通过中央和有条件、有优势的地方政府共同合资、联

合管理的方式来组织实施。目前，科技部与广东省共同签署了第一个联动实施、具有广东科技优势和适宜广东生产发展的重点研发计划协议。

我们还将加强与国务院国资委的合作，共同推动中央企业的创新发展，承担重大研发任务，提高科技创新能力；加强与民营企业的合作，鼓励和支持民营企业参与国家科技计划应用示范和共同管理；加强与金融资本的合作，建立专业化的创业投资基金。

女士们、先生们，中共“十八大”以来，党中央、国务院把科技创新作为提高社会生产力和综合国力的战略支撑，摆在国家发展全局的核心位置，深入实施创新驱动发展战略，加快推动我国从科技大国向科技强国迈进。面对新形势、新要求、新任务，我们责任重大。面对世界科技革命和产业变革的迅猛态势，我们比以往任何时候都需要宏大的科技创新力量，需要科技界、金融界、投资界、企业界紧密携手、协同创新。

同志们、朋友们，让我们发动科技创新和金融创新的强大引擎，向世界科技强国的目标乘风破浪、勇往直前！

最后，预祝本届论坛取得圆满成功！谢谢大家！

目 录

摘 要

2016 年中国创业风险投资发展态势
——新动能与新趋势

全国创业风险投资调查写作分析组[①]

2016 年，伴随着中国供给侧结构性改革深入推进、“新三板”分层制度完善，“深港通”开闸，创新创业活动高涨，中国创业风险投资（以下简称“创投”）行业又迎来了丰硕的一年，整个行业在募资、投资、退出方面出现了不同程度的增长，孕育着新的发展机会，新高能资本供给动能正在形成。

1. 2016 年中国创投行业发展的新特征

与前几年相比，总体而言，2016 年中国创投行业发展呈现出以下新特征：

1.1 机构与资本数量持续增长，专业化管理机构大幅增加

2016 年，中国创投行业机构数达到 2045 家，较 2015 年增加 270 家，增长 15.2%。其中，创业风险投资基金 1421 家，较 2015 年增加 110 家，增幅 8.4%；创业风险投资管理机构 624 家，较 2015 增加 160 家，增幅 34.5%；披露当年新募集基金 152 家，新募集基金管理资本 1016.1 亿元（见表 1）。

表 1 中国创业风险投资机构总量、增量（2007~2016）

项目 \ 年份	2007	2008	2009	2010	2011	2012	2013	2014	2015	2016
现存的 VC 机构（家）	383	464	576	867	1096	1183	1408	1551	1775	2045
其中，VC 基金（家）	331	410	495	720	860	942	1095	1167	1311	1421
其中，VC 管理机构（家）	52	54	81	147	236	241	313	384	464	624
当年新募集基金（数）	76	89	135	215	167	146	123	169	197	152
VC 机构增长（%）	11.0	21.1	24.1	50.5	26.4	7.9	19.0	10.2	14.4	15.2

① 中国科学技术发展战略研究院 2016 年“全国创业风险投资调查写作分析组”成员包括：郭戎、张明喜、张俊芳、李希义、魏世杰、朱欣乐、李日强、薛薇等。本报告执笔：张俊芳、张明喜。

一个比较明显的趋势是，创投基金采取委托管理的模式日益盛行，越来越多的基金将其日常管理与投资功能委托到专业的创投管理机构进行管理，2007~2016 年，创投管理机构由 52 家增加到 624 家，增长超过 10 倍。

2016 年，全国创业风险投资管理资本总量达到 8277.1 亿元，较 2015 年增加 1623.8 亿元，增幅为 24.4%；管理资本占 GDP 比重达到 1.11%；基金平均管理资本规模为 4.05 亿元（见表 2）。

表 2　中国创业风险管理资本总额（2007~2016）

项目＼年份	2007	2008	2009	2010	2011	2012	2013	2014	2015	2016
管理资本（亿元）	1112.9	1455.7	1605.1	2406.6	3198.0	3312.9	3573.9	5232.4	6653.3	8277.1
2015 年增长（%）	67.7	30.8	10.3	49.9	32.9	3.6	7.9	31.7	27.2	24.4
基金平均管理资本规模（亿元）	3.36	3.55	3.24	3.34	3.72	3.52	3.26	4.48	4.66	4.05

与国外相比，近年来我国创业风险投资发展迅猛，2016 年创投机构数量与管理资本规模仅次于美国。2016 年，美国创投机构数达到 2460 家（其中，创投基金 1562 家，管理机构 898 家），管理资本总额 3330 亿美元（相当于 22644 亿元），占 GDP 的 1.93%（见图 1、图 2）。

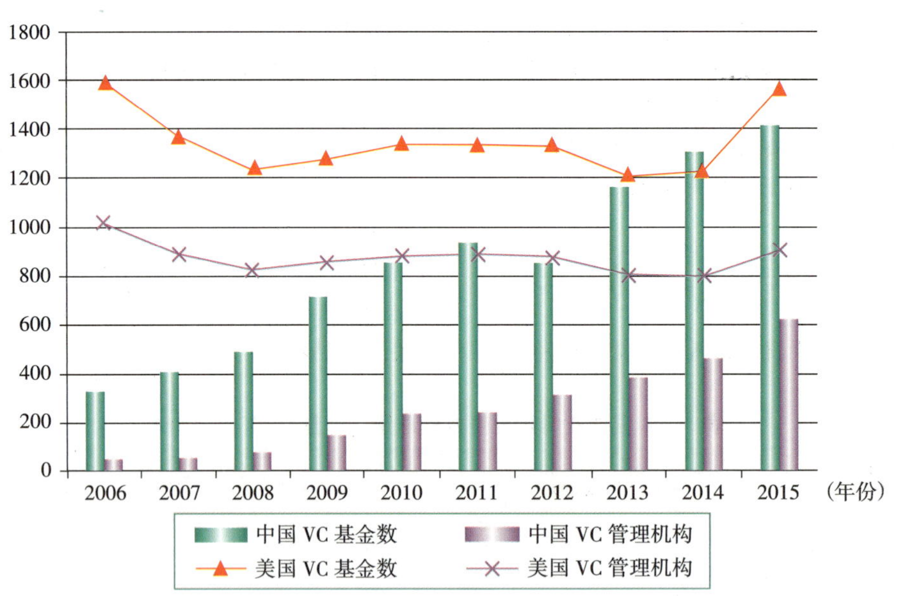

图 1　中美创业风险投资机构数对比（2006~2015）

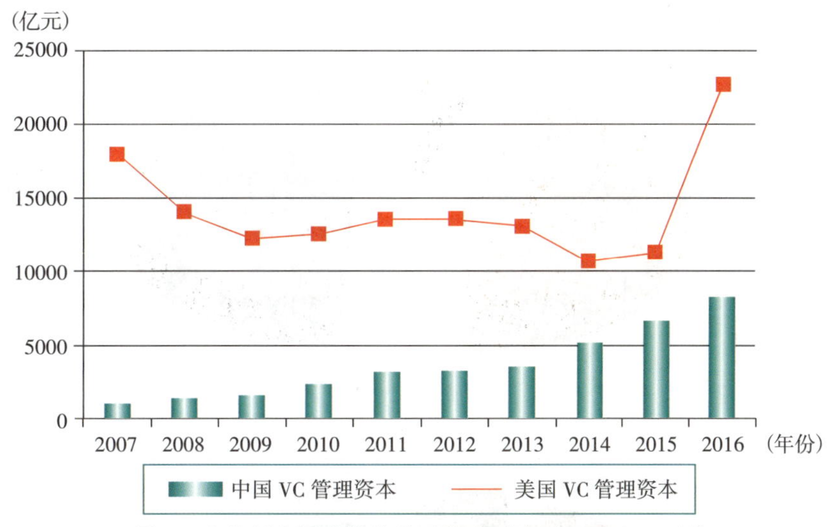

图 2 中美创业风险投资管理资本对比（2007~2016）[①]

1.2 募资来源多元化，银行等金融资本不断涌入

近年来，中国创投募资的资本结构日趋多元化。据统计，2016 年资金来源中仍以政府占主导地位，合计占比 36.13%；民营及混合所有制企业资金占比 24.02%；外资企业占比 4.42%。值得一提的是，2016 年随着相关政策的出台，银行、保险、证券等金融机构资本的占比大幅增加，社保基金也开始进入市场（见图 3）。

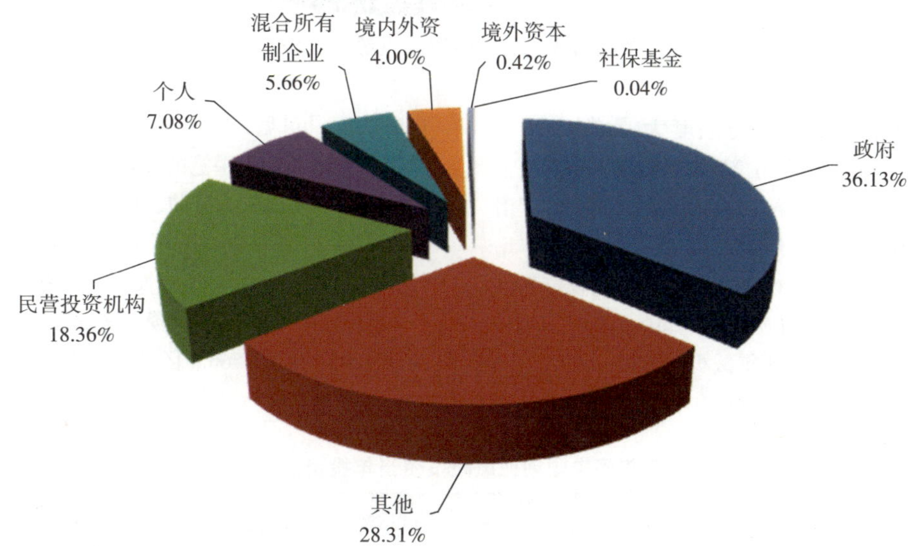

图 3 中国创业风险投资资本来源（2016）（一）

① 美国管理资本以外汇牌价 6.8 进行换算。

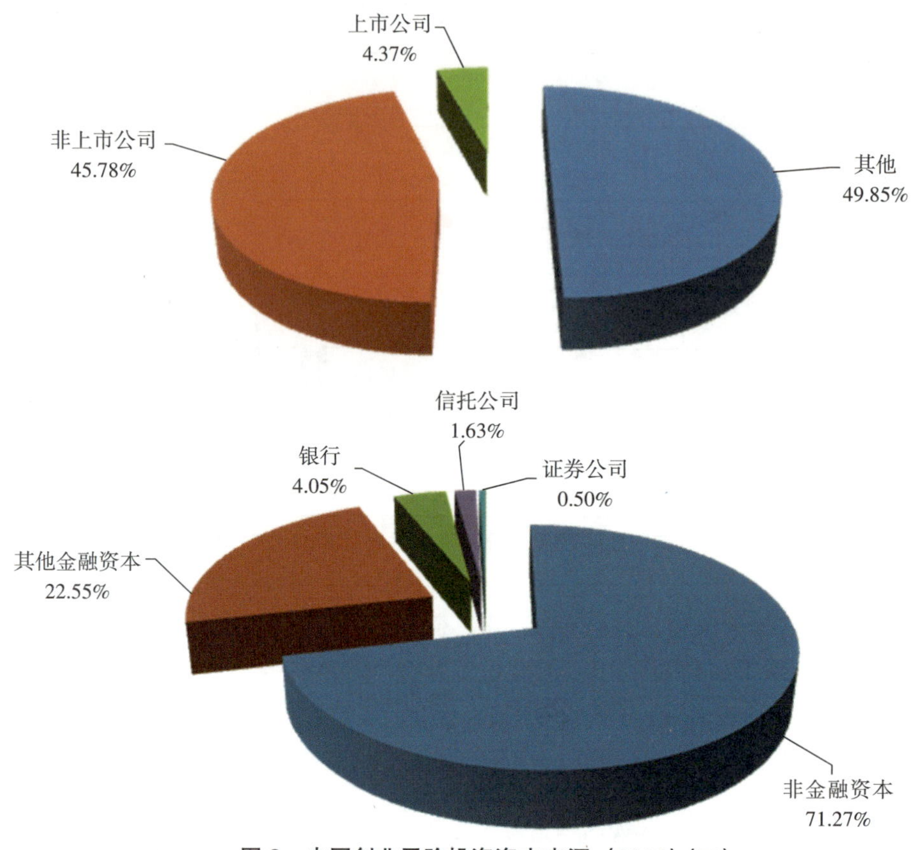

图 3 中国创业风险投资资本来源（2016）（二）

1.3 投资项目总量减少，投资强度大幅增加

2016 年，整体中国创投市场投资项目数较上年有所下滑，当年披露机构投资项目数 2744 项，较 2015 年下滑 19.8%；披露项目投资金额达到 505.5 亿元，较 2015 年增加 8.6%，占全国 GDP 比重的 0.068%，项目平均投资强度 1842 万元/项，较 2015 年增加 69.1%。其中，投资于高新技术企业项目 634 家，较 2015 年减少 23.1%；投资金额为 92.1 亿元，较 2015 年减少 21.4%，项目平均投资额为 1453 万元。可见，2016 年单笔项目投资额明显高于往年，项目估值增大，大手笔的投资有所增加；但高新技术企业项目投资期可能较为靠前，单笔项目金额略小。

截至 2016 年底，全国创业风险投资机构累计投资项目数达到 19296 项，其中投资高新技术企业项目数 8490 项，占比 44.0%；累计投资金额 3765.2 亿元，其中投资高新技术企业金额 1566.8 亿元，占比 41.6%（见表 3）。

表 3 截至 2016 年底中国创业风险投资当年投资情况（2012~2016）

年份	当年投资项目总数（项）	投资高新技术企业/项目数（项）	当年投资金额（亿元）	投资高新技术企业/项目金额（亿元）
2012	1903	850	356.0	172.6
2013	1501	590	279.0	109.0
2014	2459	689	374.4	124.8
2015	3423	820	465.6	117.2
2016	2744	634	505.5	92.1

1.4 分享经济等成为热宠，互联网经济持续发酵

按行业进行分类统计，2016 年软件和信息服务业占比大幅提升，投资金额占 47.55%；其他行业、金融保险业也成为当年创业风险投资的热点；而对新能源和环保业、医药生物业等高新技术产业领域内的投资步伐有所放缓（见表 4）。近年来，由于新商业模式的不断涌现，越来越多的产业难以再用传统的行业统计进行分类，因此，选择“其他行业”投资的占比有所增加。特别是分享经济在我国的快速发展，以共享单车为例，城市共享单车市场受到各方关注，资本纷纷涌入，摩拜单车、优拜单车、小鸣单车、ofo 等相继宣布完成新一轮融资。

表 4　中国创业风险业投资项目前十大行业分布（2015~2016）　单位：%

行业划分		2016 年		2015 年	
		投资金额	投资项目	投资金额	投资项目
软件和信息服务业	网络产业 软件产业 IT 服务业 其他 IT 产业	47.55	26.65	16.12	24.81
其他行业		12.9	13.67	10.41	10.85
金融保险业		6.97	3.12	5.71	3.09
新能源和环保业	新能源、高效节能技术 环保工程 新材料工业 核应用技术	6.84	12.51	11.00	14.86
医药生物业	生物科技 医药保健	5.54	9.81	7.5	7.52
计算机、通信和其他电子设备制造业	通信设备 光电子与光机电一体化 计算机硬件产业 半导体	4.03	7.35	23.03	10.81
传播与文化娱乐		3.02	5.26	5.5	4.32
传统制造业		1.99	3.58	3.77	4.44
建筑业		1.98	0.56	0.76	0.58
其他制造业		1.65	4.09	3.67	5.25

1.5 引导基金热度不减，为行业注入新动能

近年来，国家层面聚焦创新驱动发展，发力供给侧结构性改革，通过发展引导基金，优化资金配置方式方向。在一系列利好政策的直接推动下，引导基金迎来爆发式增长。通过带动社会资本流向创业投资领域，引导基金支持了一大批创业风险投资机构和优质创业创新项目。

调查显示，截至 2016 年底，全国创业风险投资引导基金共 448 只，累计出资 518.65 亿元，通过阶段参股、风险补助、投资保障等方式引导带动创业风险投资机构管理资金规模合计 2393.38 亿元。其中，2016 年当年新增创业风险投资引导基金 53 家。2015 年设立的三只国家大型引导基金持续发力：①国家科技成果转化引导基金，聚焦于国家科技重大专项成果转化、落实京津冀协同发展战略、培育战略性新兴产业等方面；截至 2016 年底，引导基金

出资设立了9只创业投资子基金，总规模173.5亿元，引导放大比例1∶4.5。②国家新兴产业创业投资引导基金，侧重于提升新兴产业整体发展水平和核心竞争力，主要作用于产业发展阶段，不涉及研发环节。拟发起总规模400亿元，目前，已委托3家单位作为引导基金的管理机构。③国家中小企业发展基金：基金总规模达600亿元，中央财政出资150亿元。目前，国家中小企业发展基金共设立了4只直投基金，中央财政出资49亿元，总规模达195亿元。地方层面，如浙江天使投资引导基金、西安科技创业种子投资基金、陕西省科技成果转化引导基金、黑龙江省政府创业投资引导基金等相继成立。

1.6 外资创投更加关注实体经济，布局早期项目投资

据统计，外资创投的投资领域主要集中在“其他行业”、“医药保健”、“网络产业”、“新材料工业”、“生物科技”以及“传播与文化娱乐业”，2016年六大行业合计项目占比达到63.7%。从趋势上看，随着互联网行业的兴起，近年来在该领域内的投资快速增长，到2016年投资金额占比51.7%，投资项目数占比12.7%。此外，传播与文化娱乐业也是增速较快的行业之一。受网络产业的影响，其他行业的投资占比有所下滑，但医药保健（14.5%）、新材料工业（7.3%）、生物科技（5.5%）依然是外资创投关注的投资热点。

从投资阶段来看，近年来，外资创投投资于早期项目（种子期、起步期）的占比明显增多，特别是2015年、2016年，超过半数的投资项目为早期项目（见表5）。

表5 外资、内资创业风险投资项目所处阶段（2016） 单位：%

投资阶段	投资金额		投资项目	
	外资	内资	外资	内资
种子期	9.4	4.3	24.9	19.5
起步期	23.0	30.4	38.5	38.4
成长（扩张）期	67.6	38.1	36.2	35.4
成熟（过渡）期	—	26.7	0.47	5.8
重建期	—	0.6	—	0.8

1.7 市场化的孵化平台/组织日渐成为重要的项目来源渠道

调查显示[①]，2016年中国创业风险投资的项目来源仍然以“政府部门推荐”（20.2%）、“朋友介绍”和“项目中介机构”三个渠道为主。但三者占比之和从2013年的64.5%持续下降到2016年的50.7%。值得一提的是，近年来，随着“双创”的环境营造，“众创空间（孵化器）”已经成为创业风险投资项目来源的重要渠道之一，2016年来自该渠道的占比进一步提升，达到11.3%，创投入驻创新资源（孵化器）已成为新常态（见表6）。

表6 创业风险投资机构获取项目信息来源渠道（2012~2016） 单位：%

信息渠道 年份	政府部门推荐	朋友介绍	项目中介机构	股东推荐	项目业主	银行介绍	媒体宣传	众创空间（孵化器）	其他
2012	25.2	19.2	18.6	13.2	11.5	6.9	2.2	—	3.2
2013	25.5	19.9	19.1	13.2	10.1	6.0	2.6	—	3.6
2014	24.9	17.7	17.1	14.3	11	7.4	3.9	—	3.6
2015	21.3	14.6	15.2	13.9	11.3	7.1	3.5	10.4	2.7
2016	20.2	15.4	15.1	14.1	11.5	6.1	3.5	11.3	2.7

① 有效样本数为1249份。

1.8 退出总体表现良好，长期投资、价值投资逐渐成为主流理念

2016 年，受资本市场总体平稳发展，多层次资本市场不断完善，养老金入市等积极影响，创业风险投资项目退出总体表现良好。全年共有 101 个项目通过 IPO 方式退出，与 2015 年相比大体持平，但占比略有上升，达到 17.32%。相对而言，并购交易仍然是退出的主要渠道，退出项目数达到了 173 项，占比 29.67%；此外，2016 年项目退出行情总体偏弱，回购（40.14%）与清算（8.06%）占比均较 2015 年有所增加。

总体而言，全年项目退出收益率表现良好，尽管略低于 2015 年的表现，但全行业的项目退出收益率仍然达到了 225.73%。整个行业投资退出步伐略微放缓，项目平均退出时间为 4.13 年，长期投资与价值投资日渐成为行业主流理念；整体行业平均收益率达到 29.69%（见图 4）。

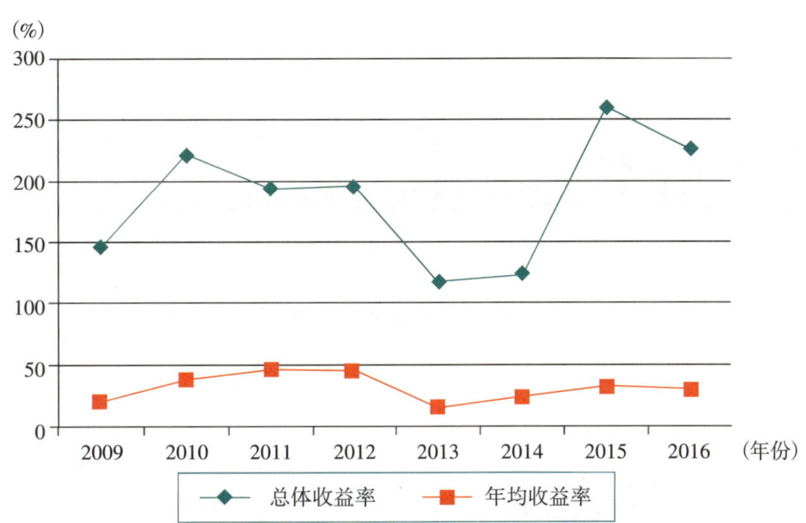

图 4 中国创业风险投资退出收益率（2009~2016）

1.9 区域集聚效应凸显，北京、上海等地成为项目的主要流入区

从地域分布看，中国创投机构分布在全国 29 个省、直辖市和自治区，且主要集聚在东部沿海和经济发达地区，2016 年，仅江苏、浙江和北京三个地区就占据了大半江山，创投机构数量与管理资本数量分别占全国的 56.23%、65.6%。中部地区的安徽、湖南、湖北、重庆等地创投发展较快，呈明显的增长态势。

调查中，通过项目所在投资机构的注册地与投资项目所在地进行分类统计，我们发现，上海、北京、广东等地成为项目的主要流入区。投资项目所在地的占比明显高于注册地，也就是说，项目流入大于流出，很多外地投资的项目向当地涌入。而安徽、重庆等地的投资项目呈流出状态，尽管创投机构数量较多，但孵化的项目并未在当地（见图 5）。

1.10 政策监管日趋规范，投资环境不断优化

近年来，我国各级政府高度重视创新创业，出台了一系列政策措施推动创业风险投资行业成长。调查显示，2016 年我国 29.2%的创投机构获得了政府提供的信息交流服务；20.3%的企业获得了各级政府的税收减免政策，17.6%的企业获得了政府的直接资金支持。

2016 年，国家深入实施创新驱动发展战略，加大推动供给侧结构性改革，进一步完善了创投行业的相关管理政策。特别是 2016 年 9 月，国务院印发了《关于促进创业投资持续健康发展的若干意见》，从投资主体、资金来源、政策扶持、法律法规、退出机制、市场环境、双向开放及行业自律与服务八个方面提出进一步促进创业投资持续健康发展的指导性意见，为促进创业风险投资做大、做强、做优提供了坚实的制度保障。此外，《关于完善股权激励和技术入股有关所得税政策的通知》进一步降低了股权激励的税收负担。银监会、科技部、人民银行等部门联合开展

的“投贷联动”试点，将进一步引导创投服务实体经济 的力度。

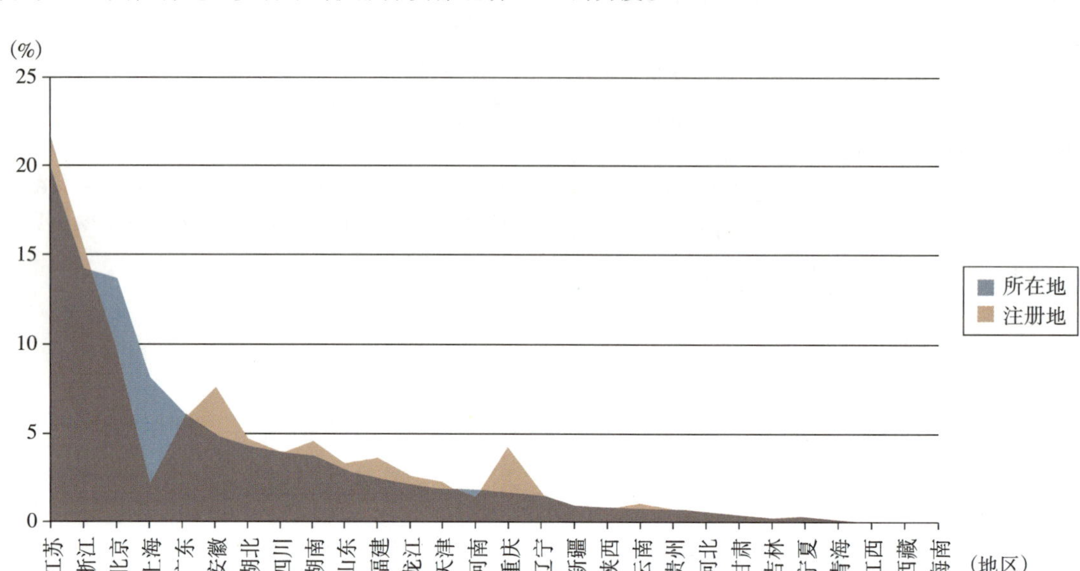

图 5 中国创业风险投资项目流动情况（2016）

2 行业景气指数分析

2016 年的调查工作，增加了行业的景气指数分析，通过行业调查，了解业内人士对行业发展的总体判断。

2.1 2017 年行业发展总体呈乐观态势

1230 家创投行业的管理者对 2017 年前景进行了预测，调查显示，认为 2017 年投资前景“非常好”和“好”的机构占比分别为 3.6%和 55.0%，总体较 2016 年提高了 5.6 个百分点。但值得注意的是，对 2017 年投资前景不确定的机构占比达到了 4.1%，较 2016 年上升了 3.3 个百分点。调查还显示，77.2%的机构认为创投行业的发展受宏观经济影响较大和非常大，因此对未来一年投资前景的不确定因素增大。

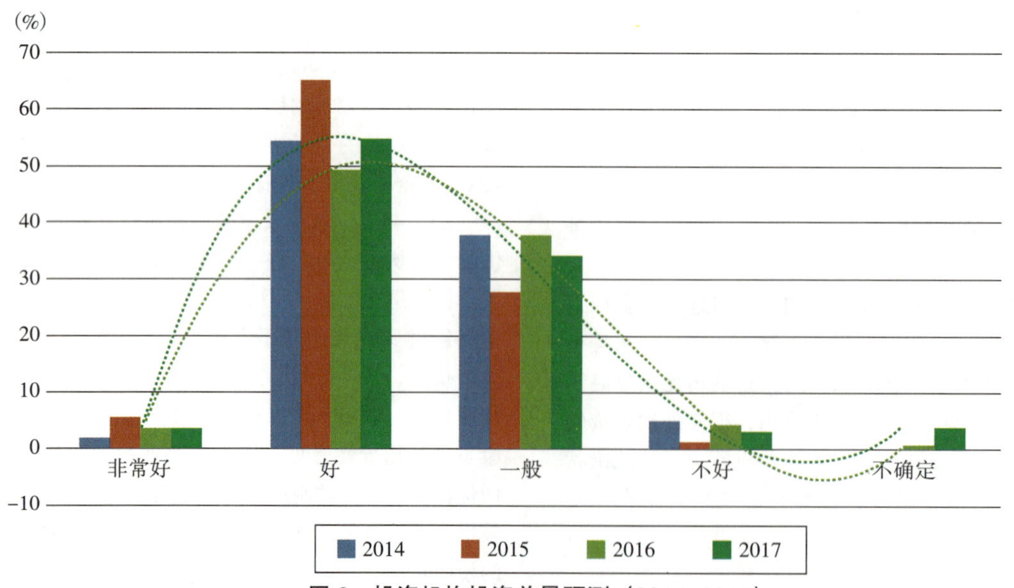

图 6 投资机构投资前景预测（2014~2017）

2.2 投资方向可能再度回归高科技企业

2016年，1232家创投机构负责人认为，“新能源、高效节能技术”、“新材料工业”和“生物科技”将成为2017年创投机构最看好的领域，占比分别为13.1%、11.3%和9.7%。与2015年相比，“医药保健”从第二位下降至第四位，但所占重仍是9.3%，“网络产业（互联网金融）”和“科技服务（包括教育）”分别位列第六位和第七位，占比均为5.1%，其中，网络产业的占比较2015年下降了2.7个百分点。从投资趋势可以看出，网络行业投资热度将有所缓解，高科技企业可能重新成为投资的主战场。

2.3 投资效果不理想主要源于“退出渠道不畅”与“政策环境变化”

2016年，1228位机构负责人填写了调查问卷，认为中国创业风险投资机构投资效果不理想的主要原因集中在“退出渠道不畅”（25.9%）、“政策环境变化”（23.5%）、“市场竞争”（17.0%）、“内部管理水平有限”（10.4%）、“后续融资不力”（9.1%）、“技术不成熟”（7.7%）以及“缺乏诚信”（2.8%）等方面。与2015年相比，并没有明显变化。可见，加强资本市场建设，建设完善、稳定、持续的政策环境，以及加强创投机构自身的内部管理建设，仍然任重道远。

2.4 税收优惠仍是业内机构最希望出台的激励政策

2016年，1214位业内人士回答了最希望政府出台的激励政策。调查表明，中国创投机构最希望出台的政府激励政策仍然是税收优惠政策，占比为43%，且与往年相比，对税收政策的诉求仍在持续提升。其次，14.8%的业内人士希望政府继续推动资本市场注册制改革，加快转板机制建设；13.1%的创业投资机构希望政府通过设立政策性基金支持创业风险投资发展，这两类诉求与2015年相比略有下滑。10.4%的创业投资机构认为应当健全符合创业风险投资行业特点和发展规律的国有创业投资管理体制，激发国有创投活力，且该项诉求较2015年略有上升。

3 对行业发展的思考与建议

总体上，2016年中国创业风险投资行业发展态势良好，业内对未来的发展持乐观态度，围绕创投发展的生态环境也在不断优化。为进一步了解行业发展的实际情况，2016年，我们多次召开业内座谈会，并通过实地走访调查等方面了解到行业发展仍存在一些障碍。在数据分析与调查研究的基础上，我们对行业未来发展提出以下思考与建议。

3.1 充分尊重行业属性，把握监管与自律的度

近年来，为防范金融风险，有关方面将创业投资业视同证券基金业纳入“新政”加强监管的范围，如从业人员必须参加“基金从业资格考试”，不备案就不能进行IPO、并购和新三板挂牌，作为类金融企业暂停挂牌新三板等措施。尽管这些措施在业内受到很大反响，引起了相关部门的高度重视，十部委联合研究发文，但相关政策尚未落地，大部分地区也未接到明确文件指示，部分地区在默许的情况下逐步放宽注册地与企业上市限制。近期，相关部委再度加紧研究，商讨建立全国自律性的行业组织，以解决行业发展问题。

建议充分尊重创投行业自身发展的属性，按照“分类监管、适度监管”的原则，把创业投资基金与证券投资基金区别对待，并从源头上建立信息共享机制，停止实质审批等不当做法；在建立行业协会的同时，要杜绝协会的行政化和官僚化。

3.2 充分了解行业内在规律，建立相适应的财政经费管理制度

近年来，政府引导基金发展迅猛，部分地方引导基金追求规模与数量，造成了财政资金结存现象严重。据2016年发布的《国务院关于2015年度中央预算执行和其他财政收支的审计工作报告》显示，通过审批的206个子基金中，有39个因未吸引到社会资本无法按期设立，已设立的167个子基金募集资金中有148.88亿元（占41%）结存未用，其中14个从未投资。究其原因，造成这一财政资金使用浪费现象的原因主要源于财政资金管理方式与创投投资市场规律间的不适应，财政资金采取了按年度预算进行审核审批的发放方式，而创投机构的投资往往需要根据项目源来确定实际投资，因此存在部分政府追求引导基金投入数量，而管理机构为了财务审计又不得不突击花钱的情况，造成了财政资金的浪费。

建议在开设财政资金专款专户的同时，加快财政资金的审批效率，既避免由于财政资金缺位而影响投资效率的现象发生，也避免由于担心多次审批而增加财政资金结余的浪费现象。从长期而言，应制定与创投管理规律相适应的财政资金管理制度。

3.3 按照“放管服”要求，提高商事服务效率

调研发现，由于各地工商局对创投机构的认识不足，

导致企业在设立和经营中遇到障碍，如工商注册手续烦琐；由于工商注销手续无法完成，而引起税收抵扣困难；部分地区禁止带有“创业投资”字样的合伙企业注册等。

建议开设创投企业工商绿色通道，简化中小企业注销及破产认定程序，取消股权变更过程中的强制评估手续，提高创投企业注册及后续变更备案的效率。

3.4 加快推进资本市场建设，提高政策的稳定性

中国资本市场的改革与发展对创业投资的发展具有深远的影响，直接关系着投资的退出收益与创投自身供血的再循环。经历了十余年的发展，目前，我国已经基本形成了多元化、低门槛的资本市场服务体系，能够为科技创新型企业提供“从创意到 IPO 再到持续成长”的全生命周期服务，中小板、创业板，以及新三板也已成为高新技术企业重要的集聚区。然而，现阶段我们仍面临着 IPO 审核的制度障碍，“堰塞湖”现象依然严重，造成了大量拥有自主知识产权、高成长潜力的创新型企业不得不寻求海外市场，创业投资的企业难以实现有效的退出等问题。

建议进一步加强资本市场建设，减少政府行政手段的干预，增强市场与政策的稳定性，使 IPO 常态化，深化创业板与场外市场的改革，加快推动科技领军企业、创新前沿企业上市等。

3.5 不断提升行业内部管理水平，加快人才队伍建设

根据调查问卷显示，“内部管理水平有限”成为制约投资效果的重要影响因素之一，占比达到 10.4%。在创投管理者最应该具备的素质调查中，“资本运作能力”、“判断力和洞察力”排在前两位，而在创投管理者最缺乏的素质调查中，“技术评估”、“资本运作”和“项目识别”依然是从事创业风险投资人员最缺乏的三个方面。可见，随着创投市场的扩张，内部管理水平和人才队伍建设还有待进一步加强。特别是，部分地方政府引导基金由政府事业单位人员运作，缺少专业投资人员，因此对基金进行专业化的运作管理较为困难，同时也难以对投资项目进行辅导。

建议进一步规范基金运作管理，加快专业化人才队伍建设。同时，鼓励政府引导基金采取市场化的运作方式，通过激励机制、投后绩效管理等方式，提高基金的专业化运作管理水平。

Executive Summary

2016 Development Trends of Venture Capital in China

—New Momentum and New Trend

National Venture Capital Survey & Writing & Analysis Group①

With further promoted supply-side structural reform, improved "New OTC Market" layering system, lunched "Shenzhen-Hong Kong Stock Connect", and upsurge in innovation and entrepreneurship activities, the year 2016 was a fruitful year for China's venture capital industry. Fundraising, investment and exit of the industry has risen in varying degrees, with potential development opportunities and emerging supply momentum of new power capital.

1. 2016 New Development Characteristics of Venture Capital Industry in China

Compared with previous years, development of China's venture capital industry in 2016 is characterized as follows:

1.1 Growing Number of Institutions and Capitals, Significantly Increased Professional Management Institutions

In 2016, the number of China's venture capital institutions reached 2045, an increase of 270 (15.2%) compared with 2015, including 1421 venture capital funds, an increase of 110 (8.4%), and 624 venture capital management institutions, an increase of 160(34.5%). 152 new fundraising funds of the year were revealed, with newly raised fund management capitals of 101.61 billion Yuan (See Table 1).

Table 1 Total Number and Increment of Venture Capital Institutions in China (2007~2016)

Items \ Year	2007	2008	2009	2010	2011	2012	2013	2014	2015	2016
Existing VC Institutions	383	464	576	867	1096	1183	1408	1551	1775	2045
Among: VC Funds	331	410	495	720	860	942	1095	1167	1311	1421
Among: VC Management Institutions	52	54	81	147	236	241	313	384	464	624
Newly Raised Funds of the Year	76	89	135	215	167	146	123	169	197	152
Grouth of VC Institutions (%)	11.0	21.1	24.1	50.5	26.4	7.9	19.0	10.2	14.4	15.2

① CASTED 2016 "National Venture Capital Investigation & Writing & Analysis Group" members: Guo Rong, Zhang Mingxi, Zhang Junfang, Li Xiyi, Wei Shijie, Zhu Xinle, Li Riqiang and Xuewei, etc. The report was prepared by: Zhang Junfang and Zhang Mingxi.

An obvious trend is that the venture capital entrusted management pattern is increasingly popular, an increasing number of funds entrusted professional venture capital institutions for investment management. 2007~2016, the venture capital management institutions increased to 624 from 52, an increase of more than 10 times.

In 2016, the total national venture capital management capitals reached 827.71 billion Yuan, an increase of 162.38 billion Yuan (24.4%) compared with 2015. The management capitals accounted for 1.11% of GDP. The average fund management capitals reached RMB 405 million Yuan (See Table 2).

Table 2 Total Venture Capital Management Capitals in China (2007–2016)

Items \ Year	2007	2008	2009	2010	2011	2012	2013	2014	2015	2016
Management Capital (RMB 100 Million Yuan)	1112.9	1455.7	1605.1	2406.6	3198.0	3312.9	3573.9	5232.4	6653.3	8277.1
A Year–on–year Increase (%)	67.7	30.8	10.3	49.9	32.9	3.6	7.9	31.7	27.2	24.4
Average Fund Management Capitals (RMB 100 Million Yuan)	3.36	3.55	3.24	3.34	3.72	3.52	3.26	4.48	4.66	4.05

Compared with foreign countries, China's venture capital developed rapidly, and the venture capital institutions and management capitals ranked only second to US. In 2016, the number of US venture capital institutions reached 2406 (including 1562 venture capital funds and 898 management institutions), with management capitals of 333 billion dollars (equivalent to 2264.4 billion Yuan), accounted for 1.93% of GDP (See Graph 1 and Graph 2).

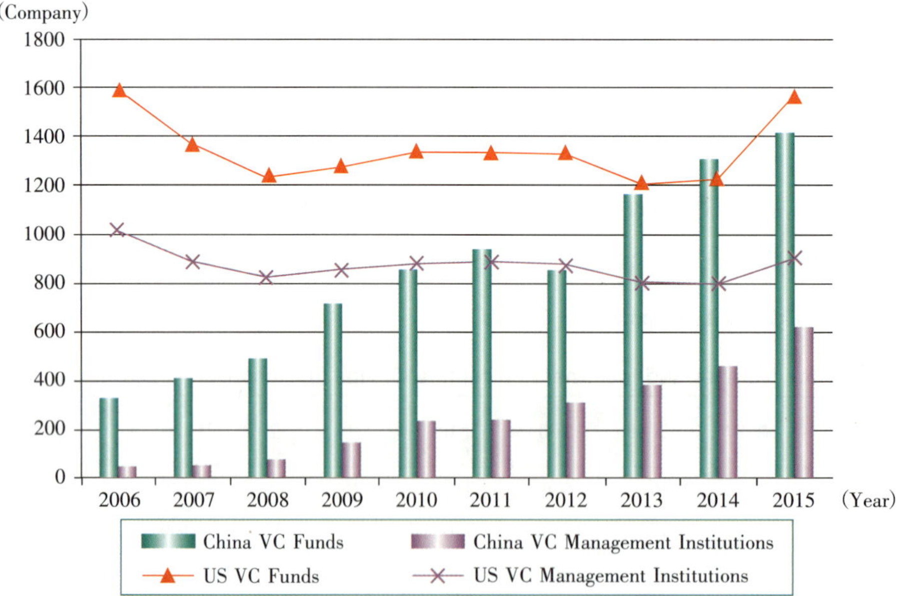

Graph 1 Comparison of Number of Venture Capital Institutors between China and US (2007–2016)

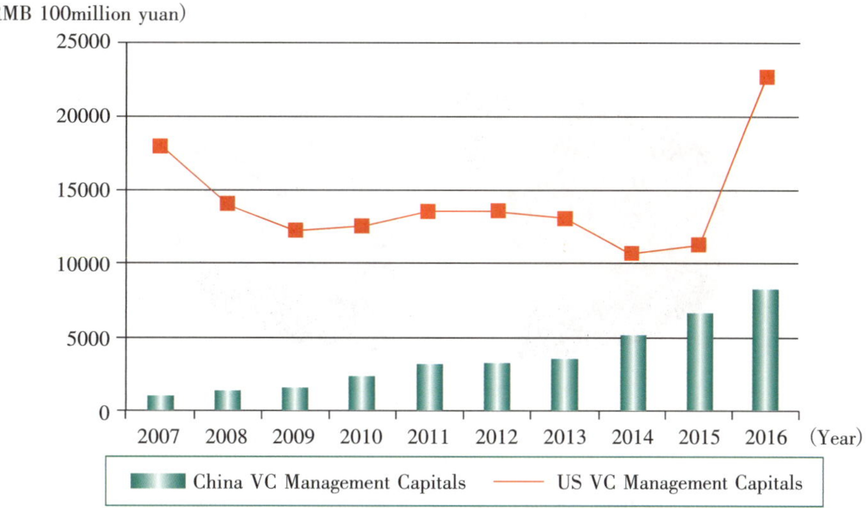

Graph 2 Comparison of Venture Capital Management Capital between China and US (2007–2016)①

1.2 Diversified Fundraising Sources, Influx of Financial Capital as Bank Capital

In recent years, capital structure of China's venture capital fundraising has been increasingly diversified. According to the statistics, government and solely state-owned units still dominated the capital sources of 2016 (accounted for 36.1%); privately owned and mixed ownership enterprises accounted for 24.02%; foreign-funded enterprises accounted for 4.42%. It is worth mentioning that the proportion of capitals of financing institutions as banks, insurance agencies and securities institutions has been significantly increased with launch of relevant policies in 2016, and the social insurance funds have entered the market (see Graph 3).

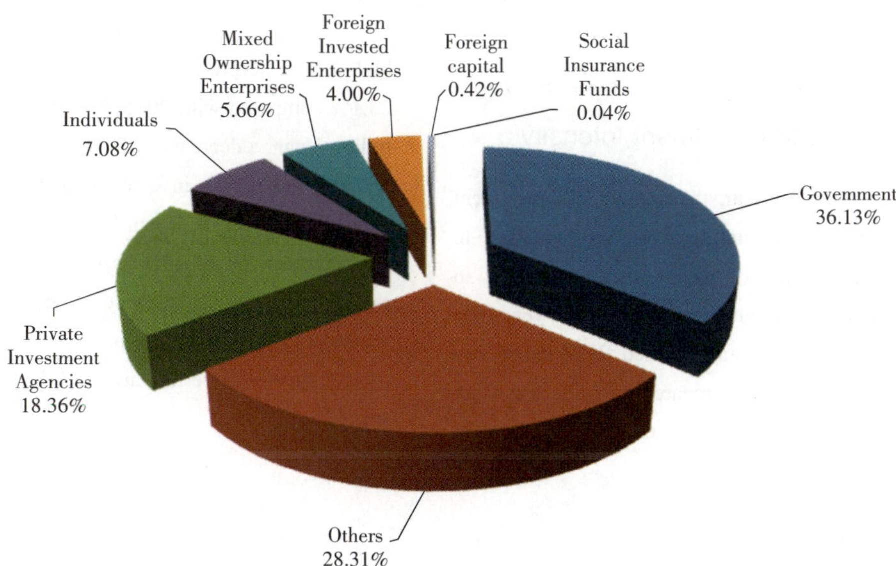

Graph 3 China Venture Capital Resources (2016) (—)

① US management capitals were converted by the foreign exchange rate 6.8.

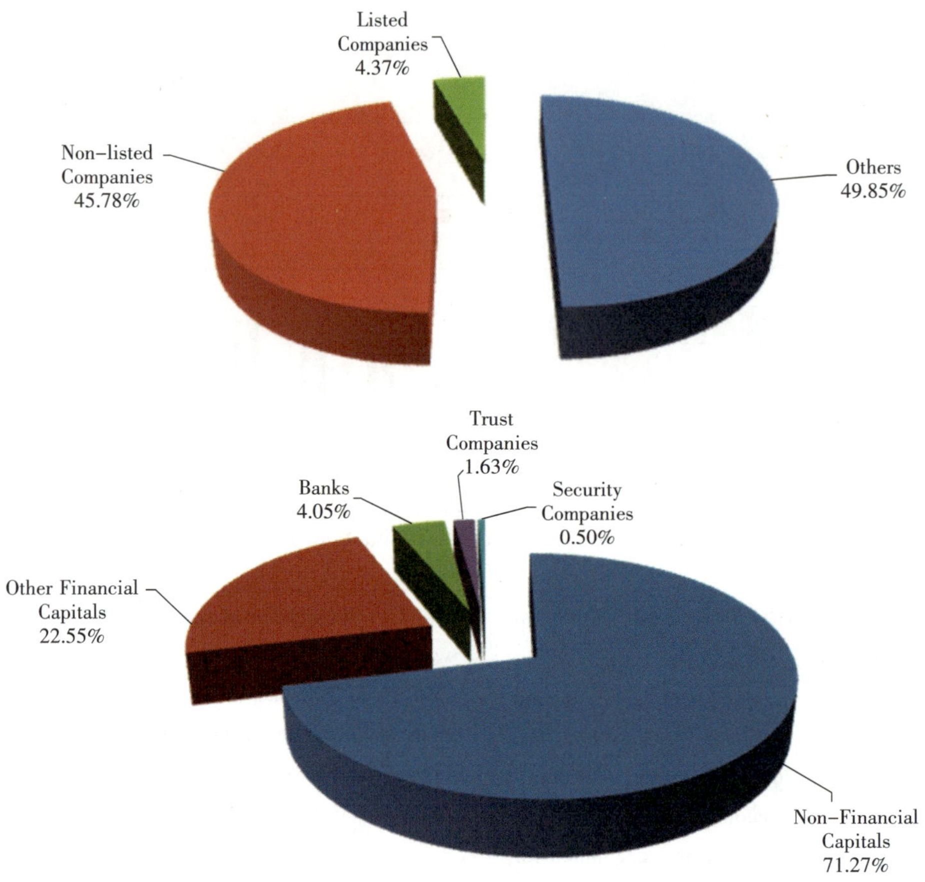

Graph 3 China Venture Capital Resources (2016) (二)

1.3 Decreased Number of Investment Projects, Significantly Increased Investment Intensity

Compared with the last year, the number of investment projects in China venture capital market was decreased in 2016. 2744 investment projects of institutions were revealed in the year, a decrease of 19.8% compared with the last year. The revealed project investment amount reached RMB 50.55 billion Yuan; an increase of 8.6% compared with the last year, and accounted for 0.068% of China's GDP. Wherein, 634 high-tech enterprise projects were invested, a decrease of 23.1% compared with 2015; investment amount of RMB 9.21 billion Yuan, a decrease of 21.4% compared with the last year, with average project investment amount of RMB 14.53 million Yuan (See Table 3). It can be seen that the single project investment amount of 2016 is significantly higher than that of previous years, with increased project valuation and the big investment. However, investment period in high-tech enterprise project may be more forward, and the single project amount is smaller.

Table 3 China Venture Capital Investment Conditions by the End of 2016 (2012~2016)

Year	Total Number of Investment Projects of the Year	Number of Investment in High-tech Enterprises/ Project	Investment amount of the year (RMB 100 million Yuan)	Investment Amount in High-tech Enterprises/Projects (RMB 100 million Yuan)
2012	1903	850	356.0	172.6
2013	1501	590	279.0	109.0
2014	2459	689	374.4	124.8
2015	3423	820	465.6	117.2
2016	2744	634	505.5	92.1

By the end of 2016, the cumulative number of investment projects of national venture capital institutions reached 19296; wherein, 8490 were invested in high-tech enterprise projects, which accounted for 44.0% . The cumulative investment amount reached RMB 376.52 billion Yuan, wherein, RMB 156.68 billion Yuan were invested in high-tech enterprises, which accounted for 41.6%.

1.4 Sharing Economy Becomes Hot Spot, Internet Economy Remains Active

According to classified statistics by industries, the propor tion of software and information service industries was significantly improved in 2016, with investment amount accounted for 47.55%; other industries, finance and insurance industry also became hot investment tips of the year. However, investment in high-tech industries as new energy and medical biology industries were slow down (See Table 4). In recently years, due to emerging business models, an increasing number of industries are hard to be classified or counted by traditional industries, and the proportion of investment in "other industries" has been increased. In particular, the sharing economy has developed rapidly in China. Take the shared bike as example; the urban bike-sharing market has received high attention, with influx of capital. MOBIKE, U-BICYCLE, XIAOMING CYCLE and OFO have announced their completion of a new round of financing (See Table 4).

Table 4 Top 10 Industrial Distribution of China Venture Capital Investment Projects (2015–2016)

Unit: %

Industrial Distribution		2016		2015	
		Investment Amount	Investment Project	Investment Amount	Investment Project
Software and Information Service Industry	Internet Software IT Service Other IT	47.55	26.65	16.12	24.81
Other Industries		12.9	13.67	10.41	10.85
Finance and Insurance Industry		6.97	3.12	5.71	3.09
New Energy and Environmental Protection Industry	New Energy and High-efficiency Energy-saving Technology Environmental Protection Engineering New Material Nuclear Application Technology	6.84	12.51	11.00	14.86

Continued

Industrial Distribution		2016		2015	
		Investment Amount	Investment Project	Investment Amount	Investment Project
Medical Biology Industry	Biotechnology Medicine and Health Care	5.54	9.81	7.5	7.52
Computer, communication and Other Electronic Equipment Manufacturing Industry	communication equipment Photoelectron and Optical Electromechanical Integration Computer Hardware Semiconductor	4.03	7.35	23.03	10.81
Communication and Cultural Entertainment Industry		3.02	5.26	5.5	4.32
Traditional Manufacturing Industry		1.99	3.58	3.77	4.44
Construction Industry		1.98	0.56	0.76	0.58
Other Manufacturing Industry		1.65	4.09	3.67	5.25

1.5 Fund of Fund Remains Hot, Inject New Momentum into the Industry

In recent years, the state has focused on innovation-driven development, promoted the supply-side structural reform, and optimized the capital allocation mode and direction by devel oping the fund of funds. Under direct promotion of a series of favorable policies, the fund of fund was ushered in the explosive growth. By leading social capitals flowing into the field of venture capital, the fund of fund has supported a large number of venture capital institutions, high quality entrepreneurship and innovation projects.

The survey showed that by the end of 2016, there were 448 government fund of fund in China, with cumulative contribution of RMB 51.865 billion Yuan, guided and stimulated venture capital institution management capitals of RMB 239.338 billion Yuan by means as stage participation, risk allowance and investment guaranty. Wherein, 53 fund of funds were newly added in 2016. Three large-scale state fund of funds established in 2015 continued to work:

① National scientific and technological achievement transformation fund of funds, focused on significant special national science and technology achievement transformation, implementation of Beijing-Tianjin-Hebei coordinated development strategy and strategic emerging industry cultivation. By the end of 2016, the fund of funds have funded and set up 9 venture capital sub-funds, with total investment amount of RMB 17.35 billion Yuan; the lever proportion of 1 : 4 : 5.

② The State venture capital funds for emerging industry focused on improving the overall development level and core competitiveness of the emerging industry, and played the role in industrial development stages, and not involved with research and development links. It is planned to initiating RMB 40 billion Yuan. Up to now, three units has been entrusted as the management institutions of the fund of funds.

③ National development funds for small and medium-sized enterprises: Fund size of RMB 60 billion Yuan, and the central budget has funded RMB 15 billion Yuan. At present, the national development funds for small and medium-sized enterprises has set up 4 direct investment funds, and the central budget has funded RMB 4.9 billion Yuan, with total size of RMB 19.5 billion Yuan. In terms of local levels, Zhejiang Angel Investment fund of fund, Xi'an technology entrepreneurship seed investment fund, Shanxi science and technology achievement transformation fund and Heilongjiang government fund of fund have been established.

1.6 Foreign Venture Capital Pays More Attention to the Real Economy; Arrange Early Project Investments

According to the statistics, the foreign venture capital are mainly concentrated in"other industries", "medicine and health care", "internet industry", "new material industry", "biotechnology" and "communication and cultural entertainment". In 2016, projects of the six industries accounted for 63.7%. In terms of the trend, with emerging internet industry, the investment in the industry has developed rapidly, and the investment amount accounted for 51.7% in 2016, with number of investment projects accounted for 12.7%. In addition, the communication and cultural entertainment industry is also one of the industries with fast growth. Affected by internet industry, proportion of investment in other industries has declined. However, medicine and health care (14.5%), new material industry (7.3%) and biotechnology (5.5%) remained the investment hot spots of foreign venture capital.

In terms of the investment stages, the proportion of foreign venture capital investment in early projects (seed stage and starting stage) has been significantly increased in recent years. Particularly, more than half of investment projects of 2015 and 2016 were early projects (See Table 5).

Table 5 Foreign and Domestic Venture Capital Project Stages (2016) Unit: %

Investment Stage	Investment Amount		Investment Project	
	Foreign Capital	Domestic Capital	Foreign Capital	Domestic Capital
Seed Stage	9.4	4.3	24.9	19.5
Starting Stage	23.0	30.4	38.5	38.4
Growth (Expansion) Stage	67.6	38.1	36.2	35.4
Maturity (Transition) Stage	—	26.7	0.47	5.8
Reconstruction Stage	—	0.6	—	0.8

1.7 Market-oriented Incubation Platforms/Organizations Becoming Important Project Source Channels

The survey① showed that "recommended by government" (20.2%), "introduced by friends" and "project intermediaries" still dominated the China's venture capital project sources in 2016. However, the proportion of three items has decreased to 50.7% in 2016 from 64.5% in 2013. It is worth mentioning that "Maker Space (Incubator)" has become one of important source channels of venture capital projects. The proportion of the channel was further improved and achieved 11.3%. The venture capital enters the innovation resource (Incubator) has become new normal (See Table 6).

Table 6 Information Source Channels of Venture Capital Institutions (2012~2016) Unit: %

Year \ Information Channel	Recommended by Government	Introduced by Friends	Project Intermediaries	Recommended by Shareholders	Project Owners	Introduced by Banks	Media Publicity	Maker Space (Incubator)	Others
2012	25.2	19.2	18.6	13.2	11.5	6.9	2.2	—	3.2
2013	25.5	19.9	19.1	13.2	10.1	6.0	2.6	—	3.6
2014	24.9	17.7	17.1	14.3	11	7.4	3.9	—	3.6
2015	21.3	14.6	15.2	13.9	11.3	7.1	3.5	10.4	2.7
2016	20.2	15.4	15.1	14.1	11.5	6.1	3.5	11.3	2.7

① There were 1249 effective samples.

1.8 The Exit Generally Performed Well, Long-term Investment and Value Investment Becoming Mainstream Concept

In 2016, under positive influence as overall stable development of capital market, continuous improvement of multi-layer capital market and pension market, the venture capital project exit generally performed well. 101 projects exited through IPO in 2016, which maintained the same level as 2015, except the proportion that was slightly increased to 17.32%. Relatively speaking, the merger transaction was still the main exit channels, with 173 projects exited, which accounted for 29.67%. In addition, the project exit conditions are generally weak in 2016. Compared with 2015, the proportions of repurchase (40.14%) and liquidation (8.06%) were increased.

In general, the project exit return rate of the year still performed well. Although slightly lower than that of 2015, the project exit return rate of the industry still reached 225.73%. The investment exit pace of the industry slowed slightly, and the average project exit time was 4.13 years. Long-term investment and value investment have gradually become the mainstream concept of the industry; the average return rate of the industry has achieved 29.69% (See Graph 4).

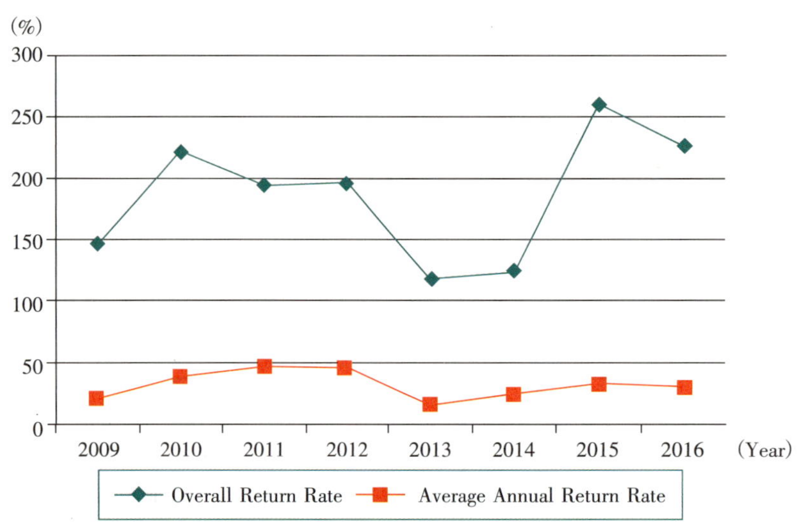

Graph 4 China Venture Capital Exit Return Rate

1.9 Prominent Cluster Effect, Regions as Beijing and Shanghai Become Main Inflow Regions

In terms of geographical distribution, China's venture capital instructions are distributed in 29 provinces, municipalities and autonomous regions, and mainly concentrated in eastern coast and developed regions of China. In 2016, Jiangsu, Zhejiang and Beijing accounted for almost half of the venture capitals, with quantities of venture capital institutions and management capitals accounted for 56.23% and 65.6% respectively of the country. Venture capitals developed fast in the middle parts of China as Anhui, Hunan, Hubei and Chongqing, and assumed an obvious growth trend.

In survey, we conducted the classified statistics on registration places of the investment institutions and the location of the investment projects, and found that regions as Shanghai, Beijing and Guangdong were main inflow regions of the pro jects. The proportion of the project location was significantly higher than the registration places. In other words, the project inflow was higher than the project outflow. A lot of investment projects flows into these regions. However, projects of regions as Anhui and Chongqing are outflow. Despite considerable venture capital institutions, their incubation projects were in other places (See Graph 5).

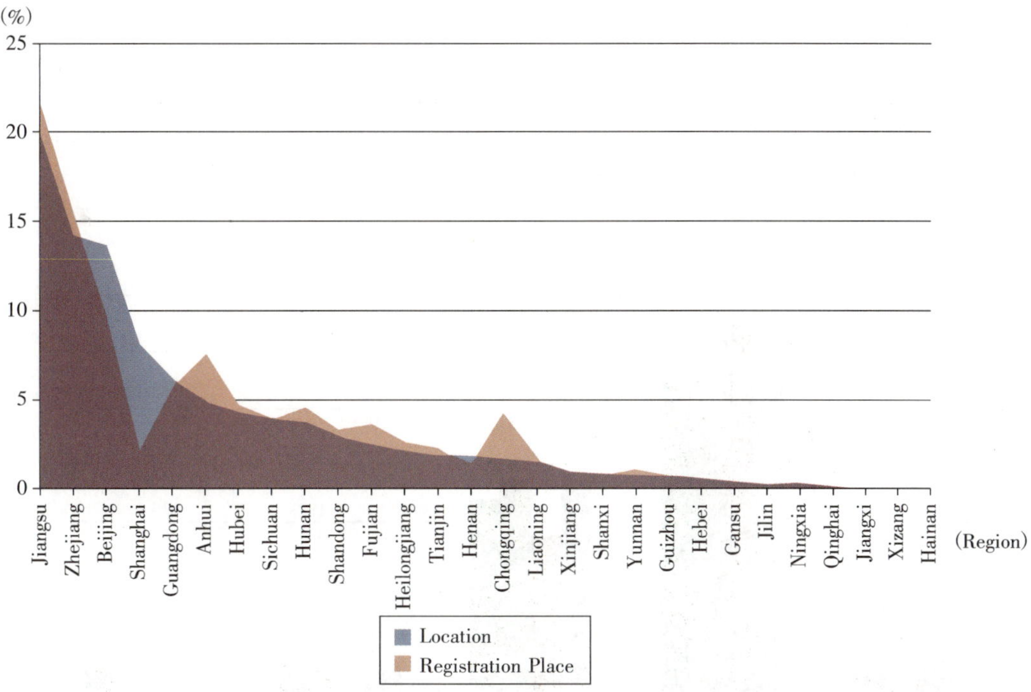

Graph 5 China Venture Capital Project Flow (2016)

1.10 Policy Supervision Gradually Regulated, Investment Environment Constantly Improved

In recent years, China's government have attached great importance to innovation and entrepreneurship at all levels, and issued a series of policy measures to promote the growth of the venture capital industry. The survey showed that 29.2% of China's venture capital institutions received information communication services provided by the government; 20.3% of enterprises enjoyed taxation reducing policies provided by government at all levels; 17.6% of enterprises obtained direct financial support from the government.

In 2016, the state fully implemented the innovation-driven development strategy, promoted the supply-side structural reform and further improved management polices related to the venture capital industry. In particular, the *Opinions on Promoting the Sustainable and Healthy Development of the Venture Capital* issued by the State Council in September, 2016 has offered the directive opinions on further promoting the Sustainable and Healthy Development of the venture capital from eight aspects: investment subjects, capital sources, policy support, law regulations, exit mechanism, market environment, two-way opening, and industry self-discipline and service, and provided Solid institutional guarantee for making the venture capital strengthened and better. In addition, the *Notice on Income Tax Polices Related to Improving Share Incentive* and *Technology Investment* has further reduced the tax burden of share incentive. The "investment and loan union" pilot project jointly conducted by departments as China Banking Regulatory Commission, Ministry of Science and Technology and People's Bank of China would further guide the real economy of venture capital services.

2 Analysis on Industrial Condition Index

The analysis on industrial condition index was added in the survey work of 2016. Learn global judgment of industry insiders on the industry development through the industry survey.

2.1 2017 Industry Development is Generally Optimistic

Managers from 1230 venture capital institutions predicated the prospect of the venture capital industry in 2017. The survey showed that the institutions that believed the investment prospect to be "very good" and "good" accounted for 3.6% and 55.0% respectively, and increase of 5.6% compared with the last year. It is worth noting that the intuitions uncertain of the investment prospect of 2017 accounted for 4.1%, an increase of 3.3% compared with the last year. The survey also indicated that 77.2% of institutions believed the development of the ven ture capital industry were significantly or greatly affected by the macro economy, the uncertain factors of the investment prospect for the next year was thus increased (See Graph 6).

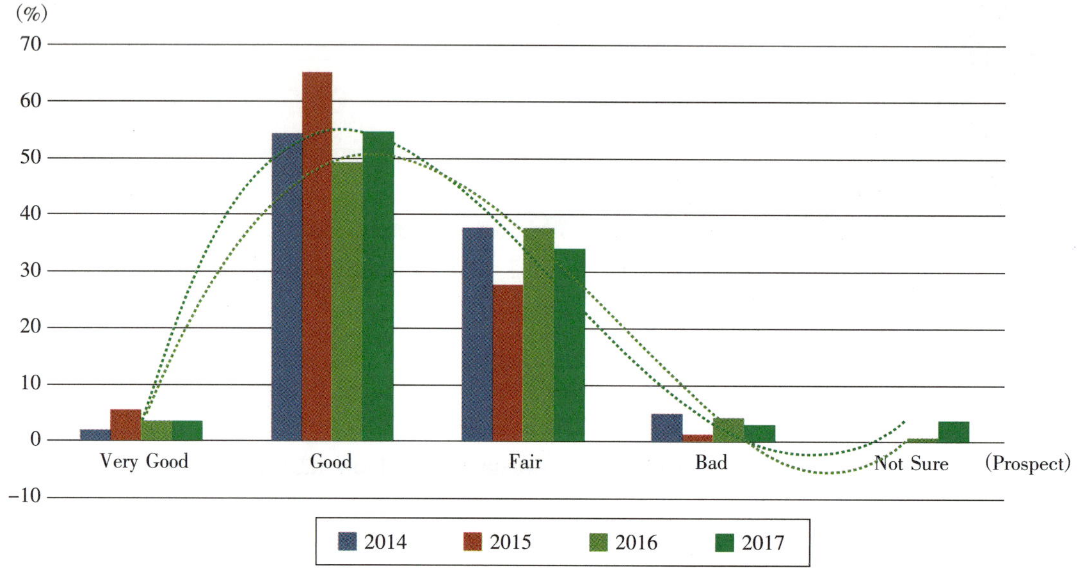

Graph 6 Investment Prospect Forecast by Investment Institutions (2014~2017)

2.2 Investment may return to High-Tech Enterprises

In 2016, principals of 1232 venture capital institutions believed that "New energy and energy-efficient technology", "new material industry" and "biotechnology" would be the most promising fields for venture capital institutions in 2017, which accounted for 13.1%, 11.3% and 9.7% respectively. Compared with 2015, "medicine and health care" dropped to the forth place from the second place, but its proportion remained to be 9.3%. "Internet industry (Internet finance)" and "science and technology service (education included)" ranked the sixth place and the seventh place respectively, and both accounted for 5.1%, wherein, the proportion of the internet industry dropped by 2.7% compared with the last year. It can be seen from the investment trend that investment popularity in internet industry would be decrease, and the high-tech enterprises may become the main battlefield of the investment again.

2.3 Unsatisfactory Investment Results Mainly caused by "Impeded Exit Channels" and "Changed Policy Environment"

In 2016, 1232 venture capital institution principal filled in the questionnaire, and believed that the unsatisfactory investment results of China's venture capital institutions were mainly caused by "impeded exit channels" (25.9%), "changed policy environment"(23.5%), "market competition" (17.0%), "limited internal management" (10.4%), "poor follow-up financing" (9.1%), "immature technology" (7.7%), "lack of in tegrity" (2.8%) and others. Compared with 2015, no significant changes were found. It is thus clear that to strengthen the construction of capital market, establishing a perfect, stable and sustainable policy environment, and strengthening the internal management of venture capital institutions remain a daunting task.

2.4 Tax Preference Remains the Incentive Policy that Most Wanted by Institutions of the Industry

In 2016, 1214 insiders gave the answer to the incentive policy they most wanted to be issued by the government. The survey showed that the incentive policy that the tax preference remained the incentive policy that most wanted by China's venture capital institutions, which accounted for 43%. Compared with previous years, their demands for the tax policy were still growing. Secondly, 14.8% of insiders hoped that the government could keep promoting the reform of capital market regis tration system, and accelerating the construction of board switch mechanism; 13.1% of venture capital institutions hoped that the government could support the venture capital development by setting up policy funds. Compared with 2015, these two demands were slighted declined. 10.4% of venture capital institutions believed that the state-owned venture capital management system conforming to features and development rules of the venture capital industry shall be improved, to stimulate the vitality of the state-owned venture capital. Compared with 2015, the demand was slightly increased.

3 Thoughts and Suggestions on the Industry Development

In general, China's venture capital industry developed well in 2016, and the insiders were optimistic about the future development. The ecological environment has also been optimized around the venture capital development. To further understand the actual development of the industry, we held many times of industry forums in 2016. Combined with field survey, we learned that obstacles still existed during the development of the industry. Based on data analysis and research, we proposed thoughts and suggestions on the future development of the industry as follows:

3.1 Fully Respect Industry Attributes, Grasp the degree of Regulation and Self-discipline

In recent years, the venture capital industry was included into the scope where the supervision should be strengthened as the security fund industry, e.g. practitioners shall participate in the "fund qualification examination"; IPO, merger and acquisition and "New OTC Market" listing can only be conducted with registration; measures as suspend the "New OTC Market" listing of similar financial enterprises. Although these measures have made a big splash in the industry, attracted high attention from relevant departments, and joint research and report by ten ministries and commissions of the nation, relevant policies has not been implemented. Most regions have not received a clear file instructions, and the restorations on registration place and listing of enterprises has been gradually relaxed in the case of acquiescence in some areas. Recently, relevant ministries and commissions have pushed ahead the research, to discuss the establishment of national self-regulatory organization of the industry for solving the development problems of the industry.

It is suggested to fully respect the development attributes of the venture capital industry, and make a difference between venture capital funds and securities investment funds in accordance with "classified and moderate supervision" principle. Establish the information sharing mechanism at the source and stop inappropriate practices as substantial approval, and avoid administration and bureaucratization when establishing the industry association.

3.2 Fully Understand Inherent Laws of the Industry, Establish Corresponding Financial Management System

In recent years, the government fund of funds has developed rapidly, and some local funds pursued scale and quantity, which has result in severe financial fund balance. According to the *Audit Report of the State Council on Implementation of the Central Budget and Other Financial Revenue and Expenditure of* 2015 issued in 2016, 39 of 206 approved sub-funds could not be set up on time due to fails in attracting social capitals, and RMB 14.888 billion Yuan (41%) of raised funds of 167 established sub-funds remained unused, and 14 sub-funds have never invested. Such financial fund waste was mainly caused by the incompatibility between the management modes of the financial funds and the rules of the venture capital market. The financial fund was distributed by audit and approval based on annual budget, while venture capital institutions generally determined the actual investment by projects. Therefore, some governments may pursue the input quantity of the guidance funds, while management institutions have to make budget flush for the financial audit, and caused the waste of financial funds.

It is suggested to open special account of financial funds, and accelerate the approval efficiency, which may avoid impact of lack of financial funds on investment efficiency, or financial fund balance increased due to multiple approvals. In the long term, the financial fund management system conform ing to the rules of venture capital management shall be estab lished.

3.3 Improve Commercial Service Efficiency in Accordance with " Streamline Administration and Institute Decentralization, Delegate Power and Strengthen Regulation, and Optimized Services"

The survey showed that insufficient recognition of local industrial and commercial bureaus about the venture capital institutions caused obstacle in establishment and operation of the enterprises, e.g. cumbersome business registration; difficulty in tax credit caused by incomplete business cancellation procedure; and registration of partnership enterprises with "venture capital" were prohibited in some areas, etc.

It is suggested to establish enterprises business green channels, simplify cancellation and bankruptcy recognizing procedures for middle and small-sized enterprises, eliminating mandatory assessment procedure during equity changes and improving the registration and subsequent change records of venture capital enterprises.

3.4 Accelerate the Construction of Capital Market, Improve the Policy Stability

The reform and development of China Capital Markets have a profound impact on the development of the venture capital, and directly relate to the exit return of the investment and the recycling of the venture capital. After more than ten years of development, a diversified and low-threshold capital market service system has been basically formed in China, and may provide technology-based venture enterprises with full life cycle services "from idea, IPO to sustainable growth", while small and medium enterprise board, growth enterprise market and New OTC Market have also become the important cluster of high-tech enterprises. However, we still have IPO audit system obstacle, and severe "barrier lake" phenomenon. A large number of high potential innovative enterprises with proprietary intellectual property rights have to look overseas, and it is difficult for venture capital enterprises to have effective exit.

It is suggested to further strengthen the construction of capital market, reducing administrative intervention of government, making IPO normal, deepening the reform of the growth enterprise market and OTC market, and accelerating the listing of leading technology enterprises and innovating enterprises, etc.

3.5 Keep Improving Internal Management Level of the Industry, Accelerating the Talent Team Construction

The questionnaire showed that the "limited internal management" has become one of important factors that restrict the investment results, and accounted for 10.4%. In the survey on most important qualities that venture capital managers should possess, "capital operation capacity" and "judgment and insight" ranked the top two, while in the survey on qualities that are most lacking in venture capital managers, "technology assessment", " capital operation" and " project identification" remained the top three. It can be seen that with the expansion of the venture capital market, internal management level and talent team construction need to be further strengthened. In particular, some local government guidance funds are operated by the staff of government institutions other than professional investors. Therefore, it is difficult to have professional operation and management on funds, or have counseling for investment projects.

It is suggested to further standardize the operation and the management of funds, and accelerate the construction of professional talent team. In the same time, encourage the adoption of market-oriented operation for government guidance funds, and improve professional operation and management level of funds through means as incentive mechanism and post-investment performance management.

1 中国创业风险投资机构与资本

1.1 2016 年度调查概述

2016 年 11 月，科技部、商务部、国家开发银行等部门联合启动第 15 次全国创业风险投资年度调查工作。2017 年 1~4 月，按照国家统计局要求（国统制〔2017〕4 号），组织了全国 35 个省（市、自治区）、53 个调查实施机构和 135 名调查员进行网上填报。在此期间，各类创业风险投资机构对调查工作给予了大力的配合，认真贯彻实施国家《统计法》。经过多年努力，本项统计调查工作为中央引导地方科技发展专项资金、引导基金申报，以及创业风险投资年度评奖等工作提供了有效的数据支持，也为我国创投业内重要政策的出台提供了有力支撑，成为我国科技金融工作的重要组成部分。

2016 年度报告所调查的创业投资机构主要包括以下三类：①创业风险投资基金，包括创业投资引导基金。②创业投资管理企业，其受创业投资基金委托，筛选投资项目，提出投资决策建议，并受托进行投资后管理。③少量从事创业风险投资业务的政府部门及其附属机构，包括以政府资金直接投资项目，或采用引导基金的方式参股创业风险投资，或对创业风险投资企业给予某种形式的激励。

截至 2016 年底，“中国创业风险投资信息系统”（www.ivcc.cn）有 5218 家机构参加过调查（包括关停并转等注销机构），其中 2016 年首次参与调查的新注册企业 970 家。根据创业风险投资的标准概念，我们对以下样本进行了剔除：①行业性和综合性投资公司，如电力投资、公交投资集团、投资主业模糊不清的投资类公司等。②以大项目为投资主业的产业投资基金。③信托公司等不以创业风险投资为主业经营的金融机构。④主要从事担保业务的担保公司，但持续地开展了创业风险投资业务的担保公司除外。⑤转业而不再从事创业风险投资业务的机构。⑥在境外注册设立、在境内仅以办公室形式开展商业活动的私募股权机构。此外，随着我国创业风险投资的业态不断复杂化，很多大型创业风险投资机构以母基金（包括引导基金）的模式出现，简单相加则会带来管理资本的重复计算，因此，在调查过程中，对相关资本的重复计算部分进行了剔除。同样，对于创业风险投资企业与创业风险投资管理机构，当存在委托与受托关系时，对相关资本和项目的重复计算部分也进行了剔除。

1.2 创业风险投资机构和管理资本

2016 年，伴随着“十三五”规划出台，“新三板”分层制度的完善，“深港通”开闸，创新创业活动高涨，中国创投行业又迎来了丰硕的一年，整个行业在募资、投资、退出方面出现了不同程度的增长。

2016 年，中国创业风险投资机构数达到 2045 家[①]，较 2015 年增加 270 家，增长 15.2%。其中，创业风险投资基金 1421 家，较 2015 年增加 110 家，增幅 8.4%；创业风险投资管理机构 624 家，较 2015 增加 160 家，增幅 34.5%；披露当年新募集基金 152 家（见表 1–1、图 1–1）。

① 实际存量机构数，主要包括：创业投资企业（基金）、创业投资管理企业以及少量从事创业投资业务的事业单位。该数据已剔除不再经营创投业务或注销的机构数。

表 1-1 中国创业风险投资机构总量、增量（2007~2016）①

项目 \ 年份	2007	2008	2009	2010	2011	2012	2013	2014	2015	2016
现存的 VC 机构（家）	383	464	576	867	1096	1183	1408	1551	1775	2045
其中，VC 基金（家）	331	410	495	720	860	942	1095	1167	1311	1421
其中，VC 管理机构（家）	52	54	81	147	236	241	313	384	464	624
当年新募集基金（家）②	76	89	135	215	167	146	123	169	197	152
VC 机构增长（%）	11.0	21.1	24.1	50.5	26.4	7.9	19.0	10.2	14.4	15.2

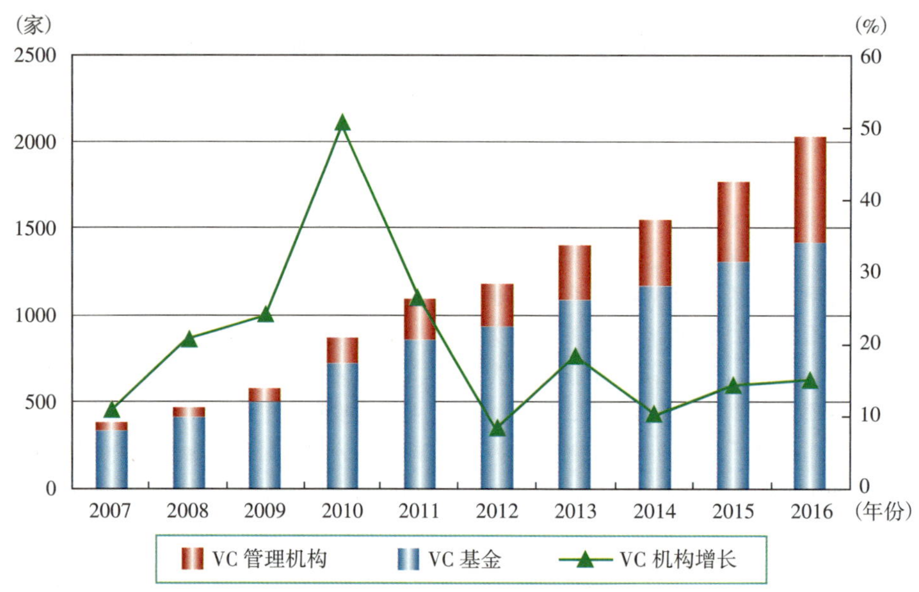

图 1-1 中国创业风险投资机构总量、增量（2007~2016）

近年来，创投基金采取委托管理的模式日益盛行，越来越多的基金将其日常管理与投资功能委托给专业的创投管理机构进行管理，2007~2016 年，创投管理机构由 52 家增加到 624 家，增长超过 10 倍。截至目前，管理资金规模最多的创投管理机构管理资本达到 600 亿元。

2016 年，全国创业风险投资管理资本总量达到 8277.1 亿元，较 2015 年增加 1623.8 亿元，增幅为 24.4%；基金平均管理资本规模为 4.05 亿元（见表 1-2、图 1-2）；披露当年新募集基金 1016.1 亿元。2016 年，全国市场母基金规模进一步扩大，据统计，最大母基金管理的子基金数达 19 家。

表 1-2 中国创业风险投资管理资本总额（2007~2016）

项目 \ 年份	2007	2008	2009	2010	2011	2012	2013	2014	2015	2016
管理资本总额（亿元）	1112.90	1455.70	1605.10	2406.60	3198.00	3312.90	3573.90	5232.40	6653.30	8277.10
较上年增长（%）	67.70	30.80	10.30	49.90	32.90	3.60	7.90	31.70	27.20	24.40
基金平均管理资本规模（亿元）	3.36	3.55	3.24	3.34	3.72	3.52	3.26	4.48	4.66	4.05

① 由于我国创投行业的迅猛发展，基金形态日趋多样化，从 2010 年起，按照国际惯例区分基金和基金管理公司，并对前期数据进行了追溯调整。

② 在实际统计中当年新募基金数量存在一定偏差，存在当年进入统计而实际为前几年募集成立基金的情形，因此每年对前期新募基金数据进行调整。

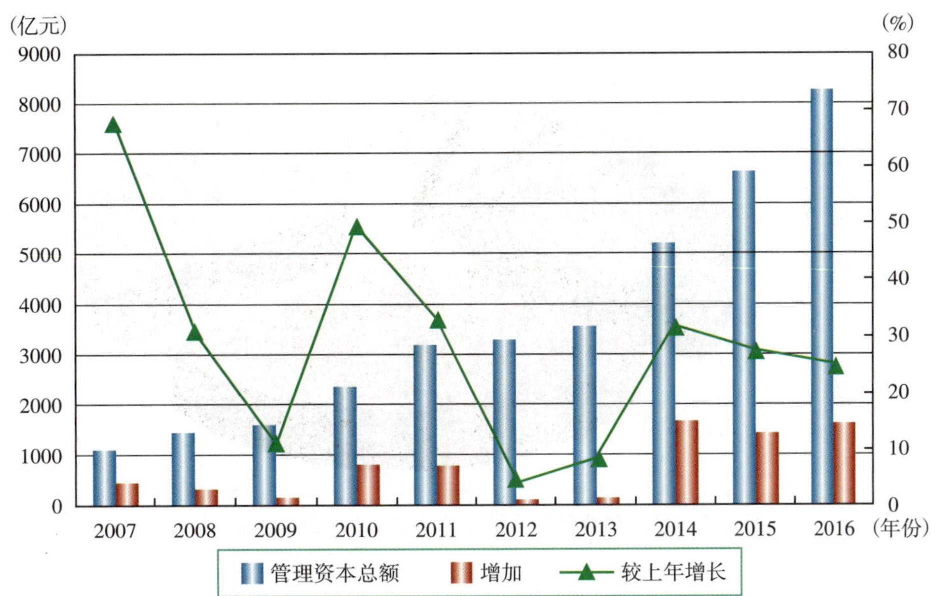

图 1–2 中国创业风险投资管理资本总额(2007~2016)

1.3 创业风险投资的资本来源

从 2016 年调查工作开始，考虑到不同资本来源属性之间的交叉关系，我们按照三个维度对我国创业风险投资的资本来源进行了重新划分。第一个维度采用了传统的分类方法，分类如下：①政府资金。包括各级政府（包括事业单位）对创业风险资本的直接资金支持。②国有独资公司资金，指国有独资公司直接提供的资金。③混合所有制企业资金。④民营所有制企业资金。⑤社保基金。⑥自然人。⑦境内外资，指通过已在中国大陆境内注册并运作的外商独资（含港、澳、台）和合资合作企业取得的创业风险投资资本。⑧境外资金，是指境外机构获得的创业风险投资资本。⑨其他资金。

据统计，2016 年中国创业风险投资的构成中，政府与国有独资合计占比 36.13%，较 2015 年上升 0.8 个百分点；民营及混合所有制企业资金占比 24.02%，较 2015 年上升 4.2 个百分点；个人投资占比 7.08%，较 2015 年有所下滑；外资企业占比 4.42%，较 2015 年升 2.3 个百分点；此外，社保基金占比 0.04%（见图 1–3）。

按照企业是否从上市融资进行划分，2016 年各类企业资金合计占比 50.15%，其中，上市企业仅占 4.37%，大量的资本以未上市企业为主，占比 45.78%（见图 1–4）。

按照资金来源的金融属性划分，银行、保险、证券等金融机构资本合计占比 6.18%，其中，银行资本较上年大幅上升；其他金融资本占比 22.55%；大量资金来源于非金融资本，占比 71.27%（见图 1–5）。

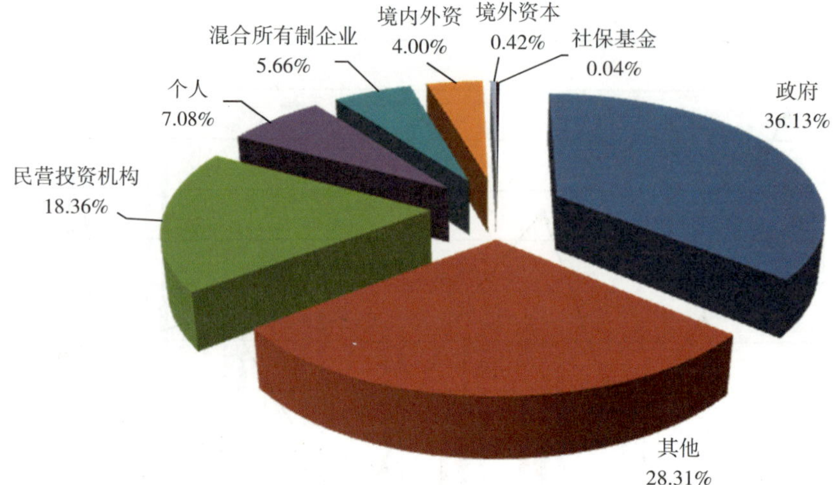

图 1-3 中国创业风险投资资本来源（2016）（分类一）①

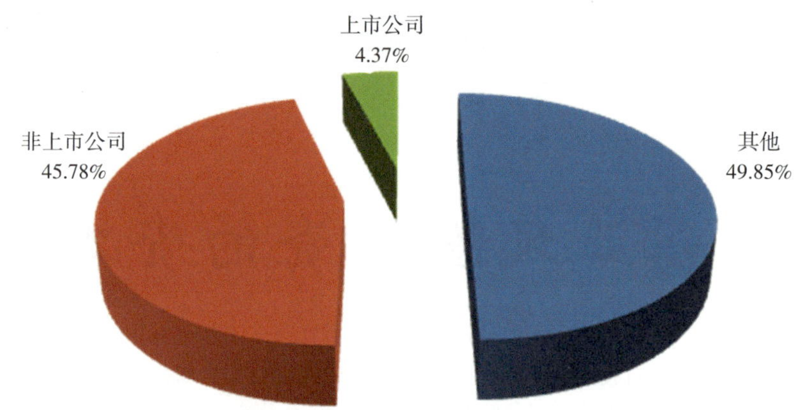

图 1-4 中国创业风险投资资本来源（2016）（分类二）②

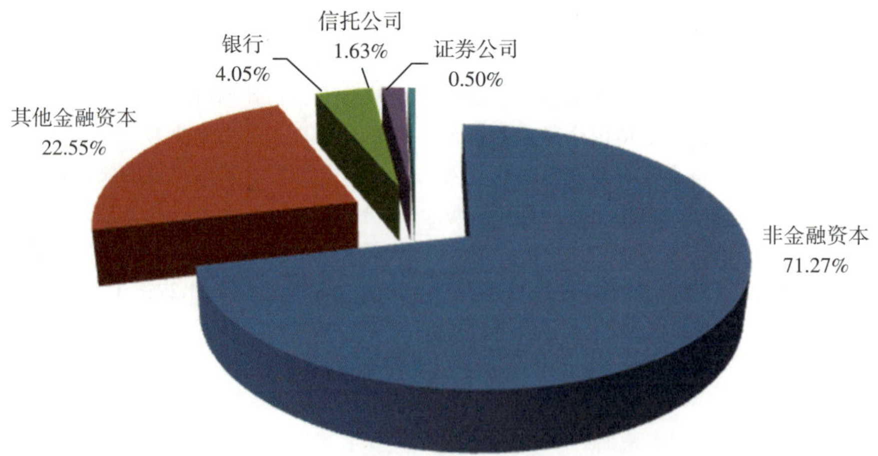

图 1-5 中国创业风险投资资本来源（2016）（分类三）③

① 有效样本数为 1352 份。
② 有效样本数为 1344 份。
③ 有效样本数为 1343 份。

1.4 创业风险投资机构的资本规模及分布

总体而言，2016 年创业风险投资机构的平均管理规模较 2015 年略有减少。从资金分布情况看，管理资金在 5000 万元以下的创业风险投资机构占机构总数的 30.5%，较 2015 年上升 2.4 个百分点；管理资金在 5000 万~5 亿元的机构合计占比 57.1%，各资金段规模企业占比均较 2015 年略有下降；整体趋势表现出了管理资金规模缩小的趋势。但也出现了个别企业管理规模扩张的情况，规模在 5 亿元以上的管理资金占比为 12.5%，较 2015 年略有上升（见图 1-6）。

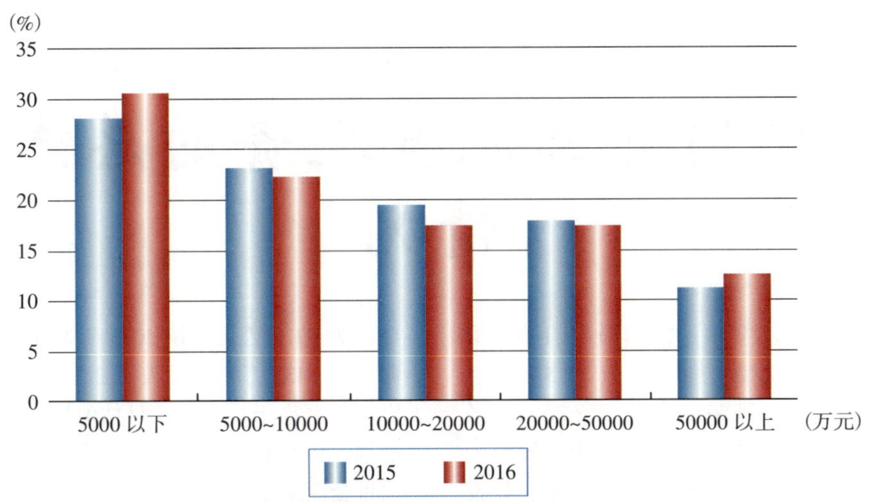

图 1-6 中国不同规模创业风险投资机构分布（2015~2016）①

按管理资金规模划分，2016 年创投机构管理资金规模略有缩小，管理资金规模在 5000 万元以下的机构仅掌握着 1.4%的创业风险投资总资本，规模在 5000 万~1 亿元的机构掌握了 3.1%的份额，规模在 1 亿~2 亿元的机构掌握了 4.6%的总资金，规模在 2 亿~5 亿元的机构所占管理资本的份额为 9.1%，均较 2015 年的占比略有下滑；81.8%的管理资本掌握在规模在 5 亿元以上的机构手中（见图 1-7），资本集聚效应更为明显。

① 有效样本数为 2968 份。

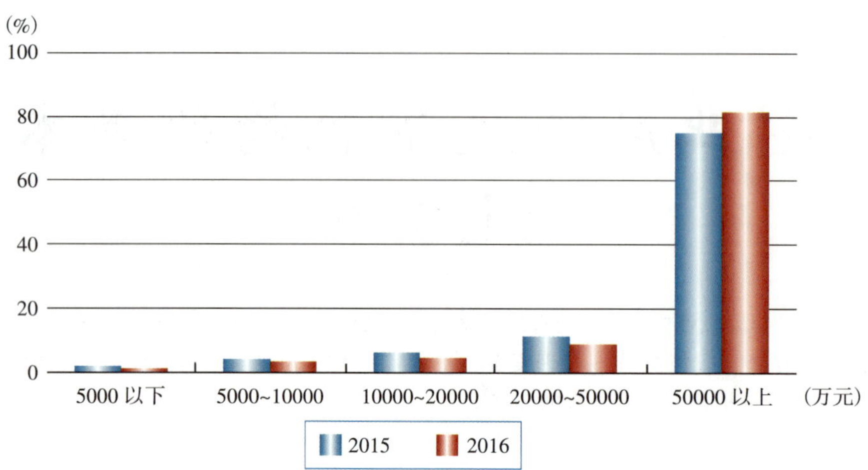

图 1-7 中国不同规模创业风险投资机构管理资本分布（2016）①

1.5 中国创业风险投资的总体投资情况

2016 年，中国创投市场投资项目数整体较上年有所滑落，当年披露机构投资项目数为 2744 项，较 2015 年下滑 19.8%；披露项目投资金额达到 505.5 亿元，较 2015 年增加 8.6%，项目平均投资额为 1842 万元。其中，投资于高新技术企业项目 634 项，较 2015 年减少 23.1%；投资金额为 92.1 亿元，较 2015 年减少 21.4%，项目平均投资额为 1453 万元（见表 1-3）。可见，2016 年单笔项目投资额略高于往年，项目估值增大，大手笔的投资有所增加；但高新技术企业项目投资期可能较为靠前，单笔项目金额略小。

表 1-3 截至 2016 年底中国创业风险投资当年投资情况（2011~2016）

年份	当年投资项目总数（项）	投资高新技术企业/项目数（项）	当年投资金额（亿元）	投资高新技术企业/项目金额（亿元）
2011	2399	1250	545.3	229.8
2012	1903	850	356.0	172.6
2013	1501	590	279.0	109.0
2014	2459	689	374.4	124.8
2015	3423	820	465.6	117.2
2016	2744	634	505.5	92.1

截至 2016 年底，全国创业风险投资机构累计投资项目数达到 19296 项，其中投资高新技术企业项目数 8490 项，占比 44.0%；累计投资金额 3765.2 亿元，其中投资高新技术企业金额 1566.8 亿元，占比 41.6%（见表 1-4）。

① 有效样本数为 2968 份。

表 1-4　截至 2016 年底中国创业风险投资累计投资情况（2011~2016）

年份	累计投资项目总数（项）	投资高新技术企业/项目数（项）	累计投资金额（亿元）	投资高新技术企业/项目金额（亿元）
2011	9978	5940	2036.6	1038.6
2012	11112	6404	2355.1	1193.1
2013	12149	6779	2634.1	1302.1
2014	14118	7330	2933.6	1401.9
2015	17376	8047	3361.2	1493.1
2016	19296	8490	3765.2	1566.8

2 中国创业风险投资的投资分析

2.1 中国创业风险投资行业特征

2.1.1 中国创业风险投资行业分布

从投资金额来看，2016 年中国创业风险资本主要集中在网络产业、其他行业、软件产业、金融保险业、医药保健，这五个行业集中了 67.13%的资金投资，其集中度较 2015 年上涨 19.23 个百分点。

从投资项目数看，2016 年中国创业风险投资项目主要集中在其他行业、网络产业、软件产业、IT 服务业、新材料工业，这五个行业集中了当年 44.83%的项目，集中度较 2015 年上涨 4.42 个百分点（见表 2–1、图 2–1、图 2–2）。

表 2–1 中国创业风险投资项目行业分布：投资金额与投资项目（2015~2016）① 单位：%

投资行业	2016 年		2015 年	
	投资金额	投资项目	投资金额	投资项目
网络产业	34.03	11.35	5.07	10.61
其他行业	12.90	13.67	10.41	10.85
软件产业	9.58	7.58	7.54	7.41
金融保险业	6.97	3.12	5.71	3.09
医药保健	3.65	5.44	5.37	4.05
新材料工业	3.36	5.53	5.66	5.48
IT 服务业	3.30	6.70	3.03	5.75
传播与文化娱乐	3.02	5.26	5.50	4.32
传统制造业	1.99	3.58	3.77	4.44
建筑业	1.98	0.56	0.76	0.58
新能源、高效节能技术	1.97	3.77	2.95	4.17
生物科技	1.89	4.37	2.13	3.47
其他制造业	1.65	4.09	3.67	5.25
科技服务	1.61	4.51	1.76	3.05
交通运输仓储和邮政业	1.60	0.88	1.86	0.89
环保工程	1.47	3.12	2.31	5.17
消费产品和服务	1.43	3.07	2.14	2.66

① 有效样本数为 2150 份。

续表

投资行业	2016 年		2015 年	
	投资金额	投资项目	投资金额	投资项目
计算机硬件产业	1.27	1.91	1.65	1.81
农林牧副渔	0.96	1.91	0.65	2.01
半导体	0.96	1.30	1.94	1.16
通信设备	0.95	2.00	18.59	5.79
社会服务	0.90	1.95	3.42	3.09
光电子与光机电一体化	0.85	2.14	0.85	2.05
其他 IT 产业	0.64	1.02	0.48	1.04
批发和零售业	0.43	0.70	1.24	1.08
房地产业	0.37	0.23	0.94	0.35
水电煤气	0.24	0.05	0.46	0.31
核应用技术	0.04	0.09	0.08	0.04
采掘业	0.01	0.09	0.06	0.04

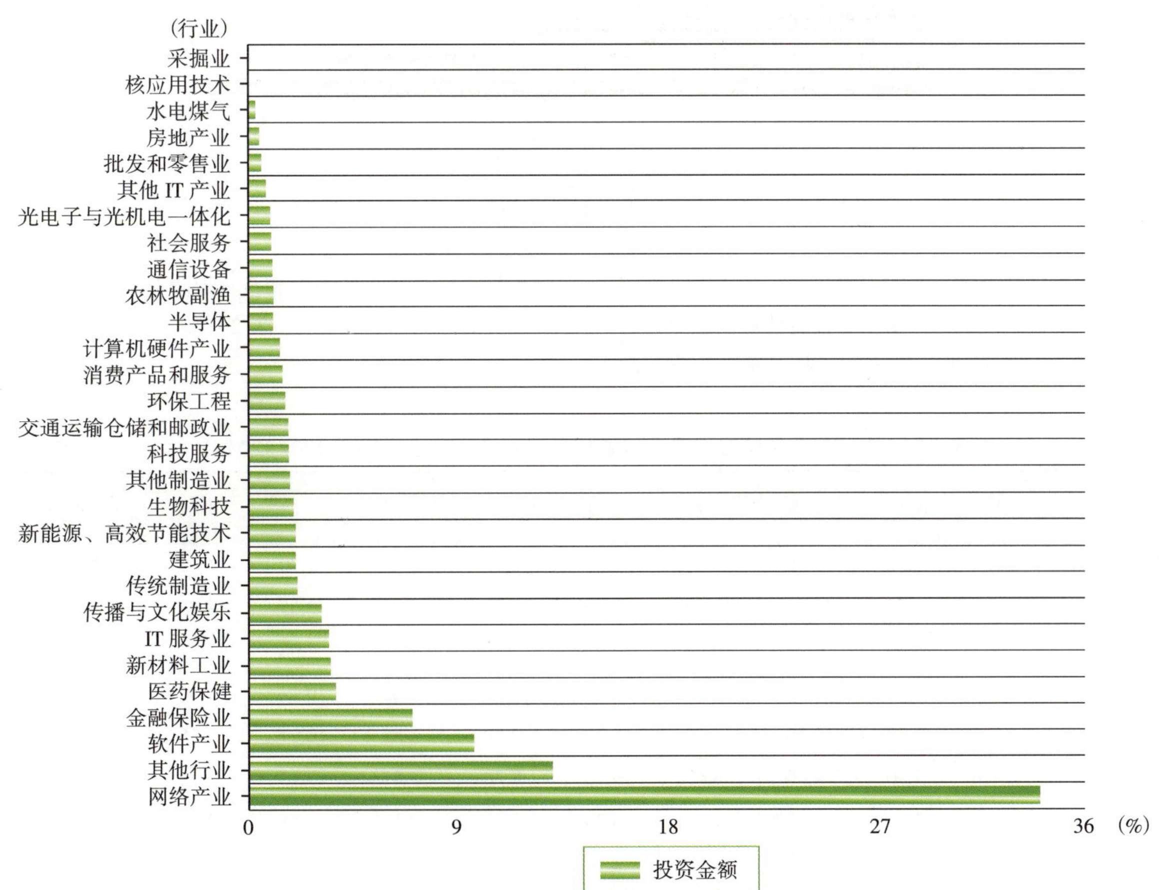

图 2-1 中国创业风险投资业投资项目按投资金额的行业分布（2016）

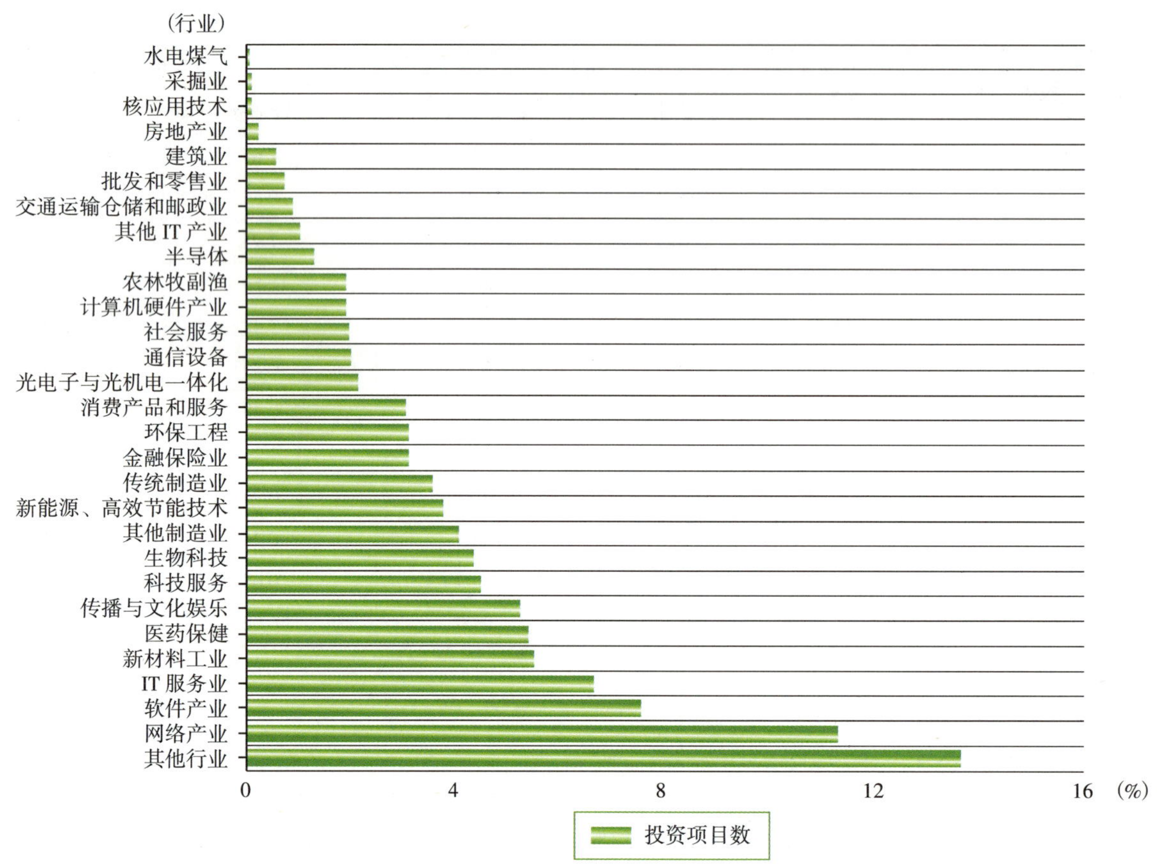

图 2-2 中国创业风险投资业投资项目行业分布（2016）

从我国创业风险投资行业变化趋势看，创业风险投资金额和投资项目数量表现为：由主要投资传统制造业转向投资网络产业、软件产业、新材料工业等新兴产业；同时，其他行业、IT 服务业和金融保险业等不断获得创业风险投资的青睐（见表 2-2、表 2-3）。

表 2-2 中国创业风险投资产业投资项目投资金额行业分布（2007~2016） 单位：%

投资行业 \ 年份	2007	2008	2009	2010	2011	2012	2013	2014	2015	2016
网络产业	0.50	2.70	1.80	2.80	2.50	2.05	1.90	4.02	5.07	34.03
其他行业	8.30	12.70	10.00	15.70	11.20	7.62	2.65	8.45	10.41	12.90
软件产业	16.00	6.20	10.90	2.90	2.10	2.41	2.02	7.37	7.54	9.58
金融保险业	22.10	8.20	15.20	7.80	2.40	5.42	10.12	2.86	5.71	6.97
医药保健	2.00	2.50	4.90	5.30	3.80	4.85	10.04	7.35	5.37	3.65
新材料工业	7.90	4.40	6.40	9.30	8.70	7.81	7.13	3.72	5.66	3.36
IT 服务业	1.00	4.60	1.50	3.20	2.80	3.14	3.58	3.00	3.03	3.30
传播与文化娱乐	2.20	1.80	2.50	2.10	2.20	6.35	6.16	5.44	5.50	3.02
传统制造业	12.60	15.60	11.90	10.10	7.70	10.10	7.19	7.64	3.77	1.99

续表

投资行业＼年份	2007	2008	2009	2010	2011	2012	2013	2014	2015	2016
建筑业	—	—	—	—	1.60	1.94	1.32	0.62	0.76	1.98
新能源、高效节能技术	4.60	7.70	8.50	8.30	6.20	7.19	8.69	2.94	2.95	1.97
生物科技	2.30	5.70	2.50	3.90	3.90	2.80	2.27	3.68	2.13	1.89
其他制造业	—	—	—	—	8.20	4.83	5.30	3.31	3.67	1.65
科技服务	4.90	2.10	2.00	2.30	1.60	1.64	1.02	2.18	1.76	1.61
交通运输仓储和邮政业	—	—	—	—	1.40	0.35	2.57	0.18	1.86	1.60
环保工程	1.50	1.30	1.80	3.30	2.60	2.81	2.89	2.83	2.31	1.47
消费产品和服务	1.40	3.90	4.30	7.10	9.40	6.27	5.00	1.57	2.14	1.43
计算机硬件产业	0.60	3.40	0.10	1.10	0.70	1.10	0.68	4.15	1.65	1.27
半导体	1.30	2.90	2.30	1.20	1.30	1.44	1.40	1.35	0.65	0.96
农林牧副渔	1.20	2.60	3.50	4.10	4.10	6.07	6.33	2.00	1.94	0.96
通信设备	2.90	1.80	1.90	1.00	2.80	3.63	3.11	13.76	18.59	0.95
社会服务	—	—	—	—	0.70	1.09	1.86	2.36	3.42	0.90
光电子与光机电一体化	2.10	4.00	4.10	4.20	3.30	3.49	4.62	1.89	0.85	0.85
其他 IT 产业	1.30	2.30	2.20	1.20	1.50	1.68	0.36	1.02	0.48	0.64
批发和零售业	1.10	0.00	0.30	0.70	1.20	0.85	0.50	3.82	1.24	0.43
房地产业	—	—	—	—	4.90	1.24	0.21	1.99	0.94	0.37
水电煤气	—	—	—	—	0.10	0.29	0.25	0.44	0.46	0.24
核应用技术	0.00	0.00	0.10	0.00	0.40	0.24	0.17	0.06	0.08	0.04
采掘业	1.90	3.60	1.50	2.50	0.60	1.30	0.51	0.00	0.06	0.01

表 2-3 中国创业风险投资业投资项目数行业分布（2007~2016） 单位：%

投资行业＼年份	2007	2008	2009	2010	2011	2012	2013	2014	2015	2016
其他行业	9.20	10.40	9.70	11.70	8.40	7.26	3.74	8.14	10.85	13.67
网络产业	2.40	2.00	3.10	4.80	3.20	2.82	3.74	8.88	10.61	11.35
软件产业	17.10	9.70	13.90	7.00	3.50	3.12	5.32	9.40	7.41	7.58
IT 服务业	2.60	3.80	3.30	4.20	4.10	3.42	4.17	5.67	5.75	6.70
新材料工业	9.60	6.60	7.20	10.10	9.50	8.76	7.61	5.93	5.48	5.53
医药保健	3.30	4.80	6.00	5.80	4.40	6.18	9.99	5.28	4.05	5.44
传播与文化娱乐	2.00	1.70	2.10	1.90	2.40	5.28	5.24	3.81	4.32	5.26
科技服务	2.00	4.50	2.70	2.50	1.80	2.58	1.94	2.60	3.05	4.51
生物科技	5.60	6.10	5.50	5.60	3.30	4.80	4.17	4.11	3.47	4.37
其他制造业	—	—	—	—	8.30	4.98	4.67	4.11	5.25	4.09

续表

投资行业 \ 年份	2007	2008	2009	2010	2011	2012	2013	2014	2015	2016
新能源、高效节能技术	5.70	5.10	6.30	7.80	6.00	7.20	6.75	4.16	4.17	3.77
传统制造业	13.80	14.20	9.40	7.30	8.00	8.82	6.03	4.98	4.44	3.58
环保工程	2.20	2.20	2.70	3.30	3.20	3.06	3.95	3.03	3.09	3.12
金融保险业	5.00	4.90	5.40	4.10	2.00	4.20	6.54	3.59	5.17	3.12
消费产品和服务	1.90	2.80	3.10	4.10	7.20	3.54	3.45	2.56	2.66	3.07
光电子与光机电一体化	4.50	5.90	5.10	6.00	4.60	3.78	4.89	2.86	2.05	2.14
通信设备	2.70	3.90	3.00	2.50	3.20	3.72	3.16	8.32	5.79	2.00
社会服务	—	—	—	—	1.30	2.34	1.87	1.65	3.09	1.95
计算机硬件产业	1.10	1.30	0.40	1.40	1.30	1.50	1.22	1.69	1.81	1.91
农林牧副渔	1.20	2.60	2.30	3.20	4.80	4.74	3.66	2.73	2.01	1.91
半导体	3.00	2.70	3.80	2.50	1.70	1.44	2.51	1.78	1.16	1.30
其他 IT 产业	2.60	3.20	3.70	2.30	2.40	1.92	1.01	1.60	1.04	1.02
交通运输仓储和邮政业	—	—	—	—	0.80	0.24	1.15	0.17	0.89	0.88
批发和零售业	1.20	0.20	0.30	0.70	1.20	0.72	0.36	1.86	1.08	0.70
建筑业	—	—	—	—	1.80	1.62	1.22	0.56	0.58	0.56
房地产业	—	—	—	—	0.30	0.54	0.29	0.22	0.35	0.23
采掘业	1.20	1.50	1.00	1.20	0.70	0.48	0.57	0.04	0.04	0.09
核应用技术	0.00	0.00	0.10	0.00	0.50	0.48	0.29	0.04	0.04	0.09
水电煤气	—	—	—	—	0.10	0.42	0.29	0.22	0.31	0.05

按行业大类统计，信息传输、软件和信息服务业，其他行业以及金融保险业是 2016 年创业风险投资的热点领域。从趋势看，2016 年创业风险投资对计算机、通信、其他电子设备制造业，新能源和环保业，医药生物业的投资步伐略有放缓（见表 2–4）。

表 2–4 中国创业风险业投资项目前十大行业分布（2015~2016）

单位：%

行业划分（代码）			2016 年		2015 年	
			投资金额	投资项目	投资金额	投资项目
I	信息传输、软件和信息服务业	IT 服务业	47.55	26.65	16.12	24.81
		其他 IT 产业				
		软件产业				
		网络产业				

续表

行业划分（代码）			2016年		2015年	
			投资金额	投资项目	投资金额	投资项目
O	其他行业		12.9	13.67	10.41	10.85
J	金融保险业		6.97	3.12	5.71	3.09
C9	新能源和环保业	核应用技术	6.84	12.51	11.00	14.86
		环保工程				
		新材料工业				
		新能源、高效节能技术				
C8	医药生物业	生物科技	5.54	9.81	7.50	7.52
		医药保健				
C7	计算机、通信和其他电子设备制造业	半导体	4.03	7.35	23.03	10.81
		光电子与光机电一体化				
		计算机硬件产业				
		通信设备				
N	传播与文化娱乐		3.02	5.26	5.50	4.32
CA	传统制造业		1.99	3.58	3.77	4.44
E	建筑业		1.98	0.56	0.76	0.58
C12	其他制造业		1.65	4.09	3.67	5.25

2.1.2 中国创业风险投资对高新技术产业与传统产业的投资比较①

按照高新技术产业和传统产业对被投资项目进行划分，可以看出，中国创业风险投资对高新技术产业的投资金额和投资项目占比在经历2015年的下滑后，2016年均实现一定程度的回升。其中，2016年中国创业风险投资对高新技术产业的投资金额占比大幅提升。可见2016年中国创业风险投资对高新技术产业保持着较高的投资热情（见表2-5、图2-3、表2-6、图2-4）。

表2-5 中国创业风险投资项目年度行业分布：高新技术产业与传统产业（2007~2016） 单位：%

产业 \ 年份	2007	2008	2009	2010	2011	2012	2013	2014	2015	2016
高新技术产业	65.5	63.2	67.7	67.0	53.4	55.3	61.3	65.4	59.0	60.9
传统产业	34.5	36.8	32.3	33.0	46.6	44.7	38.7	34.6	41.0	39.1

① 有效样本数：高新项目样本数为1310份；传统项目样本数为840份。

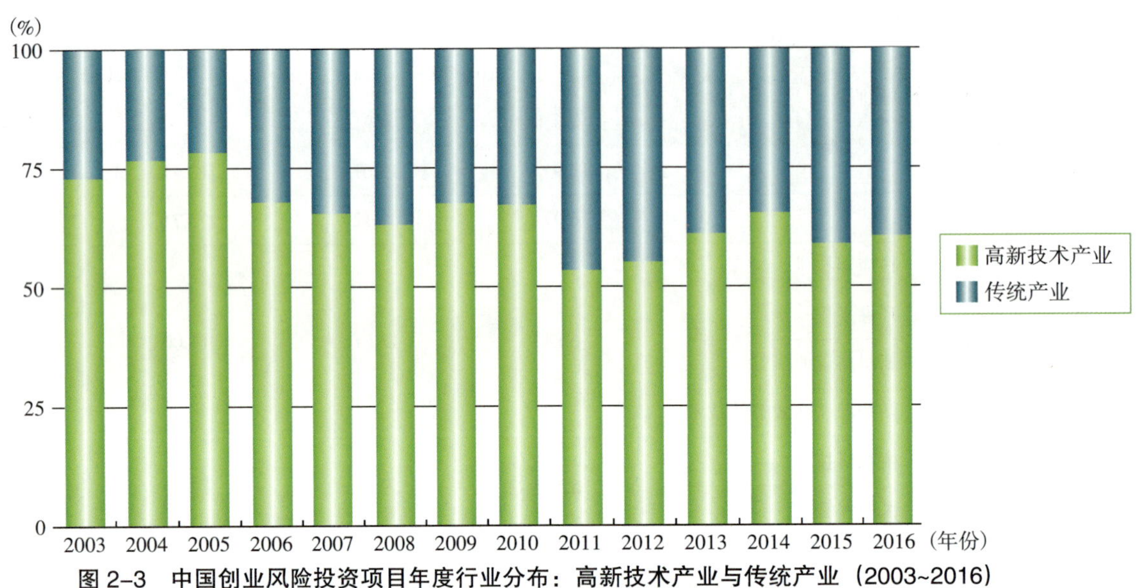

图 2-3 中国创业风险投资项目年度行业分布：高新技术产业与传统产业（2003~2016）

表 2-6 中国创业风险投资金额年度行业分布：高新技术产业与传统产业（2007~2016） 单位：%

产业 \ 年份	2007	2008	2009	2010	2011	2012	2013	2014	2015	2016
高新技术产业	51.1	55.2	52.3	52.4	44.9	47.6	50.4	59.3	58.2	65.6
传统产业	48.9	44.8	47.7	47.6	55.1	52.4	49.6	40.7	41.8	34.4

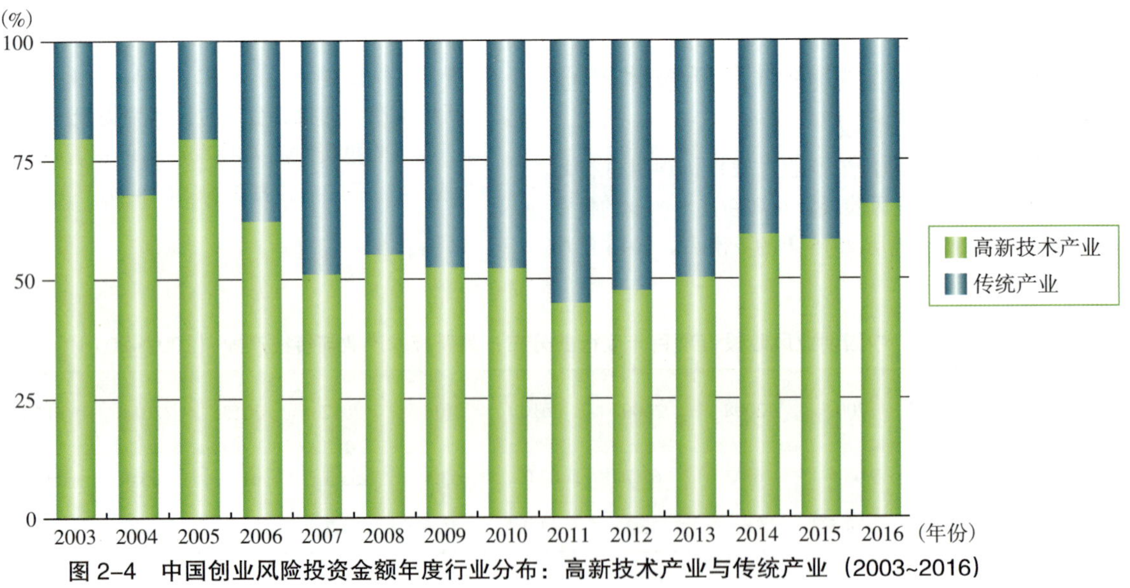

图 2-4 中国创业风险投资金额年度行业分布：高新技术产业与传统产业（2003~2016）

2.2 中国创业风险投资的投资阶段

2.2.1 中国创业风险投资所处阶段总体分布[①]

2016年，中国创业风险投资机构的投资金额主要集中在起步期、成长（扩张）期和成熟（过渡）期。与2015年相比，起步期和成熟（过渡）期的投资金额大幅上升，分别提高8.8个百分点和11.1个百分点。投资机构对成长（扩张）期的投资金额依然保持最多，但其比重较2015年下降15.9的百分点。

2016年中国创业风险投资机构的投资项目主要集中在起步期、成长（扩张）期和种子期。相比2015年，种子期的投资项目小幅提升，上涨1.4个百分点。创业风险投资对成长（扩张）期的投资项目数则回落5.1个百分点（见表2-7、图2-5、表2-8、图2-6、表2-9、图2-7）。

表2-7 中国创业风险投资项目所处阶段总体分布：投资金额与投资项目（2016） 单位：%

成长阶段	投资金额	投资项目
种子期	4.3	19.6
起步期	30.3	38.9
成长（扩张）期	38.5	35.0
成熟（过渡）期	26.3	5.7
重建期	0.6	0.8

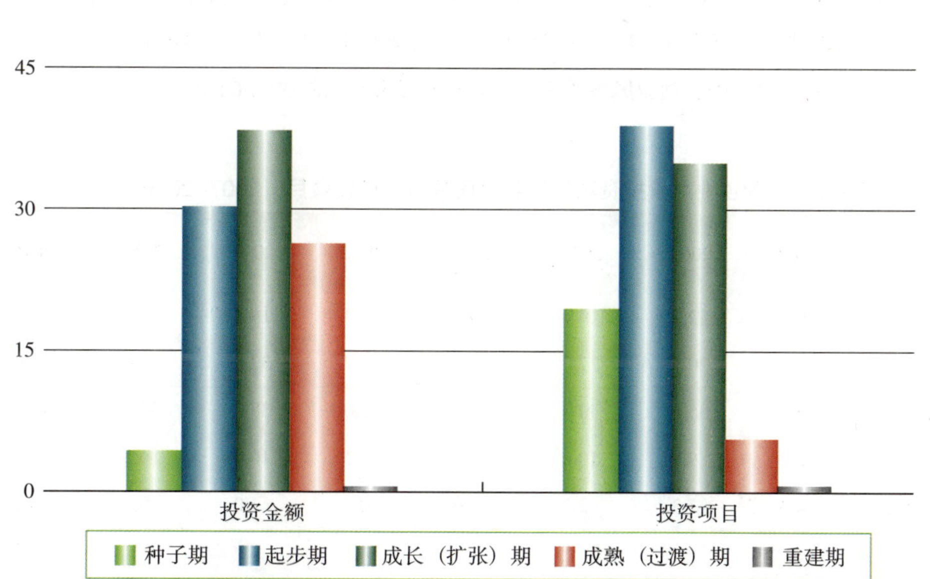

图2-5 中国创业风险投资项目所处阶段总体分布：投资金额与投资项目（2016）

① 有效样本数为2120份。

表 2-8 中国创业风险投资项目所处阶段分布：投资金额（2007~2016） 单位：%

年份 阶段	2007	2008	2009	2010	2011	2012	2013	2014	2015	2016
种子期	12.7	9.4	19.9	10.2	4.3	6.6	12.2	5.6	8.1	4.3
起步期	8.9	19.0	12.8	17.4	14.8	19.3	22.4	25.2	21.5	30.3
成长（扩张）期	38.2	38.5	45.1	49.2	55.0	52.0	41.4	59.0	54.4	38.5
成熟（过渡）期	35.2	26.5	18.5	20.2	22.3	21.6	22.8	10.1	15.2	26.3
重建期	5.0	6.6	3.7	3.0	3.6	0.6	1.2	0.1	0.7	0.6

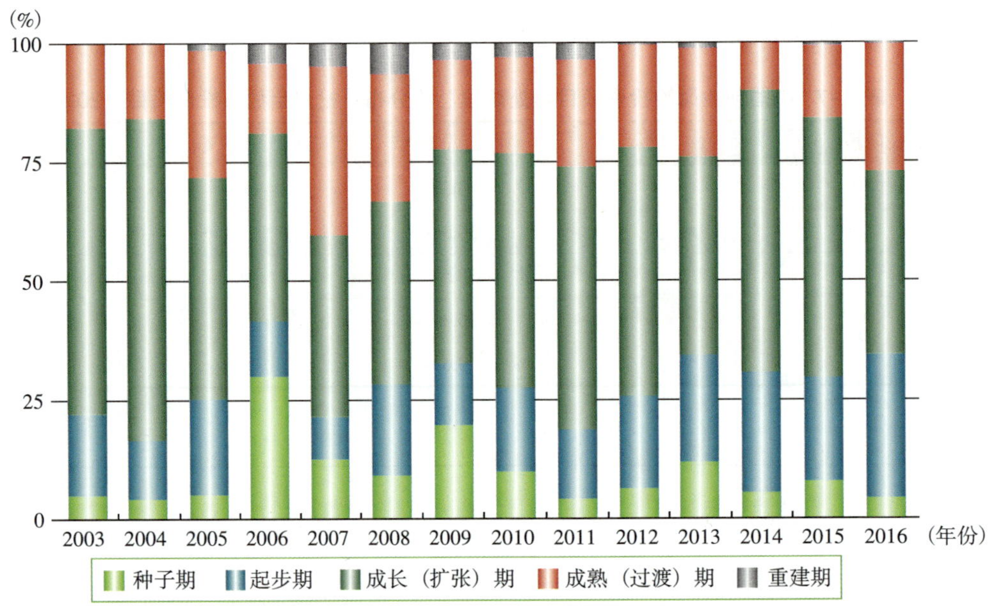

图 2-6 中国创业风险投资金额所处阶段分布（2003~2016）

表 2-9 中国创业风险投资项目所处阶段分布：投资项目（2007~2016） 单位：%

年份 阶段	2007	2008	2009	2010	2011	2012	2013	2014	2015	2016
种子期	26.6	19.3	32.2	19.9	9.7	12.3	18.4	20.8	18.2	19.6
起步期	18.9	30.2	20.3	27.0	22.7	28.7	32.5	36.6	35.6	38.9
成长（扩张）期	36.6	34.0	35.2	40.9	48.3	45.0	38.2	35.9	40.2	35.0
成熟（过渡）期	12.4	12.1	9.0	10.0	16.7	13.2	10.0	6.5	5.4	5.7
重建期	5.4	4.4	3.3	2.2	2.6	0.8	1.0	0.3	0.7	0.8

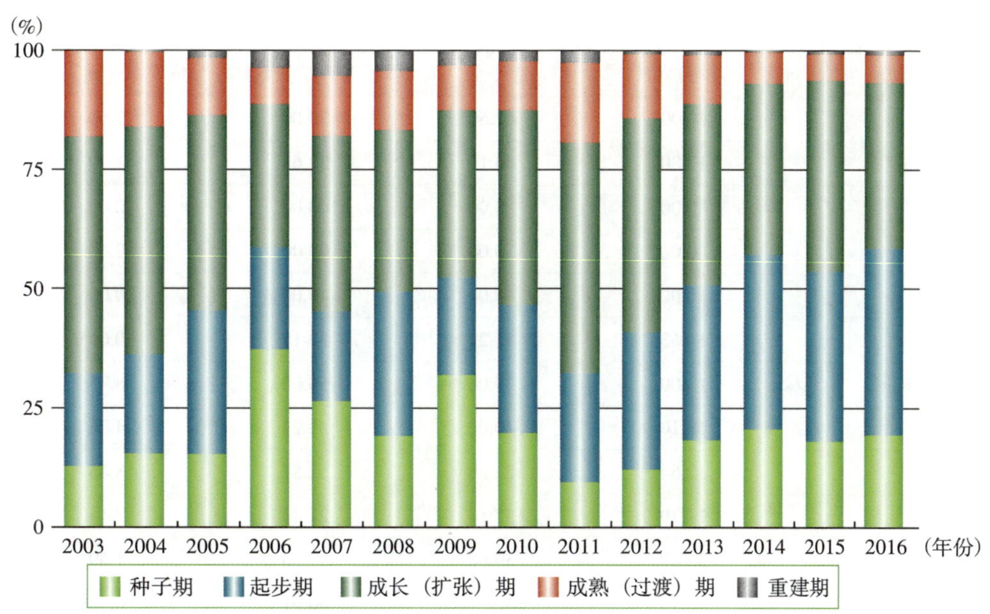

图 2-7　中国创业风险投资项目所处阶段分布（2003~2016）

2.2.2　中国创业风险投资在主要行业投资项目的阶段分布

从分行业的投资项目阶段分布看，2016 年，采掘业、软件产业、光电子与光机电一体化、消费产品和服务以及医药保健的项目数量中种子期比重较高；批发和零售业、采掘业、IT 服务业、医药保健和金融保险业的投资金额中种子期比重较高。其中，采掘业、光电子与光机电一体化和医药保健在这一阶段的投资金额和项目数均保持较高比重，一定程度上说明投资者对这三个行业早期投资价值的肯定。半导体、IT 服务业、社会服务、生物科技、金融保险业等起步期的项目得到普遍关注。核应用技术、水电煤气、采掘业、批发和零售业、环保工程、其他制造业等资金密集型产业在成长（扩张）阶段获得的创业风险投资较多关注（见表 2-10、表 2-11）。

表 2-10　中国创业风险投资项目主要行业的投资阶段分布：投资项目（2016）①　　单位：%

投资行业	种子期	起步期	成长（扩张）期	成熟（过渡）期	重建期
医药保健	23.89	35.4	32.74	7.96	0.00
传统制造业	12.99	19.48	54.55	12.99	0.00
软件产业	35.63	23.13	38.13	3.13	0.00
新材料工业	17.54	40.35	34.21	7.89	0.00
采掘业	50.00	0.00	50.00	0.00	0.00
其他行业	18.48	46.74	27.90	5.07	1.81
IT 服务业	23.36	52.55	18.98	4.38	0.73
批发和零售业	14.29	28.57	57.14	0.00	0.00
科技服务	23.40	46.81	24.47	5.32	0.00
交通运输仓储和邮政业	21.05	21.05	42.11	10.53	5.26

① 有效样本数为 2150 份。

续表

投资行业	种子期	起步期	成长（扩张）期	成熟（过渡）期	重建期
计算机硬件产业	20.00	42.50	30.00	7.50	0.00
网络产业	17.80	46.19	32.63	3.39	0.00
核应用技术	0.00	0.00	100.00	0.00	0.00
水电煤气	0.00	0.00	100.00	0.00	0.00
房地产业	0.00	40.00	40.00	20.00	0.00
社会服务	14.63	51.22	34.15	0.00	0.00
新能源、高效节能技术	10.00	30.00	50.00	8.75	1.25
传播与文化娱乐	18.10	40.00	35.24	4.76	1.90
其他制造业	12.64	22.99	52.87	8.05	3.45
半导体	14.29	57.14	21.43	7.14	0.00
消费产品和服务	25.40	39.68	33.33	1.59	0.00
其他 IT 产业	18.18	40.91	40.91	0.00	0.00
农林牧副渔	7.89	34.21	44.74	13.16	0.00
金融保险业	23.21	48.21	23.21	5.36	0.00
建筑业	9.09	27.27	45.45	18.18	0.00
环保工程	13.43	23.88	52.24	5.97	4.48
通信设备	14.63	36.59	34.15	14.63	0.00
光电子与光机电一体化	33.33	28.89	35.56	2.22	0.00
生物科技	18.48	51.09	28.26	2.17	0.00

表 2-11 中国创业风险投资项目主要行业投资阶段分布：投资金额（2016）[①] 单位：%

投资行业	种子期	起步期	成长（扩张）期	成熟（过渡）期	重建期
医药保健	9.64	32.03	48.08	10.25	—
采掘业	13.79	—	86.21	—	—
其他行业	7.27	63.38	19.58	7.60	2.17
新材料工业	5.34	33.34	35.77	25.56	—
IT 服务业	12.06	50.35	34.60	1.43	1.56
批发和零售业	35.13	11.42	53.46	—	—
科技服务	6.05	34.83	29.21	29.91	—
交通运输仓储和邮政业	1.97	77.93	13.12	3.52	3.47
计算机硬件产业	3.37	27.71	67.95	0.98	—
网络产业	1.33	24.46	22.73	51.49	—
核应用技术	—	—	100.00	—	—
水电煤气	—	—	100.00	—	—

① 有效样本数为 2066 份。

续表

投资行业	种子期	起步期	成长（扩张）期	成熟（过渡）期	重建期
房地产业	—	1.72	94.55	3.73	—
社会服务	2.31	27.34	70.34	—	—
传播与文化娱乐	4.74	32.27	46.25	15.71	1.03
其他制造业	6.53	14.80	60.27	15.02	3.38
新能源、高效节能技术	0.94	25.04	51.62	21.46	0.94
半导体	5.14	47.95	14.05	32.86	—
其他 IT 产业	0.67	13.03	86.31	—	—
消费产品和服务	4.13	20.37	72.88	2.61	—
农林牧副渔	1.22	20.10	66.82	11.86	—
金融保险业	8.72	27.38	21.15	42.75	—
建筑业	0.10	1.82	85.18	12.90	—
环保工程	4.34	17.50	60.49	13.85	3.81
通信设备	6.77	19.42	40.29	33.52	—
光电子与光机电一体化	8.28	39.90	47.71	4.11	—
生物科技	7.94	58.37	27.78	5.91	—
传统制造业	6.39	26.81	45.89	20.91	—
软件产业	3.33	6.79	80.61	9.28	—

2.3 中国创业风险投资的投资强度

2.3.1 中国创业风险投资强度的变化趋势与行业差异[①]

自 2011 年以来，我国创业风险投资强度呈现持续下降趋势，2016 年也持续了这一趋势，投资强度为 1014.76 万元/项（见表 2-12、图 2-8）。

表 2-12 中国创业风险投资的投资强度（2007~2016） 单位：万元/项

年份	2007	2008	2009	2010	2011	2012	2013	2014	2015	2016
投资强度	973.37	1041.25	1059.77	1356.53	1550.53	1322.66	1282.12	1129.53	1089.26	1014.76

① 有效样本数为 2261 份。

图 2-8 中国创业风险投资的投资强度（1995~2016）

按行业划分，2016 年创业风险投资对金融保险业、医药保健、通信设备、环保工程、其他行业等行业的项目平均投资强度较大（见表 2-13、图 2-9）。

表 2-13 中国创业风险投资不同行业的投资强度（2007~2016） 单位：万元/项

行业 \ 年份	2007	2008	2009	2010	2011	2012	2013	2014	2015	2016
医药保健	884.0	678.8	1052.5	1409.3	1444.5	1144.5	1351.0	1429.6	1190.4	1212.9
新能源、高效节能技术	1152.4	1447.4	1156.6	1302.8	1647.8	1373.0	1420.2	1059.2	1054.3	1089.9
新材料工业	938.3	867.6	1212.9	1376.6	1639.7	1224.5	1444.0	1006.4	1416.6	1033.1
消费产品和服务	1010.6	1774.1	1435.8	2463.2	2102.0	2036.9	1712.8	1053.3	1260.2	781.0
网络产业	309.0	1186.7	805.5	925.8	1487.4	1028.8	721.0	742.8	794.4	1007.9
通信设备	964.9	580.8	671.0	726.0	1791.6	1439.3	1704.3	1540.4	1268.5	1200.5
生物科技	594.0	878.0	612.0	805.1	1369	904.5	960.5	1059.2	1130.9	1091.2
软件产业	979.1	732.4	788.4	756.2	976.3	1029.8	677.8	945.0	907.7	751.3
其他行业	1089.0	1155.6	1189.9	1542.2	1628.9	1110.4	1075.7	1400.5	1156.7	1179.8
其他 IT 产业	696.5	942.3	827.4	980.7	1297.0	1171.2	616.4	971.1	849.4	695.7
批发和零售业	1273.1	30.0	1673.3	1988.2	1642.8	1810.3	2410.0	1638.7	947.8	1075.6
农林牧副渔	1411.2	1327.8	1580.6	2054.7	1505.4	1836.0	1516.6	1036.7	1517.0	1073.9
科技服务	456.4	600.8	785.9	1400.8	1391.7	842.4	944.0	903.1	854.1	708.9
金融保险业	1498.1	1537.0	1964.0	1326.1	977.6	1653.0	1885.6	929.0	1216.9	1469.1
计算机硬件产业	840.4	782.1	495.0	997.3	1117.0	799.6	581.5	1225.9	1067.8	908.0
环保工程	982.2	760.8	893.7	1501.4	1368.9	1402.3	1268.6	1559.3	1311.4	1184.6
核应用技术	—	—	1200.0	—	1517.3	757.4	1008.3	2500.0	4000.0	1176.0

续表

年份 行业	2007	2008	2009	2010	2011	2012	2013	2014	2015	2016
光电子与光机电一体化	670.3	898.9	879.1	1075.8	1420.0	1288.3	1294.2	863.4	769.8	708.2
传统制造业	1286.5	1320.7	1481.1	2057.8	1754.9	1390.3	1409.1	1032.4	1115.1	1122.4
传播与文化娱乐	765.7	671.5	1437.6	1413.1	1458.1	1398.6	1441.9	1543.3	961.0	907.5
采掘业	1037.6	1850.5	1211	1633.2	1184.3	2130.4	1537.8	200.0	3002.0	290.0
半导体	626.4	1407.6	688.7	895.4	1608.3	1312.6	963.9	1322.8	856.4	1064.9
IT 服务业	607.3	791	609.1	1002.1	1208.5	1216.5	963.0	843.4	895.5	854.1
水电煤气	—	—	—	—	866.7	1050	1512.5	1232.5	1845.4	—
社会服务	—	—	—	—	1150.3	728.5	1370.1	1147.2	752.7	771.4
其他制造业	—	—	—	—	1825.3	1483.5	959.4	1181.2	1107.6	921.1
交通运输仓储和邮政业	—	—	—	—	2163.9	2244.7	1432.4	1762.5	1633.9	1148.4
建筑业	—	—	—	—	1466.7	1834	1989.3	1346.9	1181.1	700.3
房地产业	—	—	—	—	1492.2	1523.9	1237.5	511.0	2193.6	365.0

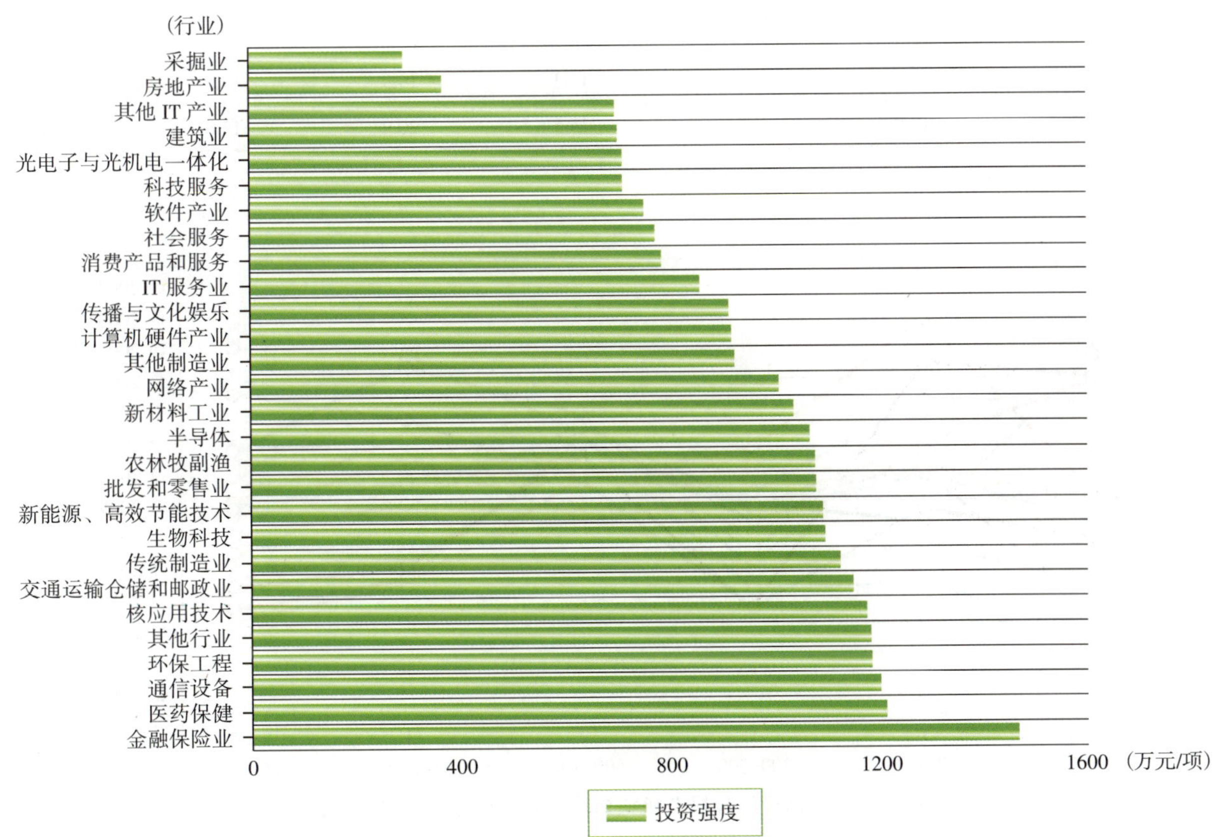

图 2-9 中国创业风险投资不同行业的投资强度（2016）

2.3.2 中国创业风险投资机构单项投资规模分布[①]

2016 年，中国创业风险投资机构单项投资金额中，500 万~1000 万元的投资项目所占比重最大，达 20.9%；其次是 100 万~300 万元的投资项目，占比为 18.1%。与 2015 年相比，1000 万~2000 万元及 2000 万元以上的项目单项投资金额占比都出现一定程度的下降；100 万元以下、100 万~300 万元、300 万~500 万元以及 500 万~1000 万元的项目单项投资金额占比都有不同程度的增加（见表 2-14、图 2-10）。

表 2-14 中国创业风险投资机构单项投资金额分布（2007~2016） 单位：%

年份＼金额（万元）	<100	100~300	300~500	500~1000	1000~2000	>2000
2007	16.1	17.6	18.3	18.1	17.4	12.5
2008	17.1	22.0	11.7	15.0	18.9	15.2
2009	11.7	22.4	12.6	20.3	17.3	15.7
2010	13.4	15.5	8.9	17.5	21.5	23.2
2011	6.8	10.6	10.2	20.6	25.7	26.2
2012	10.2	13.1	11.3	21.2	24.7	19.5
2013	8.4	17.6	14.6	20.0	20.1	19.3
2014	12.3	19.1	13.9	18.3	20.4	15.9
2015	14.5	17.5	15.3	19.9	17.2	15.6
2016	15.9	18.1	15.5	20.9	15.8	13.8

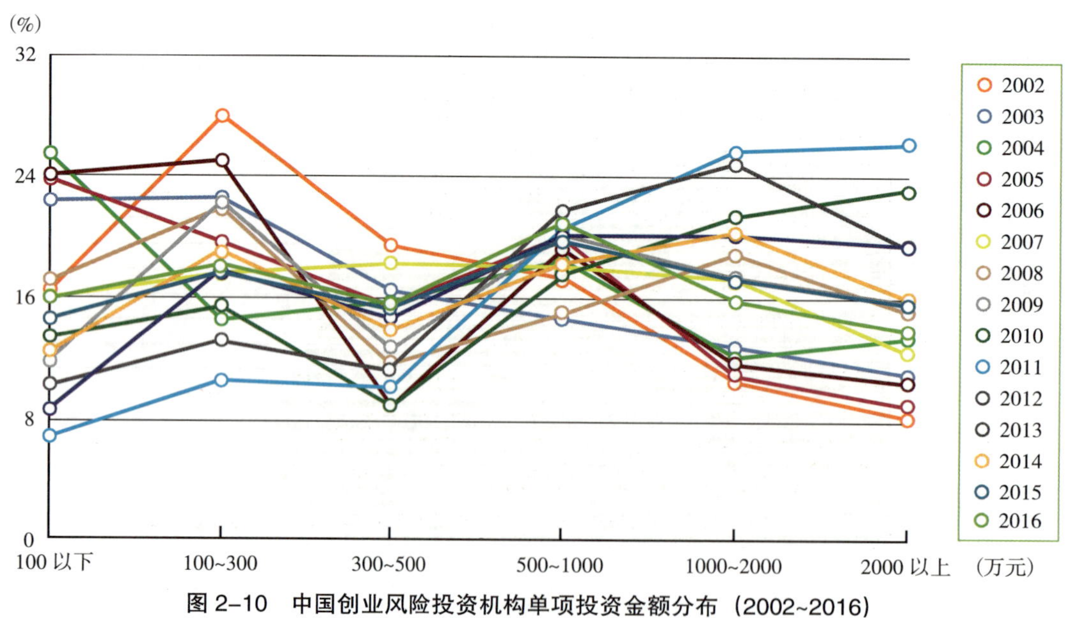

图 2-10 中国创业风险投资机构单项投资金额分布（2002~2016）

① 有效样本数为 2261 份。

2.3.3 中国创业风险投资的投资策略（联合投资）

联合投资是指两家及以上的创业风险投资机构共同投资于同一家创业企业。联合投资通过合作分享其他创业风险投资伙伴的专业知识和技能，有效分散创业风险投资机构的投资风险，实现资金使用效率的最大化，最终优化项目选择，提升投资组合整体价值。数据显示：2016 年创业风险投资机构和其他创业风险投资主体联合投资的项目中，100 万~500 万元规模的项目所占比重最高，占比为 32.5%。其次为 2000 万元以上的项目，占比为 21.8%。相比 2015 年，100 万元以下、100 万~500 万元和 2000 万元以上的项目占比都有一定程度的提高，而 500 万~1000 万元、1000 万~2000 万元的项目占比出现较大幅度下降（见表 2-15、图 2-11、表 2-16、图 2-12）。

表 2-15 中国创业风险投资联合投资的单项投资金额分布（2007~2016）① 单位：%

年份 \ 金额（万元）	<100	100~500	500~1000	1000~2000	>2000
2007	9.1	39.4	9.1	30.3	12.1
2008	19.0	31.6	13.9	20.3	15.2
2009	13.0	28.0	21.0	19.0	19.0
2010	10.3	15.4	24.1	23.1	27.2
2011	6.1	22.0	18.3	25.6	28.0
2012	13.0	28.7	20.9	20.0	17.4
2013	12.0	32.0	28.0	12.0	16.0
2014	16.0	27.6	10.4	23.3	22.7
2015	11.4	28.5	23.2	21.3	15.6
2016	14.6	32.5	20.4	10.7	21.8

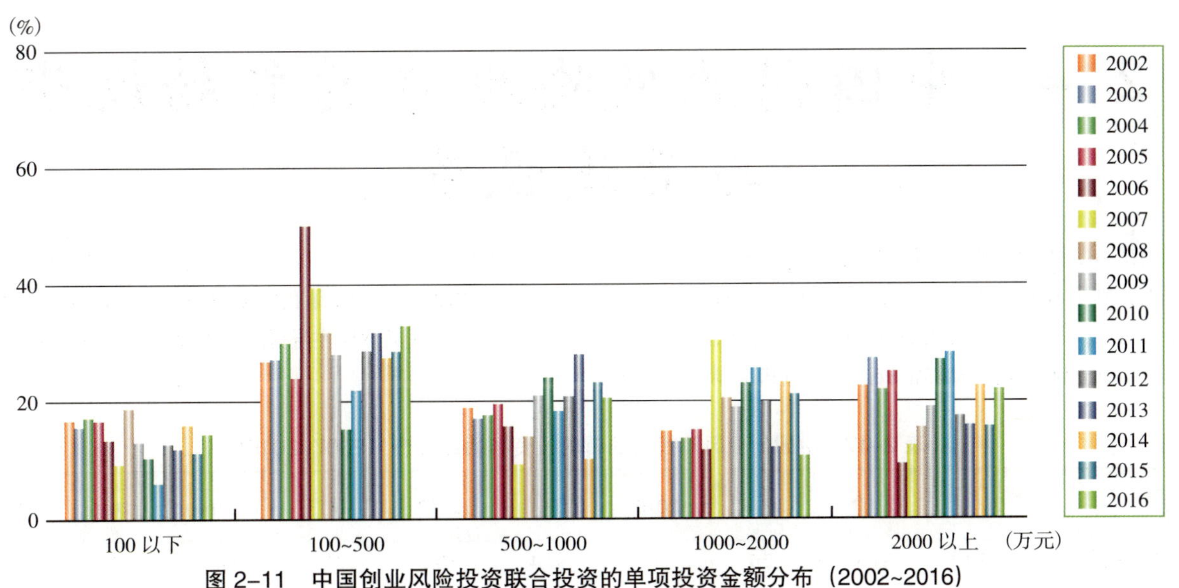

图 2-11 中国创业风险投资联合投资的单项投资金额分布（2002~2016）

① 有效样本数为 280 份。

表 2-16 中国创业风险投资机构与其他类型投资机构的联合投资（2016）① 单位：%

投资额分布（万元）	<100	100~300	300~500	500~1000	1000~2000	>2000
创业风险投资机构的投资额	0.93	4.41	7.37	19.32	26.34	41.62
其他类型投资机构的投资额	0.84	3.27	6.00	14.15	13.7	62.04

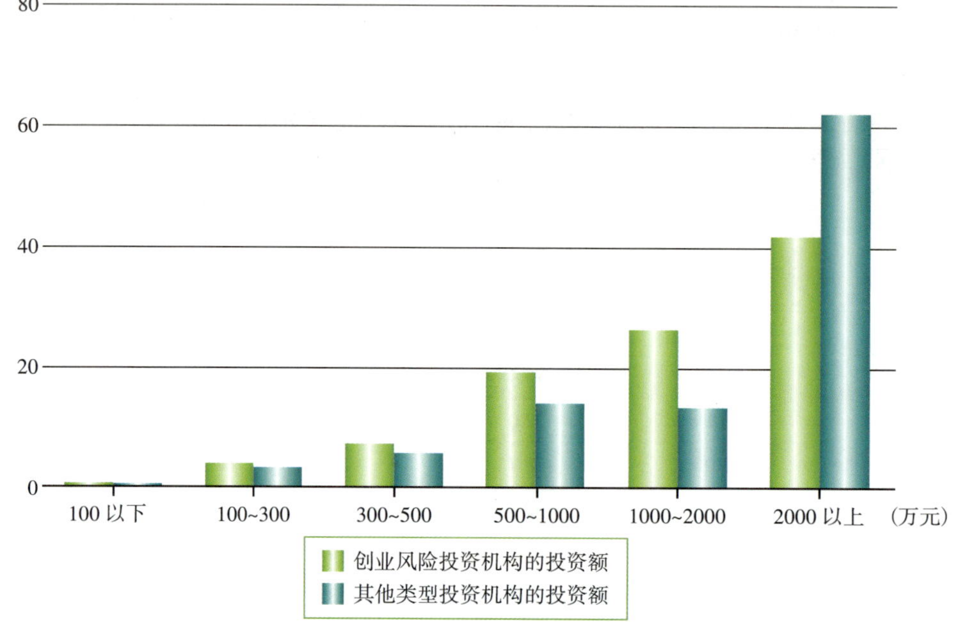

图 2-12 中国创业风险投资机构与其他类型投资机构的联合投资（2016）

2.4 中国创业风险投资的首轮投资与后续投资②

2016 年，中国创业风险投资项目的首轮投资和后续投资占比分别为 69%和 31%。与 2015 年相比，首轮投资占比提高 6.3 个百分点，提升幅度较大。可能原因之一是 2016 年我国创业创新活动热情较高，投资机会增加。后续投资占比在经历 2010 年以来的持续上升后 2016 年出现回落。总体而言，2016 年我国创业风险投资机构对被投资项目的首轮投资仍然居主导地位（见表 2-17、图 2-13）。

表 2-17 中国创业风险投资的首轮投资和后续投资（2007~2016） 单位：%

年份 项目	2007	2008	2009	2010	2011	2012	2013	2014	2015	2016
首轮投资	83.1	84.5	82.7	86.2	83.4	80.1	77.5	68.1	62.7	69.0
后续投资	16.9	15.5	17.3	13.8	16.6	19.9	22.5	31.9	37.3	31.0

① 创业风险投资机构样本数为 1757 份，其他类型投资机构样本数为 280 份。
② 有效样本数为 1947 份。

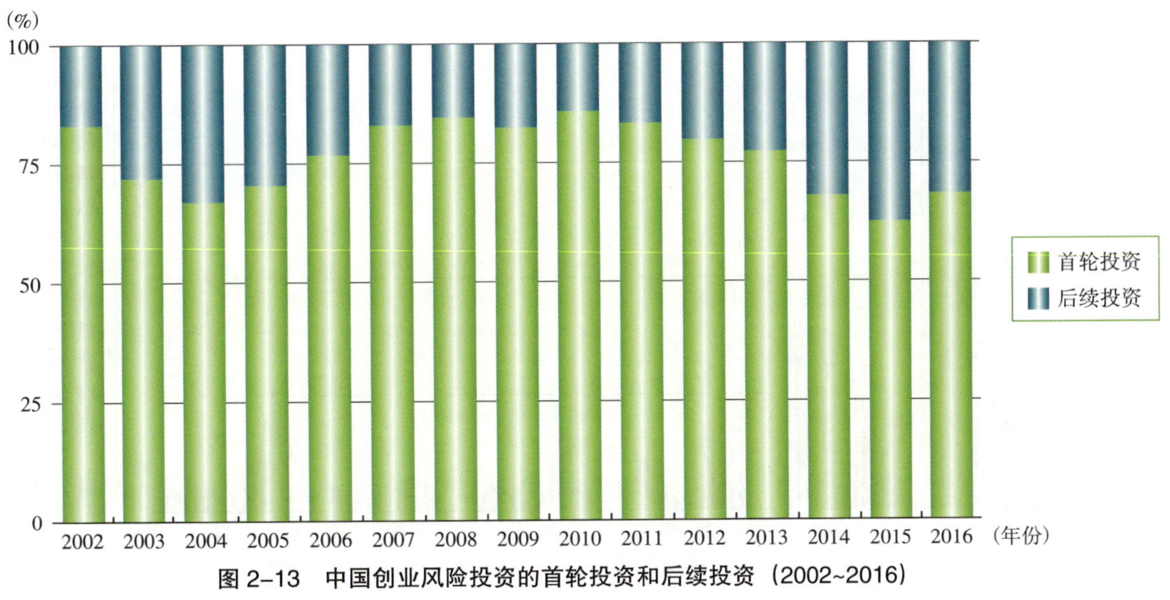

图 2-13 中国创业风险投资的首轮投资和后续投资（2002~2016）

2.5 中国创业风险投资机构持股结构[①]

2016 年中国创业风险投资机构的持股结构仍然延续了多元化趋势，参股和相对控股仍是主要投资方式。统计数据显示，2016 年创业风险投资机构的投资项目中，持股比例在 10%以下的项目所占比例高达 66.97%，与往年相比，这一数据继续上升。而持股比例在 50%以上的项目占比仅为 3.13%，与 2015 年相比小幅下降。数据表明，不谋求控股始终是创业风险投资机构的主导经营策略（见表 2-18、图 2-14）。

表 2-18 中国创业风险投资机构持股结构分布（2007~2016） 单位：%

股权比例（%）/年份	<10	10~20	20~30	30~40	40~50	>50
2007	43.33	20.32	14.44	8.41	4.92	8.57
2008	42.92	23.65	10.95	8.61	6.13	7.74
2009	44.6	22.77	13.64	5.98	5.14	7.87
2010	50.99	25.15	10.85	6.17	3.14	3.70
2011	61.04	20.46	7.08	4.38	2.24	4.80
2012	56.29	22.57	9.07	4.70	3.00	4.37
2013	50.32	25.60	11.60	4.40	2.88	5.20
2014	50.79	26.43	9.30	5.55	4.60	3.33
2015	63.47	21.88	6.10	2.96	2.14	3.46
2016	66.97	19.16	5.03	3.29	2.41	3.13

① 有效样本数为 1947 份。

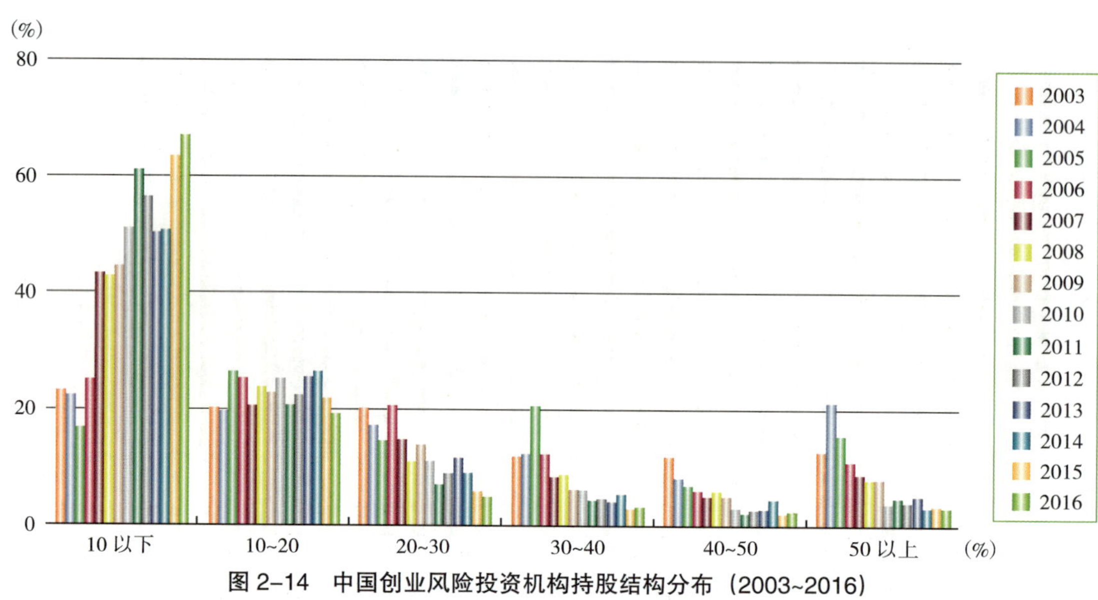

图 2-14 中国创业风险投资机构持股结构分布（2003~2016）

2.6 中国创业风险投资项目特征

2.6.1 中国创业风险投资项目的资本规模①

从被投资项目的实收资本来看，2016 年规模在 500 万元以下和 5000 万元以上的项目依然是中国创业风险投资的重点选择对象。与 2015 年相比，500 万元以下的中小投资项目占比减少 1.36 个百分点；5000 万元以上的投资项目占比增加 1.21 个百分点。从长期来看，中国创业风险投资项目规模分布的基本趋势表现为，对中小项目的投资有所上升，对大型项目的投资略有下降，其他规模项目的比重大致稳定。就 2016 年来看，所有规模项目的比重与 2015 年基本一致（见表 2-19、图 2-15）。

表 2-19 中国创业风险投资项目的实收资本规模分布（2007~2016） 单位：%

资本规模（万元） 年份	<500	500~1000	1000~3000	3000~5000	>5000
2007	26.82	12.83	20.41	13.12	26.82
2008	18.90	15.70	26.50	12.20	26.70
2009	21.60	13.90	23.50	15.40	25.60
2010	26.40	12.43	23.42	13.06	24.68
2011	15.23	11.50	24.23	13.56	35.48
2012	16.93	14.49	26.09	13.18	29.32
2013	19.49	15.25	23.74	14.44	27.07
2014	35.38	12.07	20.82	9.77	21.97
2015	33.10	12.58	20.65	10.89	22.78
2016	31.74	12.53	20.69	11.05	23.99

① 有效样本数为 1213 份。

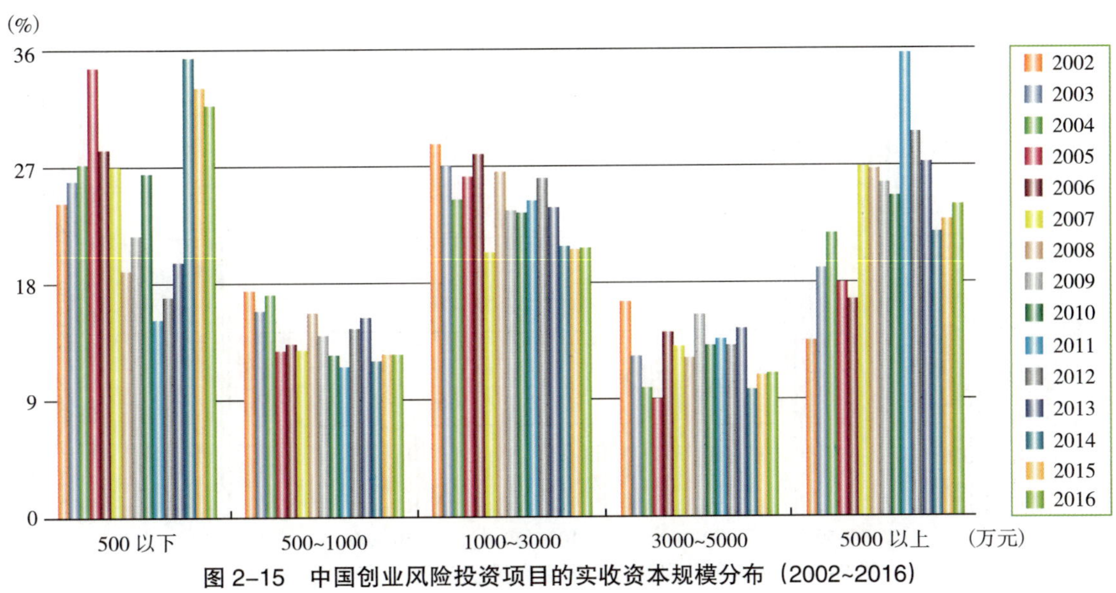

图 2-15 中国创业风险投资项目的实收资本规模分布（2002~2016）

2.6.2 中国创业风险投资项目的雇员规模①

就被投资项目雇员规模而言，2016 年中国创业风险投资机构首选雇员人数在 10~50 人的项目，占比达到 37.89%；其次为雇员规模在 10 人以下和 200 人以上的项目，占比分别为 21.84% 与 14.25%。从总体趋势上看，2016 年中国创业风险投资项目雇员规模分布与 2015 年相比波动不大（见表 2-20、图 2-16）。

表 2-20 中国创业风险投资项目雇员规模分布（2007~2016） 单位：%

年份 \ 雇员规模（人）	<10	10~50	50~100	100~150	150~200	>200
2007	14.7	26.1	12.9	8.5	7.0	30.1
2008	14.6	29.9	14.4	7.5	3.4	29.9
2009	21.8	36.7	9.8	6.2	4.8	19.9
2010	14.6	28.9	13.9	8.2	5.9	27.5
2011	11.3	24.3	13.3	8.9	6.9	34.1
2012	12.88	25.96	13.39	11.76	8.62	27.38
2013	13.75	30.38	13.97	10.2	7.43	24.28
2014	18.52	32.46	14.78	8.75	5.1	20.39
2015	19.07	38.14	15.11	5.91	4.98	16.79
2016	21.84	37.89	14.06	7.79	4.18	14.25

① 有效样本数为 1053 份。

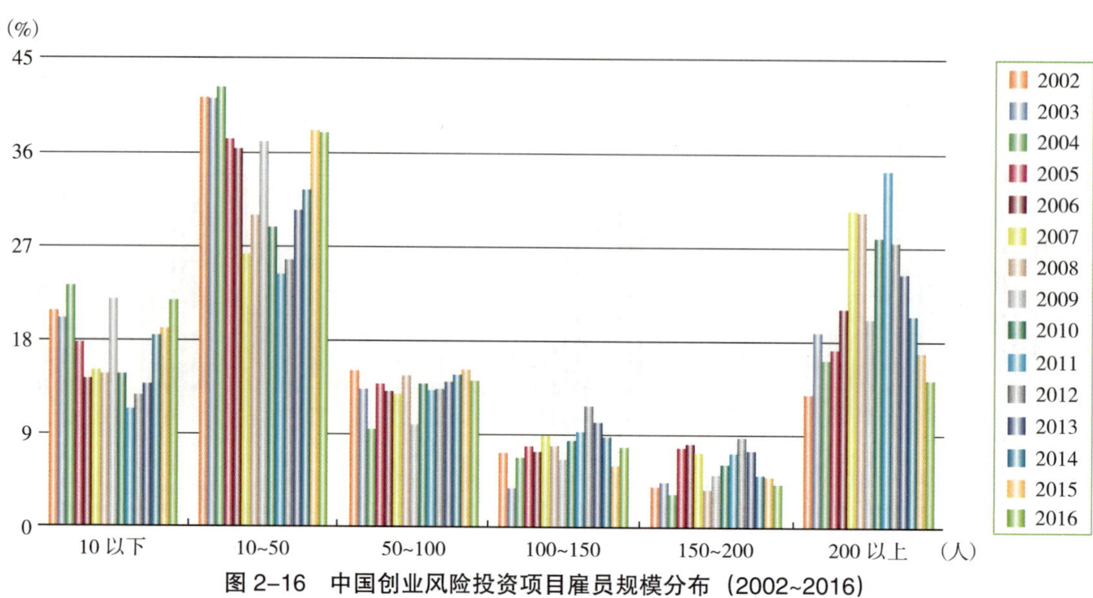

图 2-16 中国创业风险投资项目雇员规模分布（2002~2016）

2.6.3 中国创业风险投资项目的经营时间①

从被投资项目的经营时间看，2016 年创业风险投资机构仍然偏好比较稳健的成熟项目。其中，成立时间超过 5 年的被投资企业占比最高，达到 37.85%，相比 2015 年该数据继续上升。其次是成立时间在 1~3 年的初创期企业和成立时间小于 1 年的企业，占比分别为 29.31%和 20.38%。结合被投资项目的注册资本金额、雇员分布情况可以发现，这三组数据对 2016 年中国创业风险投资行为的描述大体一致（见表 2-21、图 2-17）。

表 2-21 中国创业风险投资项目经营时间分布（2007~2016） 单位：%

经营时间（年） 年份	<1	1~3	3~5	>5
2007	24.2	17.4	15.8	42.7
2008	17.3	24.3	19	39.4
2009	40.2	16.7	12.3	30.8
2010	13.6	28.8	13.6	43.9
2011	11.8	20.1	16.3	51.8
2012	14.25	20.51	15.19	50.05
2013	19.54	21.54	17.21	41.71
2014	29.29	22.21	16.14	32.35
2015	21.01	27.95	14.95	36.09
2016	20.38	29.31	12.46	37.85

① 有效样本数为 1276 份。

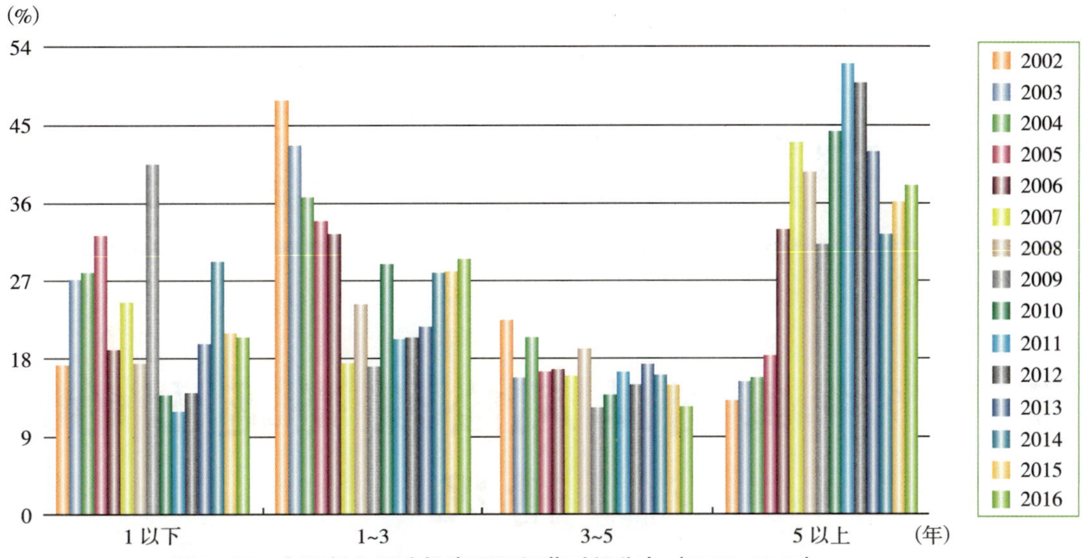

图 2-17 中国创业风险投资项目经营时间分布（2002~2016）

3 中国创业风险投资的退出

3.1 中国创业风险投资退出的基本情况①

2016 年以来，证监会发审呈现从严监管的态势，建立了首发企业现场检查机制，严格实施 IPO 各环节的全过程监管，促使发行人、保荐机构、证券服务机构等各尽其责。数据显示，截止到 2016 年 12 月 31 日，A 股市场累计共有 3052 家企业完成 IPO，2016 年当年 IPO 项目 240 项，筹资额 1600.05 亿元；其中，中小板市场 46 家，筹资额 221.21 亿元；创业板市场 78 家，筹资额 257.64 亿元。据科技部专项调查显示，2016 年创业风险投资机构参与的企业中共有 101 个项目通过 IPO 方式退出。

受资本市场行情影响，中国创业风险投资市场全年退出项目的收入规模总体上有所减少。2016 年，中国创业风险投资行业披露了 537 个退出项目的收入分配情况，其中退出项目收入在 2000 万元以上的项目占到了 29.3%，较 2015 年减少 4.9 个百分点；收入在 100 万元以下的项目比重较 2015 年显著提高，增加 6.5 个百分点（见表 3–1、图 3–1）。

表 3–1 中国创业风险投资项目的退出收入分布（2009~2016） 单位：%

收入规模（万元）/年份	<100	100~500	500~1000	1000~2000	>2000
2009	26.8	27.5	15.7	12.4	17.6
2010	27.3	19.7	13.7	13.7	25.7
2011	22.9	24.1	11	10.6	31.4
2012	19.2	17.1	10.5	17.4	35.8
2013	21.8	19.8	10.6	11.8	35.9
2014	15.7	24.7	14.4	12.7	32.4
2015	10.3	22.4	13.8	19.3	34.2
2016	16.8	22.3	15.3	16.3	29.3

① 有效样本数：有效样本数为 537 份。

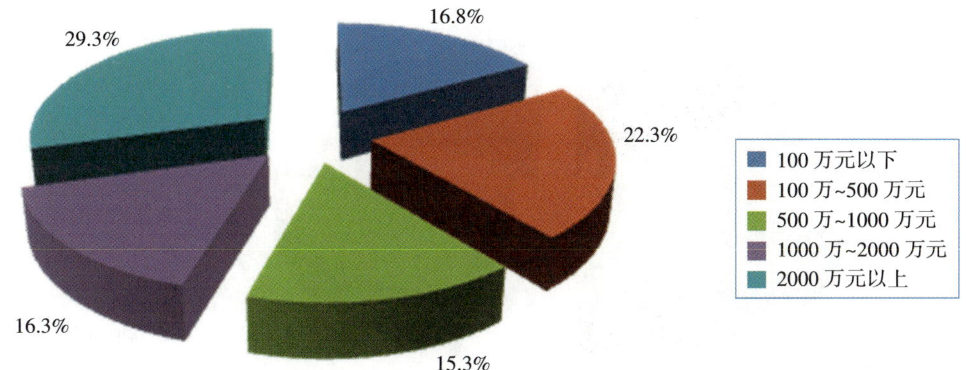

图 3–1 中国创业风险投资项目的退出收入分布（2016）

3.2 中国创业风险投资的退出方式[①]

3.2.1 中国创业风险投资的主要退出方式

据统计数据显示，2016 年全年共 583 笔退出交易披露了退出方式。按照退出渠道划分，创业风险投资的企业中共有 101 个项目通过 IPO 方式退出，与 2015 年相比大体持平，但占比略有上升，达到 17.32%。这主要源于 2016 年的资本市场行情较为稳定。相对而言，并购交易仍然是退出的主要渠道，退出项目数达到了 173 项，占比为 29.68%；此外，2016 年项目退出行情总体偏弱，回购占比与清算占比均较 2015 年有所增加（见表 3–2、图 3–2）。

表 3–2 中国创业风险投资的退出方式分布（2009~2016） 单位：%

退出方式 / 年份	上市（IPO）	并购	回购	清算	其他（含新三板）
2009	25.30	33.00	35.30	6.30	0.00
2010	29.80	28.63	32.82	6.87	1.91
2011	29.40	29.97	32.28	3.17	5.19
2012	29.41	15.86	45.01	6.65	3.07
2013	24.33	23.75	44.83	4.60	2.49
2014	20.72	36.02	36.02	4.83	2.41
2015	15.51	31.02	37.52	6.50	9.45
2016	17.32	29.68	40.14	8.06	4.80

① 有效样本数为 583 份。

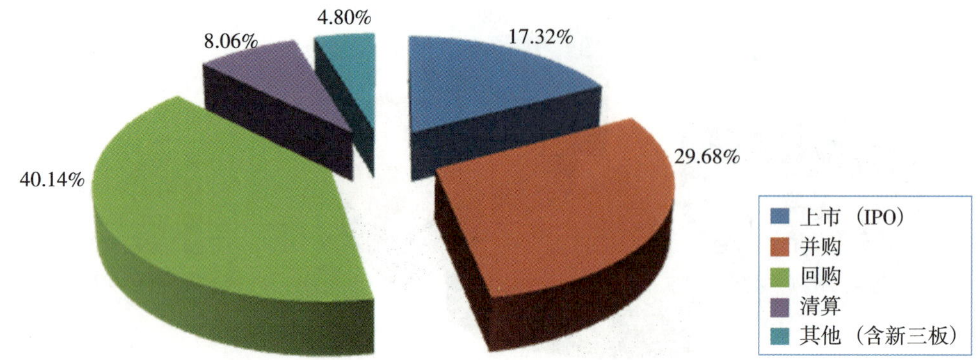

图 3-2 中国创业风险投资的退出方式分布（2016）

3.2.2 中国创业风险投资的 IPO 退出情况

随着我国多层次资本市场的建设，目前已形成主板、中小板、创业板以及新三板市场的构架。2016 年 12 月，“深港通”开闸，进一步加快完善我国多层次资本市场的建设步伐。据统计显示，2016 年披露项目中，共 101 个项目通过 IPO 实现退出收益；与 2015 年接近，境内主板市场成为 IPO 退出的主要渠道，占比达到 48.51%（见表 3-3）；此外，29.71% 的企业通过境内创业板退出，18.81%的企业通过境内中小板市场退出，较 2015 年占比略有提升（见图 3-3）。

表 3-3 中国创业风险投资 IPO 分布（2011~2016）① 单位：%

年份	境内主板上市	境内创业板上市	境内中小板上市	境外上市
2011	14.71	30.39	49.02	5.88
2012	21.74	38.26	36.52	3.48
2013	21.26	40.94	30.71	7.09
2014	22.33	42.72	21.36	13.59
2015	48.48	28.28	16.16	7.07
2016	48.51	29.71	18.81	2.97

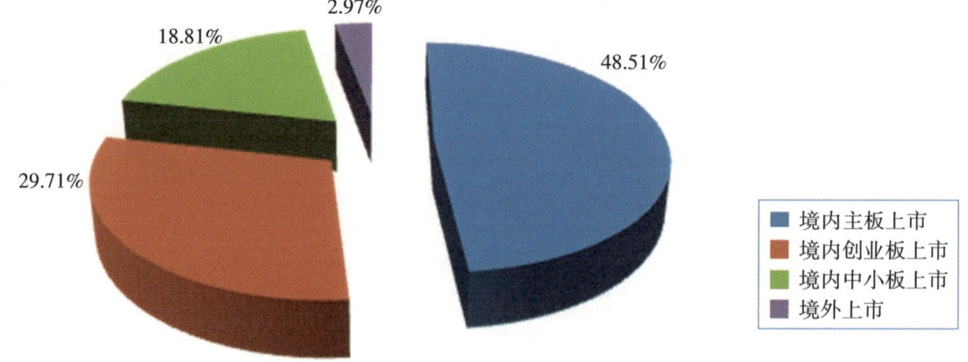

图 3-3 中国创业风险投资 IPO 分布（2016）

① 有效样本数为 101 份。

3.3 中国创业风险投资的退出项目行业分布[①]

从一级行业划分情况来看，2016 年，软件和信息服务业行业投资热度减少，其退出占比明显下滑，下降了 4.4 个百分点，减少到 15.9%。新能源和环保产业再度超过了软件和信息服务业，成为退出最多的行业，占比达到 17.6%。此外，生物医药产业，传播与文化娱乐行业的退出占比明显提高，再度成为投资回报热点（见表 3-4、图 3-4）。

表 3-4 中国创业风险投资退出项目的行业分布（2009~2016） 单位：%

行业分类 \ 年份	2009	2010	2011	2012	2013	2014	2015	2016
软件和信息服务业[②]	26.7	15.9	12.9	9.4	11.5	11.6	20.3	15.9
新能源和环保业[③]	12.7	24.5	16.7	22.2	16.2	15.2	15.7	17.6
计算机、通信设备制造业[④]	18.1	14.2	14.4	10.6	14.0	14.2	9.9	10.9
传统制造业	12.2	7.9	11.3	14.3	17.5	12.2	9.3	8.5
医药生物业[⑤]	9.0	11.0	13.5	11.1	12.5	8.3	8.7	10.8
其他制造业	0.0	0.0	5.3	6.2	8.2	4.1	7.5	4.7
其他行业	9.5	11.4	5.0	6.2	3.9	8.7	7.3	12.5
农林牧渔业	1.4	4.7	6.0	6.5	3.7	4.3	3.2	3.3
金融保险业	2.7	3.1	2.2	2.2	3.9	1.8	2.9	1.6
科技服务	2.7	1.6	0.6	2.2	0.6	1.2	2.8	2.4
传播与文化娱乐	0.9	1.6	1.9	3.0	2.7	5.5	2.3	5.9
社会服务	0.0	0.0	0.6	1.6	0.8	1.4	1.5	1.6

① 有效样本数为 577 份。
② 包括原有的网络产业、IT 产业、软件产业、其他 IT 产业四个细分的二级行业。
③ 包括原有的新材料工业、新能源/高效节能技术、核应用技术、环保工程四个细分的二级行业。
④ 包括原有的通信设备、半导体、计算机硬件产业、光电子与光机电一体化四个细分的二级行业。
⑤ 包括原有的医药保健、生物科技两个细分的二级行业。

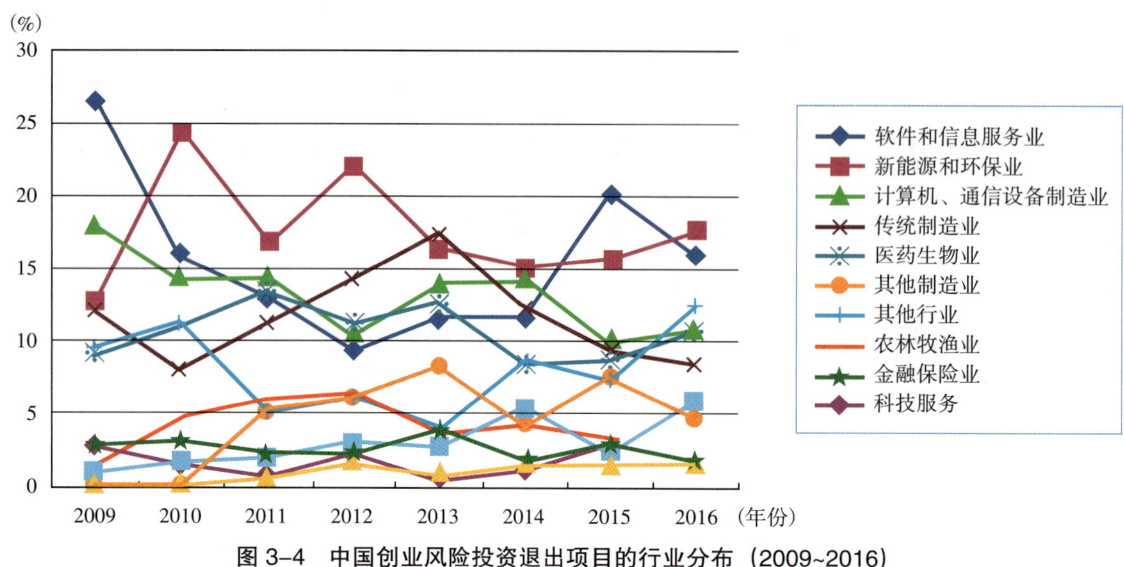

图 3-4 中国创业风险投资退出项目的行业分布（2009~2016）

从二级行业划分的情况来看，2016 年，中国创业风险投资实现项目退出最多的行业是其他行业①，占比为 12.5%。其次是传统制造业，但较 2015 年占比下滑了 0.8 个百分点。此外，医疗保健、新材料工业、环保工程，以及文化娱乐产业实现项目退出的占比有所增加，软件、网络产业的退出有所减少。排名前 10 的行业合计实现退出的项目占全部退出项目的 67.8%，集中度较 2015 年上升 2.2 个百分点（见表 3-5）。

表 3-5 中国创业风险投资退出项目的行业分布（2015~2016） 单位：%

行业分类 \ 年份	2015	2016
其他行业	7.3	12.5
传统制造业	9.3	8.5
医药保健	5.5	8.0
新材料工业	6.1	7.5
软件产业	7.0	6.1
传播与文化娱乐	2.3	5.9
新能源、高效节能技术	6.1	5.2
环保工程	3.2	4.7
网络产业	6.9	4.7
其他制造业	7.5	4.7
通信设备	3.2	3.6
IT 服务业	5.0	3.5
农林牧副渔	3.2	3.3
半导体	0.9	2.9

① 近年来，随着越来越多新模式的出现，行业界限变得模糊，不少行业融合了多个行业特点，难以再用传统的分类方式进行划分，因此选择“其他行业”的比例有所增多。

续表

行业分类 \ 年份	2015	2016
光电子与光机电一体化	4.7	2.8
生物科技	3.8	2.8
科技服务	2.8	2.4
消费产品和服务	2.3	1.9
建筑业	1.2	1.7
计算机硬件产业	1.1	1.6
金融保险业	2.9	1.6
其他 IT 产业	1.4	1.6
社会服务	1.5	1.6
批发和零售业	0.9	0.7
交通运输仓储和邮政业	1.4	0.3

3.4 中国创业风险投资退出项目的地区分布①

近年来，中国创业风险投资退出项目的地区分布总体没有较大变化，其分布与创业风险投资机构投资分布情况较为一致，东部地区因创业风险投资发展相对成熟，退出项目占比较高，其中江苏、浙江、北京、广东等地区的项目退出占比长期处于领先地位。此外，2016 年山东地区的退出项目增幅较大。

2016 年，退出项目占比排名前 10 的地区合计占比 85.8%，较上一年度集中度提升了 4.8 个百分点，区域集聚效应仍然较为明显（见表 3-6、图 3-5）。

表 3-6 中国创业风险投资退出项目的地区分布前 10 名（2009~2016） 单位：%

2009 年	地区	江苏	广东	浙江	北京	陕西	安徽	上海	四川	湖北	天津
	比例	26.4	17.4	10.0	7.5	5.5	5.0	4.0	4.0	3.5	3.0
2010 年	地区	江苏	湖北	广东	浙江	上海	山东	北京	新疆	湖南	天津
	比例	26.6	16.7	12.4	9.0	6.4	3.4	3.0	3.0	2.6	2.6
2011 年	地区	江苏	上海	浙江	广东	天津	北京	河南	山东	湖北	福建
	比例	27.6	11.5	11.2	9.6	8.1	6.5	3.4	2.8	2.8	2.2
2012 年	地区	江苏	浙江	广东	湖北	北京	上海	河北	天津	安徽	湖南
	比例	35.6	9.8	8.4	7.6	7.3	5.4	3.8	3.8	3.8	3.5

① 有效样本数为 576 份。

续表

2013 年	地区	江苏	浙江	上海	广东	北京	天津	安徽	山东	湖北	重庆
	比例	35.0	10.6	8.1	7.7	5.4	5.2	3.3	3.1	2.9	2.7
2014 年	地区	江苏	浙江	广东	上海	北京	湖北	辽宁	湖南	山东	天津
	比例	20.4	13.5	13.3	10.2	9.8	3.8	3.3	3.1	2.9	2.7
2015 年	地区	江苏	北京	浙江	广东	上海	河南	安徽	天津	湖北	四川
	比例	24.3	13.2	10.4	8.6	5.3	4.2	4.2	4.1	3.6	3.1
2016 年	地区	江苏	浙江	北京	广东	上海	山东	天津	安徽	福建	湖南
	比例	29.7	12.7	11.8	8.0	6.1	4.3	4.0	3.5	2.9	2.8

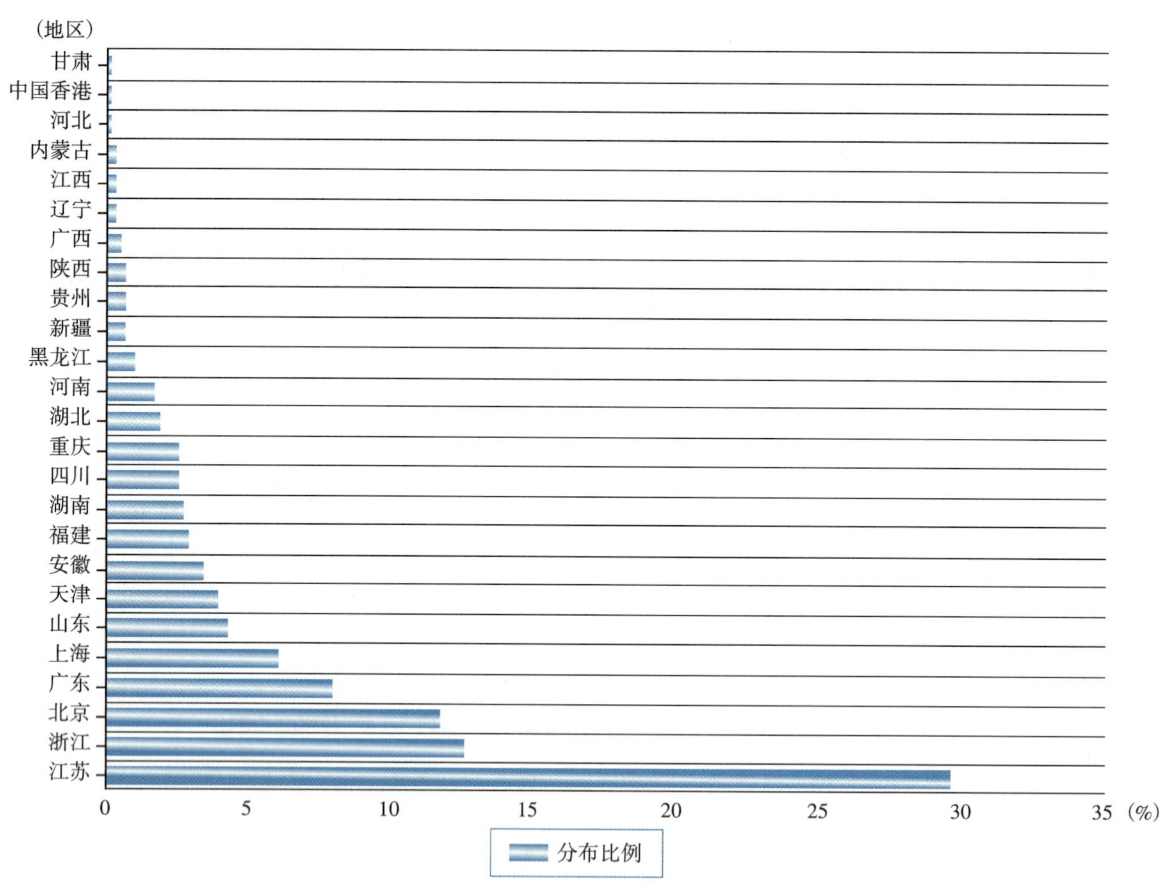

图 3-5 中国创业风险投资退出项目的地区分布情况（2016）

3.5 中国创业风险投资项目退出绩效

3.5.1 中国创业风险投资退出的总体绩效表现

2016 年，受资本市场总体平稳发展，多层次资本市场不断完善，养老金入市等积极影响，创业风险投资项目退出收益率表现良好，尽管略低于 2015 年的表现，但全行业的项目退出收益率仍然达到了 225.73%。整个行业投资退出步伐略微放缓，项目平均退出时间为 4.13 年，略高于 2015 年表现；整体行业平均收益率达到 29.69%（见表 3-7、图 3-6）。

表 3-7 中国创业风险投资退出收益率（2009~2016）①

单位：%

年份	2009	2010	2011	2012	2013	2014	2015	2016
总体收益率	144.89	221.87	193.71	196.35	117.7	123.04	260.18	225.73
年均收益率	19.33	37.82	45.62	44.01	13.85	23.46	32.39	29.69

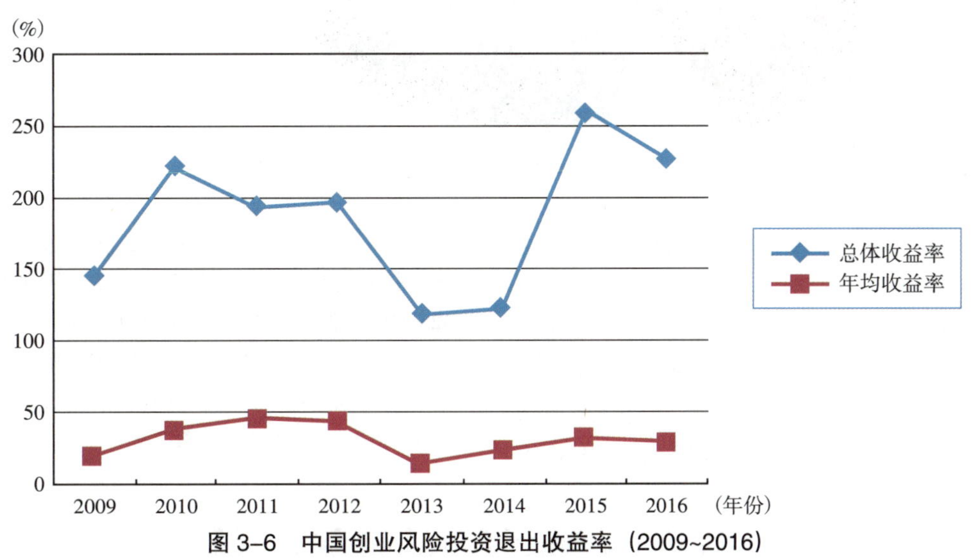

图 3-6 中国创业风险投资退出收益率（2009~2016）

退出项目的投资收益分布趋势情况显示（见表 3-8、图 3-7）：导致 2016 年总体收益率低于 2015 年的主要原因源于亏损项目增多。2016 年亏损退出的项目数高达 57.0%；此外，投资收益在各个收益分布阶段的项目占比均小于 2015 年，整体收益下滑。

① 有效样本数为 2636 份。

表 3-8 中国创业风险投资退出收益率分布（2009~2016）①　　单位：%

年份	亏损	0~15	15~20	20~50	50~100	>100
2009	63	4.8	3.2	10.6	4.2	14.3
2010	63.2	8.0	1.9	4.7	4.2	17.9
2011	47.9	9.9	3	10.6	6.5	22.1
2012	47.0	8.6	3.5	10.5	4.5	25.9
2013	67.1	2.4	2.7	8.7	2.2	16.9
2014	56.9	4.7	4.1	9.4	11.6	13.3
2015	48.9	12.1	3.5	11.8	7.4	16.2
2016	56.9	9.7	2.6	9.9	5.8	15.1

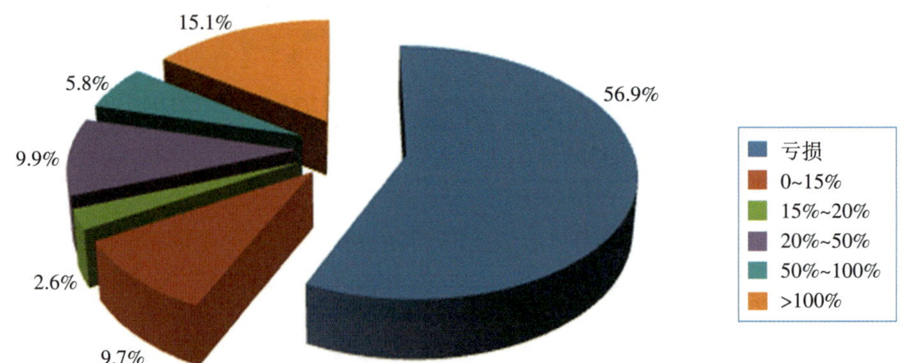

图 3-7 中国创业风险投资退出收益率分布（2016）

3.5.2 中国创业风险投资不同退出方式的绩效表现

总体而言，创业风险投资行业的投资收益主要由少数上市退出项目收益弥补多数项目的损失。2016 年，我国资本市场上证指数在 2700 点至 3100 点波动，资金面临流动性压力，A 股上涨空间有限，但上市退出收益率仍然高达 922.12%，即平均账目回报 9.2 倍，达到历史最高水平；通过并购退出的项目收益率也出现大幅度提高，收益率达 323.41%；但清算项目亏损较为严重，项目亏损达到了 43.62%。值得一提的是，“新三板”市场表现突出，成为创投项目成功退出的又一有效渠道，退出项目收益率达到了 193.82%（见表 3-9、图 3-8）。

表 3-9 不同渠道的创业风险投资退出项目总体收益率（2009~2016）②　　单位：%

年份	上市	并购	回购	清算	新三板挂牌交易
2009	327.75	4.74	-29.47	-42.66	—
2010	736.68	44.71	-21.19	-24.43	48.85
2011	799.38	41.47	-30.51	-65.37	63.19
2012	486.1	198.29	29.18	-15.34	32.48
2013	448.03	15.27	-34.28	-43.47	89.79

① 有效样本数为 537 份。
② 有效样本数为 2636 份。

续表

年份	上市	并购	回购	清算	新三板挂牌交易
2014	601.66	63.55	-34.43	-34.43	27.23
2015	779.27	135.55	19.01	-15.60	16.86
2016	922.12	323.41	3.02	-43.62	193.82

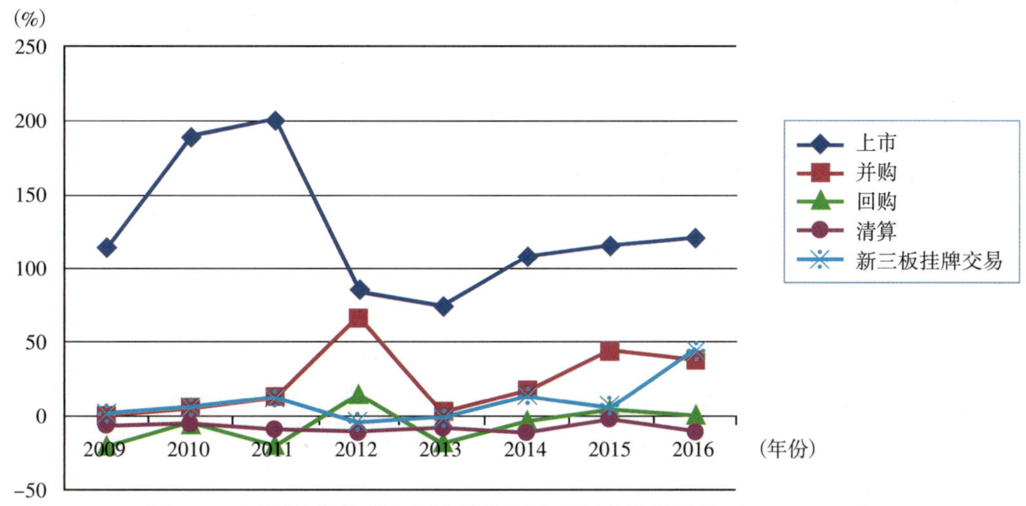

图 3-8 不同渠道的创业风险投资退出项目总体收益率（2009~2016）

一般而言，创业风险投资项目从投资到退出要经历3~7年时间，因此从年均收益率来看，创业风险投资并非一夜暴富的行业。从历年年均收益率情况来看，上市退出仍然是收益最高的退出渠道，一般年均收益率在100%左右，2011年实现最高年均收益率为200.41%，2016年实现年均收益率为120.35%。这在一定程度上说明，尽管2016年上市退出实现了历年来的最高收益率，但由于通过上市退出投资周期较长，因此年度收益率并未达到历史最高水平；此外，并购退出表现良好，年均收益率达到37.58%；新三板挂牌交易退出实现了年均收益43.89%的盈利水平（见表3-10、图3-9）。

表 3-10 不同渠道的创业风险投资退出项目年均收益率（2009~2016）[①] 单位：%

年份	上市	并购	回购	清算	新三板挂牌交易
2009	113.08	-0.37	-21.02	-6.59	—
2010	187.62	5.04	-5.35	-4.83	5.64
2011	200.41	12.99	-20.71	-8.46	13.2
2012	84.62	66.4	14.86	-10.33	-4.47
2013	73.36	2.71	-19.31	-8.26	-0.9
2014	107.19	17.49	-4.22	-11.48	12.93
2015	114.38	44.45	4.05	-2.00	6.1
2016	120.35	37.58	0.38	-10.66	43.89

① 有效样本数为2636份。

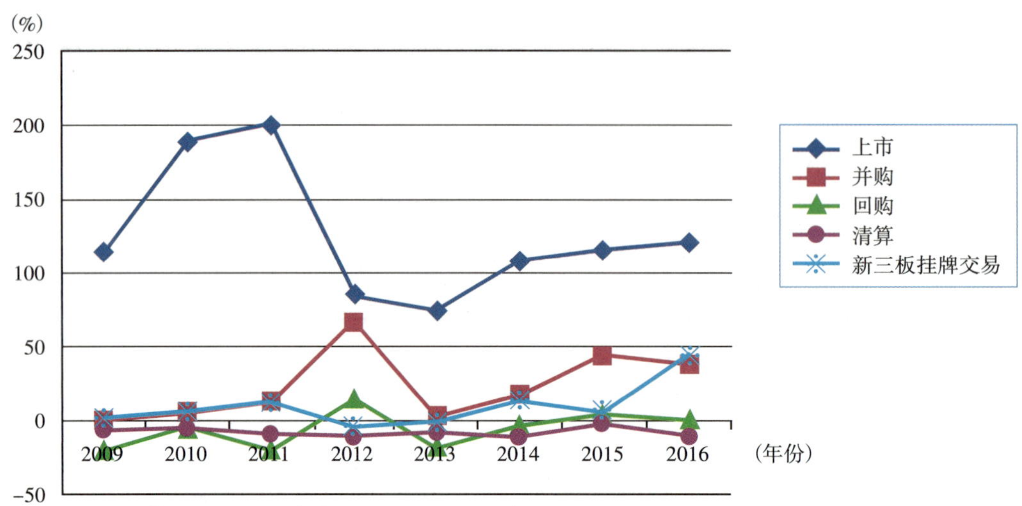

图 3-9 不同渠道的创业风险投资退出项目年均收益率（2009~2016）

3.5.3 中国创业风险投资不同行业退出的绩效表现

整个创业风险投资行业的退出绩效，大多呈现出“成三败七”的特点，通常需要用少数成功的投资项目来弥补多数的损失。但近年来，随着我国创业风险投资行业投资管理能力的逐步提升，项目的总体收益率呈现上升趋势。无论是高新技术行业还是传统行业，在经历了 2013 年的较大下滑后，项目退出的盈利水平连续回升，2016 年盈利项目超过 40%。

比较传统行业与高新技术行业的退出绩效可以看出，大部分情况下高新技术行业尽管面临着更高的投资风险，但投资盈利比例也明显高于传统行业（见表 3-11、图 3-10、表 3-12、图 3-11）。

表 3-11 高新技术行业创业风险投资的退出项目盈亏状况（2009~2016）① 单位：%

年份	2009	2010	2011	2012	2013	2014	2015	2016
盈利	37.17	37.30	52.87	55.62	32.13	47.76	51.06	44.59
亏损	62.83	62.70	47.13	44.38	67.87	52.24	48.94	55.41

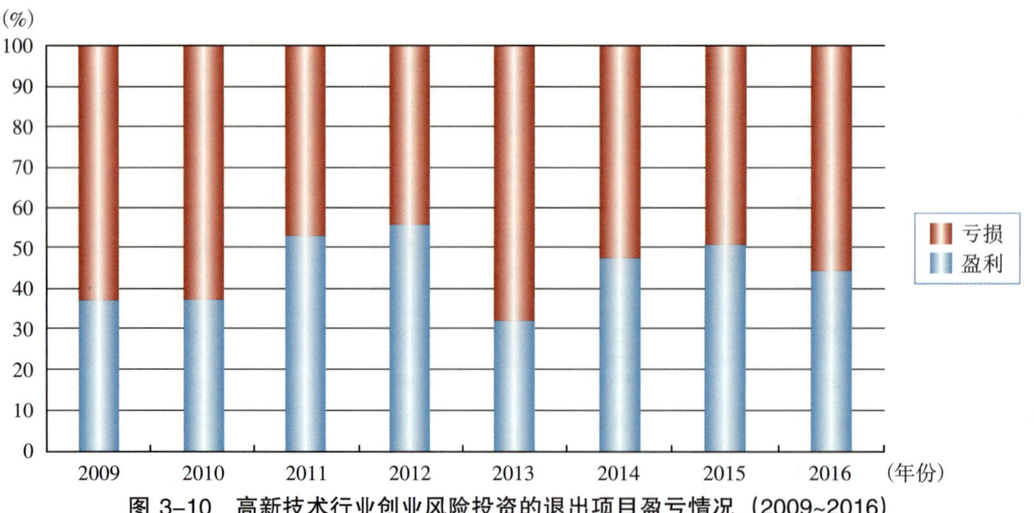

图 3-10 高新技术行业创业风险投资的退出项目盈亏情况（2009~2016）

① 有效样本数为 296 份。

表 3-12 传统行业创业风险投资的退出项目盈亏状况（2009~2016）① 单位：%

年份	2009	2010	2011	2012	2013	2014	2015	2016
盈利	39.29	36.36	48.48	50.00	35.45	38.56	50.23	40.27
亏损	60.71	63.64	51.52	50.00	64.55	61.44	49.77	59.73

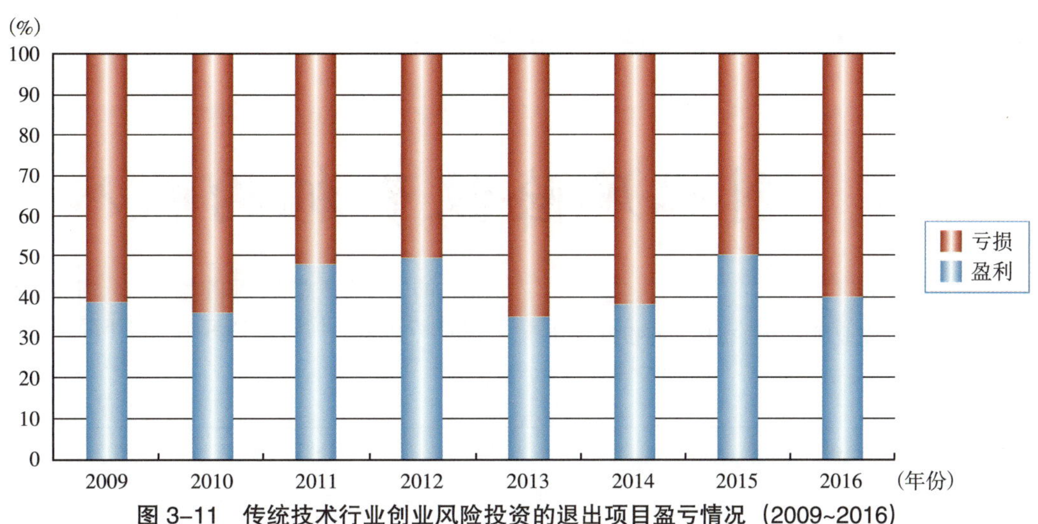

图 3-11 传统技术行业创业风险投资的退出项目盈亏情况（2009~2016）

按细分行业划分，2016 年，网络产业的退出收益水平依然高居榜首，达到了 13.5 倍。其次是新能源、高效节能技术，总体表现也好于 2015 年，账面回报率高达 7.8 倍。此外，其他 IT 产业、光电子与光机电一体化，以及环保工程的退出收益率上浮很大。这也在一定程度上解释了为什么这几类行业再度成为新一轮的投资热点（表 3-13）。

表 3-13 按细分行业划分的创业风险投资退出项目总体收益率（2015~2016）② 单位：%

行业	退出总体收益率（2015）	退出总体收益率（2016）
网络产业	1496.29	1351.87
新能源、高效节能技术	462.62	783.14
其他 IT 产业	—	307.93
传统制造业	190.95	284.38
光电子与光机电一体化	—	261.54
环保工程	52.60	207.07
其他制造业	143.06	204.14
其他行业	—	138.16
半导体	130.84	100.94
IT 服务业	—	76.61

① 有效样本数为 226 份。
② 有效样本数为 2636 份。

4 中国创业风险投资绩效

4.1 创业风险投资机构收入

4.1.1 投资机构收入

2016 年，披露信息的创业风险投资机构①与投资业务相关的主营业务总收入和平均收入分别达到 150.41 亿元和 1433.87 万元，均较 2015 年有明显下降（见图 4–1）。

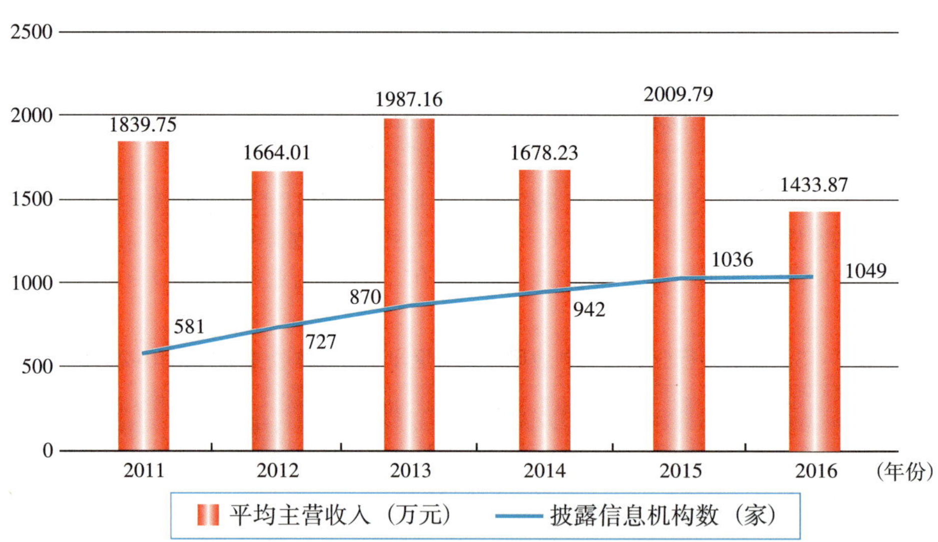

图 4–1 投资机构收入趋势（2011~2016）

（1）机构主营业务收入权重提高。2016 年，披露收入和主营业务收入的机构数量均有所增加，其中 54.72% 的机构获得与投资相关的主营业务收入，下降到 2014 年的水平，较 2015 年下降了 10 个百分点；667 家机构中有 574 家获得投资相关主营业务收入，占比高达 86.05%；主营业务收入占收入的比重仅为 64.90%，远远低于 2015 年。

（2）机构主营业务收入降低。受国内资本市场疲软的影响，2016 年创业风险投资机构的收入规模有较大幅度提升，但主营业务收入下降明显，投资相关业务带来的平均收入为近年来最低水平。

（3）基金收入远高于管理机构。分析有收入的机构发现，284 家管理机构主营业务收入 16.36 亿元，平均每家机构为 576.11 万元，765 家投资基金主营业务收入 132.84 亿元，平均每家机构为 1736.51 万元，基金的平均主营业务收入是管理机构的近 3 倍，差距较 2015 年缩小。

（4）政府支持机构收入水平更高。获得政府支持的 333 家机构平均收入达到 1598.35 万元，是未获得政府资金支持机构的 1.18 倍，差距连续两年缩小。

① 有效样本数为 1049 份。

4.1.2 不同规模投资机构收入特征[①]

按机构管理资本规模从低到高，将创业风险投资机构划分为 5 个组别，统计不同规模创业风险投资机构的平均收入及不同规模机构收入占总收入的比重（见表 4–1）。

表 4–1 不同规模投资机构的收入分布（2011~2016）

年份 \ 机构规模（亿元）		≤0.5	0.5~1	1~2	2~5	≥5
2011	平均收入（万元）	694.4	486.7	983.9	2777.6	5577.4
	占总收入比重（%）	8.7	6.4	9.8	28.6	46.4
2012	平均收入（万元）	916.0	593.1	1224.9	1190.6	6794.9
	占总收入比重（%）	10.8	7.9	13.7	14.8	52.8
2013	平均收入（万元）	443.4	945.4	1406.6	3150.7	7896.3
	占总收入比重（%）	4.7	10.1	12.3	31.9	41.1
2014	平均收入（万元）	319.8	1205.3	779.7	1299.7	7383.7
	占总收入比重（%）	4.8	17.5	9.6	16.5	51.5
2015	平均收入（万元）	374.6	985.9	1477.6	2049.1	9544.2
	占总收入比重（%）	4.6	11.0	13.2	18.9	52.3
2016	平均收入（万元）[②]	417.3	1379.6	1036.8	1494.8	6090.8
	占总收入比重（%）[③]	8.2	20.1	13.0	18.6	40.1

2016 年，中国创业风险投资机构收入分布具有如下特征：

（1）机构规模越大平均收入越高。管理资本 5000 万元以下的机构平均收入最低，为 417.3 万元，管理资本超过 5 亿元的机构平均收入最高，达到 6090.8 万元，约为前者的 15 倍；大型机构收入占比保持较高水平，管理资本 5 亿元以上的机构收入占总收入的比重超过 40%，管理资本 2 亿元以上的机构收入占比达到 58.7%，而管理资本 5000 万元以下的机构收入占比不足 10%。

（2）小规模机构收入有所提高。管理资本在 5000 万元以下的机构平均收入持续下降趋势有所改善，实现了连续两年提高；管理资本 5000 万~1 亿元的机构平均收入出现较大幅度提高，甚至高于管理资本 1 亿~2 亿元的机构，接近管理资本 2 亿~5 亿元的机构。

（3）中等规模创业风险投资机构的平均收入和收入占比波动较大，其中管理资本 2 亿~5 亿元的机构平均收入波动最大；2016 年，管理资本 1 亿~2 亿元的机构平均收入下降明显，也造成这一规模的机构收入波动曲线更加明显。

4.1.3 投资机构收入来源结构

2016 年，573 家[④]创业风险投资机构披露主营业务收入，其中，股权转让增值收入占全部收入的 50.7%，分红收入占 18.7%，管理费、咨询费收入占 10.2%，其他收入占 20.4%（见图 4–2）。与 2015 年相比，股权转让增值收入占比降低了 9.6 个百分点，分红收入占比提高了 4.2 个百分点，管理费、咨询费收入占比基本持平，其他收入占比提高了 5.5 个百分点。

① 有效样本数为 1009 份。
② 有效样本数为 991 份。
③ 有效样本数为 991 份。
④ 仅包括收入大于 0 且各项收入占比之和等于 100%的机构。

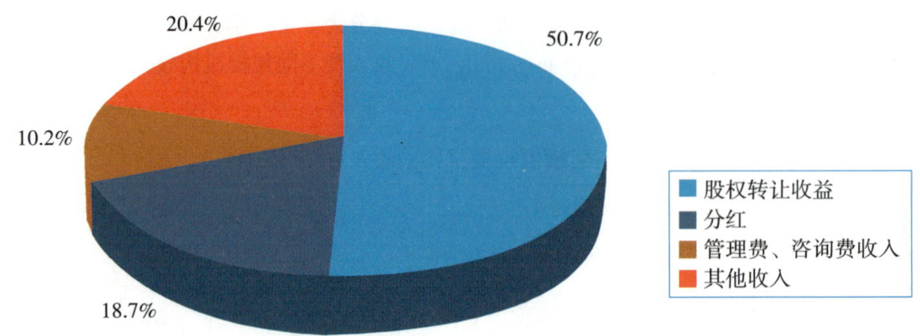

图 4-2　投资机构收入来源比例（2016）

（1）近年来，股权转让增值和分红收入对创业风险投资机构主要收入的贡献保持相对稳定的增长，但是 2016 年出现了小幅降低，其他收入占比有了明显的提高。这与 2016 年国内资本市场低迷有一定关系，机构减少股权转让或股权转让收益下降的案例增多，从而压缩了股权转让收入的占比，此外 2016 年参与调查的基金管理公司比例增高也是其原因之一。

（2）基金公司的主要收入来源是股权转让收入，占比为 56.0%，管理咨询收入占比则仅为 4.0%，分红收入和其他收入占比分别为 18.9%和 21.1%。

（3）管理公司的收入主要来源于管理咨询收入，占比高达 61.2%，而股权转让收入占比仅为 6.8%，分红收入和其他收入占比分别为 17.2%和 14.8%。

4.1.4　投资机构当年收入的最大来源①

2016 年统计调查显示，中国创业风险投资机构最大收入来源分布与往年相比未发生显著的结构变化。

（1）不同最大收入来源的机构分布。以股权转让为最大收入来源的机构占 25.8%，较 2015 年降低了 2 个百分点；以分红为最大收入来源的创业风险投资机构占 17.6%，较 2015 年降低了 1.2 个百分点；二者合计为 43.4%，较 2015 年降低了 3.2 个百分点；以管理费、咨询费等收入为最大收入来源的创业风险投资机构占比为 41.3%，再次提高了 5.4 个百分点；以其他收入为最大收入来源的创业风险投资机构占比为 15.3%，再次下降了（见图 4-3、表 4-2）。

（2）投资相关业务收入占比下降。近年来，股权转让和分红为中国创业投资机构带来了较多收益的同时，也成为更多机构的主要利润来源。2016 年，以股权转让收益和分红为第一收入来源的机构占比出现了下滑，特别是资本市场低迷造成了以股权转让收益为第一收入来源的机构占比下降较多。

（3）最大收入来源能够反映机构业务特征。管理公司和基金公司的主要收入来源也与其经营模式保持了高度一致，以管理费、咨询费等为最大收入来源的机构主要由管理机构构成，比重为 71.3%，而以股权转让和分红为最大来源的机构中，基金占比分别达到了 92.6%和 91.0%。

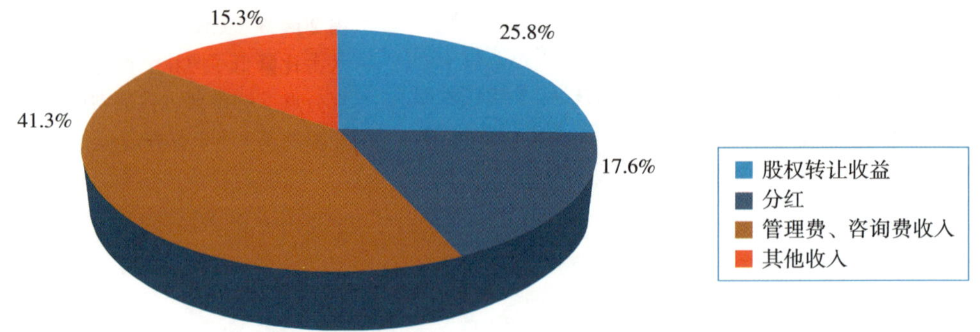

图 4-3　中国创业风险投资机构的最大收入来源（2016）

① 有效样本数为 589 份。

表 4-2 中国创业风险投资机构的最大收入来源（2007~2016） 单位：%

年份＼收入来源	股权转让	分红	管理费、咨询费等	其他
2007	42.9	14.9	31.7	10.5
2008	44.0	23.4	22.5	10.1
2009	33.8	17.4	29.8	19.0
2010	34.4	14.1	32.5	19.0
2011	36.8	15.5	30.4	17.3
2012	34.1	16.5	28.9	20.5
2013	37.1	15.0	27.4	20.5
2014	26.9	19.1	30.5	23.5
2015	27.8	18.8	35.9	17.5
2016	25.8	17.6	41.3	15.3

4.2 创业风险投资项目的收益情况

2016 年调查显示，2045 家创业风险投资机构新增投资项目 2744 项，其中 1000 余个项目披露了主营业务收入和利润信息。

4.2.1 被投资项目的主营业务收入①

创业风险投资机构新增投资项目的主营业务收入与 2015 年相比没有发生明显的变化。（见表 4-3、图 4-4）

（1）2016 年新增投资项目的主营业务收入“W 形”分布并未发生改变，其中，主营业务收入 100 万元以下和 5000 万元以上的项目占比较高，其他组别的项目分布相对平均。

（2）按主营业务收入大中小分类，占比相对平均，其中 100 万元以下为 36.8%，100 万~3000 万元为 32.0%，3000 万元以上为 31.2%。

（3）主营业务收入 100 万元以下项目占比较 2015 年上升了 1.9 个百分点，仅次于 2014 年的水平，关注小项目的趋势保持不变，其中超过 200 个项目主营业务收入为 0，利润为负。

（4）主营业务收入 5000 万元以上的项目占比较 2015 年下降了 2.6 个百分点，接近 2007 年以来的最低水平，3000 万~5000 万元的项目占比略有提高，为 4.7%。

（5）主营业务收入 500 万~1000 万元的项目占比为 6.5%，较 2015 年有小幅下降；100 万~500 万元和 500 万~1000 万元的项目占比分别出现了 0.6 个和 0.3 个百分点的下降。

表 4-3 被投资项目的主营业务收入分布（2007~2016） 单位：%

年份＼收入（万元）	<100	100~500	500~1000	1000~3000	3000~5000	>5000
2007	24.6	11.9	5.2	17.2	5.2	35.8
2008	18.8	12.1	8.1	15.1	5.6	40.3
2009	33.9	9.4	7.1	7.6	7.0	34.9
2010	29.1	6.8	5.0	12.3	4.8	41.9

① 有效样本数为 1053 份。

续表

年份 \ 收入（万元）	<100	100~500	500~1000	1000~3000	3000~5000	>5000
2011	14.9	6.7	4.7	10.0	5.4	58.3
2012	20.3	7.7	5.5	9.8	6.7	49.9
2013	29.9	10.7	4.6	10.4	5.9	38.6
2014	54.0	5.8	3.4	8.7	4.8	23.3
2015	34.9	13.9	6.8	11.1	4.2	29.1
2016	36.8	13.3	6.5	12.2	4.7	26.5

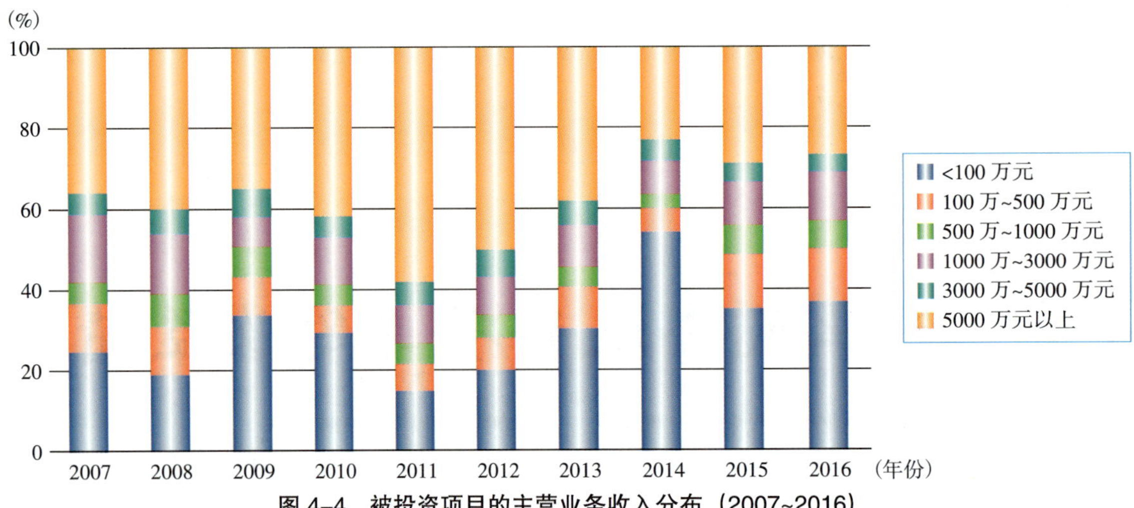

图 4-4 被投资项目的主营业务收入分布（2007~2016）

4.2.2 被投资项目的利润①

2016 年，中国创业风险投资项目的利润分布总体依然呈现为 U 形，利润超过 1000 万元和亏损的项目占比较高，分别为 19.2%和 52.0%，其他项目占比均较低（见表 4-4、图 4-5）。

（1）亏损项目所占比重提高。2016 年，被投资项目亏损比重为 52.0%，较 2015 年增加 2.1 个百分点，是近十年第二高水平，仅次于 2014 年的 61.5%。不考虑 2014 年的大面积亏损，近五年来亏损项目的比重实际上呈现逐年提高状况，一方面表现为创业风险投资机构投资行为向前端移动，另一方面则反映了中国经济的缓慢复苏。

（2）利润 100 万元以下项目占比较高。2016 年，利润 100 万元以下的盈利项目占比为 12.5%，较 2015 年低 0.1 个百分点，排在 5 类项目中的第三位。

（3）利润超过 1000 万的项目占比再次下降。2011 年以来，利润超过 1000 万元的项目占比持续下降，2016 年达到 19.2%，仅比 2014 年高 0.8 个百分点。

表 4-4 被投资项目的利润分布（2007~2016） 单位：%

年份 \ 利润（万元）	亏损	0~100	100~300	300~500	500~1000	>1000
2007	29.5	18.1	9.8	2.0	6.7	33.9
2008	24.2	17.1	9.9	5.5	7.7	35.6
2009	38.6	13.3	5.9	2.8	4.8	34.6

① 有效样本数为 1024 份。

续表

利润（万元） 年份	亏损	0~100	100~300	300~500	500~1000	>1000
2010	31.2	10.4	7.4	5.1	7.4	38.5
2011	19.6	8.1	7.3	4.2	7.6	53.2
2012	27.2	8.9	8.1	5.8	7.5	42.5
2013	39.0	9.7	8.0	5.7	5.5	32.1
2014	61.5	7.8	4.7	3.2	4.4	18.4
2015	49.9	12.6	6.7	4.3	5.9	20.6
2016	52.0	12.5	6.5	3.5	6.3	19.2

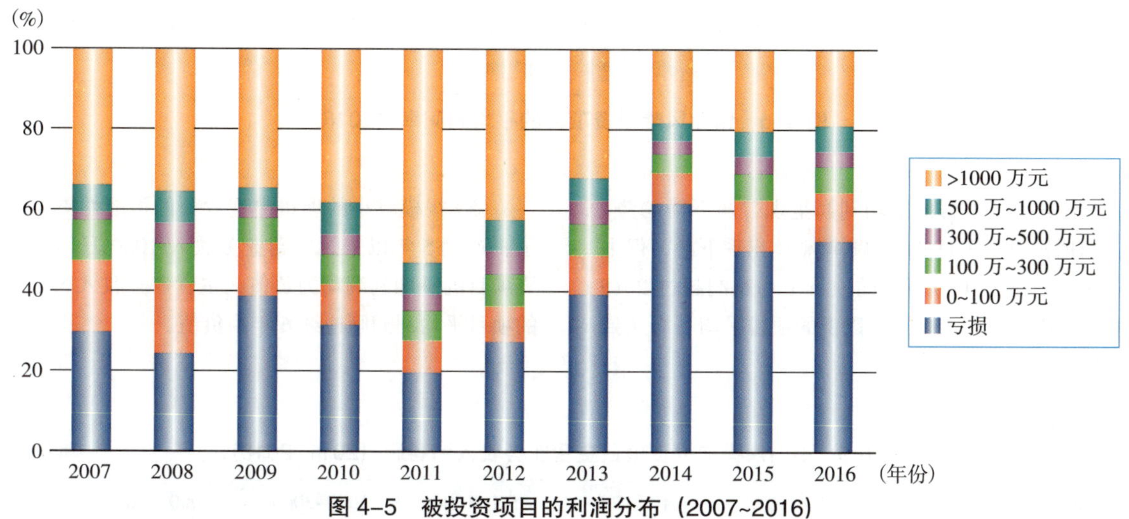

图 4-5　被投资项目的利润分布（2007~2016）

4.2.3　被投资项目主营业务收入与利润的关系

2016 年，中国创业风险投资机构投资项目[①]的平均利润率依然整体处于亏损状态，与 2015 年相比变化不大。

（1）新增投资项目整体盈利面不高。2016 年创业风险投资机构新增投资项目的盈利能力总体偏弱，但是主营业务收入 1000 万元以上的项目整体上均实现了盈利，盈利面较 2015 年有所扩大。调查显示有 48.2%的被投资项目利润为正，亏损的被投资项目占比为 33.9%。

（2）项目规模与项目利润高度相关。2016 年，不同规模新增被投资项目的平均利润率与其规模依然保持正相关。主营业务收入越大的被投资项目，平均利润率越高。其中，主营业务收入 100 万元以下的新增被投资项目平均利润率为–478.6%，主营业务收入 100 万~500 万元的新增被投资项目平均利润率为–122.4%，主营业务收入 500 万~1000 万元的新增被投资项目平均利润率为–22.6%。主营业务收入 1000 万元以上的新增被投资项目平均利润率均为正，且随收入规模增加而有所提高。

（3）不同规模新增投资项目平均利润率变化产生分化。虽然主营业务收入 1000 万元以上的项目平均利润率均为正值，但是主营业务收入 3000 万元以上的项目平均利润率有所下降，其中主营业务收入 5000 万元以上的项目平均利润率从 2015 年的 19.45%下降到 2016 年的 7.9%。主营业务收入 1000 万元以下的项目平均利润率变化也不相同，其中主营业务收入 100 万元以下的项目亏损幅度较 2015 年有所缓解，但是主营业务收入 100 万~500 万元的项目平均利润率则有明显下降。

① 有效样本数为 1020 份。

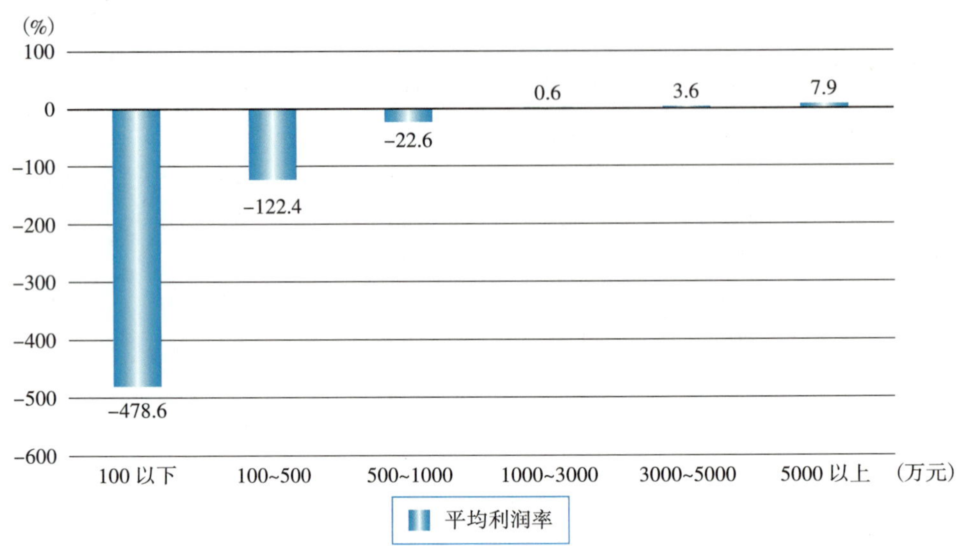

图 4-6　创业风险投资项目的平均利润率（2016）

（4）新增被投资项目的平均利润呈现普遍下滑趋势。2016 年，新增被投资项目的平均利润整体出现下滑，仅主营业务收入 1000 万~3000 万元的项目平均利润超过 2015 年，其中主营业务收入 100 万元以下的项目平均利润达到近年来最低点。

（5）规模较小的项目出现亏损的可能性更大。调查显示，连续 5 年以来，主营业务收入 1000 万元以下的被投资项目的平均利润均为负值，主营业务收入 500 万元以下的项目平均利润则连续 6 年为负值。

表 4-5　不同规模被投资项目主营业务收入和利润（2011~2016）　　单位：万元

主营业务收入（万元）		<100	100~500	500~1000	1000~3000	3000~5000	>5000
2011 年	平均主营业务收入	13.00	281.00	759.00	1971.00	3951.00	62777.00
	平均利润	-123.00	-15.00	114.00	270.00	593.00	5739.00
2012 年	平均主营业务收入	13.00	281.00	729.00	2170.00	4030.00	37292.00
	平均利润	58.00	-135.00	-52.00	316.00	497.00	4192.00
2013 年	平均主营业务收入	13.00	253.00	776.00	1915.00	4040.00	64047.00
	平均利润	-477.00	-99.00	-48.00	130.00	121.00	5266.00
2014 年	平均主营业务收入	33.02	290.00	725.00	1871.00	4028.00	775370.00
	平均利润	-226.90	-259.80	-355.70	105.00	527.00	12579.00
2015 年	平均主营业务收入	16.00	249.40	741.10	1775.40	3883.50	52008.30
	平均利润	-122.30	-171.00	-155.90	-159.50	220.20	9921.80
2016 年	平均主营业务收入①	14.60	277.90	765.20	1824.20	3948.50	33239.50
	平均利润②	-569.10	-301.50	-163.70	10.00	140.90	2653.70

① 有效样本数为 1053 份。
② 有效样本数为 1024 份。

4.3 创业风险投资项目的总体运行与趋势

4.3.1 被投资项目总体运行情况

截至 2016 年底，中国创业风险投资机构[①]累计投资项目达到 19296 项，其中，继续运行项目占 76.5%；境内外已上市项目占比为 6.9%；原股东（创业者）收购和管理层收购项目合计占比为 9.0%；被其他机构收购项目比重为 4.9%；清算的项目比重为 2.7%（见图 4-7）。

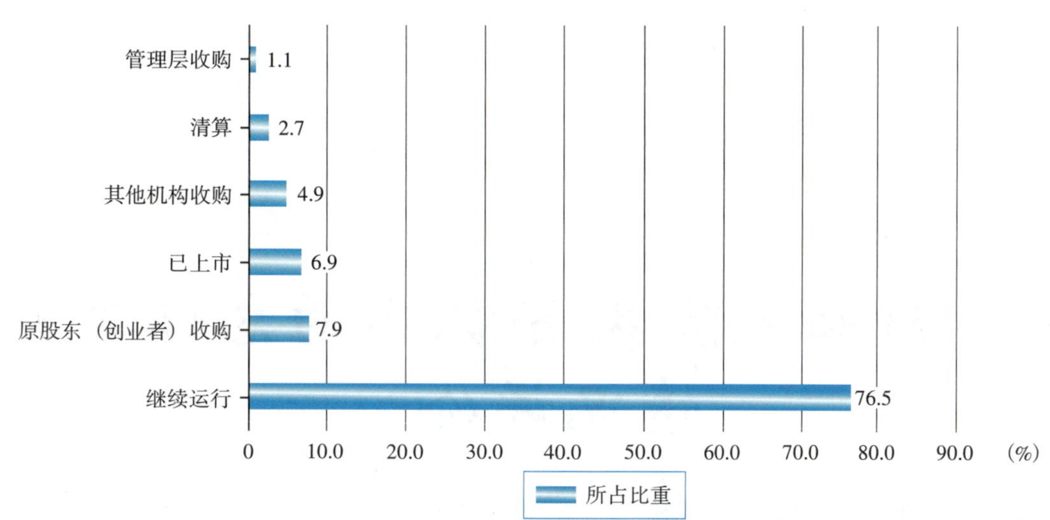

图 4-7 累计被投资项目的总体运行情况（2016）

4.3.2 被投资项目总体运行趋势

2016 年，中国创业风险投资机构累计投资项目的运行趋势表现出如下特征（见表 4-6）：

（1）资本市场不温不火，上市项目比重下滑明显。2016 年，新增投资项目大幅提高，然而国内资本市场不温不火，虽然 IPO 平稳推进，但是占比明显下降，其中国内市场 IPO 退出项目比重下降到 6.6%，境外市场 IPO 退出项目比重则下降到 0.3%。

（2）并购市场内热外冷，被投项目更受国内关注。2016 年，被境内外机构收购的项目占比为 4.9%，略低于 2015 年，但处于 2011 年以来的相对高水平，其中境内收购依然是主流，境外收购第三年下降，占比仅为 0.1%。

（3）股权回流现象普遍，原股东和管理层收购热情不减。包括创业者在内的原股东、管理层收购占比达到 9%，与 2015 年持平，其中原股东（创始人）收购占比提高了 0.3 个百分点，管理层收购下降了 0.3 个百分点。虽然与 2011 年及以前相比，股权回流的退出项目占比有所下降，但是近 3 年的比重有回升趋势。

（4）清算项目占比大幅提升。清算始终是不愿见到的投资结果，近 5 年来，清算项目比重维持在 2%以下，但是 2016 年该比重升至 2.7%，达到近 10 年的第二高位，且是连续第二年提高，这也反映了大众创业背景下，被投资项目竞争激烈、生存困难的局面。

① 有效样本数为 1290 份。

表 4-6 累计被投资项目的总体运行状况（2007~2016） 单位：%

年份＼运行情况	已上市		被收购		原股东收购	管理层收购	继续运行	清算
	境内	境外	境内收购	境外收购				
2007	3.7	2.0	6.7	0.6	13.0	1.7	70.1	2.2
2008	1.8	1.1	3.1	2.9	6.2	0.6	82.7	1.6
2009	4.6	1.8	4.5	4.0	13.2	1.0	67.6	3.3
2010	5.9	1.7	4.7	4.1	10.6	0.9	69.6	2.5
2011	6.7	1.5	3.6	0.2	8.0	1.4	76.9	1.7
2012	6.7	1.4	3.3	0.1	7.2	1.0	78.9	1.4
2013	5.7	0.9	3.8	0.1	8.7	2.7	76.4	1.7
2014	6.0	1.6	4.4	0.3	6.6	0.7	79.0	1.4
2015	8.0	1.3	4.9	0.2	7.6	1.4	74.7	1.9
2016	6.6	0.3	4.8	0.1	7.9	1.1	76.5	2.7

4.4 创业风险投资机构的总体运行情况评价

4.4.1 投资机构对自身发展状况的评价①

2016 年，1227 家创业风险投资机构对自身发展情况进行了评价，总体上持乐观评价的机构比重较 2015 年有微弱提高。

调查显示，2016 年仍然有超过一半的创业风险投资机构对自身发展持乐观态度，但是认为自身发展“非常好”的机构比重有所下降，认为自身发展“好”的机构达到近年来最高的 53.9%，二者合计为 59.0%，连续 4 年增长。对自身发展状况给予悲观评价的机构占比为 4.2%，2014 年以来保持稳定，其中认为自身发展状况“非常差”的机构比重为 0.5%，连续 4 年维持在较低水平。机构对自身发展状况评价的分布则与 2015 年保持稳定，仅仅是峰度略高而已（见表 4-7、图 4-8）。

表 4-7 投资机构对自身发展状况的评价（2013~2016） 单位：%

年份＼评价	非常好	好	一般	差	非常差	不确定
2013	3.3	47.9	42.3	6.0	0.5	—
2014	5.1	52.3	38.6	3.6	0.4	—
2015	6.3	52.1	37.0	3.8	0.5	0.3
2016	5.1	53.9	36.8	3.7	0.5	—

① 有效样本数为 1227 份。

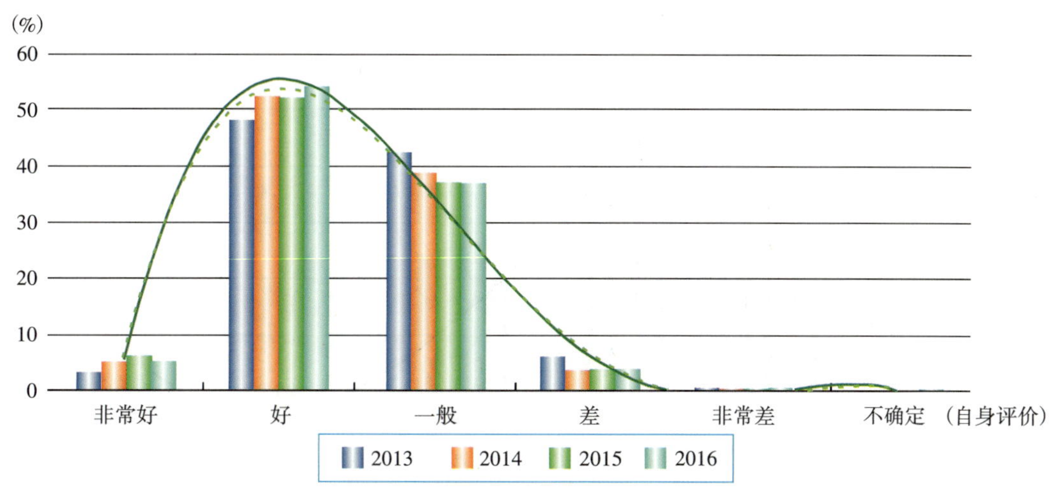

图 4-8 投资机构对自身发展状况的评价（2013~2016）

4.4.2 投资机构对全行业发展情况的评价[①]

2016 年，1225 家创业风险投资机构对全行业发展情况给出自己的评价。与 2015 年相比，中国创业风险投资机构对全行业的评价更加中庸，乐观评价比重下降了 0.2 个百分点，悲观评价下降了 1.8 个百分点。认为全行业发展"非常好"和"好"的机构比重分别上升了 0.3 个和下降了 0.5 个百分点；认为"差"和"非常差"的机构比重分别下降了 1.7 个和 0.1 个百分点；认为全行业整体发展一般的机构占比从 2015 年的 44.7%提高到了 2016 年的 45.3%，同时对行业"不确定"的机构占比上升了 1.4 个百分点（见表 4-8）。

表 4-8 投资机构对全行业的整体评价（2013~2016） 单位：%

整体评价 / 年份	非常好	好	一般	差	非常差	不确定
2013	1.3	29.3	48.1	20.0	1.3	—
2014	3.4	51.5	38.0	6.7	0.4	—
2015	2.4	42.4	44.7	7.6	1.2	1.7
2016	2.7	41.9	45.3	5.9	1.1	3.1

2016 年，中国创业风险投资机构对全行业的整体评价分布与 2015 年相比，变化不大，创业风险投资机构对整个市场的发展评价保持了高度的稳定性。对过去一年行业发展判断不置可否的比例提高并没有改变机构对行业景气判断的分化，有接近一半的机构认为 2016 年全行业发展一般，与 2015 年水平相当（见图 4-9）。

① 有效样本数为 1225 份。

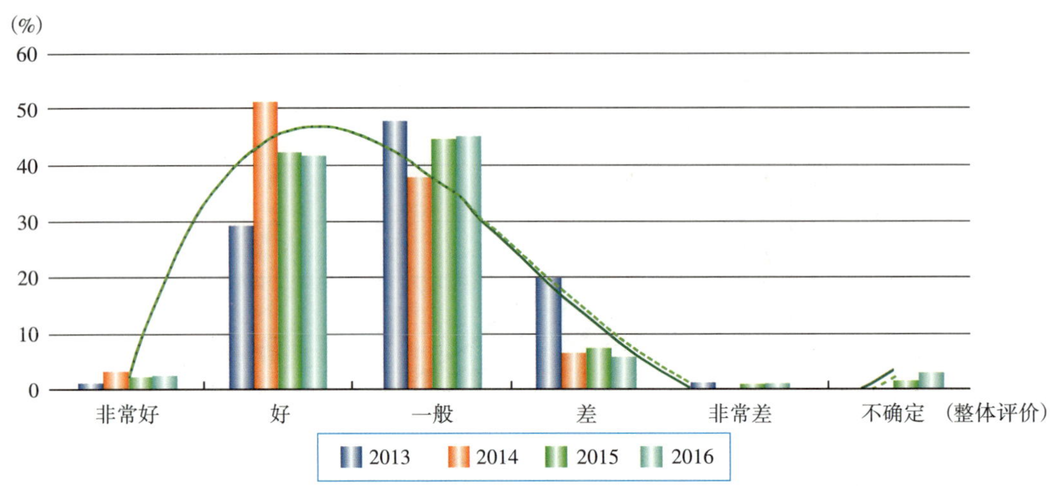

图 4-9 投资机构对全行业的整体评价（2013~2016）

与 2015 年创业风险投资机构的预测相比，2016 年的实际评价仍然存在落差，但幅度有所下降。认为 2016 年行业发展“非常好”、“好”的机构占比实际值较 2015 年的预测值分别下降了 1.0 和 7.4 个百分点；相反，悲观预测则在现实中进一步放大，上年度预测 2016 年度行业表现“差”和“不确定”的比重分别为 4.5%和 0.8%，实际认为“差”和“非常差”的机构占比则为 7%，合计上升了 1.7 个百分点。这主要是受国际、国内宏观经济不确定性的影响，此外国内资本市场继续调整可能超出了机构的预期。

4.4.3 投资机构的投资前景预测①

对于 2017 年投资前景，中国创业风险投资机构整体上给出了相对乐观的预测。与上年相比，认为 2017 年投资前景“非常好”和“好”的机构占比分别为 3.6%和 55.0%，分别较 2016 年下降了 0.1 个百分点和上升了 5.7 个百分点，从而带来乐观预期机构比例从 53%提高到了 58.6%。相应地，对 2017 年投资前景预期相对悲观的机构占比下降明显。但值得注意的是，对 2017 年投资前景“不确定”的机构占比达到了 4.1%，较 2016 年上升了 3.3 个百分点。调查还显示有 77.2%的机构认为创投行业的发展受宏观经济影响较大和非常大，因此对未来一年投资前景不确定可能源于机构对 2017 年全球市场的发展趋势更加不确定，美国、欧洲以及亚洲的政治、经济等表现都可能深刻影响全球经济。此外，2016 年机构自身和行业的实际运行情况较 2015 年预测更差也是导致企业更悲观的因素之一（见表 4-9、图 4-10）。

表 4-9 投资机构投资前景的预测（2014~2017） 单位：%

年份 \ 整体评价	非常好	好	一般	不好	不确定
2014	2.0	54.6	37.9	5.2	0.3
2015	5.6	65.2	27.7	1.3	0.2
2016	3.7	49.3	37.8	4.5	0.8
2017	3.6	55.0	34.1	3.2	4.1

① 有效样本数为 1230 份。

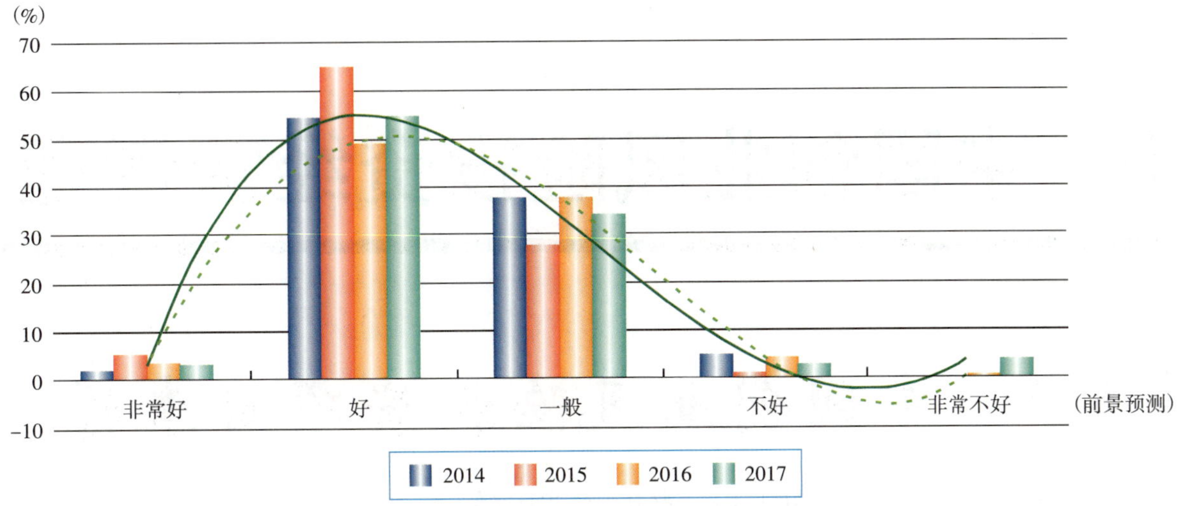

图 4-10　投资机构投资前景预测（2014~2017）

5 中国创业风险投资经营管理

5.1 中国创业风险投资项目来源

2016 年，中国创业风险投资的项目来源仍然以“政府部门推荐”、“朋友介绍”和“项目中介机构”三大主要渠道为主①（见表 5-1、图 5-1）。但三者占比之和分别从 2013 年、2014 年、2015 年的 64.5%、59.7%、51.1%继续下降到 2016 年的 50.7%。

2015 年统计调查首次将“众创空间”作为信息渠道之一，2016 年该渠道占比进一步提升，较 2015 年上升了 0.9 个百分点。

2016 年，“银行介绍”信息来源较 2014 年和 2015 年相比继续下降，从 2014 年和 2015 年的 7.4%和 7.1%，下降到 2016 年的 6.1%。

按照“自有渠道”和“中介渠道”② 划分项目来源，项目来自于自有渠道三项之和要略小于中介渠道获得项目来源。

表 5-1 创业风险投资机构获取项目信息的渠道（2008~2016） 单位：%

年份＼信息渠道	政府部门推荐	朋友介绍	项目中介机构	股东推荐	项目业主	银行介绍	媒体宣传	众创空间（孵化器）	其他
2008	25.7	17.7	16.1	13.6	15.5	5.6	2.9	—	2.8
2009	25.9	19.1	16.1	13.4	13.0	6.6	3.0	—	2.9
2010	26.2	17.9	18.5	13.2	11.3	7.2	2.9	—	2.7
2011	25.4	18.7	18.5	13.3	11.7	7.4	2.8	—	2.1
2012	25.2	19.2	18.6	13.2	11.5	6.9	2.2	—	3.2
2013	25.5	19.9	19.1	13.2	10.1	6.0	2.6	—	3.6
2014	24.9	17.7	17.1	14.3	11.0	7.4	3.9	—	3.6
2015	21.3	14.6	15.2	13.9	11.3	7.1	3.5	10.4	2.7
2016	20.2	15.4	15.1	14.1	11.5	6.1	3.5	11.3	2.7

① 有效样本数量为 1249 份。

② 自有渠道：朋友介绍、股东推荐、项目业主；中介渠道：政府部门推荐、项目中介机构、银行介绍、媒体宣传、众创空间（孵化器）以及其他。

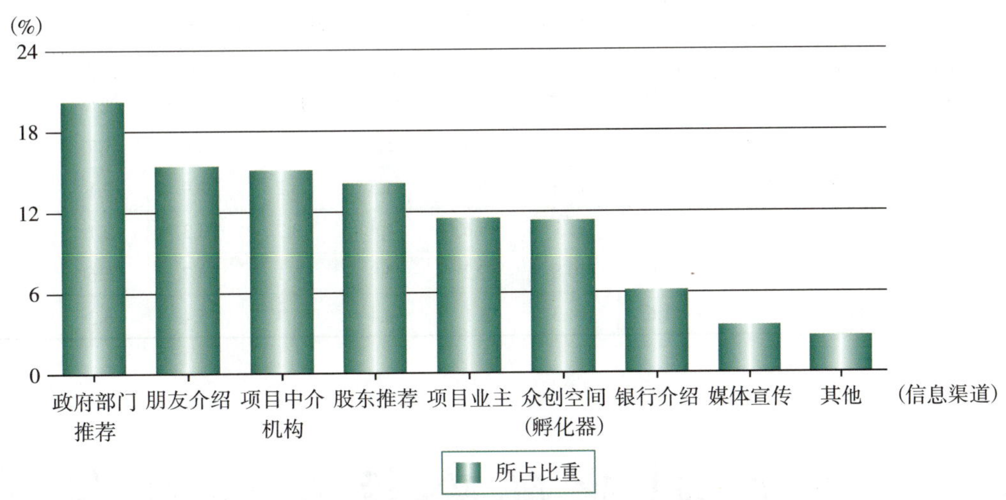

图 5-1 创业风险投资机构获取项目信息的渠道（2016）

5.2 中国创业风险投资的决策要素

根据 2016 年影响创业风险投资机构进行投资决策的因素调查①显示（见图 5-2、表 5-2）。总体看来，各决定要素所占比重逐渐趋于均衡。“市场前景”更是自 2012 年以来首次低于 20%。“市场前景”、“管理团队”和“技术因素”仍然是影响创业风险投资机构决策的三个最主要因素，但三者之和所占比重较 2015 年下降了 3.5 个百分点，为 47.7%。

与 2015 年相比较而言，“财务状况”、“公司治理结构”、“股权价格”、“资信状况”、“竞争对手情况”、“投资地点”所占比重都有所上升。其中，2016 年的“资信状况”、“竞争对手情况”、“投资地点”所占比重都较 2012 年至少翻了一番。

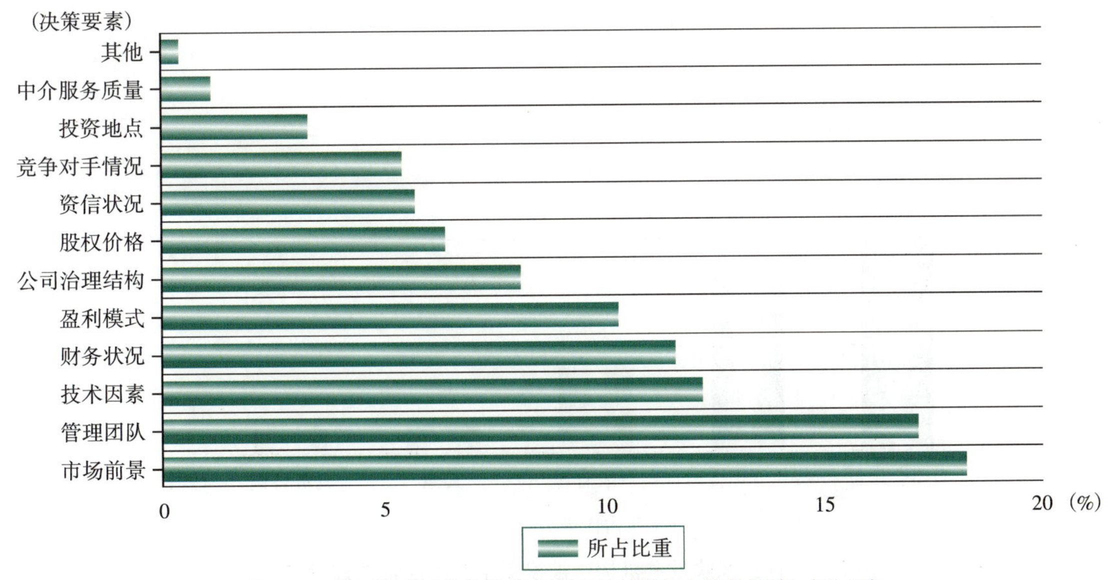

图 5-2 影响创业风险投资机构进行投资决策的因素（2016）

① 有效样本为 1249 份。

表 5-2 影响创业风险投资机构进行投资决策的因素（2012~2016）

单位：%

原因 年份	市场前景	管理团队	技术因素	财务状况	盈利模式	公司治理结构	股权价格	资信状况	竞争对手情况	投资地点	中介服务质量	其他
2012	24.3	22.5	13.0	9.2	12.4	5.4	5.2	2.9	2.9	1.7	0.3	0.2
2013	24.1	22.5	12.7	9.9	12.1	5.1	4.5	3.2	2.9	2.1	0.6	0.3
2014	24.3	21.4	13.7	8.8	11.7	5.6	4.4	3.7	3.3	2.1	0.7	0.4
2015	20.3	18.2	12.7	11.0	10.8	7.2	5.8	5.1	4.7	2.6	1.1	0.6
2016	18.3	17.2	12.2	11.6	10.3	8.1	6.4	5.7	5.4	3.3	1.1	0.4

5.3 中国创业风险投资对被投资项目的监管方式

调查显示[①]，“董事会席位”、“提供管理咨询”仍然是2016年两个主要监管方式，累计占比为74.3%，较2015年略有下降（见图5-3）。

与2015年不同的是，2016年创业风险投资机构对被投资项目的管理方式出现了明显变化，“董事会席位”所占比重较2015年有了明显提高，占比较2015年提高了3.9个百分点，占比为40.4%，并超过“提供管理咨询”成为最主要的管理方式。

2016年，“提供管理咨询”较2015年下降幅度明显，由2015年的41.5%下降到2016年的33.9%。“只限监管”占比连续三年保持上升态势，从2014年的8.3%、2015年的12.3%上升到2016年的16%。而“财务咨询”所占比重继续保持在4%左右，较2015年上升了0.5个百分点到4.8%。这在一定程度上能够反映出2016年的被投项目自身管理水平较2015年被投项目更加注重自身机构和管理的优化。

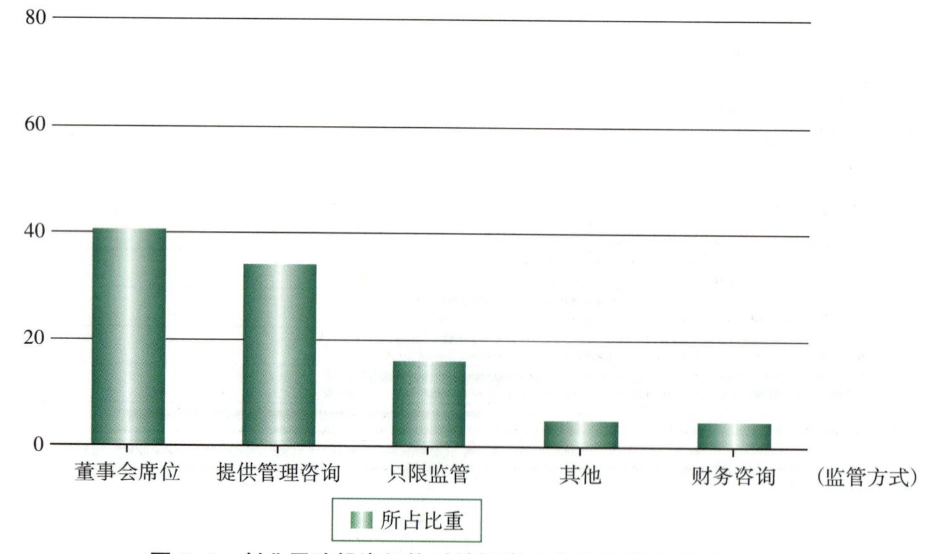

图 5-3 创业风险投资机构对被投资企业的监管方式（2016）

① 有效样本为1240份。

2016 年，创业风险投资机构依旧以“一般参股”为重点股权参与方式[①]（见表 5-3、图 5-4），“绝对控股”、“相对控股”和“一般参股”较 2015 年没有出现明显波动。其中“绝对控股”和“一般参股”所占比重分别较 2015 年下降 0.4 个和 0.5 个百分点；“相对控股”较 2015 年增长 0.85 个百分点。因变化较小所以难以做出趋势判断。

表 5-3 创业风险投资机构股权的参与程度（2008~2016） 单位：%

年份 \ 股权参与程度	绝对控股	相对控股	一般参股
2008	3.90	15.70	80.00
2009	7.70	16.10	76.30
2010	3.70	12.10	84.20
2011	4.90	8.60	86.50
2012	4.40	11.00	84.60
2013	5.20	10.20	84.60
2014	3.40	12.30	84.30
2015	3.50	7.05	89.50
2016	3.10	7.90	89.00

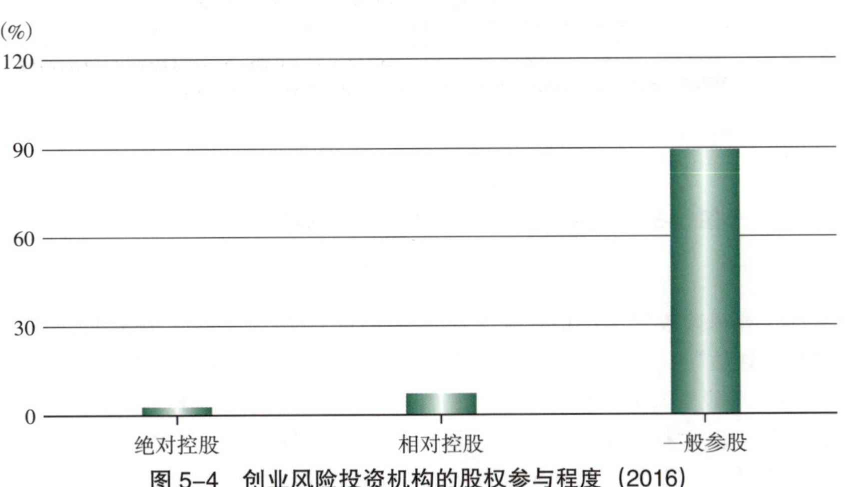

图 5-4 创业风险投资机构的股权参与程度（2016）

5.4 与创业风险投资经营管理有关的人力资源因素

通过对 2016 年从事创业风险投资人员的基本素质进行调查发现（见图 5-5）[②]，“资本运作能力”与“判断力和洞察力”是一名合格的创业风险投资人员最应该具备的两个素质。从总体排名看，2016 年各要素所占比重与

① 有效样本为 1947 份。
② 有效样本为 1240 份。

2015 年相比略有变化，“资本运作能力”、“判断力和洞察力”、“财务管理能力”和“商务谈判能力”仍然是合格创业风险投资人员应该具备的前四名；而“人际关系网络和协调能力”超过“技术背景”，成为第五项应具备的素质。

具体而言，在“资本运作能力”、“判断力和洞察力”均较 2015 年略有下降。其中，“资本运作能力”所占比重较 2015 年下降 0.1 个百分点至 20.9%，“判断力和洞察力”选项所占比重较 2015 年下降 0.6 个百分点至 18.7%，“财务管理能力”占比较 2015 年增长了 0.3%至 16.5%。

2016 年，“商务谈判能力”、“人际关系网络和协调能力”以及“技术背景”分别占比为 14.8%、14.6%和 13.9%，分别比 2015 年减少 0.7 个百分点、增长 1.5 个百分点以及与 2015 年持平。

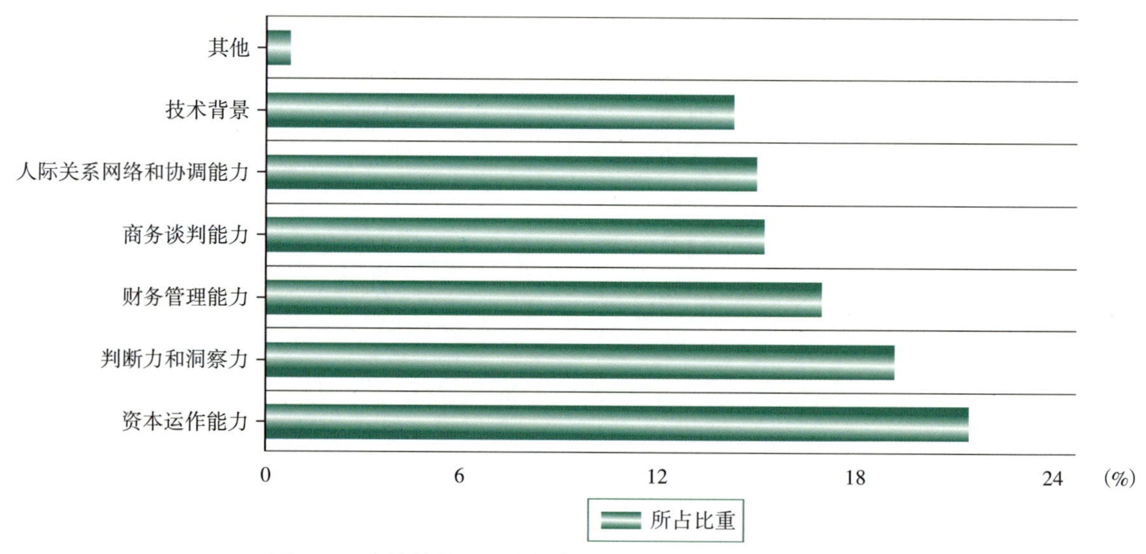

图 5-5 合格的创业风险投资人员应该具备的素质（2016）

图 5-6 给出 2016 年创业风险投资人员相对缺乏的知识的统计情况①。“技术评估”、“资本运作”和“项目识别”依然是从事创业风险投资人员最缺乏的三个专业知识。但是，相较于 2015 年，“技术评估”所占比重下降了 1.2%至 17.4%，“资本运作”所占比重无显著变化，2016 年占比为 16.2%，而“项目识别”能力略有下降至 13.6%。

此外，2016 年，“技术背景”超过“企业管理”占比，成为第四个创业风险投资人员缺乏的专业知识，从 2015 年的 12.7%增长至 2016 年的 13%，而缺乏“企业管理”所占比延续 2014 年的下降趋势，占比为 13.5%，较 2015 年下降了 0.7 个百分点。

“法律知识”、“财务管理能力”和“商务谈判能力”的排名与 2015 年相同。其中，欠缺“法律知识”所占比重继续上升，从 2015 年的 9.2%上升至 2016 年的 11.1%；“财务管理能力”和“商务谈判能力”所占比重与 2015 年变化不大，分别占比为 7.9%和 5.9%。

① 有效样本为 1237 份。

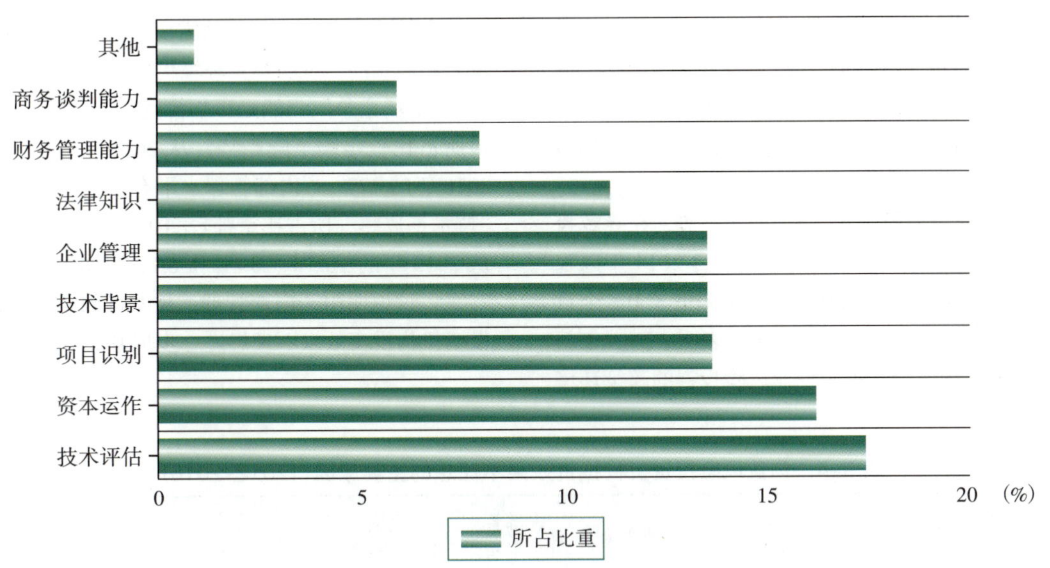

图 5-6 创业风险投资人员缺乏的专业知识（2016）

5.5 投资效果不理想的主要原因

2016 年，我国创业风险投资机构投资效果不理想的主要原因依然集中在“退出渠道不畅”、“政策环境变化”、“市场竞争”、“内部管理水平有限”、“后续融资不力”、“技术不成熟”以及“缺乏诚信”方面①（见图 5-7、表 5-4）。与 2015 年相比，并没有明显变化。

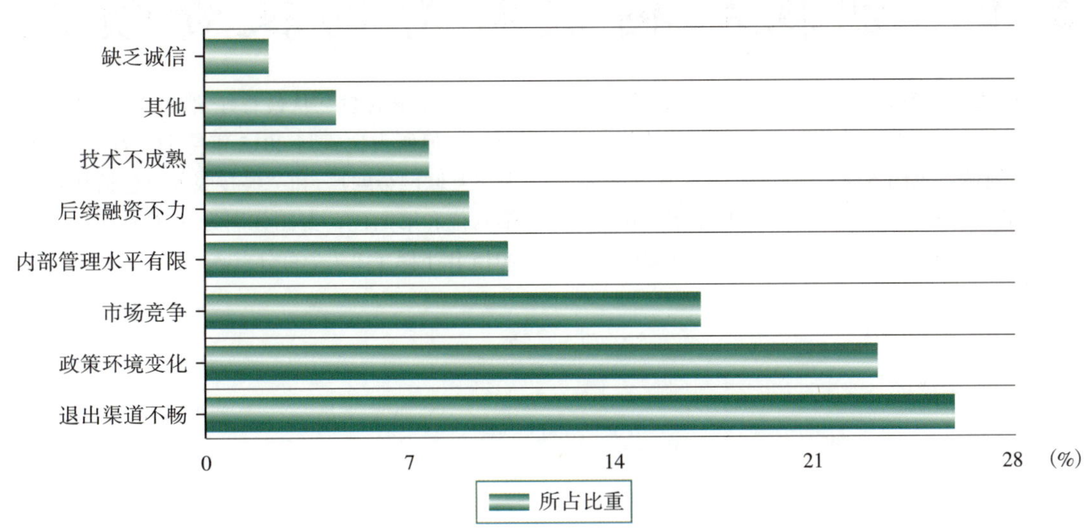

图 5-7 创业风险投资机构投资效果不理想的主要原因（2016）

① 有效样本为 1228 份。

“退出渠道不畅”仍然被创业风险投资机构选为造成投资效果不理想的最主要原因，所占比重从 2014 年的 25.4%上升至 2015 年的 26.2%后，2016 年所占比重有下降至 25.9%，仍然比排名第二的“政策变化环境”高出 2.7 个百分点。

“政策环境变化”延续 2015 年的变化态势，在导致投资效果欠佳主要因素中排名第二位，延续自 2014 年以来的占比情况，且比 2014 年和 2015 年分别降低了 0.2 个百分点和 0.5 个百分点。这也在一定程度上表明，随着创新创业整体体制机制的健全，关于创业风险投资的政策环境也越来越趋于稳定。但仍然需要认清其在影响投资效果中排名仍然靠前，说明政策环境仍然有很大优化空间。

“市场竞争”仍然是影响投资效果的第三个主要原因，但所占比重延续下降趋势，从 2015 年占比 17.6%下降至 2016 年的 17%。“内部管理水平有限”、“后续融资不力”、“技术不成熟”所占比重都较 2015 年有所上升，占比分别从 2015 年的 10.3%、8.4%和 6.7%增加到 10.4%、9.1%和 7.7%。这说明由于内部管理、技术等因素导致的创业风险投资机构投资效果不理想进一步加剧。

表 5-4 创业风险投资机构投资效果不理想的主要原因（2012~2016） 单位：%

原因 / 年份	退出渠道不畅	政策环境变化	市场竞争	内部管理水平有限	后续融资不力	技术不成熟	其他	缺乏诚信
2012	15.6	18.9	17.4	16.6	9.9	12.4	0.9	8.4
2013	26.6	26.7	18.2	8.4	5.7	6.8	4.6	3.1
2014	25.4	23.4	19.4	9.5	8.0	7.1	4.6	2.6
2015	26.2	23.7	17.6	10.3	8.4	6.7	4.7	2.4
2016	25.9	23.2	17.0	10.4	9.1	7.7	4.5	2.2

5.6 创投机构最看好的投资领域

2016 年，通过调查发现①，“新能源、高效节能技术”、“新材料工业”和“生物科技”成为 2017 年创投机构最看好的前三领域（见图 5-8）。其中，三者所占比例分别较 2015 年增长了 0.6 个百分点、1.6 个百分点和 0.6 个百分点至 2016 年的 13.1%、11.3%和 9.7%。与 2015 年相比，“医药保健”从最看好领域第二位下降至 2016 年第四位，但所占比重与 2015 年持平，都是 9.3%。“网络产业（互联网金融）”和“科技服务（包括教育）”分别位列第六位和第七位，占比分别为 5.1%和 5.1%，前者占比较 2015 年下降了 2.7 个百分点。

① 有效样本为 1232 份。

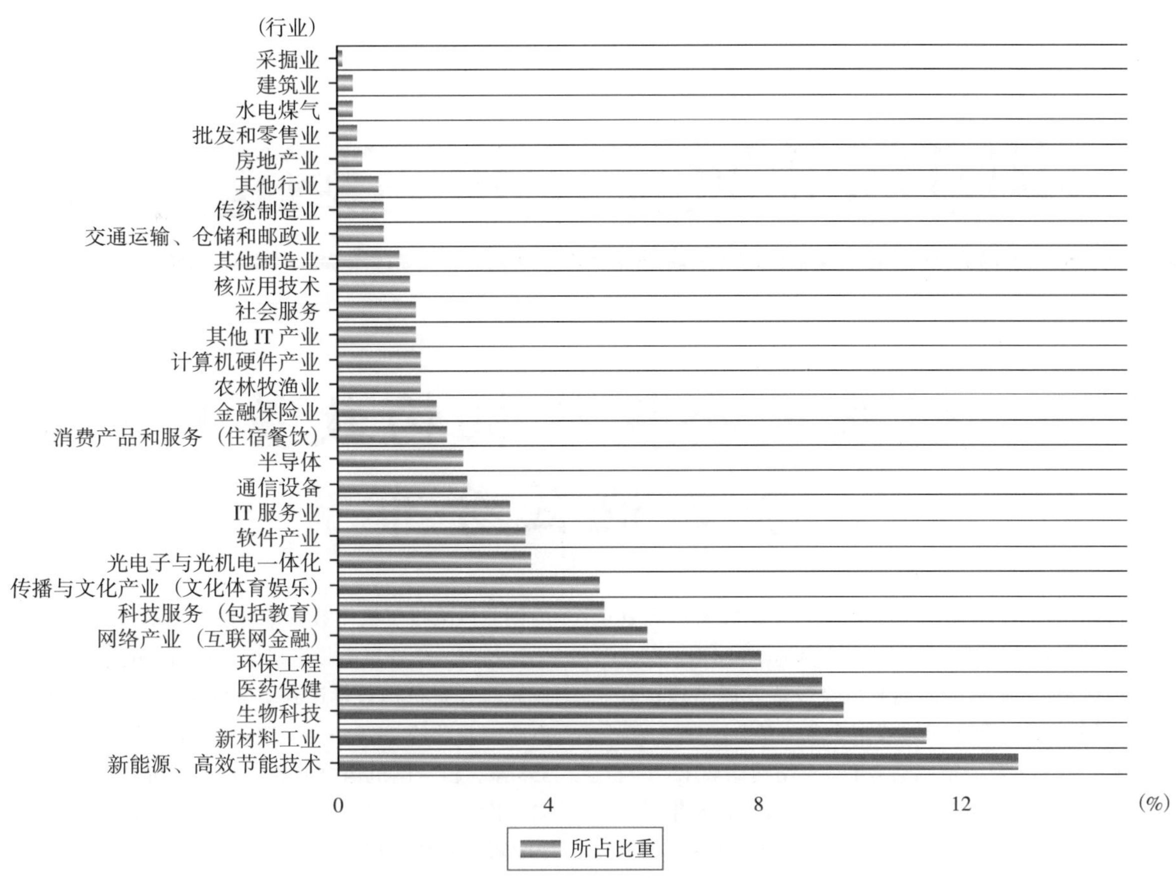

图 5-8　2017 年机构最看好的投资领域

6 中国创业风险投资区域运行状况

6.1 创业风险投资机构数量和管理资本地区分布

根据调查统计，2016 年创业风险投资机构总数达 2045 家，比 2015 年增加 271 家，增幅达 15.28%，高于 2015 年的 14.4%，显示国内创业风险投资发展迅速；在 2045 家创投机构中，创业风险投资企业（基金）1421 家，比 2015 年增加 111 家，增幅达 8.47%，增速比 2015 年有所降低；创业风险投资管理企业 624 家，较 2015 年增加 160 家，增幅 34.48%，远远高于 2015 年的 20.8%。创业风险投资管理企业继续保持了增长比例持续高于创业风险投资企业（基金）的趋势。

从地域分布看，2016 年 2045 家创业风险投资机构分布在全国 29 个省、直辖市和自治区，创业风险投资在全国的分布具有如下显著特点（见表 6–1、图 6–1）：

（1）整体看，全国创业风险投资机构仍然呈现集中在东部沿海和发达地区，中部地区创业风险投资机构崛起，而西部地区则继续保持平稳、机构数量较少的特点。另外，创业风险投资管理机构的区域分布特征表现更为明显，创投管理机构主要集中在经济发达地区，江苏、浙江和北京三地的创业风险投资管理机构明显多于国内其他地区；西部地区则主要是直接投资机构，管理类机构很少。

（2）继 2015 年之后，国内创业风险投资仍然呈现“三足鼎立”的局面。2016 年，江苏、浙江和北京，是国内创业风险投资机构数量排名前三名的地区。其中，江苏仍然是国内创业风险投资机构数量最多的地区，2016 年创业风险投资机构数量达到了 499 家，继续高居国内榜首，占全国总数的 24.4%；浙江机构数量继续排名第二，达到 353 家，占全国机构总数的 17.26%；北京与去年一样，排名继续保持第三位，但机构数量保持上升势头，达到了 298 家，占全国机构总数的 14.57%，机构数量比 2015 年增加了 117 家。上述三个地区的创业风险投资数量占全国总数的 56.23%，与 2015 年的占比基本持平。

（3）安徽、重庆、湖南、湖北、山东和上海成为 2016 年创业风险投资机构数量相对较多的地区。尤其是中部地区的安徽、湖南、湖北、重庆，其创业风险投资发展较多。2016 年，安徽创业风险投资机构数量是 98 家，比 2015 年增加 26 家，机构数量跃居全国第四；重庆有 96 家，比 2015 年增加 23 家，排名跃居全国第五位；湖南有 70 家，比 2015 年增加 23 家，排名第八；湖北有 58 家，比 2015 年增加 14 家，排名第九。

（4）部分地区的机构数量保持稳定，尤其是一些西部地区和经济欠发达地区，地区内的创业风险投资机构增长缓慢，显示这些地区的创业风险投资发展严重滞后。甘肃、宁夏、海南、青海、吉林、内蒙古和山西等地的创业风险投资机构数量都是个位数。

表 6-1 中国各地区创业风险投资机构数量（2016） 单位：家

地区	创投机构数	创投基金数	创投管理机构数
江苏	499	386	113
浙江	353	270	83
北京	298	165	133
安徽	98	80	18
重庆	96	33	63
山东	81	61	20
上海	80	53	27
湖南	70	43	27
湖北	58	27	31
广东	55	48	7
天津	54	40	14
福建	45	27	18
四川	45	31	14
河北	30	27	3
新疆	29	19	10
辽宁	28	19	9
贵州	27	20	7
黑龙江	22	17	5
河南	20	15	5
陕西	14	12	2
云南	11	5	6
海南	7	4	3
吉林	7	6	1
甘肃	6	6	0
宁夏	3	0	3
青海	3	3	0
江西	3	2	1
山西	2	2	0
内蒙古	1	0	1

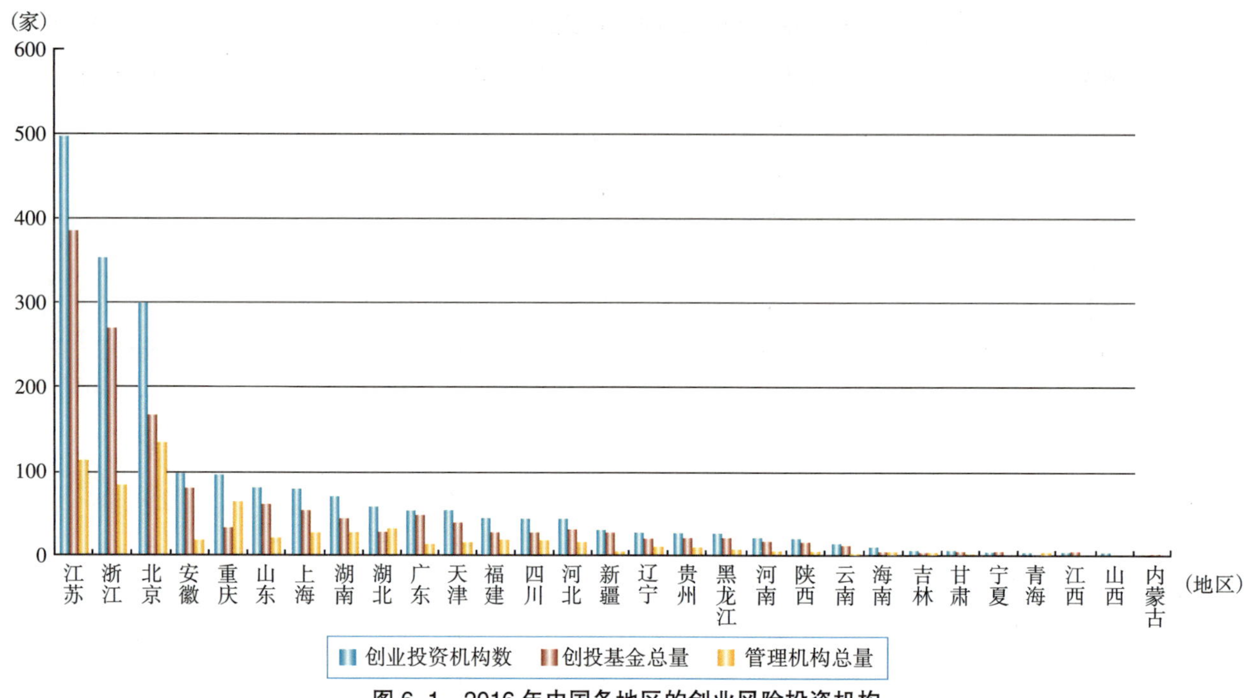

图 6–1　2016 年中国各地区的创业风险投资机构

表 6–2 和图 6–2 显示了 2016 年我国不同地区创业风险投资公司的管理资本规模。

2016 年，全国创业风险投资公司管理资金规模达 8277.06 亿元，比 2015 年增加 1623.76 亿元，增幅达 24.4 个百分点，说明进入我国创业投资行业的国内外资金大幅度增加，这与当前中央政府推动“大众创业　万众创新”以及科技、财政、金融、税务部门和地方各级政府的大力支持有关。

从地区角度看，全国创业风险投资机构管理资金具有如下特点：

（1）2016 年不同地区创业风险投资机构管理资本差距持续扩大。东部经济发达地区创业风险投资管理资金规模非常大，最高地区管理资本规模超过 2898 亿元，而部分西部地区创业风险投资管理资金规模在 1 亿~2 亿元以下，最少的内蒙古只有 7700 万元。

（2）北京、江苏、广东和浙江的创业风险投资管理资本总量位居全国前四名，尤其是北京和江苏，创业风险投资管理资本规模远远超过国内其他地区。继 2015 年之后，北京稳居国内创业风险投资机构管理资金榜首，管理资本总量达到 2898.24 亿元，比 2015 年增加 971.04 亿元，增长率达 50.39%。江苏创业风险投资管理资本总量排名第二，管理资本总量达 1954.13 亿元，比 2015 年增长 6.51%。广东[①]和浙江分别排名第三和第四。

北京创业风险投资机构的管理资金规模最大，与北京定位全国科技创新中心有直接关系，作为全国众多知名高校和研究院所的聚集地，每年产生大量的科技成果，对创业投资需求旺盛；另外，北京政府对创新创业的高度重视，大量的资金涌入创业风险投资行业。浙江创业风险投资机构数量在全国排名第二，但是由于民营投资机构数量占比较高，管理资金规模相对较小，因此创业风险投资管理资金规模与北京和江苏存在较大的差距。

（3）安徽、湖北、重庆和新疆等地区的创业风险投资管理资金规模较大，增加幅度显著。2016 年安徽创业风险投资管理资金达到了 411.87 亿元，增加 249.17 亿元，增幅达到了 153.15%，资金规模仅次于浙江，跃居全国第五位。湖北和重庆也都比上 2015 年有了较大幅度的提高。另外，内陆省份的新疆，资金规模增长明显。2016 年新疆的创业风险投资管理资本有 136.1 亿元，比 2015 年增长超过 4 倍。

（4）部分地区的创业风险投资管理资本规模较小。2016 年，青海、吉林和内蒙古创业风险投资管理资本总量都在 2 亿元以下，海南也只有 6 亿元左右。

① 由于调查原因，深圳部分创业投资机构没有填报数据，故 2016 年广东省的创业风险投资管理资金规模比 2015 年有较大程度减少。

表 6-2 中国创业风险投资管理资本的地区分布（2016） 单位：亿元

地区	管理资本总额
北京	2898.24
江苏	1954.13
广东	575.57
浙江	514.85
安徽	411.87
湖北	298.70
重庆	264.42
陕西	208.93
湖南	162.00
新疆	136.10
天津	116.80
上海	104.65
黑龙江	100.31
河南	79.83
四川	76.31
山东	70.10
福建	65.00
河北	54.41
辽宁	40.13
宁夏	36.26
甘肃	31.03
贵州	23.97
云南	22.11
江西	13.64
山西	8.15
海南	6.00
青海	1.71
吉林	1.10
内蒙古	0.77

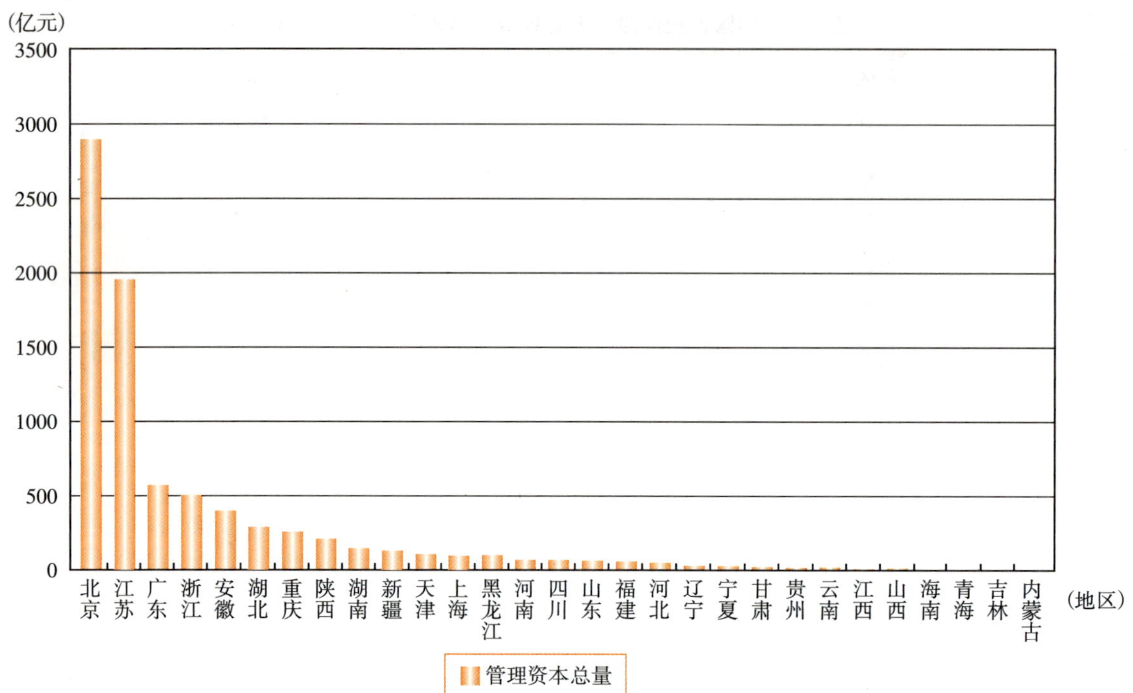

图 6-2 部分地区创业风险投资的管理资本分布（2016）

6.2 各地区创业风险投资机构的规模分布

表 6-3 和图 6-3 显示了 2016 年我国不同地区创业风险投资管理资本的规模分布。

表 6-3 各地区创业风险投资机构的管理资本规模分布（2016）

单位：%

地区	5000 万元以下	5000 万~1 亿元	1 亿~2 亿元	2 亿~5 亿元	5 亿元以上
湖南	29.31	15.52	25.86	17.24	12.07
山东	29.63	16.67	25.93	25.93	1.85
重庆	27.85	10.13	18.99	22.78	20.25
浙江	30.00	25.19	22.22	16.30	6.30
吉林	50.00	0.00	50.00	0.00	0.00
陕西	36.36	18.18	9.09	18.18	18.18
江苏	23.68	20.57	26.08	19.86	9.81
河北	26.09	17.39	26.09	17.39	13.04
海南	33.33	0.00	0.00	66.67	0.00
天津	32.65	28.57	10.2	20.41	8.16

续表

地区	5000 万元以下	5000 万~1 亿元	1 亿~2 亿元	2 亿~5 亿元	5 亿元以上
贵州	30.43	26.09	30.43	13.04	0.00
福建	37.84	5.41	29.73	18.92	8.11
辽宁	20.83	33.33	20.83	16.67	8.33
四川	10.53	23.68	36.84	18.42	10.53
湖北	7.50	12.50	32.50	25.00	22.50
广东	20.59	20.59	23.53	11.76	23.53
黑龙江	9.09	0.00	45.45	27.27	18.18
河南	23.53	23.53	11.76	29.41	11.76
青海	66.67	0.00	33.33	0.00	0.00
北京	19.07	13.56	15.25	18.22	33.9
安徽	22.78	13.92	17.72	30.38	15.19
新疆	35.29	23.53	23.53	5.88	11.76
上海	11.76	5.88	23.53	44.12	14.71
内蒙古	0.00	100.00	0.00	0.00	0.00
甘肃	0.00	0.00	40.00	40.00	20.00
云南	0.00	0.00	20.00	20.00	60.00
宁夏	0.00	0.00	33.33	33.33	33.33
山西	0.00	0.00	0.00	0.00	100.00

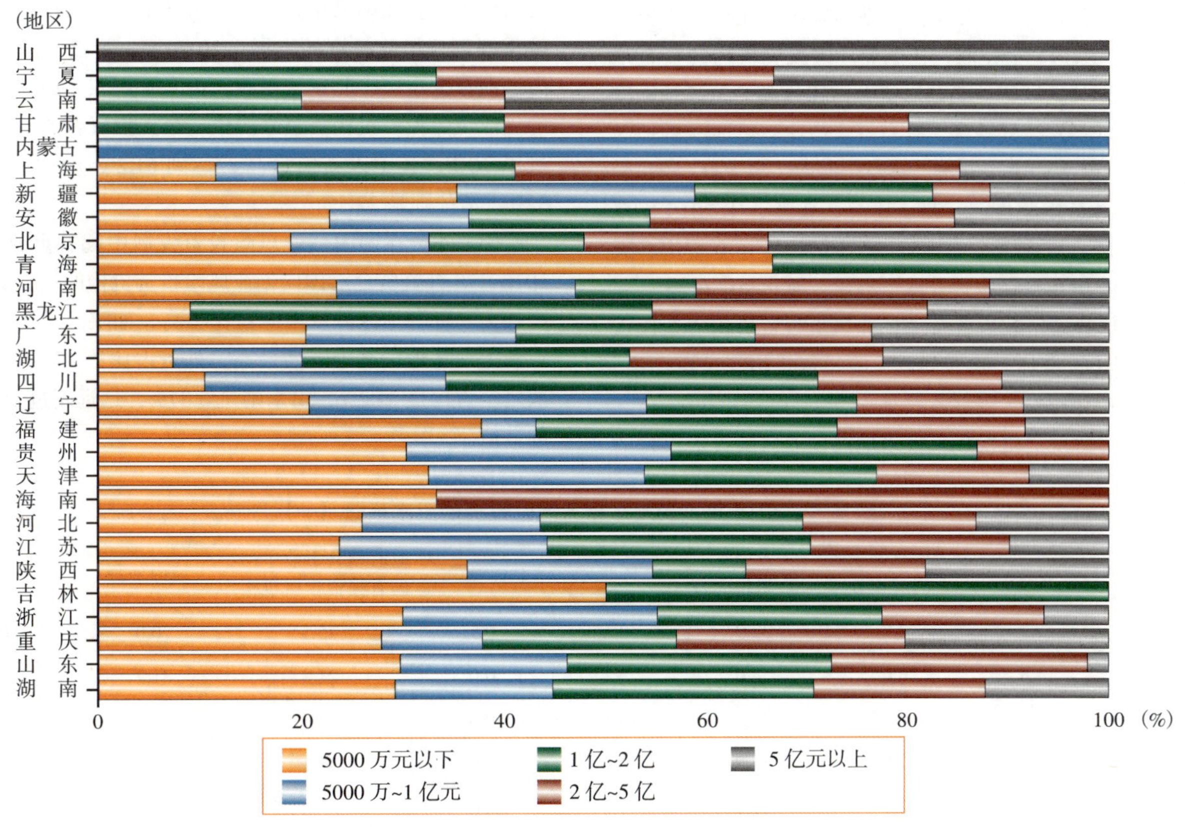

图 6–3 各地区不同规模创业风险投资机构的数量分布

整体上，2016 年，国内大部分地区创业风险投资机构中，管理资金规模以 1 亿~2 亿元和 5000 万元以下的机构占比较高，其次是 2 亿~5 亿元的机构。创业风险投资不发达的部分地区，其机构管理的资金集中在有限的几个规模水平上，包括海南、青海、山西、内蒙古、吉林、甘肃等。

创业风险投资机构管理资金规模在 5 亿元以上占比较高的地区有北京、广东，还有山西、宁夏、云南和重庆；前者是经济发达地区，地区内的创业风险投资机构筹集资金的能力较强；后者是经济相对不发达地区，创业风险投资机构大部分是由政府出资设立的，政府出资规模较大。

资金规模较少机构占比较高的地区有山东、陕西、天津、福建、青海和新疆等，其中青海的管理资金规模在 5000 万元以下的创业风险投资机构占比最高，达 66.67%。

6.3 各地区创业风险投资机构资本来源

本部分从三个角度来分析 2016 年国内创业风险投资机构的资本来源。

6.3.1 政府/个人/外资

表 6-4 显示：2016 年，全国各地区创业风险投资机构的资本来源呈现如下典型特征：

（1）政府资金依然是国内创业风险投资机构的主要资金来源。与 2015 年类似，在创业风险投资机构的资金来源中，大部分地区仍然是政府资金占比最高，尤其是经济和创业投资不发达的地区。政府资金占比超过 50%的地区有 12 个，包括甘肃、贵州、海南、河南、黑龙江、湖北、湖南、吉林、内蒙古、宁夏、青海、新疆，比 2015 年多出 3 个地区。政府资金占比超过 1/3 的地区还有重庆、天津、四川、山东、辽宁、安徽、福建、河北和广东等。

（2）部分地区政府资金占创业风险投资机构资金比重较低。浙江、吉林、陕西创业风险投资机构管理资金中，政府资金占比很低，浙江省只有 11.7%，陕西是 3.9%。

（3）民营投资机构成为很多地区创业风险投资机构的重要资金来源。2016 年，有 10 个地区的创业风险投资机构，来自民营投资机构的资金占比超过 20%，分别是江西、安徽、山东、湖北、福建、河南、四川、天津、辽宁和河北，其中江西省占比最高，达 46.7%。

（4）个人投资进一步成为全国创业风险投资机构的重要资金来源。在国家相关政策的引导下，个人投资者越来越重视创业风险投资的发展。2016 年，新疆、四川、青海、浙江、重庆、北京、福建、山东、广东、湖南、河南的创业风险投资机构资金来源中，个人投资者的比重都超过了 10%，其中以新疆最高，达到 61.2%，另外四川是 32%，浙江则是 22.3%。

（5）外资在国内创业风险投资发展中起着重要作用。2016 年，外资资金对国内创业风险投资机构的资金贡献力度加大，部分地区外资来源占比很高，如陕西、北京、山东和上海等地，其中陕西最高，外资占比达 47.7%，北京次之，占比是 31.2%，山东则是 5.87%，远远超过 2015 年的数值。

表 6-4 2016 年不同地区创业风险投资的资本来源（一） 单位：%

地区	个人	混合所有制企业（含国有成分）	民营投资机构	其他	社保基金	政府（含事业单位、国有独资投资机构）	境内外资	境外资本
安徽	2.3	4.2	33.9	13.6	0.5	45.5	0.0	0.0
北京	14.5	26.0	4.0	3.1	0.0	21.3	31.2	0.0
福建	10.9	1.5	37.3	15.1	0.0	34.7	0.5	0.0
甘肃	0.0	2.5	1.7	0.6	0.0	95.1	0.0	0.0
广东	8.9	2.3	47.7	1.8	0.0	38.6	0.3	0.2

续表

地区	个人	混合所有制企业（含国有成分）	民营投资机构	其他	社保基金	政府（含事业单位、国有独资投资机构）	境内外资	境外资本
贵州	11.5	6.6	9.9	8.9	0.0	63.1	0.0	0.0
海南	0.0	0.0	0.0	28.5	0.0	71.5	0.0	0.0
河北	42.0	0.0	14.4	9.3	0.0	33.4	0.9	0.0
河南	3.7	27.4	7.5	1.2	0.0	60.2	0.0	0.0
黑龙江	3.8	1.4	3.3	2.8	0.0	88.7	0.0	0.0
湖北	1.5	15.9	7.1	3.3	0.0	70.6	1.4	0.2
湖南	8.8	5.8	8.5	7.7	0.0	69.2	0.0	0.0
吉林	5.5	22.5	0.0	0.0	0.0	72.0	0.0	0.0
江苏	6.1	5.2	18.9	41.5	0.0	26.8	0.6	0.8
辽宁	4.2	3.7	23.6	21.2	0.0	47.1	0.0	0.2
内蒙古	0.0	0.0	0.0	0.0	0.0	100.0	0.0	0.0
宁夏	4.1	0.0	5.0	0.0	0.0	90.9	0.0	0.0
青海	19.6	0.0	13.3	0.6	0.0	66.6	0.0	0.0
山东	11.7	2.2	23.2	18.8	0.0	38.3	1.7	4.1
山西	0.0	0.0	0.0	75.4	0.0	24.6	0.0	0.0
陕西	0.6	0.0	0.7	47.5	0.0	3.9	47.3	0.0
上海	6.8	33.1	13.5	12.3	0.0	31.7	2.7	0.0
四川	15.8	5.0	24.2	10.3	0.0	44.0	0.7	0.0
天津	8.4	4.5	33.8	14.8	0.0	37.3	0.0	1.1
新疆	1.3	1.5	1.9	3.5	0.0	91.9	0.0	0.0
云南	9.5	39.4	11.3	9.0	0.0	30.8	0.0	0.0
浙江	16.6	4.8	23.2	43.5	0.0	11.7	0.3	0.0
重庆	11.4	2.8	17.9	33.8	0.0	34.1	0.1	0.0

6.3.2 上市公司/非上市公司

表 6-5 显示了 2016 年不同地区创业风险投资机构管理资本中上市公司与非上市公司的情况。

表 6-5 2016 年不同地区创业风险投资的资本来源（二） 单位：%

地区	上市公司	非上市公司	其他
安徽	1.4	55.2	43.4
北京	0.0	47.1	52.9
福建	2.0	45.9	52.0
甘肃	1.9	20.6	77.4

续表

地区	上市公司	非上市公司	其他
广东	5.3	77.2	17.5
贵州	0.0	50.2	49.8
海南	0.0	0.0	100.0
河北	8.1	17.7	74.2
河南	11.5	73.6	14.9
黑龙江	0.0	30.0	70.0
湖北	5.7	60.8	33.4
湖南	0.7	64.1	35.2
吉林	0.0	100.0	0.0
江苏	1.7	48.8	49.5
辽宁	1.2	68.8	30.0
内蒙古	0.0	0.0	100.0
宁夏	0.0	95.9	4.1
青海	0.0	69.3	30.7
山东	1.9	62.7	35.3
山西	0.0	0.0	100
陕西	14.9	15.9	69.2
上海	0.5	77.0	22.4
四川	1.5	47.0	51.5
天津	11.3	53.7	35.0
新疆	0.4	4.3	95.3
云南	5.3	70.8	24.0
浙江	9.0	36.9	54.1
重庆	9.5	36.5	54.0

整体看，非上市公司仍然是 2016 年国内各地区创业风险投资机构的主要资本来源。非上市公司资金占比超过 50%的地区有 14 家，比 2015 年多 2 家，其中最高的是吉林省，高达 100%。而上市公司出资用于创业风险投资的资金则相对较少，上市公司资金来源占比超过 10%的地区有陕西、河南、天津，其中占比最高的陕西为 14.9%。

6.3.3 金融机构/非金融机构

从金融机构/非金融机构角度来看，表 6-6 显示：2016 年，全国大部分地区创业风险投资机构的主要资金来源是非金融资本，比例最高的是甘肃和内蒙古，占比都是 100%。而金融机构投资设立创业风险投资的比例很少。

在现有的金融机构资金来源中，信托机构和银行是投资于国内创业风险投资机构最多的金融资本，河南、宁夏和重庆的创业风险投资资本来源中，信托机构的比例很高，而湖北、湖南和陕西，则银行的比例较高。至于证券资本，2016 年有 9 个地区的创业风险投资资本中有证券公司介入，河南创业风险投资资金中证券公司的资金占比很高，达到了 14.3%，另外就是新疆的 3.3%，其他地区占比都很低。至于保险资金，根据 2016 年的调查，还没有地方的保险机构涉足国内的创业风险投资。

表 6-6　2016 年不同地区创业风险投资的资本来源（三）

单位：%

地区	非金融资本	其他金融资本	信托公司	银行	证券公司	保险公司
安徽	39.5	59.1	0.4	0.8	0.2	0.0
北京	63.1	36.9	0.0	0.0	0.0	0.0
福建	74.7	24.7	0.0	0.0	0.6	0.0
甘肃	100.0	0.0	0.0	0.0	0.0	0.0
广东	88.5	6.0	0.0	4.6	0.9	0.0
贵州	95.6	4.4	0.0	0.0	0.0	0.0
海南	98.1	1.9	0.0	0.0	0.0	0.0
河北	48.1	51.9	0.0	0.0	0.0	0.0
河南	56.7	3.9	25.1	0.0	14.3	0.0
黑龙江	77.9	22.1	0.0	0.0	0.0	0.0
湖北	69.5	10.4	0.0	19.9	0.1	0.0
湖南	71.5	20.1	0.1	8.4	0.0	0.0
吉林	100.0	0.0	0.0	0.0	0.0	0.0
江苏	84	14.7	0.0	1.3	0.0	0.0
辽宁	85.6	14.4	0.0	0.0	0.0	0.0
内蒙古	100.0	0.0	0.0	0.0	0.0	0.0
宁夏	16.1	67.3	16.5	0.0	0.0	0.0
青海	100.0	0.0	0.0	0.0	0.0	0.0
山东	60.1	39.9	0.0	0.0	0.0	0.0
山西	0.0	100.0	0.0	0.0	0.0	0.0
陕西	10.9	65.8	0.0	23.2	0.1	0.0
上海	70.7	29.3	0.0	0.0	0.0	0.0
四川	83.9	15.4	0.0	0.7	0.0	0.0
天津	60	39.8	0.2	0.0	0.0	0.0
新疆	95.6	1.0	0.0	0.1	3.3	0.0
云南	43.4	55.7	0.0	0.0	0.9	0.0
浙江	89.7	7.5	0.2	2.5	0.0	0.0
重庆	53.9	21.1	21.1	2.7	1.2	0.0

6.4 各地区创业风险投资的投资特征

6.4.1 创业风险投资项目的地区分布

本部分从两个维度来分析 2016 年中国创业风险投资项目的地区分布：一是从投资机构的注册地分析当地的创业风险投资机构的投资活跃状况；二是从投资项目所在地角度分析创业风险投资最乐于选择投资的地域分布。

（1）以机构注册地划分。表 6–7 显示了以项目投资机构的注册地为标准，不同地区创业风险投资机构所投资项目的情况。

表 6–7 2016 年完成投资项目的中国创业风险投资机构地区分布

单位：%

地 区	项目数占比
江 苏	21.7
浙 江	15.2
北 京	9.9
安 徽	7.6
广 东	5.8
湖 北	4.7
湖 南	4.6
重 庆	4.3
四 川	3.9
福 建	3.6
山 东	3.3
黑龙江	2.6
天 津	2.2
上 海	2.2
辽 宁	1.6
河 南	1.5
云 南	1.0
新 疆	0.9
贵 州	0.8
陕 西	0.8
河 北	0.7
宁 夏	0.4
甘 肃	0.4
吉 林	0.2
青 海	0.2
海 南	0.1

2016 年，全国共有 26 个地区的创业风险投资机构进行了项目投资，其中江苏和浙江依然占据投资项目数量的前两名，江苏创业风险投资机构所投资的项目占比是 21.7%，与 2015 年的 22.5%基本持平；浙江的创业风险投资机构所投资的项目占比是 15.2%，比 2015 年减少约 1 个百分点。北京创业风险投资机构所投资的项目数量在全国排名第三，超越了去年的广东，但是占比只有 9.9%，较 2015 年下降了 3 个百分点。安徽创业风险投资机构所投资的项目数量占比 7.6%，增加 4.3 个百分点，超越了广东，排名第四，达到历史排名最高，显示安徽创业风险投资机构在 2016 年的投资活动非常活跃。

整体看，前四名地区的投资项目占比合计为 54.4%，项目占比集中度比 2015 年有所降低。广大的西部地区，包括新疆、陕西、宁夏、甘肃、青海、山西等地区，创业风险投资机构的活跃度相对不高，投资项目很少，项目占比都低于 1%，部分地区甚至没有投资。另外，辽宁、吉林、河北、海南地区的创业风险投资机构投资项目也非常少。值得注意的一个地区是陕西省，虽然创业风险投资机构管理的资金规模很大，但是投资项目却非常少。

（2）以项目所在地划分。表 6-8 显示了 2016 年中国创业风险投资机构当年投资项目所注册地区分布。

表 6-8　2016 年中国创业风险投资机构所投资项目的地区分布　　单位：%

地　区	项目数占比
江　苏	20.0
浙　江	14.3
北　京	13.7
上　海	8.1
广　东	6.2
安　徽	4.9
湖　北	4.3
四　川	4.0
湖　南	3.8
山　东	3.0
福　建	2.5
黑龙江	2.2
天　津	1.9
河　南	1.9
重　庆	1.7
辽　宁	1.5
新　疆	1.0
陕　西	0.8
云　南	0.8
贵　州	0.8
河　北	0.6
甘　肃	0.4
吉　林	0.3

续表

地 区	项目数占比
宁 夏	0.3
青 海	0.2
江 西	0.1
西 藏	0.1
海 南	0.1

2016 年，中国创业风险投资机构的投资项目分布在全国 28 个地区，其中投资项目集中在东部经济和科技发达地区，项目占比最多的前五名分别是江苏、浙江、北京、上海、广东，项目合计占全国总数的 62.3%，比 2015 年有所下降，显示这 5 个地区仍然是最受国内创业风险投资青睐的地区。其中，江苏辖区内的投资项目在国内仍旧高居榜首，项目占比是 20%，比 2015 年有所提高；浙江则排名第二，项目占比是 14.3%，比 2015 年略有下降；北京的排名从 2015 年的第二下降为第三，项目占比是 13.7%，比 2015 年下降 4.9 个百分点。另外，安徽、湖北的项目占比也相对较高。

相比之下，西部地区的项目占比很少，甘肃、宁夏、青海、江西、西藏等地区的项目占比都低于 0.5%；海南和吉林的项目占比很少，显示这些地区的投资环境有待改善。

6.4.2 各地区创业风险投资的投资强度

2016 年，全国 27 个地区的创业风险投资机构所投资项目的投资强度见表 6-9 和图 6-4。

整体上，2016 年全国创业风险投资机构所投资项目的投资强度地区差距较大，最高的新疆达 13720.26 万元/项，超过 2015 年山西的 1 亿元/项，最低的吉林项目平均投资资金只有 60 万元，也低于 2015 年广西最低的 200 万元/项。

除北京之外，投资强度排在前面都是内陆省份（自治区），如新疆、宁夏、云南、湖南和重庆，而投资项目较多的江苏、浙江、上海、山东和安徽等地，项目投资强度在 1000 万元/项左右。

表 6-9 2016 年各地区创业风险投资的投资强度 单位：万元/项

地 区	投资强度
新 疆	13720.26
北 京	10349.84
宁 夏	6587.23
云 南	3798.82
湖 南	3228.42
重 庆	2919.07
河 北	2703.06
海 南	2333.33
广 东	1895.38
山 西	1885.00
湖 北	1723.51
河 南	1478.55
安 徽	1427.41

续表

地　区	投资强度
贵　州	1390.96
青　海	1300.00
陕　西	1289.11
山　东	1279.35
上　海	1199.3
浙　江	1093.71
江　苏	1036.88
甘　肃	1024.33
黑龙江	992.52
天　津	824.26
辽　宁	772.04
四　川	752.00
福　建	657.99
吉　林	60.00

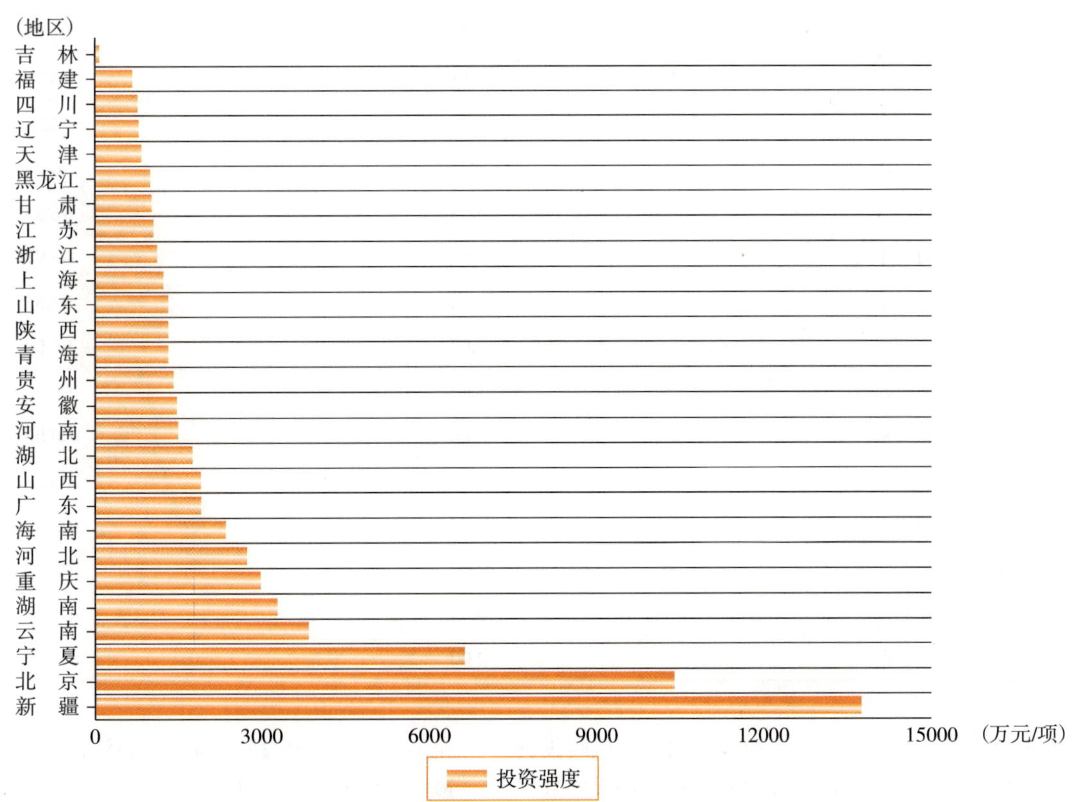

图 6-4　各地区创业风险投资的投资强度（2016）

6.4.3 各地区创业风险投资机构的项目持股结构

表 6-10 2016 年中国创业风险投资机构所投资项目持股结构的地区分布 单位：%

地 区	持股比例≥50%	持股比例<50%
吉 林	100.00	0.00
宁 夏	50.00	50.00
青 海	25.00	75.00
甘 肃	25.00	75.00
贵 州	16.67	83.33
云 南	11.11	88.89
福 建	9.41	90.59
天 津	9.09	90.91
安 徽	8.52	91.48
河 南	5.71	94.29
新 疆	5.00	95.00
辽 宁	4.76	95.24
湖 南	4.49	95.51
广 东	3.81	96.19
上 海	3.77	96.23
四 川	3.75	96.25
重 庆	3.45	96.55
山 东	3.03	96.97
江 苏	2.42	97.58
湖 北	1.92	98.08
浙 江	1.42	98.58
北 京	0.00	100.00
陕 西	0.00	100.00
海 南	0.00	100.00
河 北	0.00	100.00
黑龙江	0.00	100.00
山 西	0.00	100.00

表 6-10、图 6-5 显示：大部分地区的创业风险投资机构不寻求绝对控股，持股<50%的项目占全部投资数比重超过 90%的地区有 21 个。继 2015 年之后，2016 年完全不追求绝对控股的创业风险投资机构的地区数量持续在减少，由 8 个下降到 6 个。

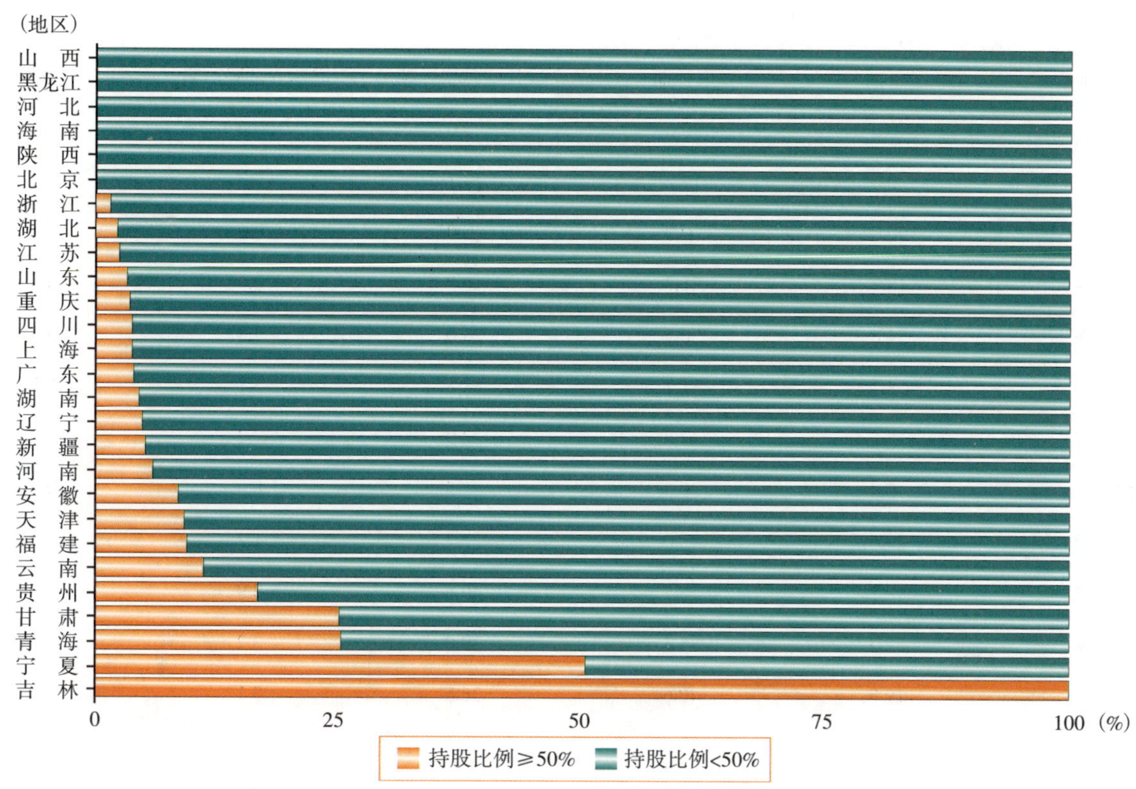

图 6-5 各地区创业风险投资机构的持股结构（2016）

6.4.4 各地区创业风险投资项目的所处阶段

表 6-11 和图 6-6 显示了 2016 年度中国各地创业风险投资机构所投资项目的所处阶段。

2016 年，中国各地创业风险投资机构所投资项目所处阶段具有如下几个主要特点：

（1）起步期和成长期（扩展）阶段的项目成为 2016 年我国大部分地区创业风险投资机构的投资重点。2016 年最明显的一个特点是：部分地区创业风险投资机构投资最多的项目为起步期阶段的项目，分别是北京、河北、黑龙江、上海、浙江、福建、湖北、广东、海南、贵州、陕西、青海和宁夏 13 个地区。

成长期（扩展）阶段占投资项目比重最高的地区有辽宁、江苏、安徽、山东、湖南、云南、重庆和新疆。

（2）越来越多地区的创业风险投资重视种子期阶段的项目。2016 年，有 13 个地区种子期阶段的项目占比超过 15%，其中最高的吉林省达到 100%。

（3）中西部地区创业风险投资在成熟（过渡）期的项目比例较高。山西、重庆、陕西和新疆在成熟（过渡）期的项目占比都高于 10%，其中最高的山西达到 100%。

（4）投资于重建期阶段项目的地区只有江苏、浙江、山东和湖北，其中山东省最高，占比达 3.9%。

表 6-11 2016 年各地区创业风险投资项目的所处阶段 单位：%

地 区	种子期	起步期	成长（扩张）期	成熟（过渡）期	重建期
北 京	15.2	43.5	36.3	4.9	0.0
天 津	44.7	21.1	31.6	2.6	0.0
河 北	0.0	70.0	30.0	0.0	0.0

续表

地　区	种子期	起步期	成长（扩张）期	成熟（过渡）期	重建期
山　西	0.0	0.0	0.0	100.0	0.0
辽　宁	0.0	19.2	73.1	7.7	0.0
吉　林	100.0	0.0	0.0	0.0	0.0
黑龙江	18.3	71.7	10.0	0.0	0.0
上　海	34.6	36.5	25.0	3.8	0.0
江　苏	23.1	31.7	37.8	7.1	0.2
浙　江	17.9	47.8	23.9	7.2	3.2
安　徽	10.4	39.3	41.5	8.9	0.0
福　建	29.6	42.0	27.2	1.2	0.0
山　东	18.2	24.7	49.4	3.9	3.9
河　南	32.3	35.5	29.0	3.2	0.0
湖　北	19.8	40.6	36.5	3.1	0.0
湖　南	18.0	31.5	46.1	3.4	1.1
广　东	14.9	63.2	17.2	4.6	0.0
海　南	0.0	66.7	33.3	0.0	0.0
四　川	38.8	24.7	35.3	1.2	0.0
贵　州	0.0	58.8	41.2	0.0	0.0
云　南	13.6	4.5	81.8	0.0	0.0
重　庆	6.1	25.5	58.2	10.2	0.0
陕　西	5.3	42.1	31.6	21.1	0.0
甘　肃	44.4	44.4	11.1	0.0	0.0
青　海	0.0	100.0	0.0	0.0	0.0
宁　夏	0.0	100.0	0.0	0.0	0.0
新　疆	9.5	33.3	42.9	14.3	0.0

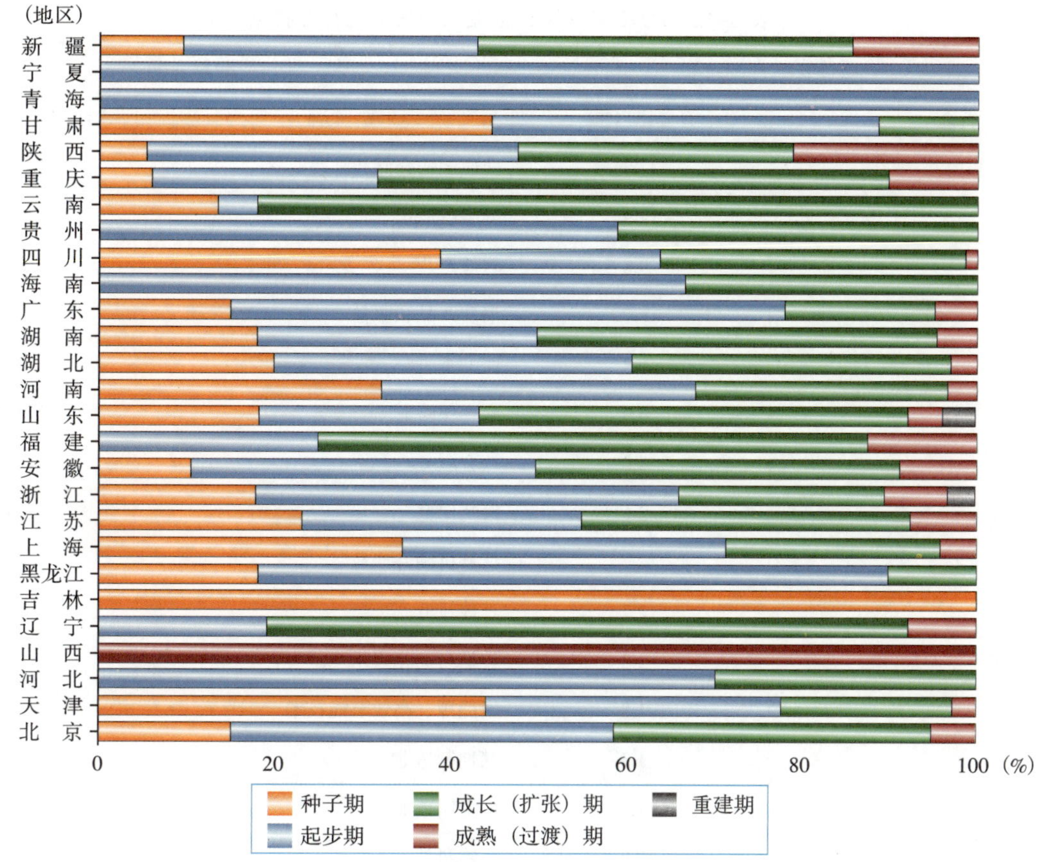

图 6-6　各地区创业风险投资项目所处阶段（2016）

6.5　部分地区创业风险投资的行业投资特征

根据 2016 年全国创业风险投资调查统计，本部分对 2016 年我国创业风险投资较为活跃的地区进行重点分析，以掌握和了解这些地区投资项目的行业分布和资金情况（见表 6-12 至表 6-20）。

2016 年，北京的创业风险投资项目分布在 19 个行业，比 2015 年减少 6 个行业，显示北京创业风险投资的投资领域更趋向于集中，主要集中在网络产业、软件产业、IT 服务业、其他行业和计算机硬件产业，其中网络产业占比 37.5%，软件产业占比 12.9%，二者合计占比超过 50%。从表 6-12 看出，北京创业风险投资在 2016 年的投资重心为互联网信息行业，这也与当前中央政府大力推动“互联网+”有很大关系。与 2015 年比较，社会服务行业占比下降幅度较大，由 11.3%下降为 4%。

至于行业投资强度，2016 年各个行业之间的投资强度差异非常大，排名前三的行业平均投资都超过了 1 亿元，其中最高的交通运输仓储和邮政业达到 6.58 亿元，排名第二的网络产业也有 2.03 亿元，第三位的软件产业也有 1.30 亿元。而其他行业的投资强度大部分是在 1000 万~2000 万元。投资强度超过 1000 万元的行业有 15 个，占总数的是 78.95%，超过 2015 年的 72%。

表 6-12 2016 年北京市创业风险投资的行业特点

项目数		投资强度	
行业	百分比（%）	行业	行业投资强度（万元）
网络产业	37.5	交通运输仓储和邮政业	65789.0
软件产业	12.9	网络产业	20306.7
IT 服务业	9.8	软件产业	12955.2
其他行业	6.7	消费产品和服务	4558.8
计算机硬件产业	6.3	IT 服务业	3371.9
医药保健	4.9	金融保险业	3277.5
社会服务	4.0	社会服务	2841.8
传播与文化娱乐	3.6	医药保健	2744.5
新能源、高效节能技术	2.7	计算机硬件产业	1983.0
生物科技	2.7	其他行业	1864.2
消费产品和服务	1.8	传播与文化娱乐	1685.0
金融保险业	1.8	新能源、高效节能技术	1500.0
其他制造业	1.3	其他制造业	1333.3
传统制造业	1.3	传统制造业	1194.6
科技服务	0.9	生物科技	1166.7
光电子与光机电一体化	0.4	新材料工业	517.4
交通运输仓储和邮政业	0.4	光电子与光机电一体化	500.0
批发和零售业	0.4	科技服务	423.7
新材料工业	0.4	批发和零售业	400.0

由表 6-13 可见，2016 年，江苏的创业风险投资项目分布在 27 个行业，比 2015 年增加 1 个；投资较多的行业是其他行业、新材料工业、网络产业、医药保健、其他制造业、软件产业和生物科技；其中，投资最多的行业仍然是其他行业，项目占比由 2015 年的 9.2%上升到 13%。

与 2015 年比较，2016 年江苏创业风险投资关注度较高的行业未发生大的变化，新材料工业、网络产业、医药保健和软件产业一直是江苏创业风险投资较多的行业。生物科技行业成为 2016 年江苏创业风险投资的关注热点之一，项目占比由 2015 年的 4.8%上升到 6.1%。

至于行业投资强度，2016 年江苏创业风险投资的行业投资强度整体低于 2015 年，最高的批发和零售业是 3250 万元，远远低于 2015 年最高的传播与文化娱乐行业的 5468.7 万元，最低的建筑业只有 100 万元，也远远低于 2015 年最低行业社会服务业的 783.3 万元。投资强度在 1000 万元以上的只有 10 个，远远少于 2015 年的 10 个行业。

表 6-13 2016 年江苏省创业风险投资的行业特点

项目数		投资强度	
行业	百分比（%）	行业	行业投资强度（万元）
其他行业	13.0	批发和零售业	3250.0
新材料工业	9.3	金融保险业	3116.6
网络产业	7.6	消费产品和服务	2100.0
医药保健	7.4	光电子与光机电一体化	1323.1
其他制造业	7.2	新材料工业	1173.1
软件产业	7.0	半导体	1159.6
生物科技	6.1	通信设备	1026.3
传统制造业	5.2	传播与文化娱乐	1017.1
新能源、高效节能技术	5.0	IT 服务业	1016.8
IT 服务业	4.6	网络产业	1007.2
光电子与光机电一体化	3.7	生物科技	968.8
传播与文化娱乐	3.0	计算机硬件产业	899.0
科技服务	2.8	医药保健	810.2
半导体	2.4	农林牧副渔	734.7
环保工程	2.2	其他行业	727.8
消费产品和服务	2.2	软件产业	706.7
农林牧副渔	2.0	新能源、高效节能技术	669.1
通信设备	1.7	其他 IT 产业	615.0
计算机硬件产业	1.5	传统制造业	612.0
社会服务	1.5	其他制造业	603.7
金融保险业	1.3	社会服务	576.4
其他 IT 产业	1.3	交通运输仓储和邮政业	544.5
批发和零售业	0.9	采掘业	500.0
交通运输仓储和邮政业	0.4	科技服务	433.3
建筑业	0.2	环保工程	420.8
核应用技术	0.2	核应用技术	300.0
采掘业	0.2	建筑业	100.0

由表 6-14 可见，2016 年，广东的创业风险投资项目分布在 20 个行业，数量比 2015 年减少 8 个；其中，投资较多的行业是其他行业、科技服务和新材料工业。与 2015 年比较，行业的关注度发生了较大变化，科技服务和新材料工业成为 2016 年广东的创业风险投资最关注的行业，其中科技服务占比达 16.7%，而 2015 年投资最多的网络产业则不在 2016 年的投资范围之内；此外，IT 服务业的项目占比也由 2015 年的 8.1%下降到 4.4%。

至于行业投资强度，与 2015 年比较，2016 年广东创业风险投资行业投资强度有所下降，最高的传播与文化娱乐行业投资强度是 8400 万元，远远低于 2015 年最高的建筑业 10200 万元，排名第二的建筑业投资强度是 7980.3 万元，也低于 2015 年水电煤气的 9100 万元。2016 年大部分行业的投资强度在 1000~4000 万元，而 2015 年大部分行业的投资强度在 1000~6000 万元。

表 6-14　2016 年广东省创业风险投资的行业特点

项目数		投资强度	
行业	百分比（%）	行业	行业投资强度（万元）
其他行业	31.1	传播与文化娱乐	8400.0
科技服务	16.7	建筑业	7980.3
新材料工业	8.9	医药保健	4000.0
IT 服务业	4.4	其他 IT 产业	3930.0
其他制造业	4.4	新材料工业	3120.3
环保工程	4.4	金融保险业	3000.0
半导体	4.4	半导体	2862.5
农林牧副渔	3.3	其他行业	2483.3
传播与文化娱乐	3.3	消费产品和服务	2333.3
消费产品和服务	3.3	生物科技	2281.6
医药保健	2.2	农林牧副渔	1446.7
传统制造业	2.2	其他制造业	1260.2
生物科技	2.2	IT 服务业	1110.1
软件产业	2.2	计算机硬件产业	990.0
新能源、高效节能技术	1.1	科技服务	970.4
金融保险业	1.1	环保工程	902.0
计算机硬件产业	1.1	传统制造业	828.7
建筑业	1.1	新能源、高效节能技术	800.0
其他 IT 产业	1.1	软件产业	399.0
光电子与光机电一体化	1.1	光电子与光机电一体化	120.0

由表 6-15 可见，2016 年，安徽的创业风险投资项目分布在 24 个行业，比 2015 年增加 2 个，投资较多的行业是其他行业，其他制造业，新能源、高效节能技术，科技服务和环保工程。与 2015 年比较，新能源、高效节能技术和环保工程一直是安徽创业风险投资机构投资较多的行业。

至于行业投资强度，2016 年安徽创业风险投资的行业投资强度差距很大，最高的其他 IT 产业平均投资是 19800 万元，最低的交通运输仓储和邮政业则只有 250 万元。有 11 个行业的投资强度在 1000 万元以下。与 2015 年比较，安徽创业风险投资的行业投资强度有所降低，投资强度在 1000 万元以上的只有 13 个行业，远远低于 2015 年的 17 个。

表 6-15　2016 年安徽省创业风险投资的行业特点

项目数		投资强度（万元）	
行业	百分比（%）	行业	行业投资强度
其他行业	25.7	其他 IT 产业	19800.0
其他制造业	8.8	网络产业	4356.4

续表

项目数		投资强度（万元）	
行业	百分比（%）	行业	行业投资强度
新能源、高效节能技术	8.1	社会服务	3500.0
科技服务	5.9	通信设备	2860.0
环保工程	5.9	光电子与光机电一体化	2800.0
传统制造业	5.1	传统制造业	2788.9
网络产业	5.1	金融保险业	2525.0
新材料工业	5.1	新材料工业	2519.4
生物科技	4.4	新能源、高效节能技术	2356.2
软件产业	3.7	环保工程	1854.1
医药保健	2.9	其他行业	1767.6
计算机硬件产业	2.9	其他制造业	1547.5
光电子与光机电一体化	2.2	医药保健	1450.0
消费产品和服务	2.2	消费产品和服务	912.5
IT 服务业	2.2	生物科技	766.7
农林牧副渔	1.5	农林牧副渔	750.0
交通运输仓储和邮政业	1.5	半导体	700.0
半导体	1.5	科技服务	653.1
金融保险业	1.5	软件产业	530.0
通信设备	0.7	传播与文化娱乐	500.0
传播与文化娱乐	0.7	计算机硬件产业	281.3
批发和零售业	0.7	IT 服务业	256.7
社会服务	0.7	批发和零售业	250.0
其他 IT 产业	0.7	交通运输仓储和邮政业	250.0

由表 6-16 可见，2016 年，浙江的创业风险投资项目分布在 26 个行业，行业数量比 2015 年多 1 个。与 2014 年、2015 年一样，网络产业持续成为浙江创业风险投资在 2016 年投资最多的行业，占比是 12.7%，说明浙江的互联网创新创业项目大量涌现，受到投资者的持续关注。2016 年浙江创业风险投资较多的还有传播与文化娱乐、IT 服务业、其他行业、科技服务、医药保健和软件产业，其中，传播与文化娱乐和 IT 服务业近两年一直是浙江创业风险投资的热点。

2016 年，浙江创业风险投资行业投资强度不是很大，最高的计算机硬件产业只有 3970.8 万元，最低的批发和零售业只有 102 万元。26 个行业中，有 15 个行业的投资强度在 1000 万元以下，除了计算机硬件产业和软件产业之外，其他大部分行业的投资强度都在 2000 万元以下。

表 6-16 2016 年浙江省创业风险投资的行业特点

项目数		投资强度	
行业	百分比（%）	行业	行业投资强度（万元）
网络产业	12.7	计算机硬件产业	3970.8
传播与文化娱乐	11.6	软件产业	3136.8
IT 服务业	9.3	建筑业	1800.0
其他行业	7.3	交通运输仓储和邮政业	1482.4
科技服务	7.3	其他行业	1442.7
医药保健	6.8	通信设备	1385.1
软件产业	6.2	半导体	1320.0
金融保险业	5.6	医药保健	1257.9
消费产品和服务	5.1	传统制造业	1171.9
新材料工业	3.7	科技服务	1155.7
生物科技	3.1	传播与文化娱乐	1104.6
传统制造业	3.1	生物科技	985.1
新能源、高效节能技术	3.1	新能源、高效节能技术	915.6
通信设备	2.5	其他 IT 产业	843.3
环保工程	2.3	新材料工业	840.4
社会服务	2.3	其他制造业	825.0
计算机硬件产业	1.7	环保工程	781.4
交通运输仓储和邮政业	1.4	房地产业	750.0
其他制造业	1.1	网络产业	588.8
其他 IT 产业	0.8	光电子与光机电一体化	586.7
光电子与光机电一体化	0.8	IT 服务业	578.5
批发和零售业	0.8	金融保险业	569.8
农林牧副渔	0.3	农林牧副渔	500.0
建筑业	0.3	消费产品和服务	402.0
半导体	0.3	社会服务	230.6
房地产业	0.3	批发和零售业	102.0

由表 6-17 可见，2016 年，湖北的创业风险投资项目分布在 23 个行业，比 2015 年多 4 个行业，投资领域更加宽泛，主要集中在新材料工业、生物科技、其他制造业、金融保险业、医药保健和传播与文化娱乐，其中新材料工业最多，占比是 11.5%。与 2015 年比较，医药保健仍是湖北创业风险投资热点，新材料工业、生物科技、金融保险业和传播与文化娱乐则是新的关注点；软件产业下降明显，由 2015 年的 14.5%下降为 2016 年的 6.3%，从排名第一下降到第八位。

整体上看，2016 年湖北创业风险投资的行业投资强度比 2105 年有较大幅度提高。有 16 个行业的投资强度在 1000 万元以上，远远高于 2015 年的 3 个行业；投资强度最高的是新能源、高效节能技术为 3941.3 万元，高于 2015 年最高的新能源、高效节能技术的 2500 万元；最低的是光电子与光机电一体化，只有 200 万元，也高于 2015 年最低的光电子与光机电一体化的 125 万元。

表 6–17　2016 年湖北省创业风险投资的行业特点

项目数		投资强度	
行业	百分比（%）	行业	行业投资强度（万元）
新材料工业	11.5	新能源、高效节能技术	3941.3
生物科技	8.3	金融保险业	3492.5
其他制造业	8.3	网络产业	2300.0
金融保险业	8.3	医药保健	2274.9
医药保健	8.3	社会服务	2088.0
传播与文化娱乐	8.3	IT 服务业	2000.1
IT 服务业	7.3	交通运输仓储和邮政业	2000.0
软件产业	6.3	批发和零售业	2000.0
通信设备	6.3	计算机硬件产业	1962.0
新能源、高效节能技术	4.2	其他制造业	1888.3
其他行业	4.2	其他行业	1667.5
科技服务	4.2	通信设备	1531.7
计算机硬件产业	2.1	软件产业	1522.2
光电子与光机电一体化	2.1	传播与文化娱乐	1377.5
传统制造业	2.1	新材料工业	1295.5
社会服务	1.0	生物科技	1046.6
建筑业	1.0	传统制造业	712.5
批发和零售业	1.0	其他 IT 产业	700.0
其他 IT 产业	1.0	建筑业	600.0
农林牧副渔	1.0	科技服务	550.0
交通运输仓储和邮政业	1.0	农林牧副渔	500.0
网络产业	1.0	消费产品和服务	500.0
消费产品和服务	1.0	光电子与光机电一体化	200.0

由表表 6–18 可见，2016 年，湖南的创业风险投资项目分布在 19 个行业，其中投资最多的是网络产业，占比达 16.7%，最低的是新能源、高效节能技术，只有 0.9%。整体看，2016 年湖南省创业风险投资集中在网络产业、其他行业、其他制造业、IT 服务业、传播与文化娱乐和金融保险业等行业。

至于投资强度，2016 年，湖南省创业风险投资在金融保险业的投资强度最大，高达 3.80 亿元。除了金融保险业之外，超过 50%的行业投资强度在 1000 万元以下，最低的科技服务业则只有 70 万元。

表 6-18 2016 年湖南省创业风险投资项目的行业特点

项目数		投资强度	
行业	百分比（%）	行业	行业投资强度（万元）
网络产业	16.7	金融保险业	37963.4
其他行业	13.0	新材料工业	3754.0
其他制造业	10.2	环保工程	2000.0
IT 服务业	9.3	医药保健	1643.3
传播与文化娱乐	6.5	生物科技	1250.0
金融保险业	6.5	传播与文化娱乐	1176.4
消费产品和服务	5.6	计算机硬件产业	1066.7
新材料工业	4.6	其他制造业	876.9
社会服务	3.7	其他行业	764.4
生物科技	3.7	半导体	666.7
医药保健	3.7	农林牧副渔	650.0
传统制造业	2.8	网络产业	440.8
计算机硬件产业	2.8	IT 服务业	431.8
半导体	2.8	新能源、高效节能技术	395.9
光电子与光机电一体化	1.9	社会服务	392.5
科技服务	1.9	传统制造业	279.5
环保工程	1.9	消费产品和服务	214.5
农林牧副渔	1.9	光电子与光机电一体化	107.5
新能源、高效节能技术	0.9	科技服务	70.0

由表 6-19 可见，2016 年，重庆的创业风险投资活动比较活跃，投资项目较多，创业风险投资项目分布在 23 个行业，比 2015 年增加 1 个；投资较多的行业是其他行业、医药保健、新材料工业、消费产品和服务。与 2015 年比较，消费产品和服务仍是重庆的创业风险投资较多的行业；医药保健、新材料工业则是 2016 年新增的投资热点。

至于投资强度，2016 年重庆创业风险投资强度差距较大，最高的行业是建筑业，达 18963 万元，其次是半导体的 16026.3 万元，而最低的其他 IT 产业只有 293 万元。与 2015 年比较，2016 年重庆创业风险投资的行业投资强度整体上呈现较大幅度的提高，超过 1000 万元的行业有 17 个行业，远超出 2015 年的 9 个，最低的其他 IT 产业为 293 万元，也远远超过 2015 年最低行业计算机硬件产业的 60 万元。

表 6-19 2016 年重庆市创业风险投资项目的行业特点

项目数		投资强度	
行业	百分比（%）	行业	行业投资强度（万元）
其他行业	16.5	建筑业	18963
医药保健	8.2	半导体	16026.3

续表

项目数		投资强度	
行业	百分比（%）	行业	行业投资强度（万元）
新材料工业	7.2	IT 服务业	3592.5
消费产品和服务	6.2	医药保健	3147.5
新能源、高效节能技术	5.2	环保工程	2704.0
环保工程	5.2	新能源、高效节能技术	2596.4
建筑业	5.2	通信设备	2300.0
传播与文化娱乐	5.2	生物科技	2020.0
软件产业	5.2	软件产业	1810.3
社会服务	5.2	交通运输仓储和邮政业	1800.0
科技服务	5.2	批发和零售业	1500.0
金融保险业	4.1	其他行业	1426.2
网络产业	4.1	科技服务	1350.2
IT 服务业	4.1	新材料工业	1312.5
生物科技	2.1	金融保险业	1240.0
批发和零售业	2.1	社会服务	1124.4
交通运输仓储和邮政业	2.1	网络产业	1008.3
计算机硬件产业	2.1	农林牧副渔	1000.0
通信设备	1.0	消费产品和服务	985.0
农林牧副渔	1.0	光电子与光机电一体化	700.0
半导体	1.0	传播与文化娱乐	647.0
光电子与光机电一体化	1.0	计算机硬件产业	550.0
其他 IT 产业	1.0	其他 IT 产业	293.0

由表 6-20 可见，2016 年，福建的创业风险投资项目分布在 20 个行业，其中投资最多的行业是网络产业，约占全部项目的 1/4。排名第二的软件产业占比也有 15.9%，前五个行业的占比合计是 69.6%，表现出较高的行业集中度。

至于投资强度，2016 年福建创业风险投资的行业投资强度相对不高，最高的是传统制造业，平均投资金额是 3383.5 万元，20 个行业中只有 6 个行业的投资强度超过了 1000 万元，大部分行业的投资强度在 500 万元以下。

表 6-20　2016 年福建省创业风险投资项目的行业特点

项目数		投资强度	
行业	百分比（%）	行业	行业投资强度（万元）
网络产业	24.4	传统制造业	3383.5
软件产业	15.9	批发和零售业	3047.0
IT 服务业	11.0	其他制造业	2000.0

续表

项目数		投资强度	
行业	百分比（%）	行业	行业投资强度（万元）
其他行业	11.0	新能源、高效节能技术	1802.0
传播与文化娱乐	7.3	其他行业	1224.7
金融保险业	6.1	金融保险业	1205.0
新能源、高效节能技术	3.7	农林牧副渔	835.1
医药保健	2.4	传播与文化娱乐	631.8
新材料工业	2.4	新材料工业	550.0
通信设备	2.4	消费产品和服务	500.0
交通运输仓储和邮政业	2.4	医药保健	500.0
环保工程	1.2	交通运输仓储和邮政业	385.0
生物科技	1.2	网络产业	375.1
其他 IT 产业	1.2	环保工程	350.0
批发和零售业	1.2	IT 服务业	303.7
农林牧副渔	1.2	生物科技	303.0
消费产品和服务	1.2	软件产业	221.3
其他制造业	1.2	其他 IT 产业	180.0
传统制造业	1.2	通信设备	130.0
房地产业	1.2	房地产业	45.0

6.6 各经济区域创业投资活动情况

本节从经济区域角度来比较、分析 2016 年我国创业风险投资的运行状况，尤其在当前中国经济发展进入新常态的情况下，通过比较经济发达、有特色的地区与经济相对不发达、创投活动不活跃地区之间的差异，一定程度上揭示创业风险投资对促进地区经济发展的重要作用，起到我国创业风险投资今后发展指南针作用。

本节的区域划分，是根据经济发展的联系紧密程度以及发展特色，并参照国家现有的经济区域划分，本着研究的连续性来进行划分。当前我国最为关注的几个经济区域增长带是珠三角地区、长三角地区以及围绕北京、天津这样的大型城市、具有知识高密度的京津冀等地区，同时还有正在重新振兴的东北三省老工业基地。因此，本节划分的区域有：

（1）京津冀地区（包括北京、天津、河北）。

（2）长三角地区（包括浙江、上海、江苏）。

（3）珠三角地区：广东（深圳）。

（4）东北三省地区（包括辽宁、吉林、黑龙江）。

（5）其他区域。

本章选取这五个区域，出发点之一是前三个区域是中国目前经济发展最快也是最有活力的区域，充分代表了当前我国创业风险投资的最新动态。东北三省地区是我国的老工业基地，国有企业比重高，人口流出严重，资源枯竭，正面临经济和产业转型，国外经验证明：创业风险投资可以鼓励民营和科技经济发展，有效提升产业转型和升级，因此把东三省地区单独列出来。

6.6.1 我国创业风险投资机构项目的区域分布

表 6–21 显示了 2016 年我国不同区域创业风险投资所投资项目的占比。与 2015 年一样，长三角地区仍然是国内创业风险投资最活跃的区域，投资项目占比是 39.1%，只是较 2015 年有所减少。京津冀和珠三角地区创业风险投资所投资项目数量占比都比 2015 年有所下降，京津冀地区减少 2.4 个百分点，珠三角地区减少 8.8 个百分点。相反，包括安徽、湖北、湖南、山东在内的其他地区，创业风险投资活跃度显著提高，所投资项目占比从 2015 年的 26.3%提高到 37.9%。东北三省地区比 2015 有所增加，投资项目占比增加了 2 个百分点。

表 6–21　2016 年中国创业风险投资项目的区域分布　　单位：%

区域	长三角	珠三角	京津冀	东北三省	其他地区
项目占比	39.1	5.8	12.8	4.4	37.9

6.6.2 我国不同区域创业风险投资的投资强度

表 6–22、图 6–7 显示：2016 年京津冀地区创业风险投资的投资强度最高，远高于其他区域，比 2015 年增加 4618 万元，显示京津冀地区创业风险投资的资金充足。珠三角地区、长三角地区和东北三省创业风险投资的投资强度都比 2015 年有所下降，其中长三角地区降幅最多，减少 400 多万元，其次是东北三省，降低了 360 多万元，珠三角地区下降最少，减少 100 多万元。不过，其他地区的创业风险投资的投资强度则比 2015 年大幅增加，由 2015 年的 1350.5 万元提高到了 2016 年的 2089.9 万元。

表 6–22　2016 年中国创业风险投资强度的区域分布　　单位：万元/项

区域	京津冀	珠三角	长三角	东北三省	其他地区
投资强度	8293.4	1895.4	1068.2	869.2	2089.9

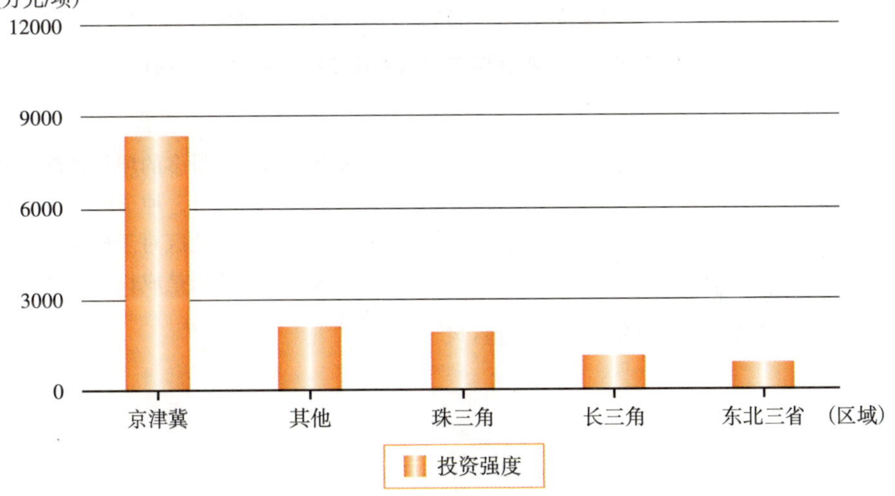

图 6–7　中国创业风险投资强度区域分布（2016）

6.6.3 不同区域创业风险投资的持股结构

表 6-23 与图 6-8 显示：与 2015 年相比，东北三省、珠三角地区和其他地区创业风险投资追求绝对控股的项目比例都有所增加，其中东北三省最高，达 7.5%，增加了一倍多，珠三角创业风险投资追求绝对控股的项目比例比 2015 年提高了 245%，达 3.8%，其他地区则由 2015 年的 4.9%提高到 2016 年的 6.3%。相比之下，京津冀和长三角地区创业风险投资追求绝对控股的项目比例都有所下降，其中长三角地区由 2015 年的 3.9%下降到 2.1%，京津冀地区则由 3.8%下降到 3.1%。

表 6-23 2016 年各经济区域创业风险投资的持股结构

单位：%

区域	东北三省	其他地区	珠三角	京津冀	长三角
持股比例≥50%	7.5	6.3	3.8	3.1	2.1
持股比例<50%	92.5	93.8	96.2	96.9	97.9

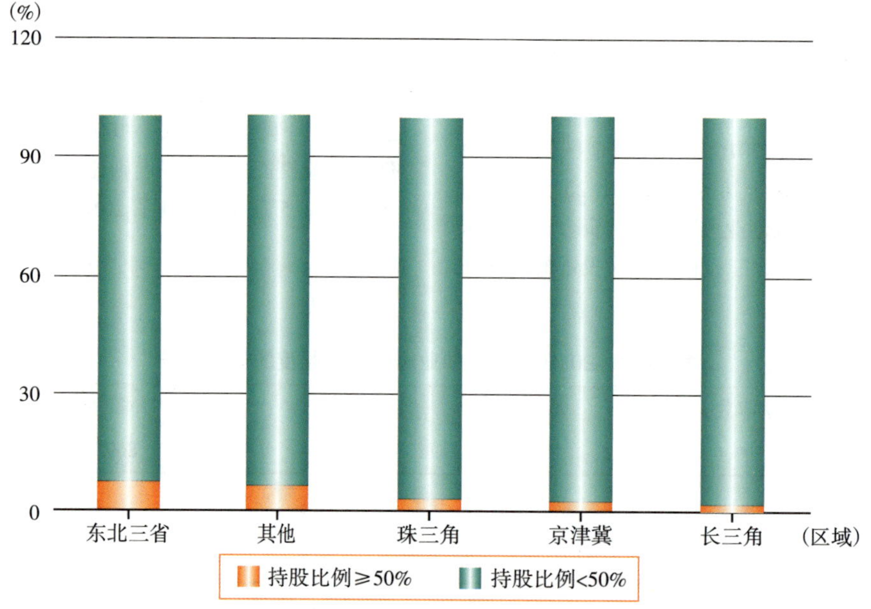

图 6-8 各经济区域创业风险投资持股结构（2016）

6.6.4 不同经济区域创业风险投资项目所处阶段

表 6-24 和图 6-9 显示了 2016 年我国各个经济区域创业风险投资项目的阶段分布情况。

2016 年，长三角、京津冀、珠三角和东北三省地区风险投资机构投资最多的项目是起步期阶段项目，其次是成长（扩张）期项目，种子期项目占比也均超过了 15%，充分显示当前这些地区对于早期阶段项目重要性的重视。其他地区最青睐的则是成长（扩张）期项目，其次是起步期项目。

表 6-24 2016 年各区域创业风险投资项目所处阶段 单位：%

区域＼所处阶段	种子期	起步期	成长（扩张）期	成熟（过渡）期	重建期
长三角	21.71	38.40	31.54	6.97	1.37
京津冀	18.82	41.33	35.42	4.43	0.00
珠三角	14.94	63.22	17.24	4.60	0.00
东北三省	17.58	52.75	27.47	2.20	0.00
其他地区	18.34	34.42	41.46	5.28	0.50

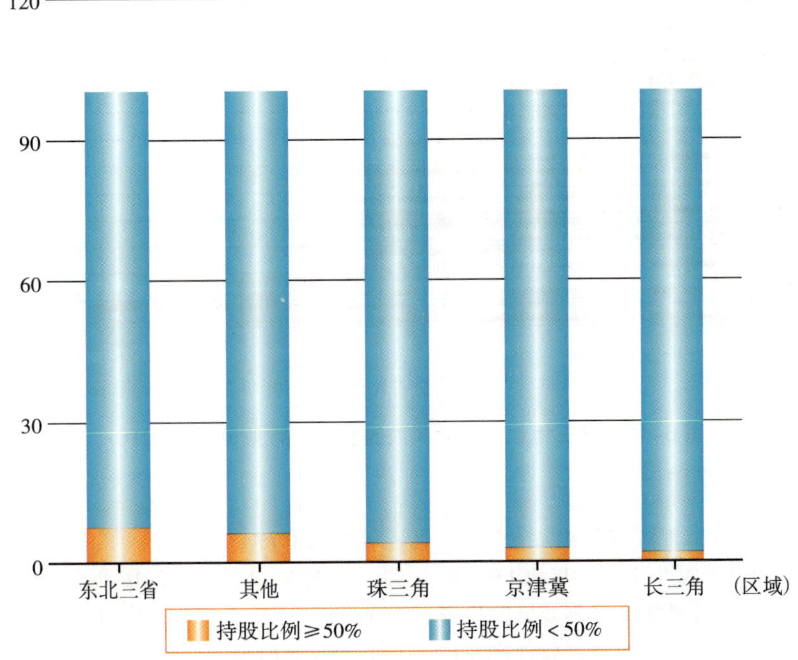

图 6-9 各经济区域创业风险投资的持股结构（2016）

6.6.5 各经济区域创业风险投资项目的行业分布

图 6-10 至图 6-14 分别显示了 2016 年我国不同经济区域创业风险投资的行业分布。

图 6-10 显示：2016 年长三角地区的创业风险投资分布在 28 个行业，行业范围比 2015 年多 1 个；长三角地区的创业风险投资所投资的行业相对分散，没有占比非常高的行业，网络产业是近年来长三角地区投资最多的行业；其次是 IT 服务业、传播与文化娱乐、医药保健、软件产业和新材料工业等占比相差较小的几个行业。

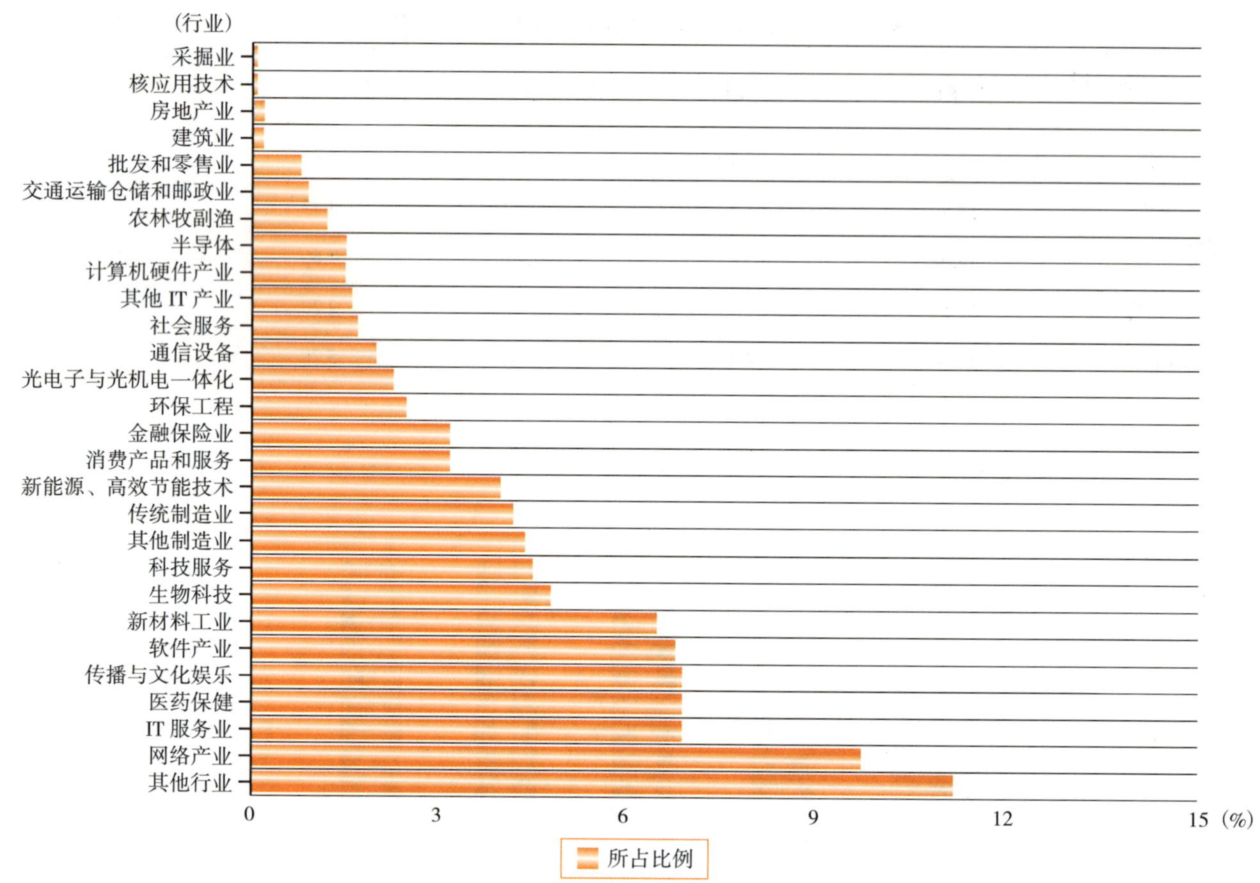

图 6-10 长三角地区创业风险投资项目行业分布（2016）

图 6-11 显示：2016 年京津冀地区创业风险投资的行业分布在 24 个行业，比 2015 年减少 2 个。与 2015 年不同的是，网络产业成为 2016 年京津冀地区创业风险投资最多的行业，几乎占全部投资的 1/3。另外，软件产业一直受到京津冀地区创业风险投资的关注，2016 年占比达 13.6%，与 2015 年基本持平。IT 服务业、医药保健和计算机硬件产业也是京津冀地区创业风险投资较多的领域。相比之下，通信设备则下降非常明显，从 2015 年的 24.1% 下降为 0.7%。

图 6-12 显示：2016 年珠三角地区创业风险投资的行业分布在 20 个行业，比 2015 年减少 8 个，显示珠三角地区创业风险投资机构关注度趋向集中。另外，一个显著的特点是，2016 年珠三角地区创业风险投资在科技服务和新材料工业的项目比例明显高于其他行业，其中科技服务占比是 16.7%，新材料工业是 8.9%。与 2015 年比较，投资最多的网络产业基本未涉及。

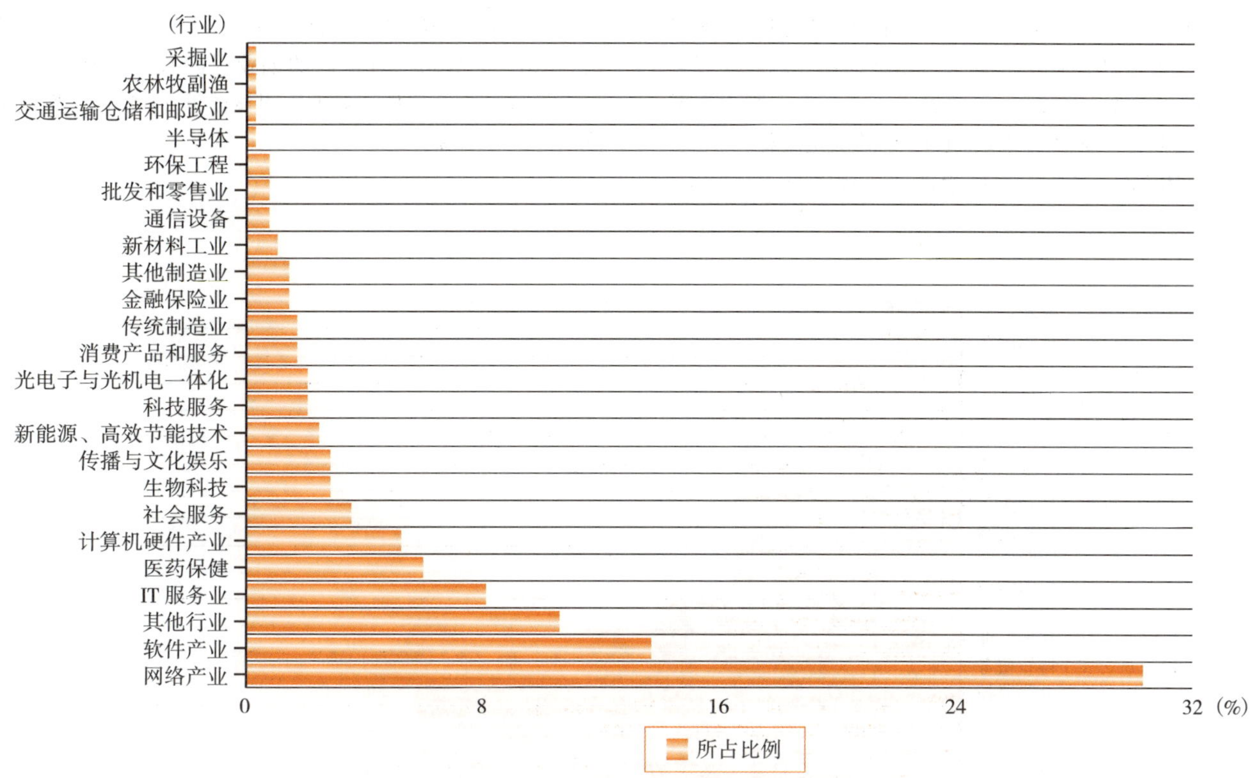

图 6-11　京津冀地区创业风险投资项目的行业分布（2016）

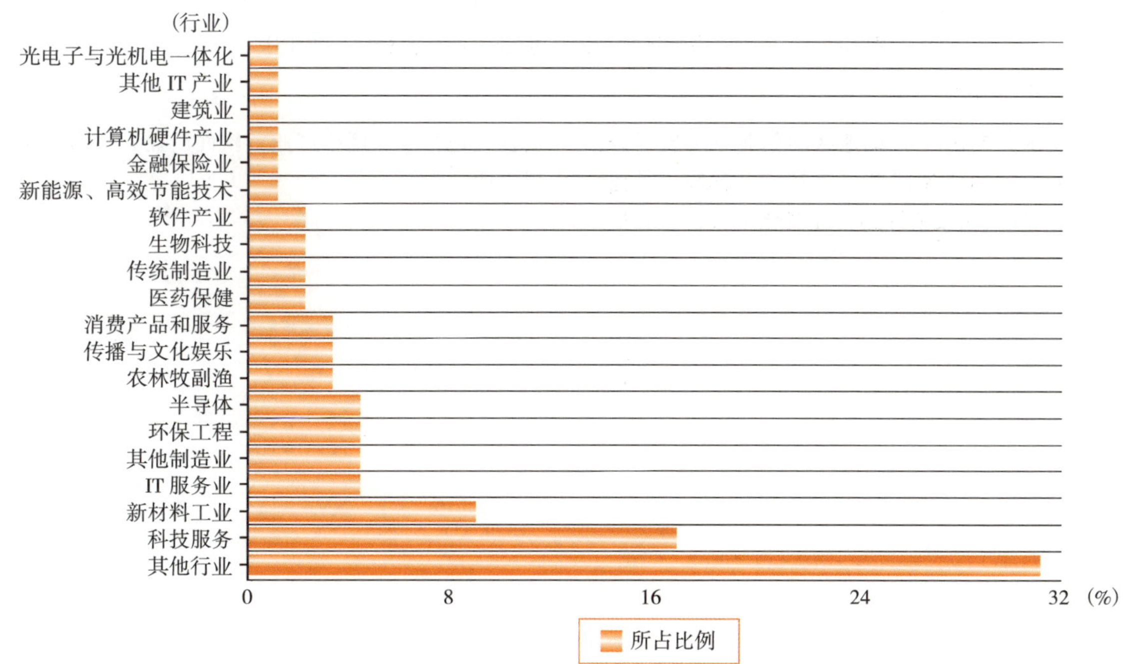

图 6-12　珠三角地区创业风险投资项目行业分布（2016）

图 6-13 显示了 2016 年东北三省地区的创业风险投资行业分布。2016 年，东北三省地区的创业风险投资分布在 20 个行业，比 2015 年增加了 4 个行业；其中投资最多的是软件产业，占比是 11.4%，其次是新材料工业，占比是 10.2%；另外，在网络产业、传播与文化娱乐、IT 服务业和生物科技上的项目也比较多。与 2015 年相比，2016 年东北三省地区的创业风险投资行业相对分散，投资最多的软件产业占比明显低于 2015 年最多的网络产业的 29.8%。

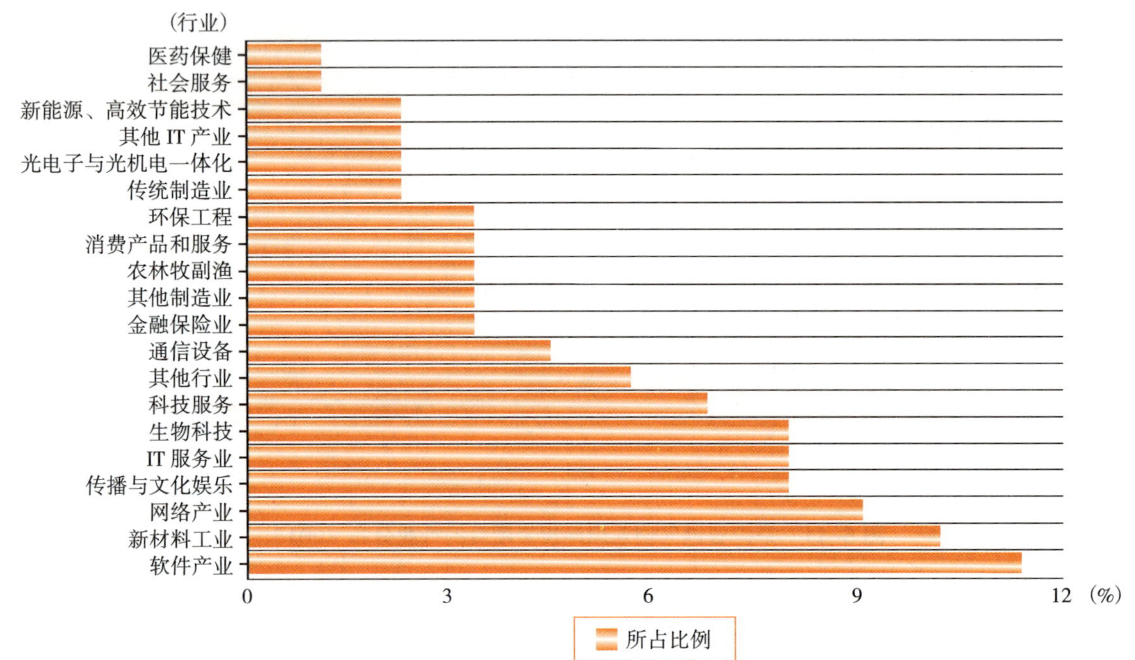

图 6-13　东北三省地区创业风险投资项目行业分布（2016）

图 6-14 显示：2016 年其他地区的创业风险投资分布在 28 个行业，与 2015 年持平；与 2015 年比较，其他区域的创业风险投资比较关注的行业变化不大，主要投资在其他行业、网络产业、软件产业、IT 服务业和新材料工业。

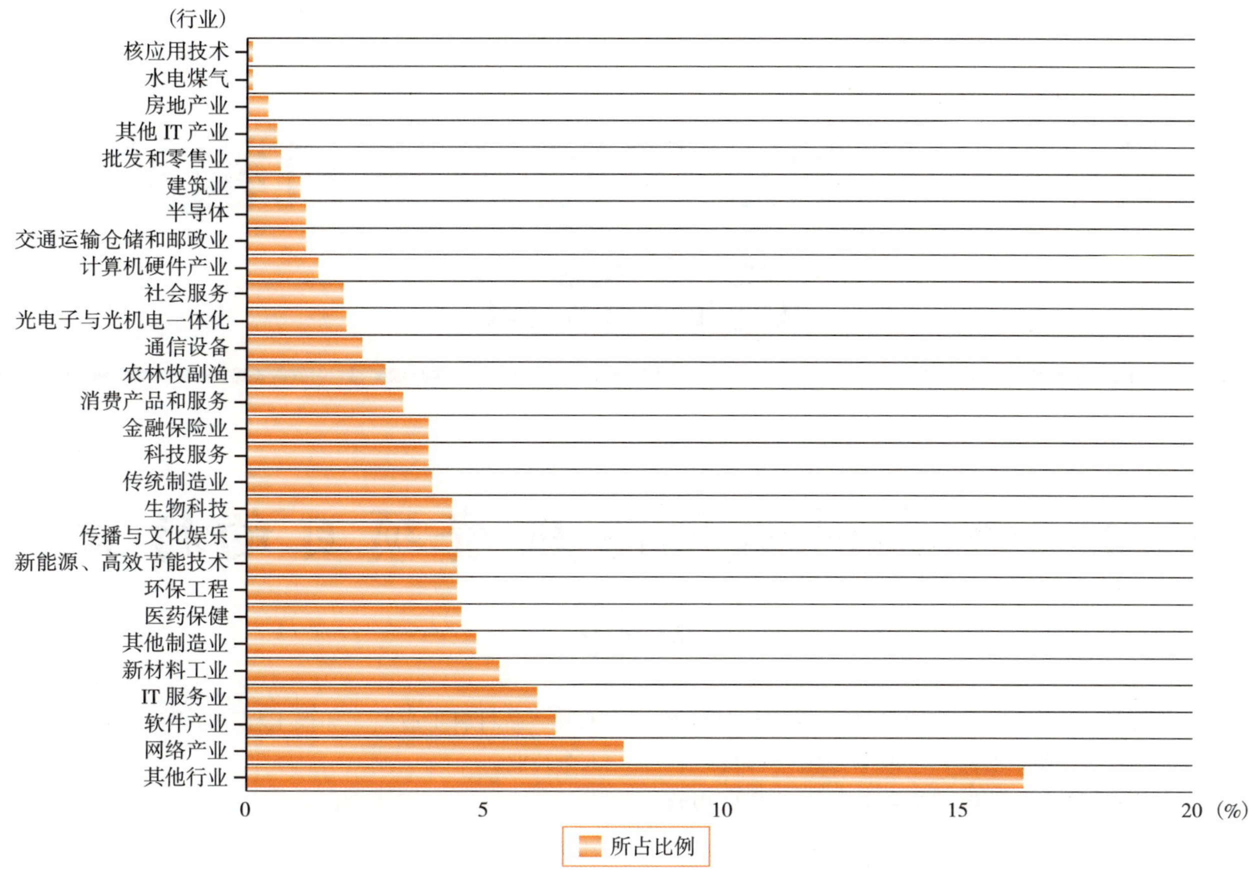

图 6-14　其他地区创业风险投资项目的行业分布（2016）

7 外资创业风险投资机构的运行状况

7.1 外资创业风险投资项目的行业分布

通过对 2016 年外资创业风险投资机构总体情况调查发现[①]，投资项目主要集中在 13 个项目领域[②]（如表 7–1 所示），相较于 2015 年新增“医药保健”、“核应用技术”、“新材料工业”、“环保工程”以及“农林牧副渔”五个行业。

表 7–1 外资创业投资项目的行业分布：投资金额与投资项目（2016） 单位：%

投资行业	投资金额占比	投资项目占比
网络产业	51.7	12.7
其他行业	13.5	18.2
医药保健	11.7	14.6
软件产业	8.5	3.6
传播与文化娱乐	3.0	5.5
核应用技术	2.5	1.8
新材料工业	2.0	7.3
生物科技	1.9	5.5
环保工程	1.6	3.6
半导体	1.3	1.8
农林牧副渔	0.7	3.6
金融保险业	0.4	3.6
通信设备	0.4	1.8

① 2016 年，我国境内共有 119 家外资创业风险投资机构，以下各部分是根据不同机构披露信息情况进行统计的结果。
② 有效样本为 55 份。

按投资金额划分[①]（见图 7-1），“网络产业”、“其他行业”和“医药保健”行业成为投资金额最多的三个领域，共占比 76.9%；与 2015 年相比，投资于“网络产业”的投资金额占比骤增，从 2015 年占比 5.2%增长到 2016 年的 51.7%，增长了近 10 倍。这可能与 2016 年资本纷纷布局共享单车、“互联网+医疗”以及网络产业高投入产出特性等原因有关。“传播与文化娱乐”行业投资金额则较 2015 年下降幅度明显，占比从 74%下降到 2016 年的 2.95%。“医药保健”作为新增投资行业，占 2016 年投资金额的 11.7%。

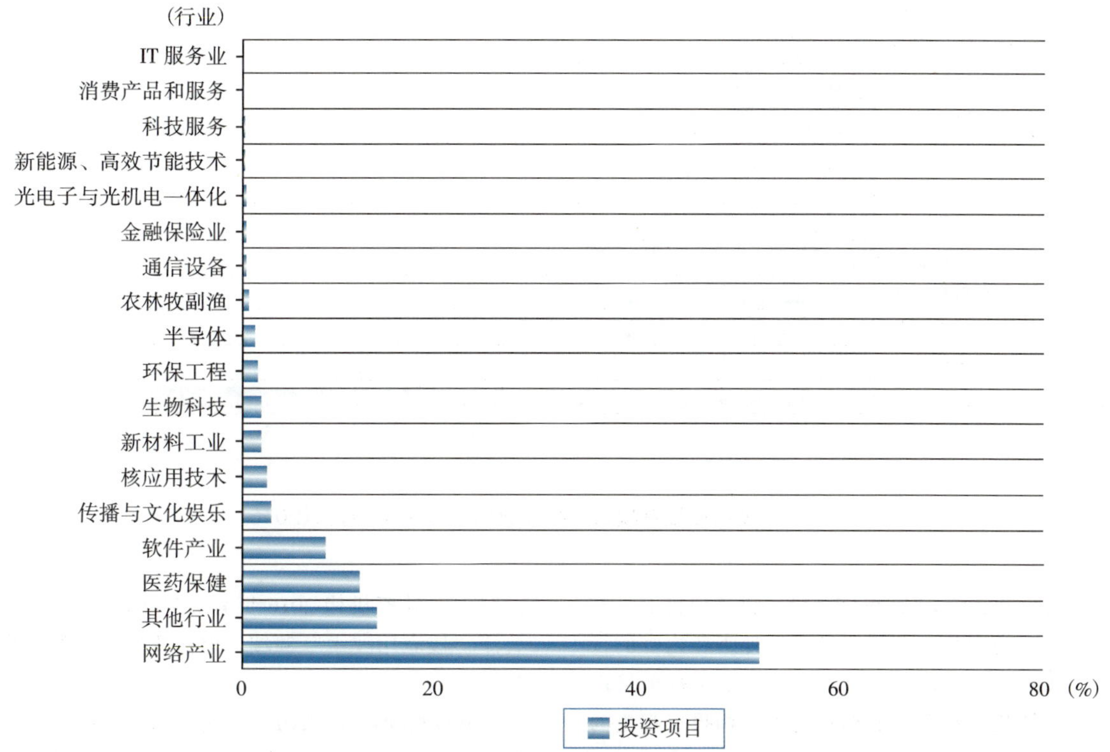

图 7-1 外资创业投资项目的行业分布：投资金额（2016）

2016 年外资创业风险投资项目数量则较为分散[②]（见图 7-2）。其中，“其他行业”以 18.2%占比最高，其次是“医药保健”以 14.6%位列第二位，“网络产业”投资项目数量占比较 2015 年略有下降了 3.3 个百分点至 12.7%。

①② 有效样本为 55 份。

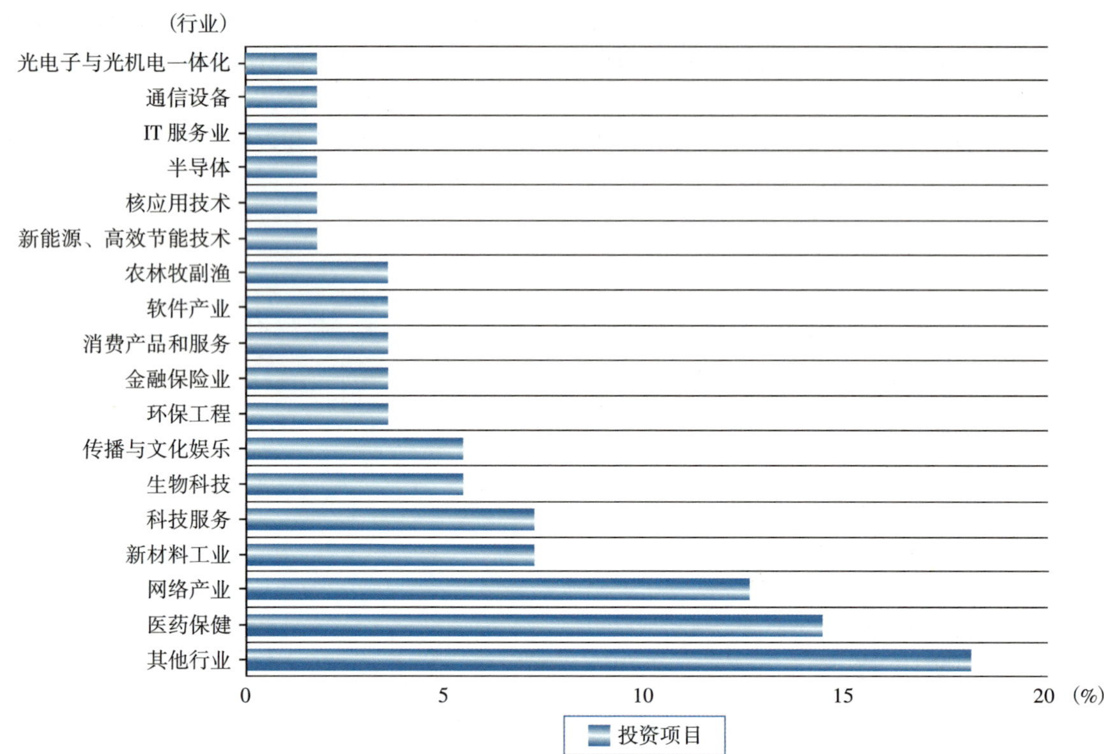

图 7-2 外资创业投资项目的行业分布：按投资项目（2016）

表 7-2 给出了 2016 年在投资金额和投资项目下，按外资创业风险投资“投资金额”排序的外资和内资的行为特征①。总体而言，无论从投资金额还是投资项目占比情况看，外资机构投资领域相较内资机构投资都更为集中。

投资金额看，2016 年外资机构投资金额前三个行业之和共占比 76.9%，内资机构前三个行业占比累计 56.3%。外资和内资机构的投资金额都大量投在“网络产业”领域，分别占比 51.7%和 33.8%。属于外资机构关注的“医药保健”和“核应用技术”则与内资机构表现出较为明显差异：“医药保健”投资金额占比位居全部行业第三位，而内资在该行业投资金额占比仅为 3.5%，二者相差 8.2 个百分点；外资机构 2016 年有 2.5%的投资金额已经开始关注“核应用技术”领域，但内资在该领域投资金额却为零。

从投资项目看，2016 年外资投资项目前三个行业之和共占比 45.4%，内资机构前三个行业占比合计 32.6%。外资机构与内资机构投资项目占比最多的都是“其他行业”，占比分别是 18.2%和 13.6%。位于外资和内资第二位的分别是“医药保健”和“网络产业”，分别占比 14.5%和 11.3%。此外，外资和内资机构表现较为不同的行业领域还有“软件产业”和“新材料工业”，其中内资机构更倾向于投资软件行业而外资机构则更偏向于投资技术领域。

表 7-2 外资、内资创业风险投资项目前十大行业分布：投资金额和投资项目（2016） 单位：%

投资行业	投资金额		投资项目	
	外资	内资	外资	内资
网络产业	51.7	33.8	12.7	11.3
其他行业	13.5	12.9	18.2	13.6

① 有效样本：外资为 55 份；内资为 2095 份。

续表

投资行业	投资金额		投资项目	
	外资	内资	外资	内资
医药保健	11.7	3.5	14.5	5.2
软件产业	8.4	9.6	3.6	7.7
传播与文化娱乐	2.9	3.0	5.5	5.3
核应用技术	2.5	0.0	1.8	0.0
新材料工业	2.0	3.4	7.3	5.5
生物科技	1.9	1.9	5.5	4.3
环保工程	1.6	1.5	3.6	3.1
半导体	1.3	1.0	1.8	1.3

注：按外资创业风险投资“投资金额”占比排序。

7.2 外资创业风险投资项目所处阶段

通过对 2016 年外资创业风险投资项目所处阶段的调查发现[①]（图 7-3），外资机构的投资金额和投资项目都不再集中于“成长（扩张期）”，其中，投资项目将重点放在了“起步期”，这较 2015 年是明显的变化。

具体而言，从投资金额角度分析，2016 年外资机构在“成长期”投资金额占比较 2015 年下降幅度明显。投资于“起步期”的金额骤增，从 2015 年的 3.3%上升至 2016 年的 23.0%。

从投资项目看，2016 年投资于“种子期”和“起步期”的投资项目更多，二者累计占比 63.4%，而这一比例在 2015 年是 31.3%，二者占比分别是 24.9%和 38.5%。

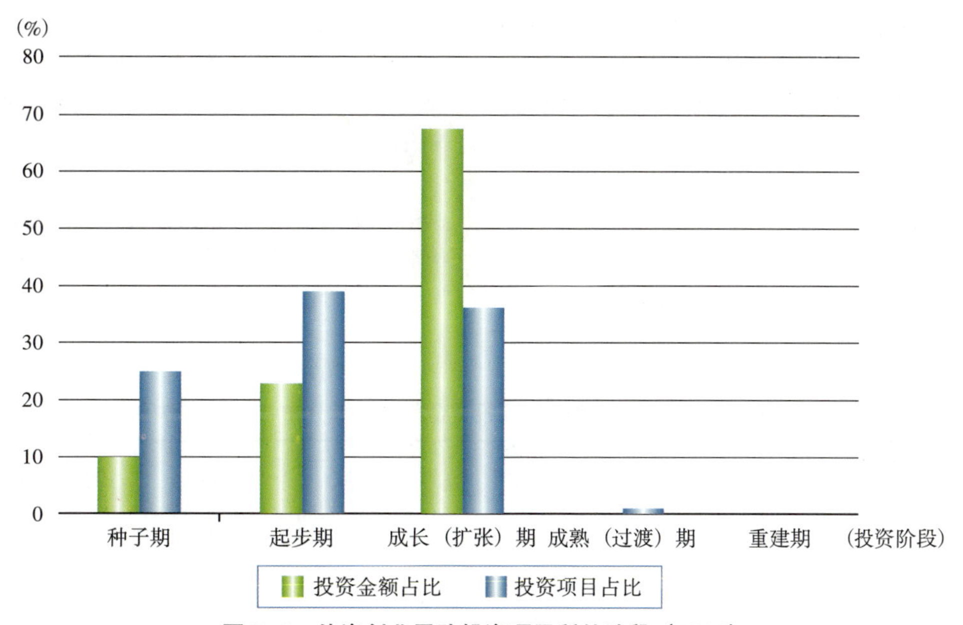

图 7-3 外资创业风险投资项目所处阶段（2016）

① 有效样本为 49 份。

对比2016年外资和内资机构投资项目所处阶段（见表7-3）可以发现[①]：

从投资金额看，外资机构和内资机构投资金额均在“成长（扩张期）”所占比重最高，分别是67.6%和38.1%，但均较2015年的94.9%和53.0%有明显下降。与2015年相比，外资机构投资项目金额在“起步期”和“种子期”累计占比从2015年的5.1%上升到2016年的32.4%。与外资机构对比而言，内资机构投资金额占比最多的也是“成长期”，“成长（扩张）期”和“成长（过渡）期”二者累计占比较外资机构低2.8个百分点；内资机构投资在“起步期”的项目金额则较外资机构高出7.4个百分点。

从投资项目看，自2013年以来，外资机构投资在“起步期”的投资项目数量首次超过“成长期”；“种子期”和“起步期”累计占比增至63.4%，远高于内资机构在该阶段累计占比。

表7-3 外资、内资创业风险投资项目所处阶段（2016） 单位：%

投资阶段	投资金额		投资项目	
	外资	内资	外资	内资
种子期	9.4	4.3	24.9	19.5
起步期	23.0	30.4	38.5	38.4
成长（扩张）期	67.6	38.1	36.2	35.4
成熟（过渡）期	—	26.7	0.47	5.8
重建期	—	0.6	—	0.8

7.3 外资创业风险投资项目情况

2016年，外资机构投资单项投资金额分布延续2011年以来特征，即单项投资金额在2000万元以上的占主要地位[②]（见表7-4、图7-4）。但与2015年以前的单项金额分布对比存在明显差异：

（1）单笔在2000万元以上的大额投资所占比例明显降低，较2015年下降了25%。

（2）单笔投资金额在“100万元以下”、“100万~300万元”、“300万~500万元”和“500万~1000万元”都是自2011年以来所占比重最高的，四种分布累计占比20.1%，较2015年增长16个百分点。

（3）单笔投资金额在1000万~2000万元的占比为18.5%，较2015年增长9.2个百分点，也是自2013年以来占比最大的一年。

针对上述数据的分析，再一次证明2016年外资投资机构的投资倾向，即相比2015年及以前，2016年外资机构都明显减少和降低了对成长期项目的关注和投资，逐渐回归创业风险投资属性。

表7-4 外资创业风险投资单项投资金额的规模分布（2011~2016） 单位：%

投资金额分布（万元）/年份	<100	100~300	300~500	500~1000	1000~2000	>2000
2011	0.0	0.2	0.3	3.3	13.9	82.3
2012	0.4	0.4	1.4	9.7	24.5	63.7
2013	0.0	0.1	1.3	4.2	16.1	78.2

① 有效样本：外资，49份，内资，2071份。
② 有效样本，57份。

续表

年份 \ 投资金额分布（万元）	<100	100~300	300~500	500~1000	1000~2000	>2000
2014	0.1	0.4	0.9	5.3	18.1	75.2
2015	0.0	1.0	0.7	2.4	9.3	86.5
2016	0.6	4.1	2.1	13.3	18.5	61.5

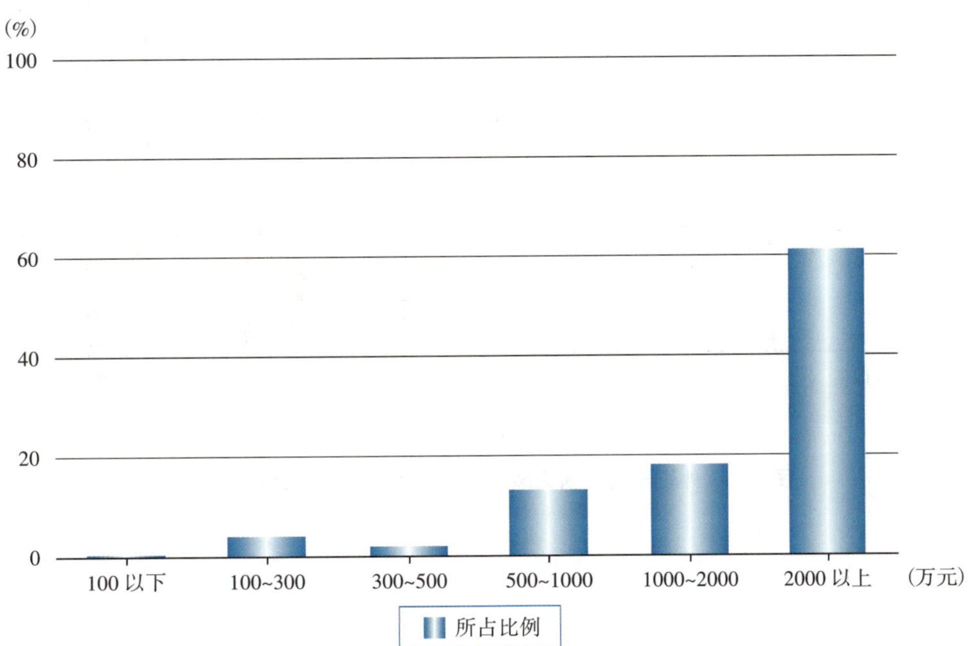

图 7-4 外资创业风险投资单位投资金额分布（2016）

通过对比外资和内资风险投资单项投资金额的规模分布[①]（见表 7-5、图 7-5）可以发现，2000 万元以上的投资项目仍然是外资和内资创业风险投资机构的主要投资方向，占比分别为 61.5%和 78.7%。2016 年，外资机构项目单笔投资金额 1000 万元以上累计占比较 2015 年下降幅度明显，从 2015 年的 95.8%下降至 2016 年的 80%；而内资机构 1000 万元以上的占比则较 2015 年小幅增长，从 2015 年的 85.2%增长至 88.5%。对比内资、外资投资机构的投资行为可以明显发现，2016 年外资机构相较 2015 年及以前增加了单笔投资金额小且早前期的项目。

表 7-5 外资、内资创业风险投资单项投资金额的规模分布（2016） 单位：%

分布比例	100 万元以下	100 万~300 万元	300 万~500 万元	500 万~1000 万元	1000 万~2000 万元	2000 万元以上
外资	0.6	4.1	2.1	13.3	18.5	61.5
内资	0.4	1.6	2.8	6.8	9.8	78.7

① 有效样本量：外资为 57 份，内资为 2328 份。

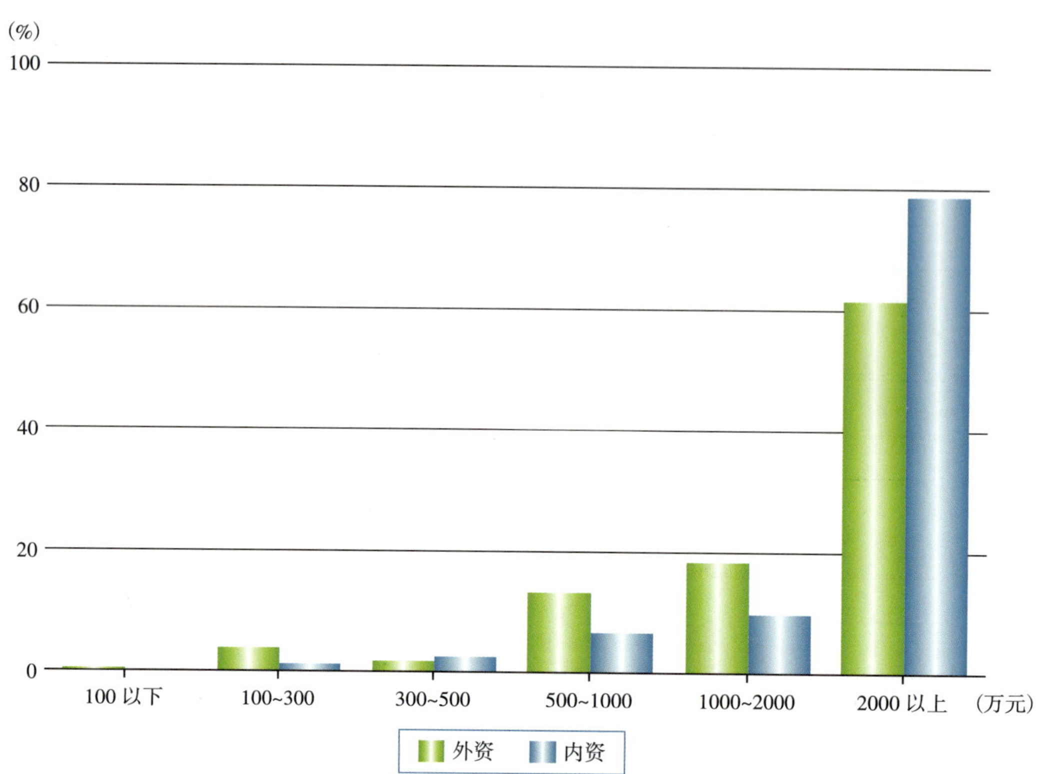

图 7-5 外资与内资创业风险投资单项投资金额分布（2016）

7.4 外资创业风险投资项目雇员情况

调查显示①（见表 7-6、图 7-6），与 2015 年相比，2016 年外资创业风险投资项目的雇员数量更为集中。根据外资机构披露数据情况，所投资项目雇员人数都在 100 人以下。其中，“10 人以下”、“10~50 人”和“50~100 人”各自所占比重分别为 36.8%、31.6%和 31.6%。

表 7-6 外资创业风险投资项目雇员人数分布（2011~2016） 单位：%

年份	10 人以下	10~50 人	50~100 人	100~150 人	150~200 人	200 人以上
2011	3.6	13.4	8.9	14.3	13.4	46.4
2012	8.3	17.9	9.5	21.4	10.7	32.1
2013	13.3	13.3	16.7	10.0	6.7	40.0
2014	10.5	19.7	10.5	15.8	6.6	36.8
2015	14.3	28.6	14.3	0.0	14.3	28.6
2016	36.8	31.6	31.6	—	—	—

① 有效样本为 19 份。

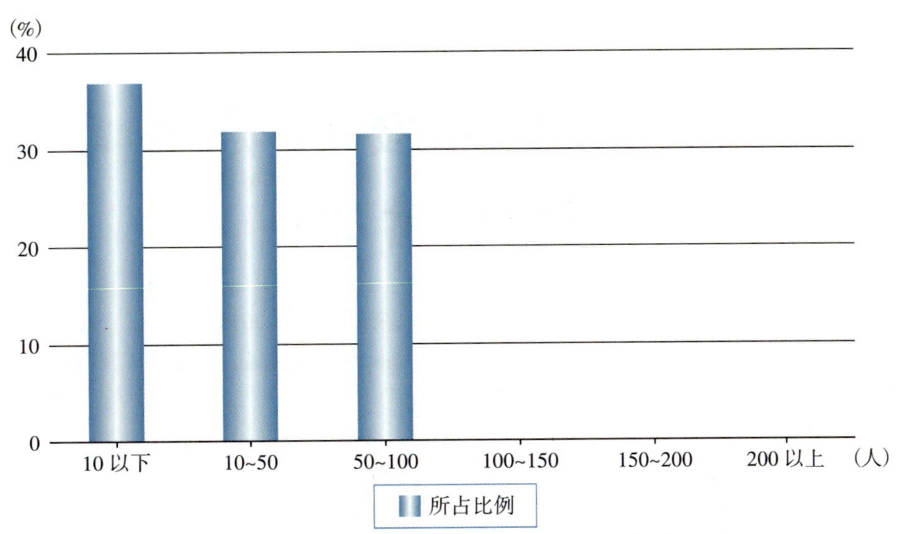

图 7-6 外资创业风险投资项目雇员人数分布（2016）

表 7-7 和图 7-7 给出了 2016 年外资与内资创业风险投资项目雇员人数分布情况[①]。对比内外资投资项目雇员情况，2016 年，外资机构投资项目雇员数量相较内资机构投资项目雇员数量而言更为集中。其中，外资机构投资项目雇员在“10 人以下”表现得更为集中；而内资机构投资项目人数则在“10~50 人”较为集中，所占比例为 38.0%，而雇员人数在 100 人以下累计占比为 73.3%，较 2015 年增长了 16.1 个百分点。这也说明了 2016 年投资机构都更倾向于规模相对较小的项目。

表 7-7 外资与内资创业风险投资项目雇员人数分布（2016）

单位：%

分布比例	10 人以下	10~50 人	50~100 人	100~150 人	150~200 人	200 人以上
外资	36.8	31.6	31.6	0.0	0.0	0.0
内资	21.6	38.0	13.7	7.9	4.3	14.5

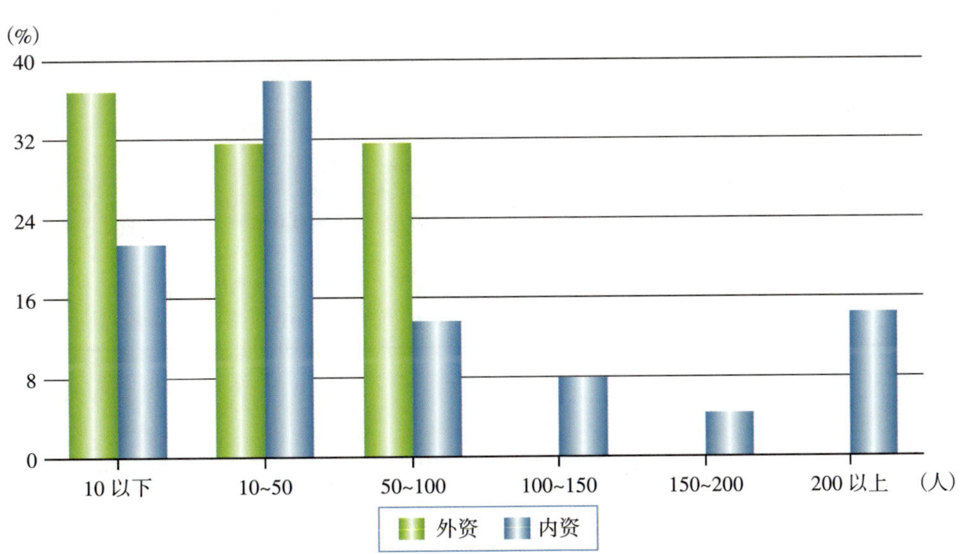

图 7-7 外资与内资创业风险投资项目雇员人数分布（2016）

① 有效样本：外资为 19 份，内资为 1034 份。

7.5 外资创业风险投资项目总体运作情况

表 7-8、图 7-8 给出了 2012~2016 年底外资创业风险投资项目运行的基本情况①。通过调查发现，2016 年外资创业风险投资的整体投资周期仍然较长，89.5%的项目仍然处于继续运行中，较 2015 年增长了 28.4%，是自 2012 年以来所占比例最高的一年，从侧面反映出外资创业风险投资机构对早前期的投资项目还在持续关注。

2016 年我国资本市场政策频出，机遇与风险并存，2016 年外资机构所投项目“已上市”比例降到自 2012 年以来最低。与 2015 年相比，2016 年“已上市”的投资项目占比降幅明显，从 15.5%骤降至 1.5%，其中“境内上市”所占比例较 2015 年减少了 14.4 个百分点。

2016 年，除“管理层收购”外，“原股东（创业者）回购”和“清算”所占比例都较 2015 年有所下降，且“原股东（创业者）回购”所占比例是近五年来最低，仅为 2.1%。

表 7-8 2012~2016 年底外资创业风险投资项目运行情况

单位：%

投资项目运作情况	已上市		准备上市		被其他机构收购			原股东（创业者）回购	管理层收购	继续运行	清算
	境内上市	境外上市	境内上市	境外上市	境内上市公司收购	境内非上市公司或自然人收购	境外收购				
2012 年	10.7		6.2		6.0			6.5	0.7	68.8	1.1
	7.6	3.1	5.1	1.1	1.1	4.9	0.0				
2013 年	10.8		7		5.1			10.0	14.0	52.0	1.1
	7.4	3.4	6.5	0.5	0.8	4.1	0.2				
2014 年	4.5		15		9.8			4.0	0.0	70.6	0.9
	3.3	1.2	9.5	5.5	0.5	5.5	3.8				
2015 年	15.5		0.0		8.8			11.8	0.2	61.1	2.6
	13.7	1.8	0.0	0.0	7.2	0.0	1.6				
2016 年	1.5		0.0		6.6			2.1	1.7	89.5	1.7
	1.1	0.4	0.0	0.0	6.6	0.0	0.0				

① 有效样本数量为 35 份。

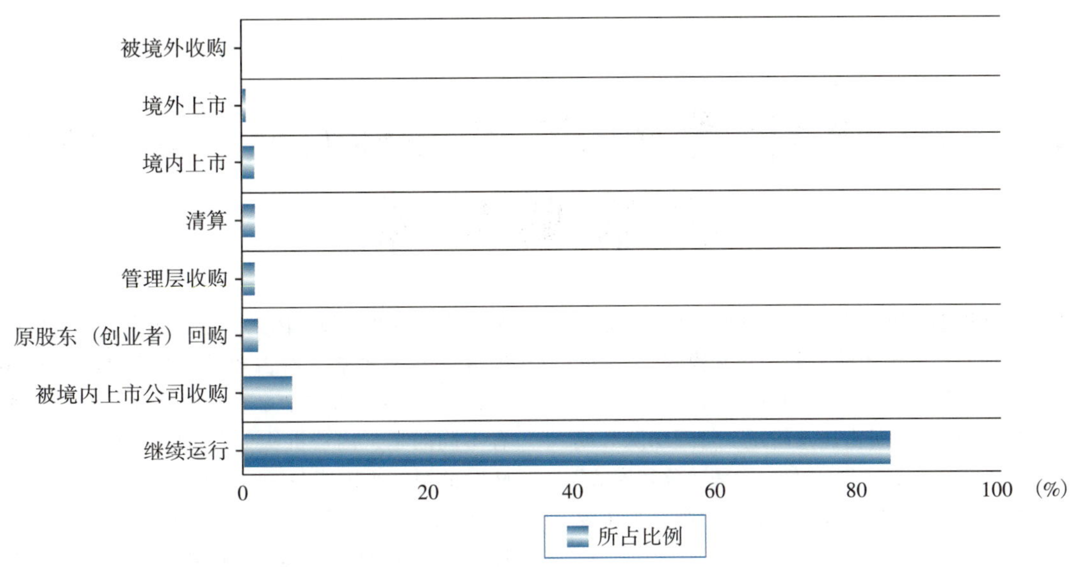

图 7-8 外资创业风险投资项目的运作情况（2016）

表 7-9、图 7-9 给出了 2016 年底外资与内资创业风险投资项目运作情况的对比。从表 7-9 中可以看出内资机构和外资机构的投资项目运作情况并没有明显的结构化差异，“继续运行”仍然是外资和内资机构投资项目的主要运行状态，与 2015 年相比，外资投资项目较内资投资项目“继续运行”占比增幅更大。

表 7-9 2016 年外资与内资创业风险投资项目运作情况

单位：%

运作情况	继续运行	其他机构收购	已上市	原股东（创业者）回购	管理层收购	清算	准备上市
外资	85.9	6.6	2.1	1.7	1.7	1.7	0.0
内资	76.4	4.9	7.0	8.0	1.1	2.7	0.0

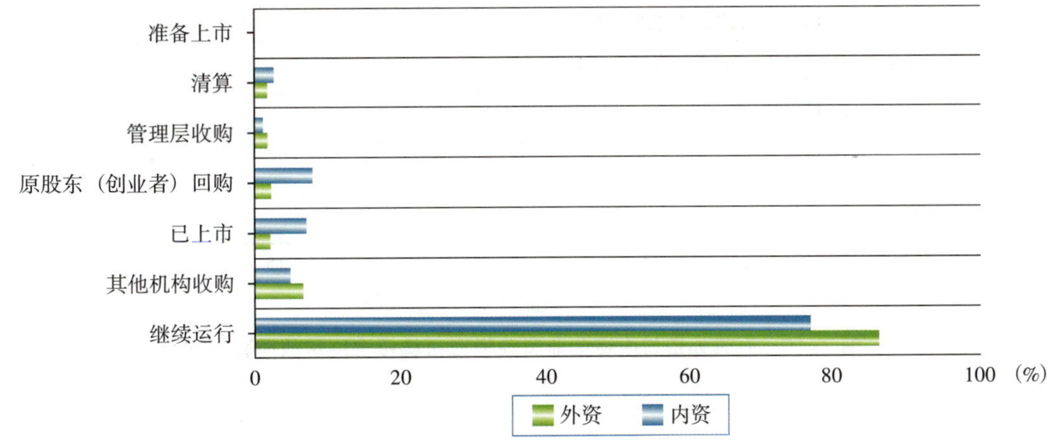

图 7-9 外资与内资创业风险投资项目的运作情况（2016）

7.6　影响外资创业风险投资机构投资决策的因素

2016 年影响外资创业风险投资机构的前三个主要原因分别是“市场前景”、“管理团队”和“盈利模式”（见图 7-10）①，占比分别为 15.2%、12.9%和 12.4%。一是与 2015 年相比，“市场前景”所占比重超过“管理团队”成为影响外资机构投资决策最主要因素；二是“盈利模式”超过“财务状况”，成为影响外资机构决策的第三个重要因素。

对比 2016 年外资和内资创业风险投资机构决策要素可以发现，“管理团队”、“市场前景”、“财务状况”、“盈利模式”以及“技术因素”是影响内资和外资投资决策的前五个共同要素，所占比重分别为 64.4%和 69.8%，较 2015 年分别降低 12.7 个和 3 个百分点。但与外资机构略有不同的是，内资机构更看重除“市场前景”、“管理团队”的第三个因素——“技术因素”，所占比重为 12.2%。此外，除了前五个最主要因素外，内资创业风险投资机构还比外资创业风险投资机构看重所投项目的“资信状况”、“投资地点”以及“中介服务质量”。

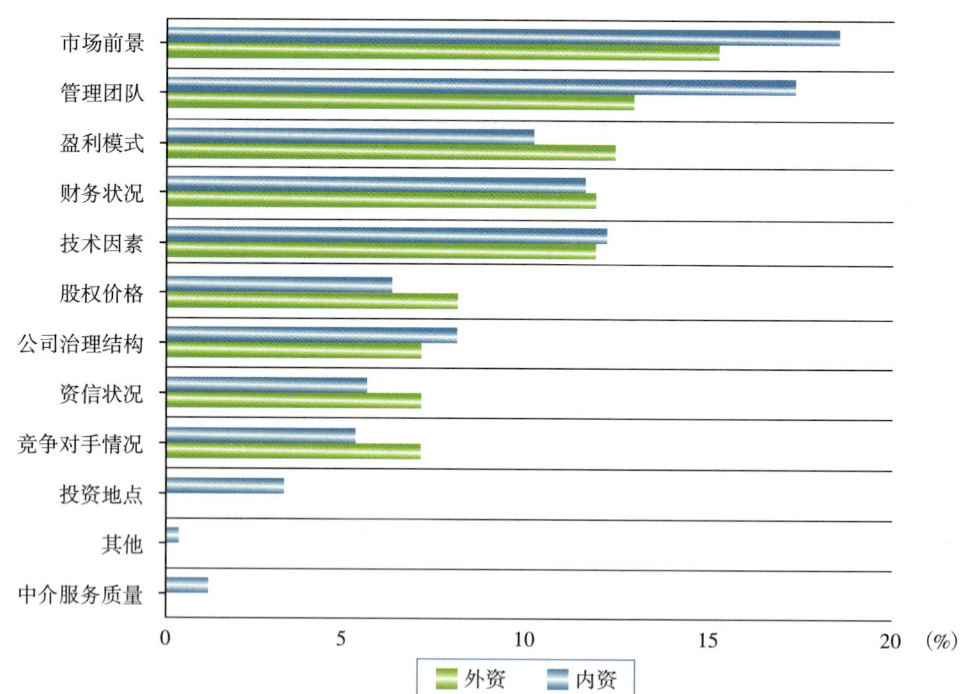

图 7-10　影响外资与内资创业风险投资机构投资决策的因素（2016）

① 有效样本量：外资为 34 份，内资为 1215 份。

7.7 外资创业风险投资机构获取信息主要渠道

通过对内资和外资创业风险投资获取信息渠道的调查发现①（见图 7-11），获取信息的主要渠道与 2015 年相比出现较大变化：

就外资机构而言，“政府部门推荐”成为外资和内资获取信息的最主要渠道，占比分别为 19.1%和 20.2%，较 2015 年排位从第三位升至第一位；而“股东推荐”从 2015 年的首要渠道成为第四位，占比由 20.3%下降到 14.1%。“项目中介机构”和“朋友介绍”分别位列第二、第三获取信息的主要渠道，占比分别 17.4%和 14.8%。

对比外资与内资机构，“政府部门推荐”、“项目中介机构”以及“朋友介绍”都位列外资和内资获取信息的主要渠道前三名，其中略有不同的是，对内资机构而言，“朋友介绍”占比较“项目中介机构”略高 0.4 个百分点，占比分别为 15.4%和 15.0%。

此外，相较于 2015 年，“众创空间（孵化器）”作为获得资金渠道所占比重明显上升。其中，内资机构上升幅度小于外资机构，外资机构信息获取来自“众创空间（孵化器）”所占比重由 2015 年的 2.5%上升到了 2016 年的 9.6%，内资则从 10.6%上升到了 11.3%。

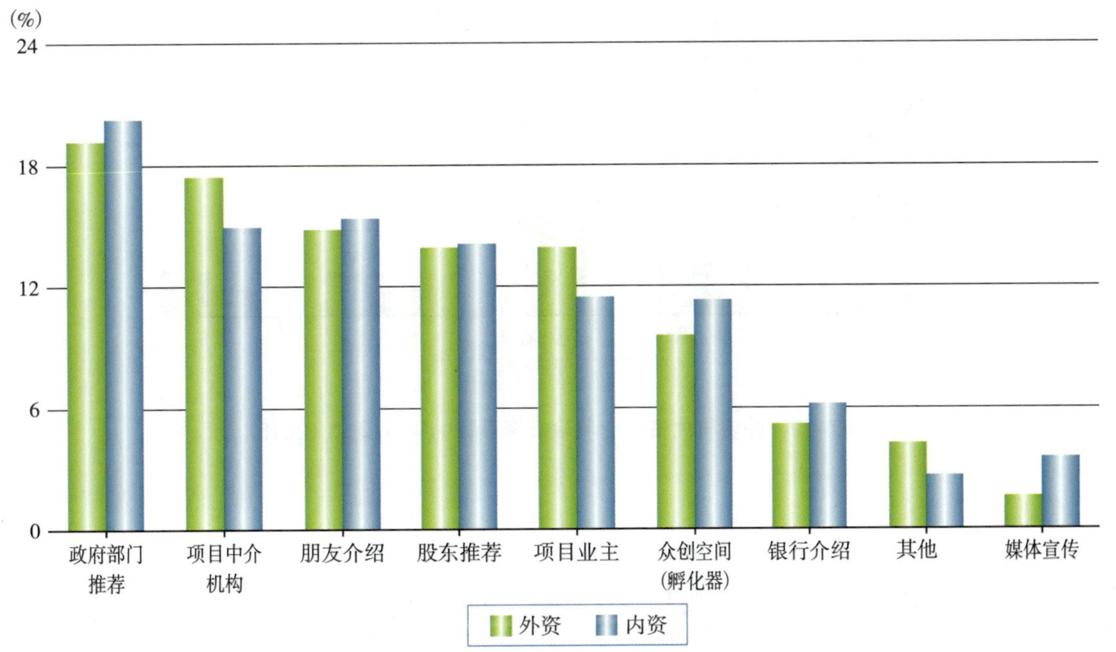

图 7-11 外资与内资创业风险投资机构获取信息的主要渠道（2016）

① 有效样本量：外资为 34 份，内资为 1215 份。

7.8 外资创业风险投资项目的监管模式

2016 年，外资创业风险投资的监管模式主要集中在“提供管理咨询”、“董事会席位”以及“只限监管”三方面[①]（见图 7–12），在投资项目中担任“董事会席位”的比重较 2015 年下降了 24 个百分点至 35.3%，与“提供管理咨询”的管理模式所占比例持平。此外，与 2015 年相比，外资机构有 2.9%的项目选择了“财务咨询”。

对比内资和外资创业风险投资项目监管模式可以发现，2016 年，内资创业风险投资机构相较于外资机构而言，更倾向于为投资项目以“董事会席位”方式进行监管，但仍比 2015 年略低 1 个百分点至 40.5%；“提供管理咨询”占比 33.8%。

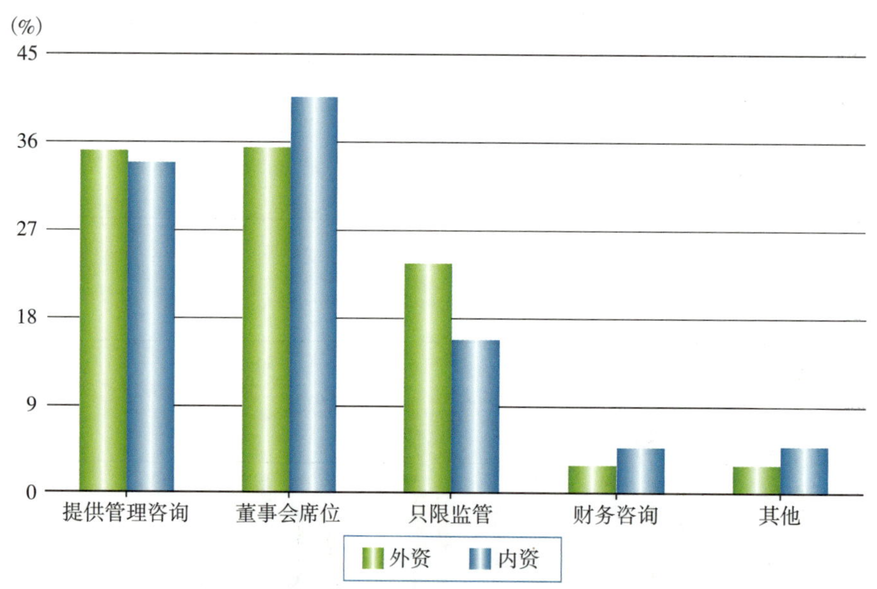

图 7–12 外资与内资创业风险投资项目的监管模式（2016）

7.9 与外资创业风险投资机构经营有关的人力资源因素

通过调查外资和内资创业风险投资机构对创业风险投资从业人员基本素质发现[②]（见图 7–13），2016 年外资机构对合格创业人员从业素质要求略有变化，但就整体而言，外资与内资机构都认为合格的创业风险投资人员应该

①② 有效样本数量：外资为 34 份，内资为 1206 份。

具备多种素质。

与 2015 年相比，“判断力和洞察力”替代“资本运作能力”，成为外资机构最看重的因素，二者占比分别为 19.9%和 17.9%；“商务谈判能力”位次与 2015 年相同，占比 17.2%；“财务管理能力”取代“技术背景”成为第四个需要具备的素质要求，占比分别为 15.9%和 14.6%；最后被看中的能力是“人际关系网络和协调能力”，占比 13.9%，该能力连续两年占比都较为靠后。

对比外资、内资机构，内资机构更看中合格创业风险投资人员具备“资本运作能力”，所占比重比外资机构在该项占比高 3.1 个百分点；而“判断力和洞察力”和“商务谈判能力”则分别位列第二、三位，所占比重分别是 18.6%和 14.8%。

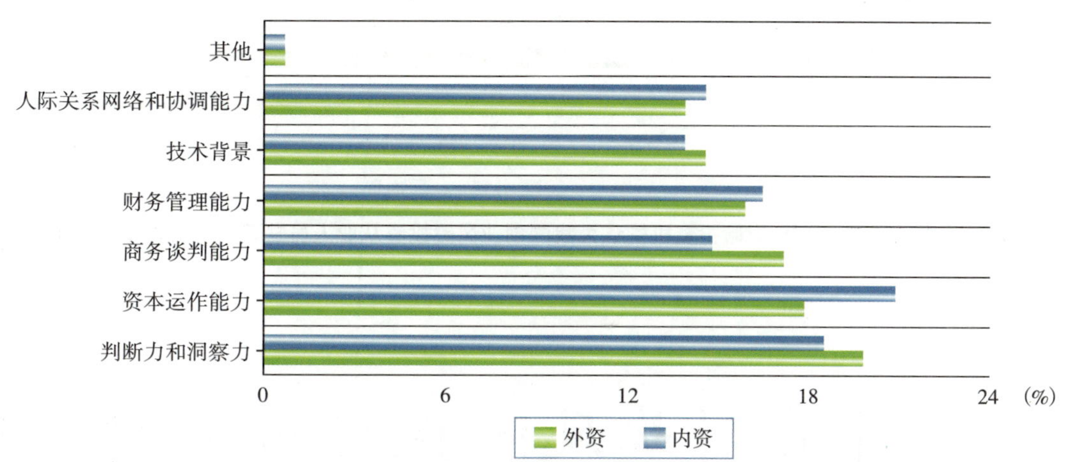

图 7-13 外资与内资创业风险投资机构对合格创业风险投资人员素质要求（2016）

通过对外资、内资机构调查我国创业风险投资人员最缺乏的专业知识发现，无论是外资还是内资机构，都对“技术评估”能力、“技术背景”等较为专业的能力提出了更高的要求。

调查显示[①]（见图 7-14），2016 年外资机构认为“技术评估”、“技术背景”以及“资本运作”是创业风险投资人员最缺乏的三项专业知识，所占比重分别为 19.8%、17%和 14.2%；缺乏“企业管理”的比重从 2015 年的第七位上升至 2016 年的第四位，所占比重为 14.2%；而“项目识别”能力所占比重则从 2015 年的第一位下降至第五位，仅占 10.4%。

对比外资创业风险投资机构对于人才的要求，2016 年内资创业风险投资机构认为从业人员最缺乏的知识依然是“技术评估”和“资本运作”，所占比重分别是 17.4%和 16.2%。而外资机构认为从业人员缺乏的“技术背景”技能，在内资创业风险投资机构认为我国创业风险投资从业人员缺乏的专业知识中排名第三，占比为 13.4%。

① 有效样本量：外资为 34 份，内资为 1206 份。

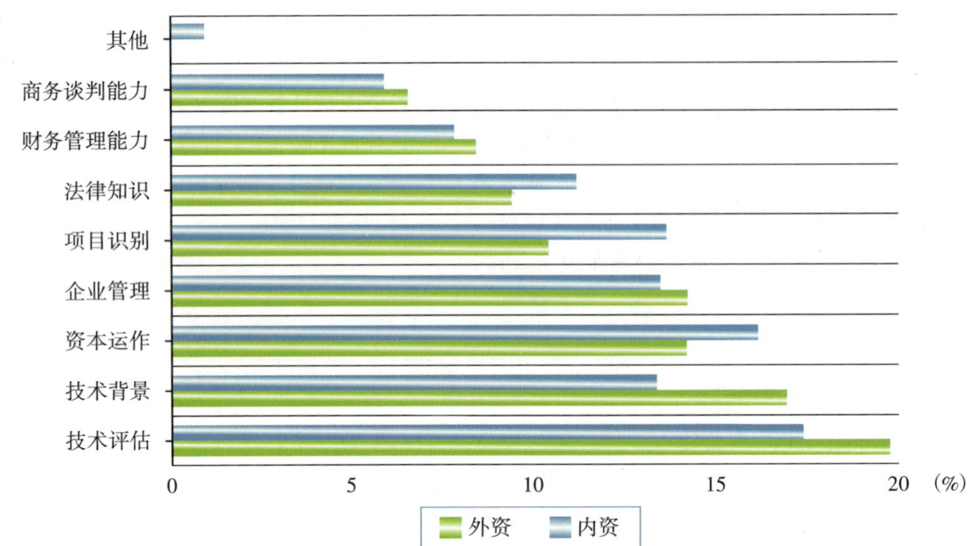

图 7-14 外资与内资创业风险投资机构认为我国创业风险投资从业人员缺乏的专业知识（2016）

7.10 外资创业风险投资机构对总体发展环境的评价

根据对外资创业风险投资机构关于投资效果是否理想的调查①（见图 7-15），“退出渠道不畅”超过“政策环境变化”成为 2016 年外资认为投资效果不理想的主要原因，所占比重分别是 32.3%和 12.4%；而“市场环境”成为第二项影响投资效果是否理想的因素，所占比重为 19.4%。

对比内资、外资创投机构可以发现，二者对政策环境的评价稍微存在差异。内资创业风险投资机构虽然同样认为“退出渠道不畅”，但“政策环境变化”是内资机构认为影响投资效果的第二重要因素，所占比重分别为 25.7%和 23.5%；“市场竞争”则被内资机构认为是导致效果不佳的第三个因素，占比 17%。

① 有效样本数量：外资为 31 份，内资为 1197 份。

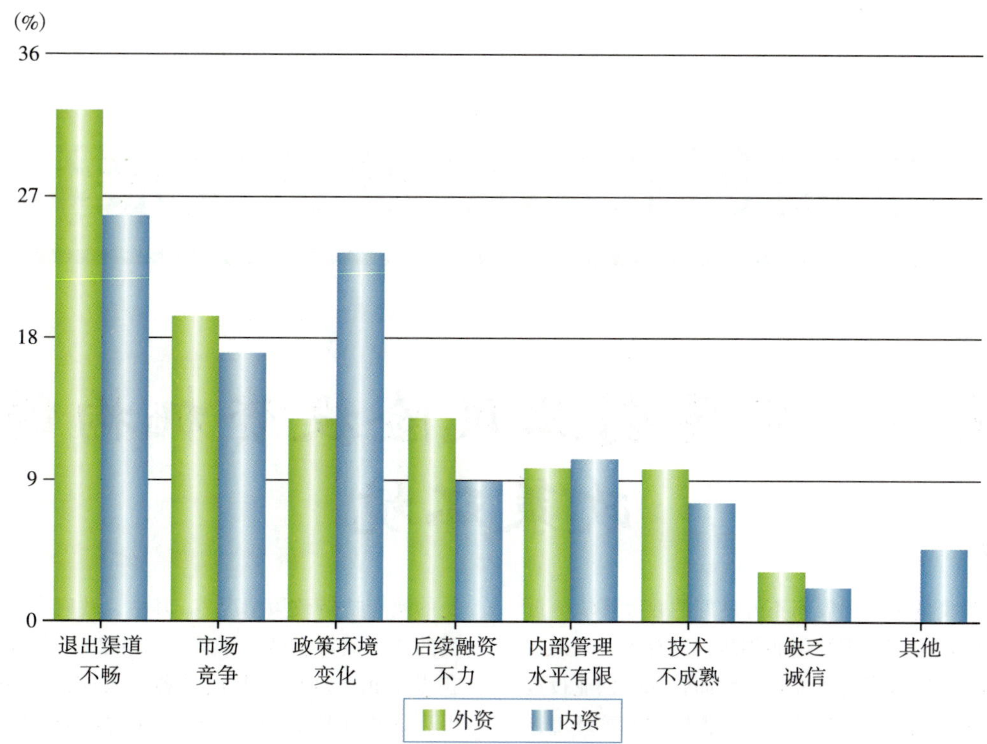

图 7-15　外资与内资创业风险投资机构认为投资效果不理想的原因（2016）

8 中国创业风险投资发展环境

8.1 中国创业风险投资机构的政策环境

创业风险投资的蓬勃发展离不开良好的政策环境。近年来，我国各级政府高度重视创业创新，出台了一系列政策措施推动创业风险投资行业成长。然而，我国创业投资行业健康持续发展尚需更加规范的制度保障和政策环境建设。本部分将重点阐述 2016 年我国创业风险投资机构所处的政策环境，分析其享受的主要税收政策及缴税情况，最后梳理创业风险投资机构的政策需求。

8.1.1 中国创业风险投资机构可以享受的政府扶持政策

图 8-1 列示了 2016 年我国创业风险投资机构能够享受的政府扶持政策情况[①]。其中，政府提供的信息交流方面的扶持政策支持居于首位，29.2%的创业风险投资机构获得了相关环境；其次是各级政府的所得税减免政策，得到该项扶持的创业投资企业占比为 20.3%；政府的直接资金支持位居第三，能够享受此项政策的创业风险投资机构占 17.6%，与 2015 年相比进一步降低；14.5%的创业风险投资机构在人员培训上获得了政府支持，12.8%的创业风险投资机构享受了其他扶持政策。总体来看，2016 年我国政府对创业风险投资机构的扶持以间接服务和税收政策为主。

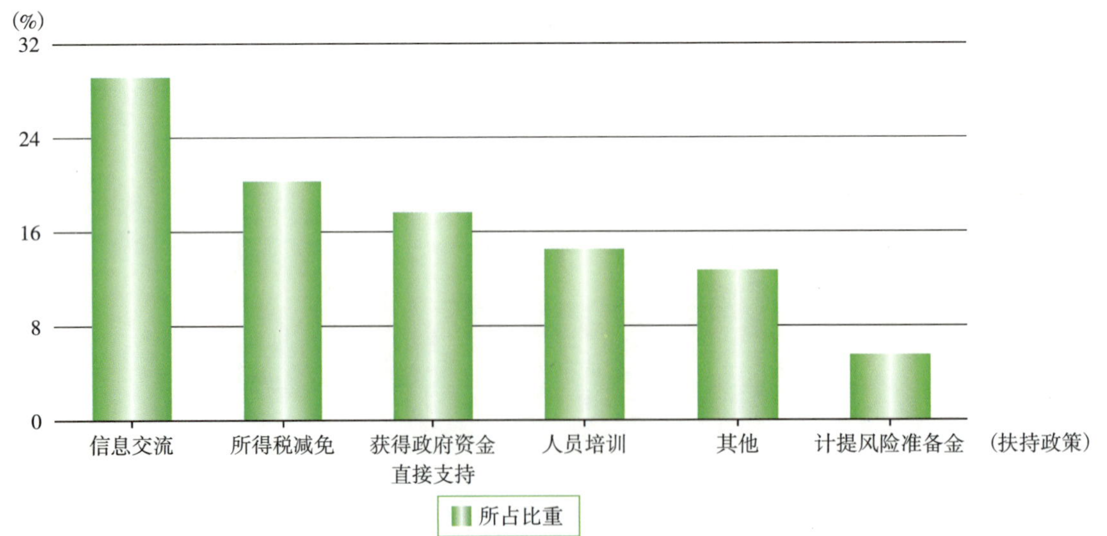

图 8-1 创业风险投资机构可以享受的政府扶持政策（2016）

① 有效样本数为 1180 份。

图 8-2[①]、图 8-3[②] 按照政府层级对 2016 年我国创业风险投资机构能够享受的扶持政策情况做了进一步划分。如图 8-2 所示，在中央政府扶持政策中，创业风险投资机构享受的信息交流服务与所得税减免分列前两位，占比分别为 29.4%和 19.9%；其他政策扶持则排在第三位，占比 16.1%；15.3%的企业享受到中央政府的直接资金支持。在地方层面（见图 8-3），29.1%的创业投资企业得到了地方政府的信息交流支持，20.7%的创业投资企业享受了地方政府的税收优惠；获得地方政府资金直接支持的创业风险投资机构占 19.5%。通过图 8-2 与图 8-3 的对比，不难发现，2016 年中央政府与地方政府在促进创业投资发展的政策导向上存在一定差异，与中央政府相比，地方政府对创业风险投资机构的直接扶持力度较大。

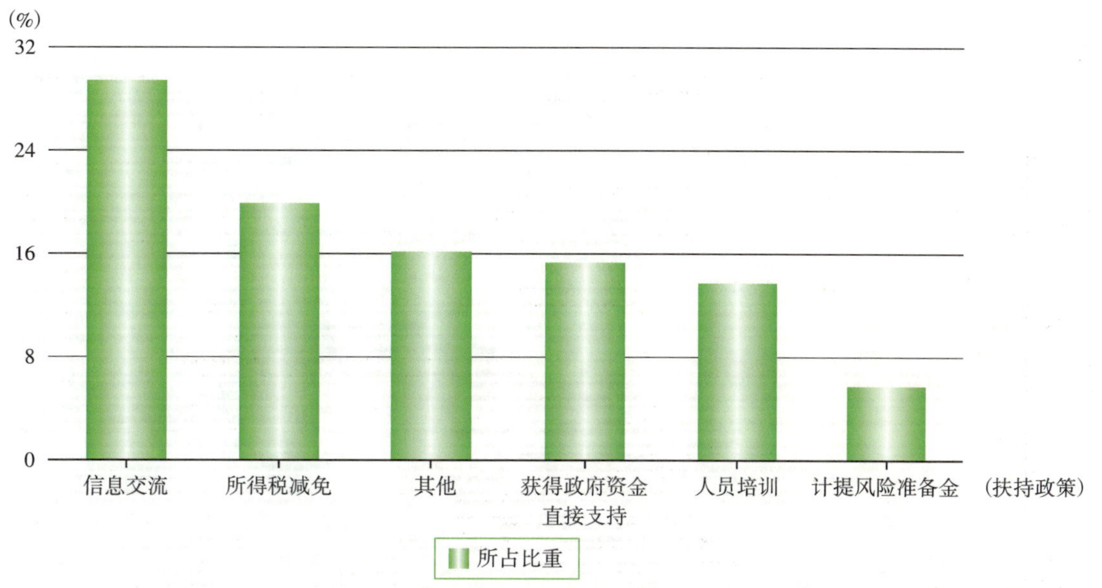

图 8-2 创业风险投资机构可以享受的中央政府扶持政策（2016）

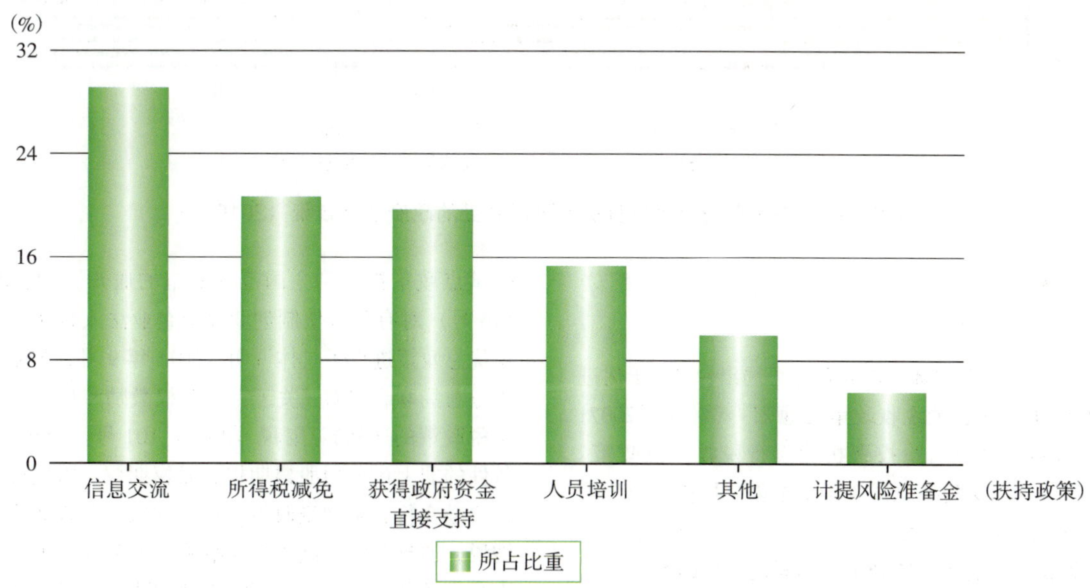

图 8-3 创业风险投资机构可以享受的地方政府扶持政策（2016）

① 有效样本数为 1114 份。
② 有效样本数为 1158 份。

按地域划分，2016 年我国创业风险投资机构享受政府扶持政策情况如图 8–4 所示①。可以看出，2016 年各地创业投资机构获得的各类型扶持政策并不均衡。重庆、山东、江苏、北京、广东等创业投资较为活跃的地区，能够享受各项政策的创业风险投资机构分布相对平均，山西、青海、海南、甘肃等地的创业风险投资企业获得的政策扶持相对单一。信息交流服务和所得税减免是各地创业风险投资机构享受的主要政策形式。其中，甘肃、宁夏、青海等 22 个地区的创业投资企业得到信息交流支持的比重超过了 25%，山西、天津、新疆等 11 个地区超过 20%的创业风险投资机构获得了所得税优惠。山西、青海、北京、内蒙古、黑龙江、云南等地区的创业投资机构获得政府资金直接支持的比重均超过了 30%，吉林、陕西、河北等地的创业投资企业则可以通过计提风险准备金降低投资风险和投资成本。

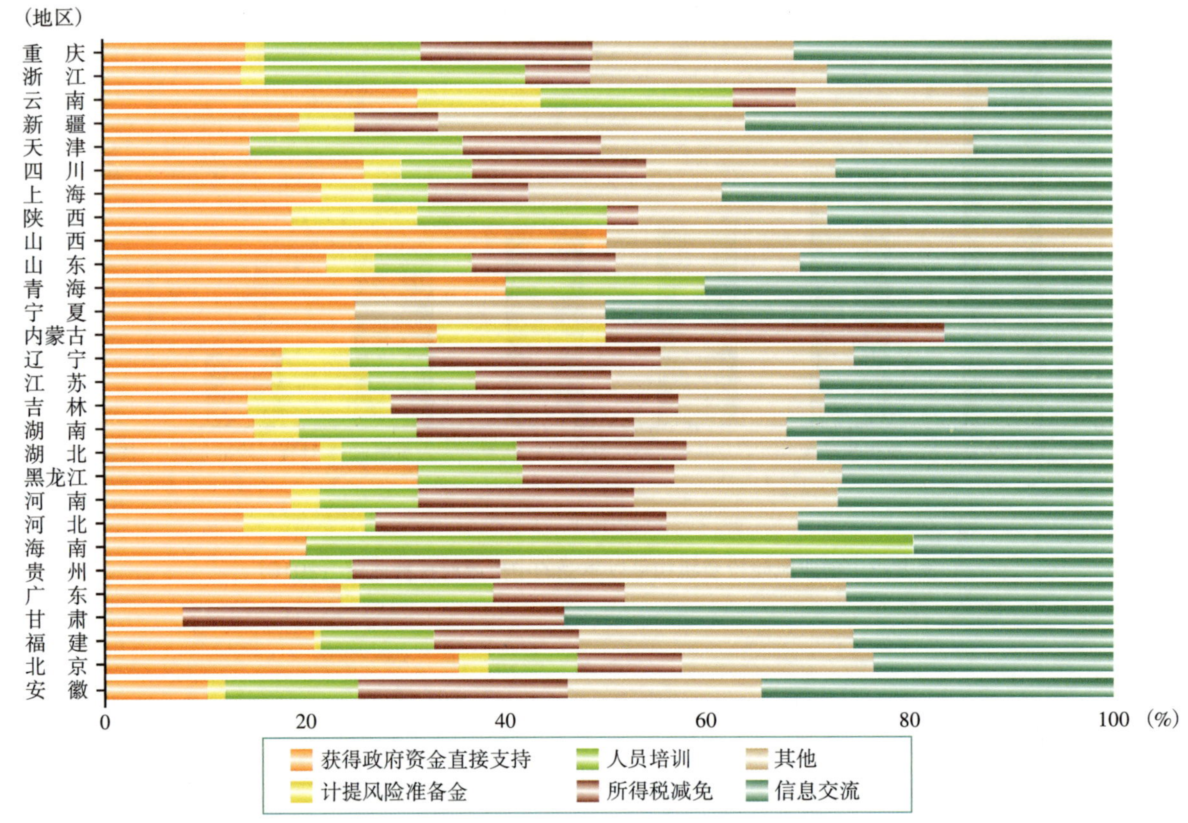

图 8–4 各地创业风险投资机构可以享受的政府扶持政策（2016）

8.1.2 中国创业风险投资机构享受的主要税收政策及缴税情况②

2007 年 2 月，财政部、国家税务总局出台《关于促进创业投资企业发展有关税收政策的通知》（财税〔2007〕31 号），明确对创业风险投资机构实行税收优惠政策。2009 年 4 月，《国家税务总局关于实施创业投资企业所得税优惠问题的通知》（国税发〔2009〕87 号）就创业投资企业所得税优惠的有关问题做了具体规定。2015 年 10 月，《财政部国家税务总局关于将国家自主创新示范区有关税收试点政策推广到全国范围实施的通知》（财税〔2015〕116 号）对有限合伙制创业投资企业法人合伙人企业所得税优惠政策进行了具体说明。2016 年 9 月，财政部、国家税务总局联合发布《关于完善股权激励和技术入股有关所得税政策的通知》（财税〔2016〕101 号）指出："对符合条件的非上市公司股票期权、股权期权、限制性股票和股权奖励实行递延纳税政策，员工在取得股权激励时可暂不纳税，递延至转让该股权时纳税，税率降低为 20%；对上市公司股票期权、限制性股票和股权奖励延长纳税期限，

① 有效样本数为 1180 份。
② 有效样本数为 1054 份。

个人可自股票期权行权、限制性股票解禁或取得股权奖励之日起，在不超过 12 个月的期限内缴纳个人所得税；对技术成果投资入股实施选择性税收优惠政策”。

2016 年统计数据显示，国内披露缴税情况的创业风险投资机构 1054 家，合计缴税金额 17.89 亿元，其中，享受投资中小高新技术企业所得税减免的创业风险投资机构共 50 家。

8.1.3 中国创业风险投资机构的政策需求①

图 8-5 列示了 2016 年中国创业风险投资机构最希望出台的政府激励政策，主要类型如下：

（1）完善创投税收优惠政策。统计数据显示，2016 年中国创业风险投资机构最希望出台的政府激励政策是税收优惠类，占比为 43%。与往年相比，创业投资企业的税收政策诉求仍在持续提升。

（2）设立政策性基金。13.1%的创业投资企业希望设立政策性基金，并通过市场化的运作方式支持创业风险投资发展，与 2015 年相比，这一数据略有降低。

（3）鼓励科研人员创新创业。数据显示，5.6%的创业投资机构认为政府应当出台鼓励科研人员创新创业的相关政策，进一步激发创新创业热情，促进科技成果转化。

（4）加快注册制改革，建立转板机制。希望政府继续推动资本市场注册制改革，加快建立场内外市场之间的转板机制的创业风险投资企业占比为 14.8%。与 2015 年相比，该项诉求下降了 5.3 个百分点。

（5）完善和落实相关法律。根据调查统计，6%的创业风险投资机构希望政府能够完善和落实创业投资的相关法律，营造规范的制度环境。

（6）理顺国有创投管理体制。10.4%的创业投资机构认为应当健全符合创业风险投资行业特点和发展规律的国有创业投资管理体制，激发国有创投活力，提高国有创投运行效率。该项诉求较 2015 年略有上升。

（7）发展众创空间等新型孵化器。6%的创业投资机构希望政府加大众创空间等新型孵化器的扶持力度，进一步加快推进大众创新创业。

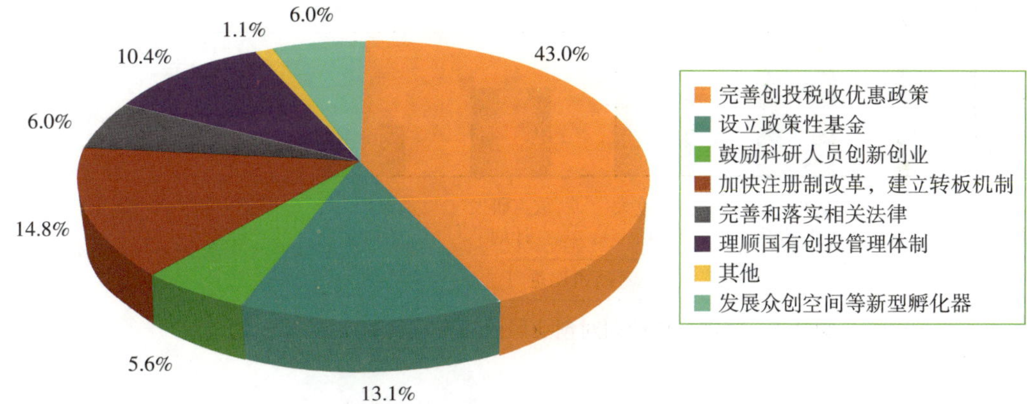

图 8-5 创业风险投资机构希望的政府激励政策（2016）

8.2 国家科技计划支撑创业风险投资发展

8.2.1 国家科技计划对创业风险投资项目支持情况②

统计数据显示，2016 年约 4.5%的创业风险投资项目获得了国家科技计划的支持，低于 2015 年的 5.49%。其中，0.84%的项目获得了技术创新引导专项的支持，低于 2015 年的 1.12%；重点研发计划支持了 0.63%的创业投资

① 有效样本数为 1214 份。

② 2016 年有效样本数为 2385 份，2015 年有效样本数为 2850 份。

项目，比 2015 年高 0.31 个百分点；0.75%和 0.38%的创业风险投资项目分别受到了科技重大专项与基地和人才专项的资助，1.89%的项目则获得了其他国家级计划的支持（见表 8-1、图 8-6）。

表 8-1 国家科技计划对创业风险投资项目的支持（2015~2016） 单位：%

国家科技计划 / 年份	其他国家级计划	技术创新引导专项	科技重大专项	重点研发计划	基地和人才专项	自然科学基金
2015	2.85	1.12	0.81	0.32	0.35	0.04
2016	1.89	0.84	0.75	0.63	0.38	0.00

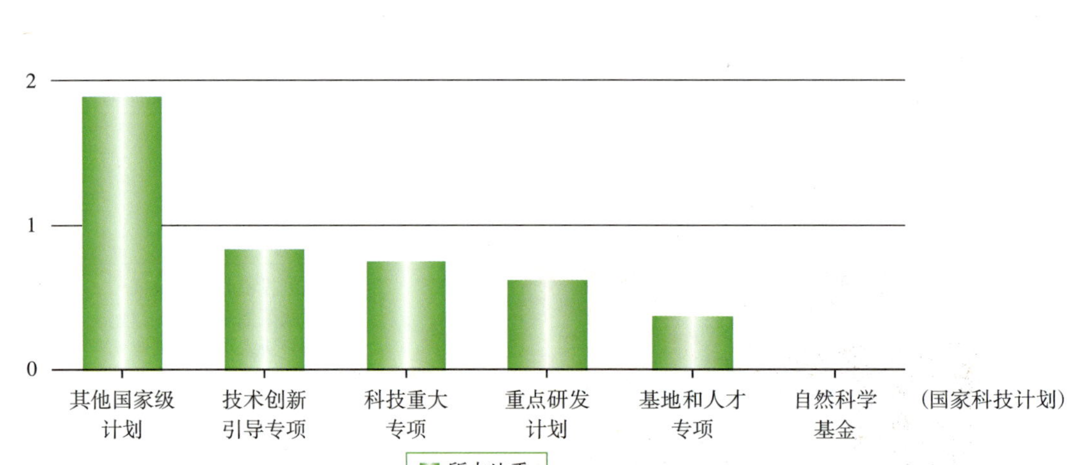

图 8-6 国家科技计划对创业风险投资项目的支持（2016）

8.2.2 国家科技计划与创业风险投资项目对接的关键因素①

2016 年统计数据显示，33%的创业风险投资机构认为加大基础、应用和开发投入是国家科技计划与创业风险投资项目对接的首要因素。与 2015 年相比，这一比重略有提升；26%的创业风险投资机构认为应当尽快设立科技型中小企业上市的绿色通道，高于 2015 年的 24%；22%的创业风险投资机构认为需要创业风险投资项目给予直接资助，低于 2015 年的 26%；11%的创业风险投资机构认为应鼓励、资助创业风险投资与孵化器之间的合作，比 2015 年的 10%略高；5%的创业投资机构要求加大科技项目信息的公开度，这一比重与 2015 年基本持平；仅有 3%的创业风险投资机构认为应当对科技类投资项目提供培训、管理咨询，比 2015 年的 3%略低（见图 8-7）。

① 有效样本数为 1207 份。

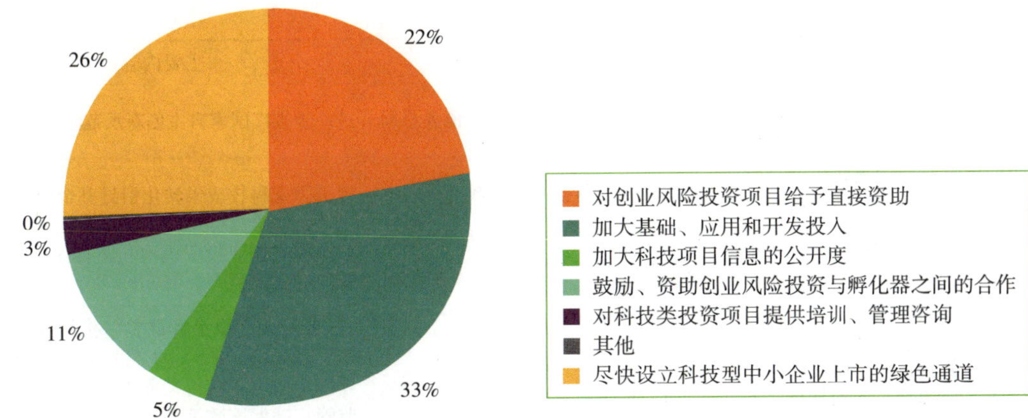

图 8-7 国家科技计划与创业风险投资良好对接的关键因素（2016 年）

8.3 中国促进创业风险投资发展主要政策

政府部门的政策支持是创业风险投资发展的直接助推器。自 1999 年国务院办公厅转发科技部等七部门联合出台的《关于建立风险投资机制的若干意见》开始，我国各有关部门相继出台了一系列支持创业风险投资发展的政策，涉及外商投资、监督管理、税收优惠、商事制度、国有股转持、引导基金等方面，有效推动了我国创业风险投资事业的前进。本部分将对近五年来国家层面出台的促进中国创业风险投资发展的相关文件进行梳理（见表 8-2）。

表 8-2 近年来中国促进创业风险投资发展主要政策文件

文件名称	发布时间	发布机构	主要内容（或主要目标）
《非上市公众公司监督管理办法》	2012 年	证监会	将非上市公众公司纳入合法监管，有利于中小企业融资，对促进创业风险投资投资中小企业有积极意义
《全国中小企业股份转让系统有限责任公司管理暂行办法》	2013 年	证监会	进一步完善多层次资本市场建设，有利于创业风险投资机构股权退出
《中小企业发展专项资金管理办法》	2014 年	财政部、工业和信息化部、科技部、商务部	进一步完善科技型中小企业创业投资引导基金管理模式和支持方式
《私募投资基金监督管理暂行办法》	2014 年	证监会	将创投等以私募性质募集资金的投资基金纳入备案监管
《基金从业资格考试管理办法（试行）》	2015 年	证监会	加强基金从业人员资格考试管理工作，完善基金从业资格考试管理流程
《私募投资基金募集行为管理办法（试行）（征求意见稿）》	2015 年	证监会	加强对基金募集行为的规范管理
《关于推广中关村国家自主创新示范区税收试点有关问题的通知》	2015 年	财政部、国家税务总局	将中关村关于股权奖励个人所得税政策、有限合伙制创业投资企业法人合伙人企业所得税政策等推广到国家自创区

续表

文件名称	发布时间	发布机构	主要内容（或主要目标）
《关于将国家自主创新示范区有关税收试点政策推广到全国范围实施的通知》	2015 年	财政部、国家税务总局	进一步推广国家自主创新示范区关于创业投资的优惠政策
《关于印发国家科技成果转化引导基金贷款风险补偿管理暂行办法的通知》	2015 年	科技部、财政部	规范国家科技成果转化引导基金贷款风险补偿工作
《国务院关于取消和调整一批行政审批项目等事项的决定》	2015 年	国务院	豁免国有创业投资机构和国有创业投资引导基金国有股转持义务审核
《关于取消豁免国有创业投资机构和国有创业投资引导基金国有股转持义务审批事项后有关管理工作的通知》	2015 年	财政部	《国务院关于取消和调整一批行政审批项目等事项的决定》（国发〔2015〕11 号）要求，对豁免创投机构和引导基金国有股转持义务事项不再进行审批。为加强后续监管，确保该政策顺利实施，并避免对国有股转持政策造成不利影响，从资质条件、办理程序、国有股回拨和监督管理有关事项做了详细规定
《政府投资基金暂行管理办法》	2015 年	财政部	明确政府应当设立投资基金支持创新创业，增加创业投资资本供给
《关于财政资金注资政府投资基金支持产业发展的指导意见》	2015 年	财政部	对创业投资引导基金支持战略性新兴产业等新兴产业及中小企业提出指导意见
《国家创新驱动发展战略纲要》	2016 年	中共中央、国务院	对实施创新驱动发展战略、推进新时期创新工作做出顶层设计和系统谋划。鼓励拓展多层次资本市场支持创新功能，积极发展天使投资，壮大创业投资规模
《关于做好国家新兴产业创业投资引导基金参股基金推荐工作的通知》	2016 年	发改委办公厅、财政部办公厅	按照国务院批复的《国家新兴产业创业投资引导基金设立方案》有关要求，为加快推进国家新兴产业创业投资引导基金设立及运行工作，推荐一批国家新兴产业创业投资引导基金参股基金方案
《关于促进创业投资持续健康发展的若干意见》	2016 年	国务院	对创业投资的投资主体、资金来源、政策扶持、法律法规、退出机制、市场环境、双向开放及行业自律与服务等提出指导性意见
《关于完善股权激励和技术入股有关所得税政策的通知》	2016 年	财政部、国家税务总局	调整股权激励和技术入股税收政策，从税率和纳税时点两方面进一步降低股权激励税收负担
《政府出资产业投资基金管理暂行办法》	2016 年	发改委	明确政府出资产业投资基金募集和登记管理、投资运作和终止、绩效评价、行业信用建设、监督管理等事宜

2016 年，国家深入实施创新驱动发展战略，加大推动供给侧结构性改革，针对创新创业密集出台了多部系统性、高级别、纲领性政策文件。

2016 年 9 月 20 日，国务院印发《关于促进创业投资持续健康发展的若干意见》（以下简称《意见》），从投资主体、资金来源、政策扶持、法律法规、退出机制、市场环境、双向开放及行业自律与服务八个方面提出进一步促进创业投资持续健康发展的指导性意见：

一是培育多元创业投资主体。以形成各具特色、多元化的投资机构体系为目标，鼓励各类机构投资者和个人依法设立公司型、合伙型创业投资企业，鼓励行业骨干企业等机构参与创业投资，鼓励包括天使投资人在内的各类个人从事创业投资。

二是拓宽创业投资资金来源。培育各类合格投资者，推动发展投贷联动、投保联动、投债联动等新模式，支持银行业金融机构开展并购贷款业务，支持发行企业债券和其他债务融资工具。

三是加大政策扶持力度。完善创业投资企业投资抵扣税收优惠政策，建立创业投资与政府项目对接机制，研究鼓励长期投资的政策措施，进一步发挥政府资金的引导作用。

四是完善相关法律法规。进一步完善促进创业投资发展相关法律法规，落实和完善国有创业投资管理制度，积极探索市场化投资机构的激励约束、股权转让、跟投等机制与国有体系的结合。依法依规豁免国有创业投资企业和国有创业投资引导基金国有股转持义务。

五是完善退出机制。充分发挥主板、创业板、全国中小企业股份转让系统以及区域性股权市场功能，完善全国中小企业股份转让系统交易机制，鼓励创业投资以并购重组等方式实现市场化退出，改善市场流动性。

六是优化市场环境。实施更多的普惠性支持政策措施，严格保护知识产权，优化监管、商事、信用环境。

七是推动创业投资行业双向开放。鼓励外资扩大创业投资规模，引导和鼓励创业投资企业加大对境外及中国港、澳、台地区高端研发项目的投资，积极分享高端技术成果。

八是完善行业自律和服务体系。加快推进依法设立全国性创业投资行业协会，健全创业投资服务体系。

《意见》是迄今为止针对创业风险投资发展的最为全面系统的纲领性文件，是创业风险投资领域的顶层设计和新里程碑。《意见》的出台为我国创业风险投资行业健康发展和制定具体政策提供了基本遵循，为进一步扩大创业风险投资规模、促进创业风险投资做大、做强、做优提供了坚实的制度保障。

9 中国创业风险投资引导基金发展情况

9.1 创业风险投资引导基金支持创业投资发展概况

近年来，国家层面聚焦创新驱动发展，发力供给侧结构性改革，通过发展引导基金，优化资金配置方式方向。在一系列利好政策的直接推动下，引导基金迎来爆发式增长。通过带动社会资本流向创业投资领域，引导基金支持了一大批创业风险投资机构和优质创业创新项目。

本项调查结果显示①，截至 2016 年底，全国创业风险投资引导基金共 448 只，累计出资 518.65 亿元，通过阶段参股、风险补助、投资保障等方式引导带动创业风险投资机构管理资金规模合计 2393.38 亿元。其中，2016 年当年新增引导基金 53 家。

2016 年调查结果显示，获得引导基金支持的创业风险投资机构平均管理资本规模达到 56358.1 万元，比 2015 年的 49675.8 万元增长 13.5%。未获得引导基金支持的创业风险投资机构平均管理资本规模为 60988 万元，比 2015 年的 47714.1 万元增长 27.8%（见图 9-1）②。

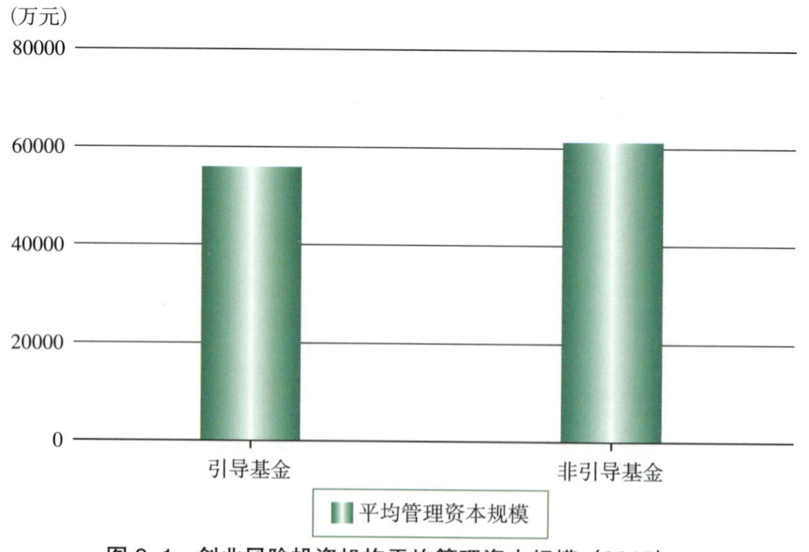

图 9-1 创业风险投资机构平均管理资本规模（2016）

① 有效样本数为 621 份。
② 有效样本数为：获得引导基金支持创投 327 份、未获得引导基金支持创投 1258 份。

对 2016 年创业风险投资机构的资金来源进行分类，分别见图 9-2、图 9-3、图 9-4。

按机构所有制性质进行划分，2016 年度数据显示，在获得引导基金支持的创业风险投资机构资本构成中，政府资本（含事业单位、国有独资投资机构）居于首位，占比高达 49.9%，较 2015 年的 30.7%提升了 19.2 个百分点；其次是民营投资机构的资金支持，占比为 19.6%，较 2015 年的 12.7%上涨了 6.9 个百分点。其他资金位列第三位，但较 2015 年比重出现大幅下滑。未获得引导基金支持的创业风险投资机构资本则主要来源于其他与政府部门，占比分别为 33.1%与 31.4%，相比 2015 年二者占比变化不大。总体来看，不论是否获得引导基金支持，政府部门的支持依旧是当前我国创业投资企业发展的重要推手。

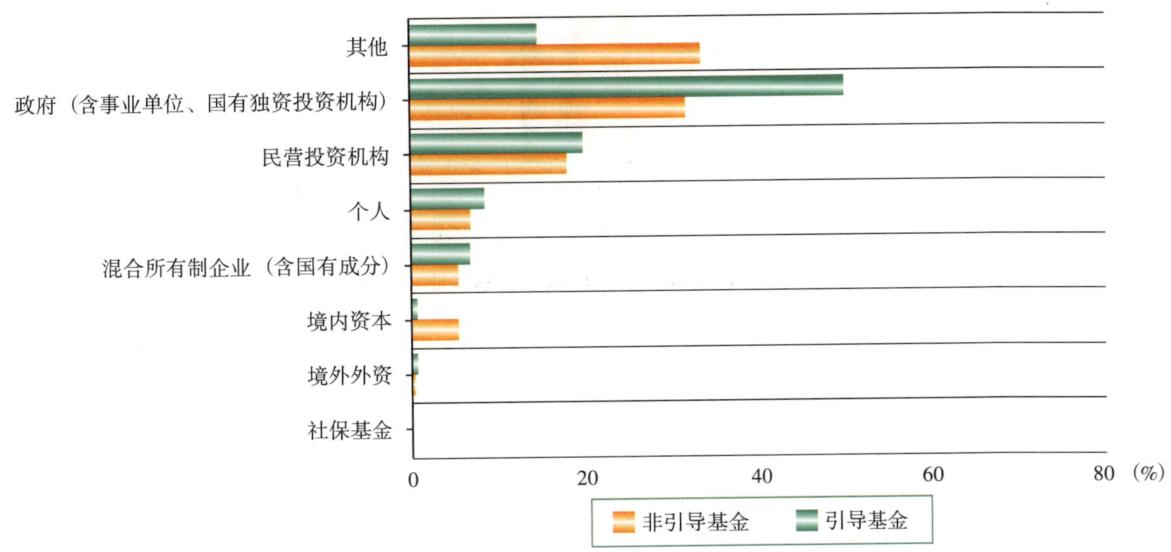

图 9-2　2016 年创业风险投资机构的资本构成（分类一）

按组织形式划分的 2016 年创业风险投资机构资本构成如图 9-3 所示。不难发现，非上市公司是创业投资机构的主要资金供给方。其中，在获得引导基金支持的创业风险投资机构资本构成中，非上市公司占比 55.3%，较 2015 年的 48.1%提高 7.2 个百分点。未获得引导基金支持的创业投资机构资本构成中，非上市公司占比 42.7%，但相比 2015 年的 56.8%出现明显下降。相比未获得引导基金支持的创业投资机构，获得引导基金支持的创业风险投资机构得到了更多非上市公司的资金支持。

按金融资本属性划分的 2016 年创业风险投资机构资本构成见图 9-4。结果显示：获得引导基金参与的创业投资机构资本构成中非金融资本占比 79.9%，其他金融资本占比 17.6%，而银行、信托、证券等金融资本占比微乎其微。未获得引导基金参与的创业投资机构资本构成中，非金融资本占比 68.5%，其他金融资本占比 24.1%。这一分布态势与 2015 年度一致，非金融资本更看重获得引导基金支持的创业风险投资机构。

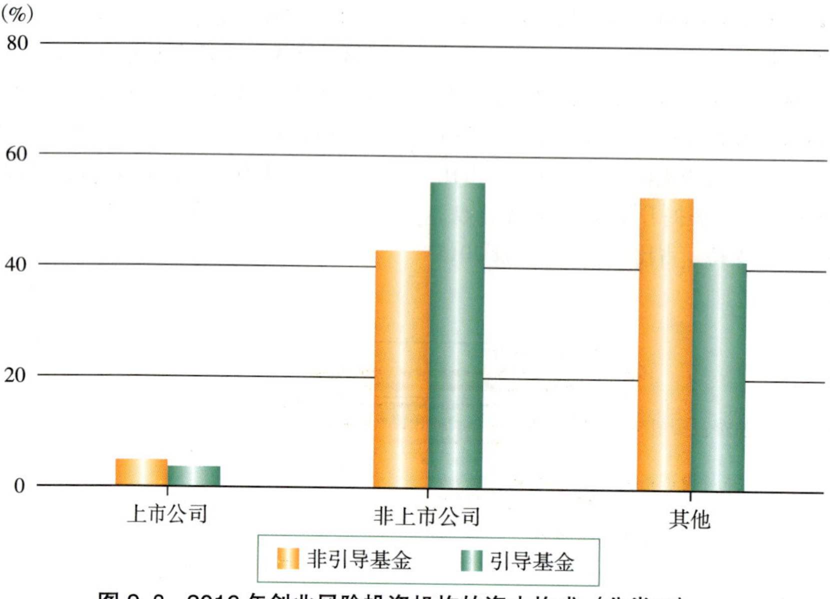

图 9-3　2016 年创业风险投资机构的资本构成（分类二）

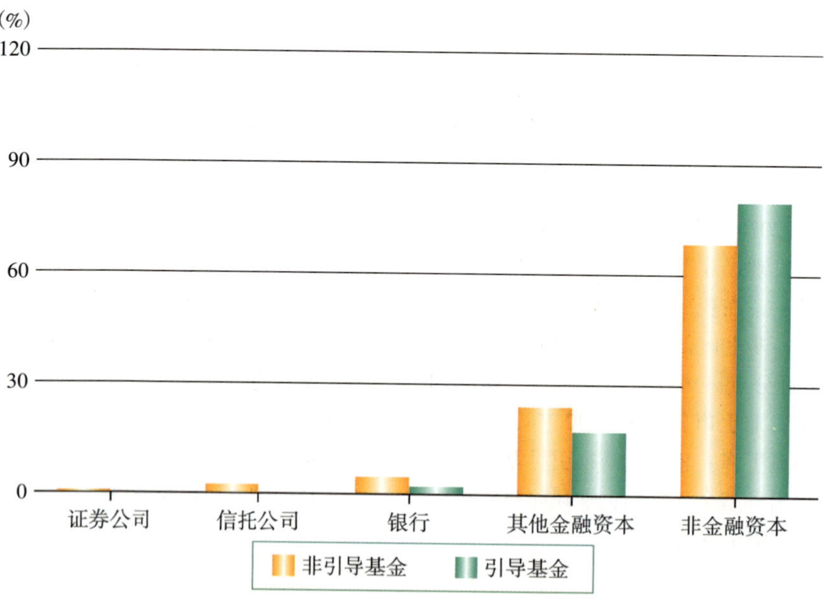

图 9-4　2016 年创业风险投资机构的资本构成（分类三）

9.2 中国创业风险投资引导基金投资项目的行业分布[①]

按照项目的投资金额进行统计，2016 年，引导基金支持的创业风险投资机构，其投资资金主要集中在其他行业、医药保健、传播与文化娱乐、新材料工业、传统制造业，这五个行业合计投资金额占比达到 54.8%。

按照投资项目数进行统计，引导基金支持的创业风险投资机构投资项目主要集中于其他行业、医药保健、网络产业、传播与文化娱乐、软件产业等，上述行业集中了当年 40.7%以上的项目。

总体上看，与投资金额分布相比，获得引导基金支持的创业风险投资机构在投资项目数量上更加分散（见图 9-5、图 9-6）。

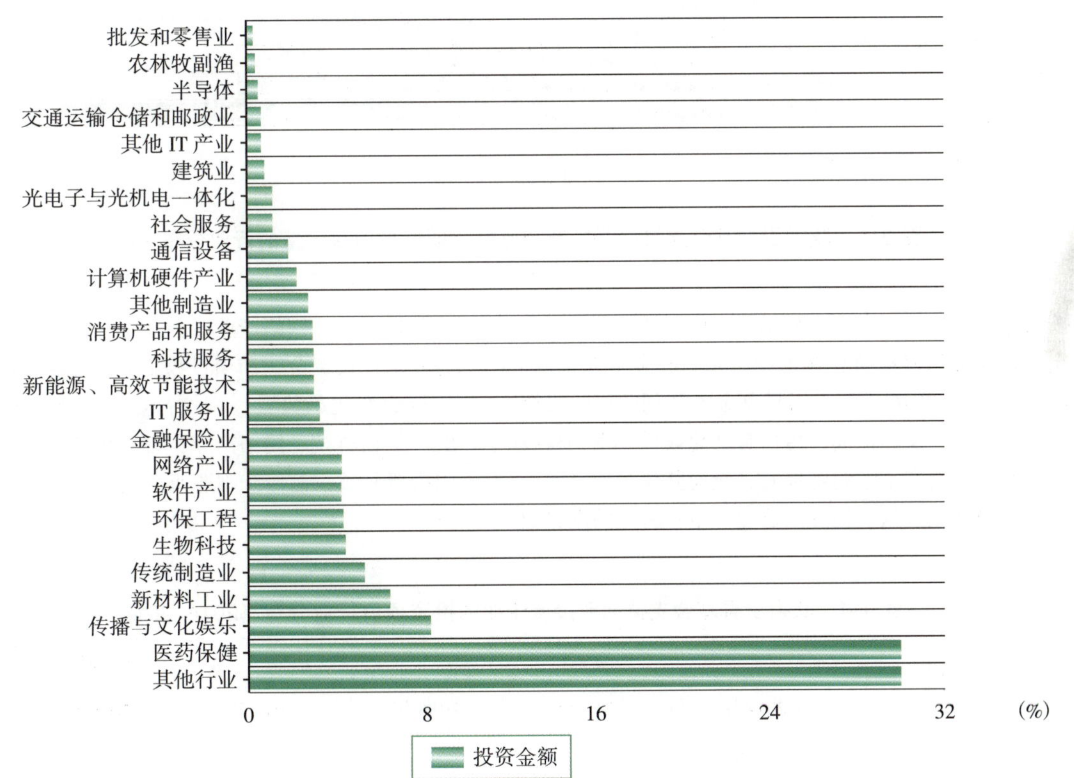

图 9-5 获得引导基金支持创业投资企业投资项目按投资金额的行业分布（2016）

① 2016 年有效样本为 710 份，2015 年有效样本为 1076 份，2014 年有效样本为 960 份。

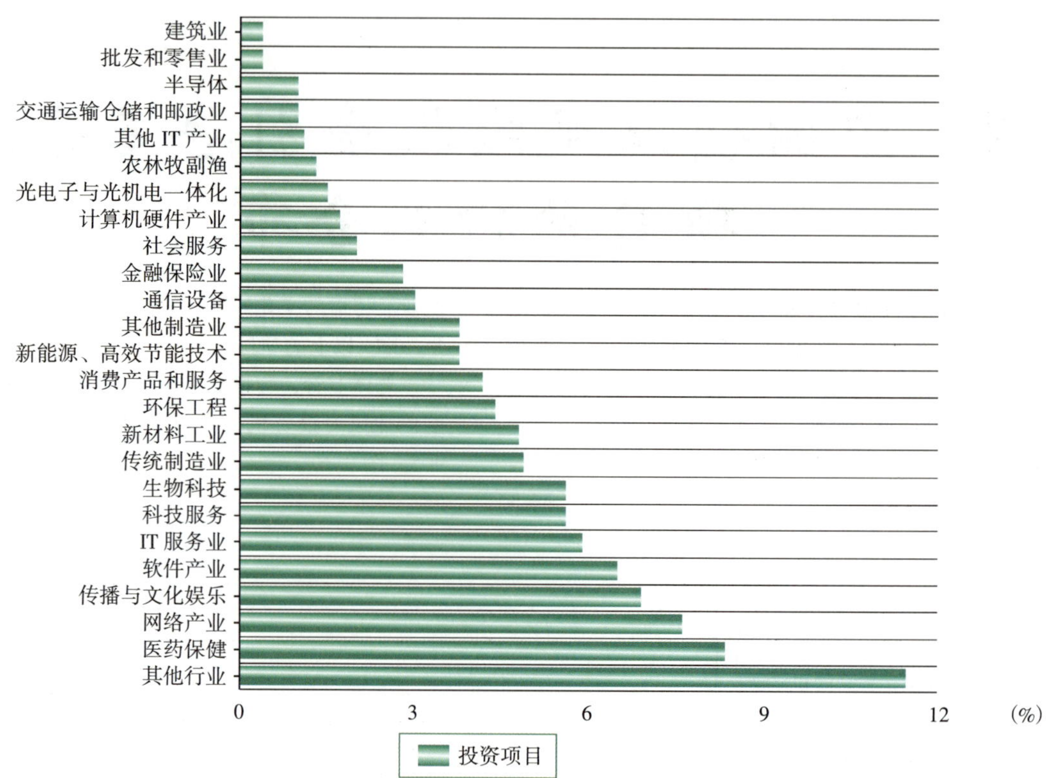

图 9-6 获得引导基金支持创业投资企业投资项目按项目数量的行业分布（2016）

按趋势进行统计，表 9-1 列示了 2014~2016 年获得引导基金支持创业风险投资机构的投资项目行业分布情况。与 2015 年相比，2016 年获得引导基金支持创业风险投资机构在其他行业、医药保健、传播与文化娱乐、生物科技在投资金额占比上有了大幅度提升；投向其他行业、医药保健、传播与文化娱乐、传统制造业、生物科技的项目数量明显增加。网络产业，新能源、高效节能技术，其他制造业则在投资金额和项目数量上均出现了回落。综合近三年行业变化趋势看，其他行业的占比大幅上升，医药保健、生物科技、网络产业，以及传播与文化娱乐始终是热门投资领域，而传统制造业的受关注程度则持续下滑。

表 9-1 获得引导基金支持创业投资企业的投资项目行业分布（2014~2016）① 单位：%

投资行业	投资金额			投资项目		
	2014 年	2015 年	2016 年	2014 年	2015 年	2016 年
其他行业	6.6	9.2	30.1	6.5	9.3	11.4
医药保健	14.8	5.2	8.3	7.2	4.6	8.3
传播与文化娱乐	4.1	4.2	6.5	4.6	4.7	6.9
新材料工业	5.4	12.3	5.4	6.8	6.3	4.8
传统制造业	11.7	2.7	4.5	4.7	2.3	4.9
生物科技	4.8	3.0	4.4	4.9	3.8	5.6

① 行业分类在国家统计局颁布的国民经济行业分类标准（GB/T 4754-2011）基础上适度调整，按照 2016 年投资金额比例由高到低列示。

续表

投资行业	投资金额			投资项目		
	2014 年	2015 年	2016 年	2014 年	2015 年	2016 年
环保工程	2.2	4.6	4.3	3.2	4.5	4.4
软件产业	3.0	4.9	4.2	7.5	7.4	6.5
网络产业	4.7	9.1	3.6	11.5	16.1	7.6
金融保险业	2.5	5.4	3.5	2.5	3.4	2.8
IT 服务业	5.1	3.8	3.3	7.0	6.0	5.9
新能源、高效节能技术	3.9	5.6	3.1	4.5	5.1	3.8
科技服务	2.2	2.4	3.1	2.6	3.5	5.6
消费产品和服务	2.7	4.2	3.0	3.3	3.2	4.2
其他制造业	4.1	5.4	2.8	4.2	5.3	3.8
计算机硬件产业	1.0	0.5	2.3	2.1	1.0	1.7
通信设备	3.5	3.0	1.9	2.8	2.3	3.0
社会服务	1.6	2.5	1.2	1.7	3.1	2.0
光电子与光机电一体化	4.4	1.3	1.2	3.6	1.9	1.5
建筑业	0.3	0.2	0.8	0.3	0.2	0.4
其他 IT 产业	1.4	0.3	0.7	1.7	1.0	1.1
交通运输仓储和邮政业	0.1	4.0	0.7	0.2	0.9	1.0
半导体	2.7	1.3	0.5	2.7	1.5	1.0
农林牧副渔	2.3	1.9	0.4	2.7	1.0	1.3
批发和零售业	0.0	0.1	0.3	0.7	0.2	0.4

与未获得引导基金支持创业风险投资机构的投资项目行业分布情况进行对比（见图 9-7）①，结果显示：2016 年获得引导基金支持的创业风险投资机构倾向于其他行业、医药保健、网络产业、传播与文化娱乐、软件产业、IT 服务业等领域；未获得引导基金支持的创业风险投资机构倾向于投资其他行业、网络产业、软件产业、IT 服务业、新材料工业、传播与文化娱乐等领域。

① 有效样本数为：获得引导基金支持创投为 710 份、未得引导基金支持创投为 1439 份。

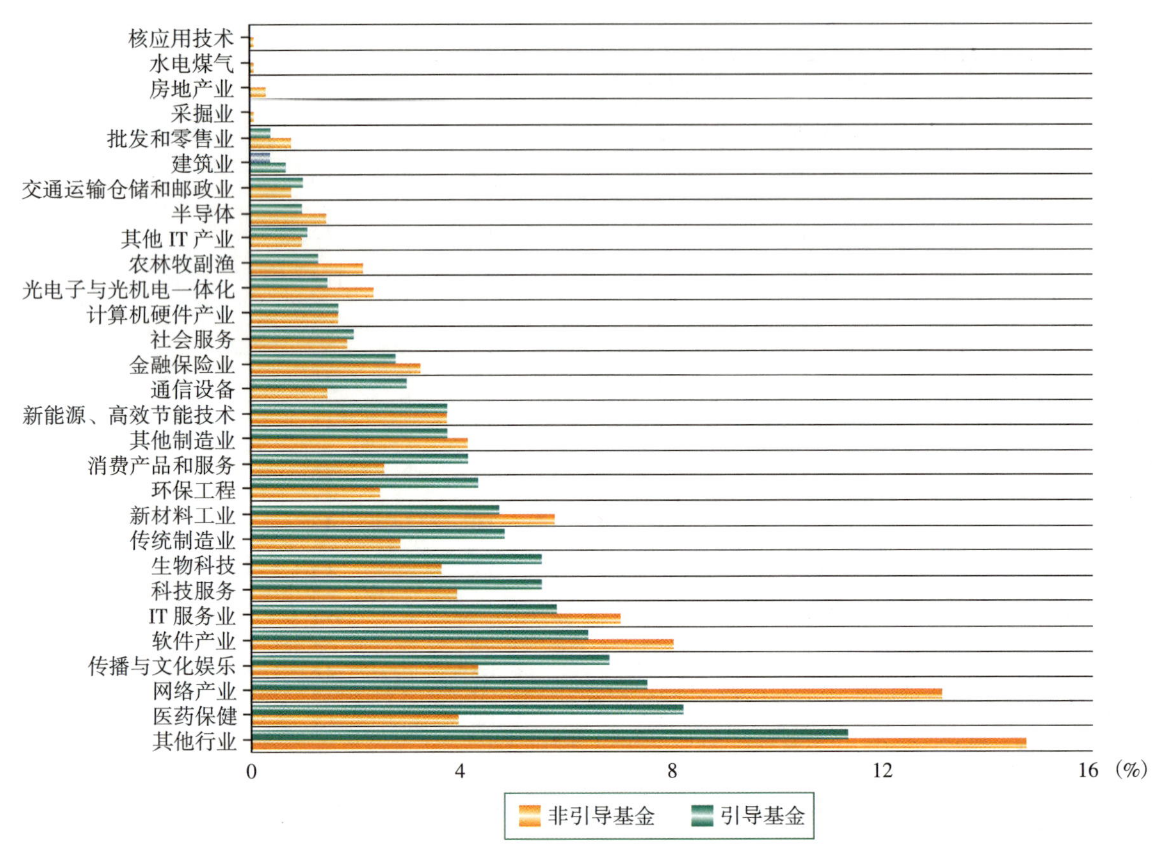

图 9-7 创业风险投资机构投资项目的行业分布（2016）

9.3 中国创业风险投资引导基金投资项目所处阶段①

2016 年度获得引导基金支持创业风险投资机构的投资项目所处阶段分布见表 9-2、图 9-8。统计结果显示：2016 年，获得引导基金支持的创业风险投资机构主要投资处于种子期和起步期项目，投资金额分别占 5.8% 和 41.3%，合计 47.1%。与 2015 年相比，种子期和起步期的投资金额占比合计大幅上升，其中投资于起步期的项目金额占比同比上涨超过 15 个百分点；种子期和起步期投资项目数量占比分别为 17.2% 和 34.3%，合计 51.5%。与 2015 年相比，二者占比合计小幅下降。这在一定程度上说明，2016 年获得引导基金支持的创业风险投资机构投资于创业早期的项目单笔金额同比有所增加。

表 9-2 获得引导基金支持创业风险投资机构的投资项目所处阶段（2016） 单位：%

成长阶段	种子期	起步期	成长（扩张）期	成熟（过渡）期	重建期
投资金额	5.8	41.3	38.2	13.3	1.3
投资项目	17.2	34.3	40.4	6.8	1.4

① 有效样本数为：获得引导基金支持创投为 738 份、未获得引导基金支持创投为 1381 份。

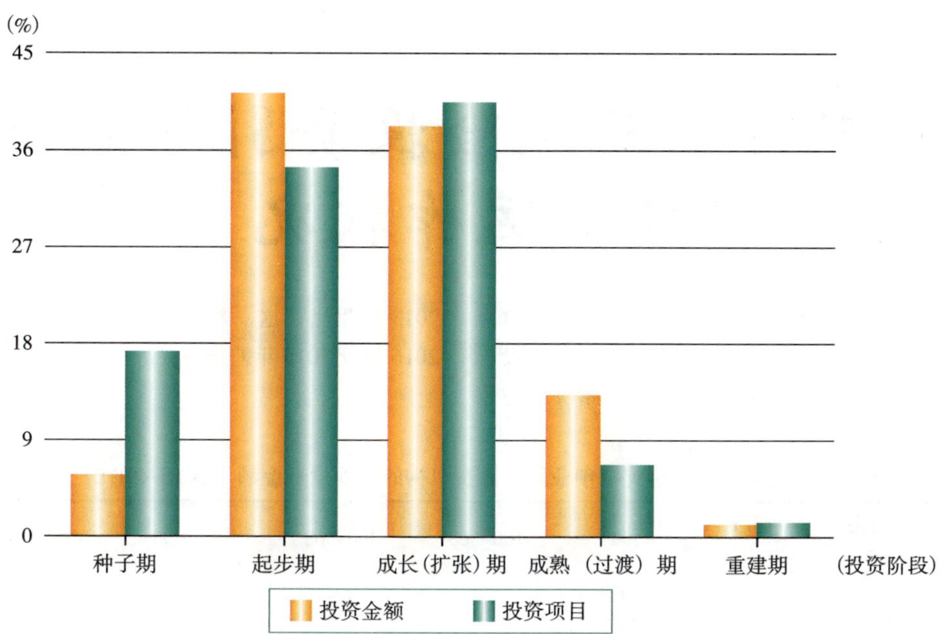

图 9-8 获得引导基金支持创业风险投资机构的投资项目所处阶段分布（2016）

数据显示，与未获得引导基金支持的创业风险投资机构相比，2016 年获得引导基金支持的创业风险投资机构更加倾向于投资种子期和起步期等初创期企业，投资金额占比明显高于未获得引导基金支持创业风险投资机构的 29.8%（见图 9-9）。

上述统计数据表明：近年来引导基金不断加大对创新能力强、市场前景好的中小企业的扶持力度，通过引导创业投资企业投资于种子期、起步期等初创期企业，较好地体现了其引导资金投资方向、扶持创新中小企业的政策导向。

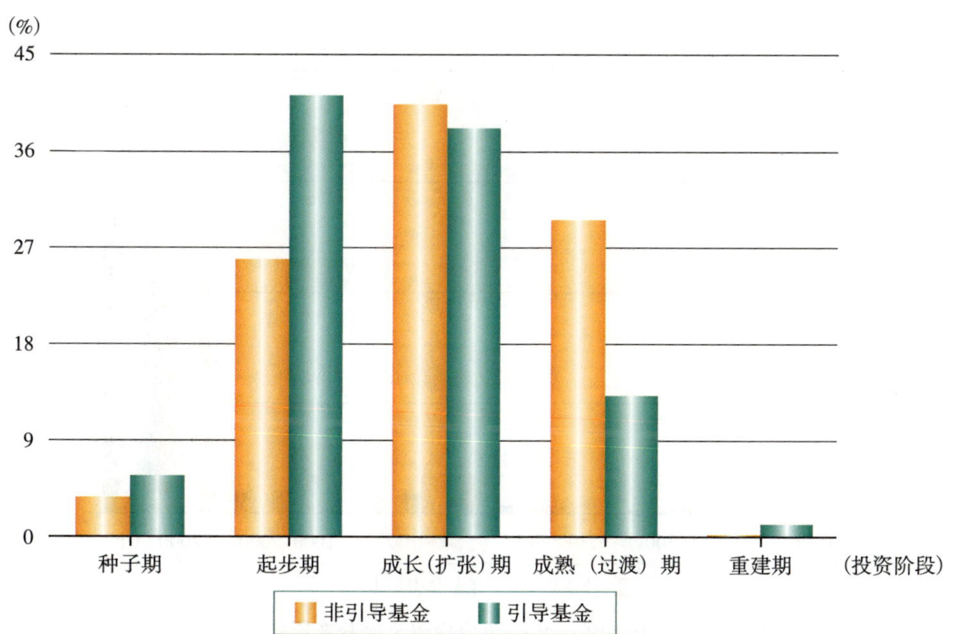

图 9-9 创业风险投资机构投资项目按投资金额计算的所处阶段分布对比（2016）

9.4 中国创业风险投资引导基金投资项目运作状况

2016年，获得引导基金支持的创业风险投资机构在单项投资金额上的分布情况见表9-3①。数据显示，单笔投资金额在1000万元以上的项目所占比重超过80%，与2015年相比，这一数据略有上升。在总体分布态势上，2016年较2015年差异不大。

表9-3 获得引导基金支持创业风险投资机构的单项投资金额（2015~2016） 单位：%

年份 \ 单项投资金额（万元）	<100	100~300	300~500	500~1000	1000~2000	>2000
2015	0.4	2.7	4.8	11.9	18.8	61.3
2016	0.3	2.4	4	11.1	19.2	63

2016年，获得引导基金支持的创业风险投资机构与未获得引导基金支持的创业风险投资机构在投资强度上存在一定差异。相比于获得引导基金支持的创业风险投资机构，未获得引导基金支持的创业风险投资机构单项投资金额在1000万元以上的比重更高，已超过90%。对于在500万~1000万元的单项投资，获得引导基金支持的创业风险投资机构较未获得引导基金支持的创业风险投资机构高5.6个百分点。这在一定程度上说明，获得引导基金支持创业投资企业的单项投资金额更小，更倾向于投资早前期项目（见图9-10）②。

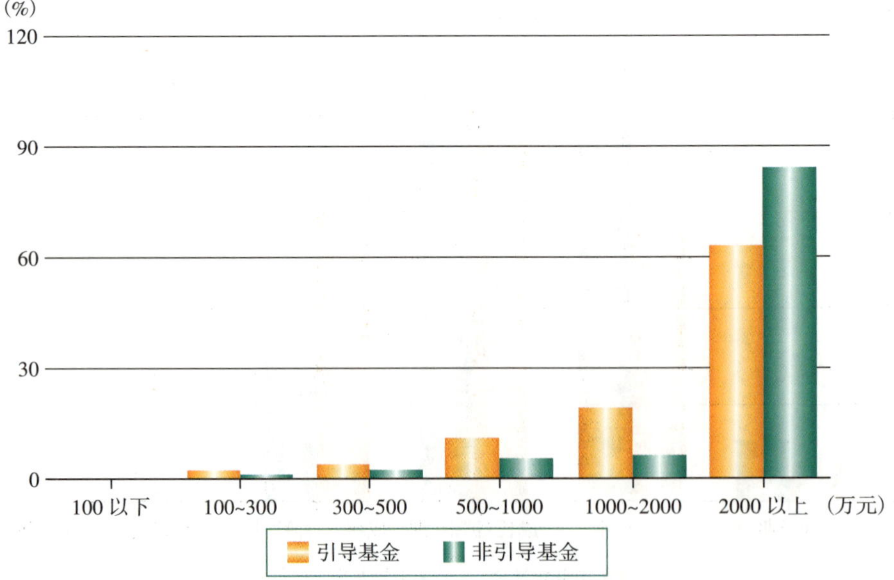

图9-10 创业风险投资机构单项投资金额分布比较（2016）

① 2016年有效样本数为794份，2015年有效样本数为1147份。
② 有效样本数为：获得引导基金支持创投为794份、未获引导基金支持创投为1381份。

统计数据显示，2016年获得引导基金支持的创业风险投资机构共计投资了198家高新技术企业，占总投资项目数的24.9%；未获得引导基金支持的创业风险投资机构共计投资了271家高新技术企业，占总投资项目数的17%。可以看出，获得引导基金支持的创业投资机构更倾向于选择高新技术企业投资。与2015年相比，获得引导基金支持的创业投资机构投资于高新技术企业的项目数占比有所下降，同时平均投资金额较2015年有所减少（见表9-4）①。

表9-4 创业风险投资机构投资项目中投资高新技术企业情况（2016）

企业分类	投资高新技术企业数（家）	投资高新技术企业项目数占比（%）	平均投资金额（万元）
未获得引导基金支持的VC	271	17	1241.4
获得引导基金支持的VC	198	24.9	1550.4

表9-5、图9-11对比了2016年获得引导基金支持创业风险投资机构和未获得引导基金支持创业风险投资机构的项目运作状况②。结果显示，获得引导基金支持创业风险投资机构的投资项目中股东回购、境内上市、被境内上市公司收购等比例相对较高，未获得引导基金支持企业投资项目中清算的比例更高。同时，不论是否获得引导基金支持，继续运行依然是2016年创业投资机构的主要选择，与2015年相比，这一比例继续提高。

表9-5 创业风险投资机构投资项目运作状况（2016） 单位：%

运作情况	继续运行	原股东（创业者）回购	境内上市	被境内上市公司收购	清算	管理层收购	境外上市	被境外收购
获得引导基金支持的VC	75.4	8.6	7.1	5.0	1.7	1.6	0.4	0.1
未获得引导基金支持的VC	76.9	7.7	6.4	4.7	3	0.9	0.3	0.1

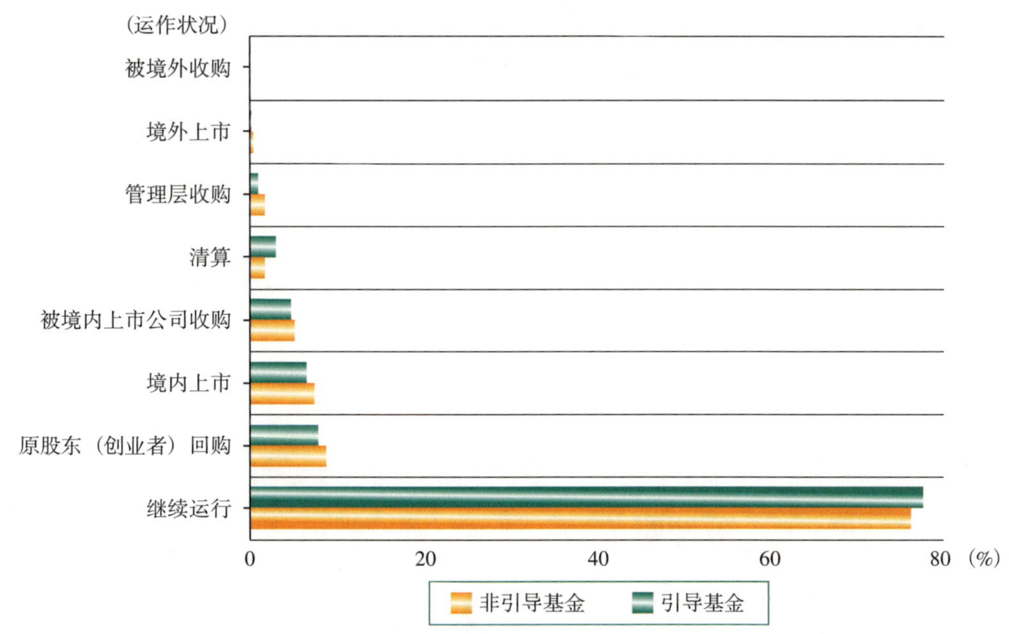

图9-11 创业风险投资机构投资项目运作状况（2016）

① 有效样本数为：获得引导基金支持创投为198份、未获得引导基金支持创投为271份。
② 有效样本数为：获得引导基金支持创投为316份、未获得引导基金支持创投为1085份。

附录 1　2016 年美国创业风险投资综述

一、总体概括

近年来，随着风险投资公司、风险投资基金和资产管理规模增加，美国风险投资行业呈现稳步增长。2016 年数据显示，现有 898 家风险投资管理公司，管理着 1562 家活跃的风险投资基金，管理资产规模约 3330 亿美元。

2016 年当年，253 个风险投资基金募集了 416 亿美元投入到有前途的初创公司，创十年新高。2016 年，少数基金集中了大量管理资金，推动了风险投资管理基金规模中位值高达 7500 万美元（自 2008 年以来最高）。

2016 年，7750 多家公司获得了 691 亿美元的风险投资资金，这些初创公司拥有近 37 万雇员。其中，首轮融资下滑至 2340 家公司，总额达 66 亿美元。天使/种子期和早期风险投资交易数及金额分别占到 81%和 44%。软件行业吸引了大量风险投资（330 亿美元，占风投资金总额的 48%）。

2016 年，风险投资的退出环境仍具挑战，仅 39 家公司进行首次公开募股（IPO）。全年共 726 家企业实现退出，其中，披露的并购交易数占 82%，披露的退出值共计 468 亿美元。

二、行业资源

风险投资行业一直持续增长。2016 年，数据显示，在过去 8 年里，现存的风险投资管理企业共 898 家。在 2016 年底，这 898 家风险投资公司管理了 1562 家的风险投基金，其管理资产约 3330 亿美元。

风险投资行业的增长与美国快速成长的初创公司的需求相吻合，这些初创公司在风险投资公司的运营资金和战略指导与帮助下，开发创新产品和创新服务。2016 年，2105 家风险投资公司在美国的一家创业公司完成了至少一项投资，其中 738 家公司参与了初创公司的第一轮机构融资。同时，风险投资基金上升至 7500 万美元（见附表 1–1）。

附表 1–1　美国创业风险投资（VC）总体情况统计

年份 / 指标	2004	2010	2016
现存 VC 机构数量（家）	872	898	898
现存 VC 基金数量（家）	1670	1294	1562
首次 VC 基金募集数量（家）	37	34	22
当年募集资金的 VC 基金数量（家）	158	153	253

续表

指标＼年份	2004	2010	2016
VC 当年募集的资本额（十亿美元）	17.6	19.6	41.6
VC 管理资本金额（十亿美元）	166.9	251.5	333.5
平均 VC 管理资本额（百万美元）	110.5	215.5	243.6
截至目前的 VC 基金平均规模（百万美元）	116.5	134.8	138.3
当年新增 VC 基金平均规模（百万美元）	117.1	137.8	170.6
VC 管理机构管理资金规模中位值（百万美元）	190.6	197.4	130.9
截至目前 VC 基金规模中位值（百万美元）	51.0	56.0	50.8
当年 VC 基金规模中位值（百万美元）	50.0	45.3	75.0
截至目前最大 VC 基金募集额（百万美元）	2322.0	4300.0	4300.0

这一行业增长和创业需求连续三年为企业投资了近 700 亿美元。风险投资水平在 2015 年达到顶峰之后，2016 年进行重新调整，并恢复稳定的投资步伐。此外，募资和退出也对美国风险投资生态系统的整体健康产生重要影响。

在全球范围内，美国继续吸引大量的风险投资。不过，近十年来，由于世界各国不断完善国内创业生态系统后，美国的风险投资份额比十年前的水平有所下降（见附表 1-2、附表 1-3、附表 1-4）。

附表 1-2　美国风险投资募资在全球风险投资的占比　　单位：%

分类＼年份	2004	2005	2006	2007	2008	2009	2010	2011	2012	2013	2014	2015	2016
金额	77	74	73	64	63	53	53	52	62	66	72	64	65
项目	68	60	48	46	44	37	40	34	46	57	69	65	68

资料来源：NVCA 2017 年鉴，PitchBook 提供数据。

附表 1-3　美国风险投资交易量在全球风险投资的占比　　单位：%

分类＼年份	2004	2005	2006	2007	2008	2009	2010	2011	2012	2013	2014	2015	2016
金额	85	81	81	78	76	75	69	70	69	69	64	56	54
项目	77	73	69	68	68	67	64	62	61	59	58	58	60

资料来源：NVCA 2017 年鉴，PitchBook 提供数据。

附表 1-4　美国风险投资退出在全球风险投资的占比　　单位：%

分类＼年份	2004	2005	2006	2007	2008	2009	2010	2011	2012	2013	2014	2015	2016
金额	77	63	70	69	71	65	70	69	86	58	71	63	68
项目	67	63	62	60	61	64	61	61	63	60	57	55	57

资料来源：NVCA 2017 年鉴，PitchBook 提供数据。

三、资金募集

2016 年，美国风险投资行业迎来十多年来募资最快的一年，与 2015 年相比，2016 年风险投资募资增长了 18%，共有 253 家基金募集了 416 亿美元，这证明了风险投资在财务回报和创新经济方面吸引了越来越多的有限合伙人。

尽管是风险投资基金募集资金辉煌的一年，但 2016 年交易的基金总额连续第二年略有下降。全年共有七家公司筹集风险投资基金 10 亿美元，大约占总募集资金总量的 1/4，推动了年度风险投资基金规模中位数增加到 7500 万美元，这是自 2008 年以来的最高的中位数（见附图 1-1、附表 1-5）。

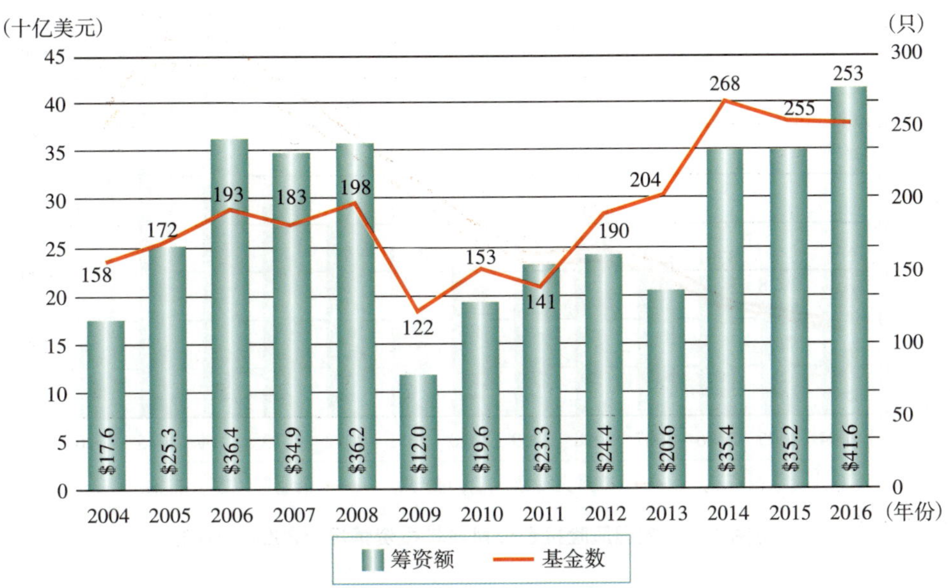

附图 1-1 美国创业风险投资基金募集情况（2004~2016）

附表 1-5 2016 年十大美国风险投资基金

基金名	基金规模（百万美元）	交易日期	基金所在州
TCVIX	2500	8/1/16	加利福尼亚州
安德森·霍洛维茨基金 V	1576	6/10/16	加利福尼亚州
创始人基金 VI	1300	3/17/16	加利福尼亚州
诺维斯特风险投资公司 XIII	1200	1/20/16	加利福尼亚州
格雷洛克 XV	1105	10/11/16	加利福尼亚州
KPCB 数据成长型基金 III	1000	6/29/16	加利福尼亚州
GSRGo 全球基金	1000	4/18/16	加利福尼亚州
GGV 风险投资 VI	900	4/12/16	加利福尼亚州
General Catalyst 集团 VIII	845	2/4/16	马萨诸塞州
光速风险投资基金 XI	715	3/8/16	加利福尼亚州

资料来源：NVCA 2017 年鉴，PitchBook 提供数据。

四、投资活动

截至 2016 年上半年，美国风险投资活动继续以 2015 年风起云涌的风波投入高潮，风险投资活动达到顶峰。但是，下半年的活动开始放缓。2016 年整年，投资者在美国投资了 691 亿多美元，7750 多家公司募集 8136 笔资金（见附图 1–2）。

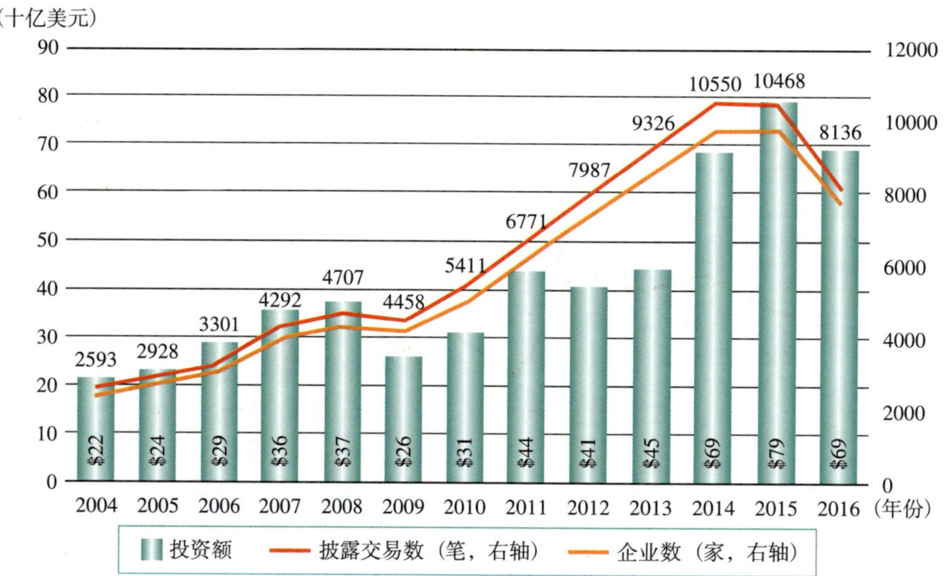

附图 1–2 美国风险投资公司当年投资情况（2004~2016）

（一）投资行业

2016 年，软件公司吸引了大量的风险投资，共有 3100 家公司获得 330 亿美元投资，相当于总投资的 48%和达成交易的 38%。在软件领域，一些社交/平台软件公司一马当先，其中包括交通移动应用 Uber Technologies、照片信息移动应用 Snap，按需乘车和共享乘车平台 Lyft，房屋租赁市场 Airbnb 和商业智能云服务平台 Domo。2016 年，虽然风险投资的整个行业有所下降，但软硬件信息技术领域却是唯一同比增长的行业。

然而，生命科学公司（制药与生物技术和医疗设备和用品）的投资项目（1016 项）和风险投资（116.5 亿美元）同比下降。2016 年，该领域内风险投资交易的份额上升到 12.5%。其投资企业类型包括：Moderna、遗传性疾病制药商、血友病和补血因子以及肿瘤学；人类寿命、基因组学和细胞治疗的诊断和治疗技术开发人员；CVRx、治疗高血压和心脏衰竭的可植入型技术等（见附表 1–6）。

附表 1–6 按行业分类统计的投资状况（2016）

行业分类	交易额（十亿美元）	占比（%）
软件	32.98	47.7
制药与生物技术	7.79	11.3
医疗设备和用品	3.86	5.6

续表

行业分类	交易额（十亿美元）	占比（%）
商业服务	3.46	5.0
医疗服务和系统	3.32	4.8
IT 硬件	2.52	3.6
消费品与娱乐	2.13	3.1
媒体	1.42	2.1
能源	1.35	2.0
其他行业	10.27	14.9

（二）投资阶段

与 2015 年相比，在每个投资阶段，2016 年达成的交易数量和投资金额均有所下降。天使/种子阶段的投资分别占投资数量的 51%，投资金额的 9.6%。2016 年，1525 家后期投资的资金达到 384 亿美元，同比分别下降 14%和 17%。此外，由于投资者对约 2500 家早期投资（同比下降 17%）投入了 240 亿美元（同比下降 2%），所以对刚刚起步的公司的投资资金下降幅度较小（见附表 1-7、附图 1-3）。

虽然去年的天使/种子投资和早期投资有所减少，但交易的规模却增加了，这使得天使/种子投资的中位值从 2015 年的 80 万美元增长到 2016 年的 100 万美元。同样，早期投资的中位值从 2015 年的 450 万美元增长到 2016 年的 530 万美元。

附表 1-7 美国风险投资的当年投资阶段（2004~2016）（按交易量划分）

阶段＼年份	2004	2005	2006	2007	2008	2009	2010	2011	2012	2013	2014	2015	2016
天使/种子期	234	292	431	744	902	1141	1672	2603	3556	4641	5452	5683	4115
早期	1452	1660	1812	2224	2322	1941	2223	2519	2707	2873	3147	3013	2496
后期	907	976	1058	1324	1483	1376	1516	1649	1724	1812	1951	1772	1525

资料来源：NVCA 2017 年鉴，PitchBook 提供数据。

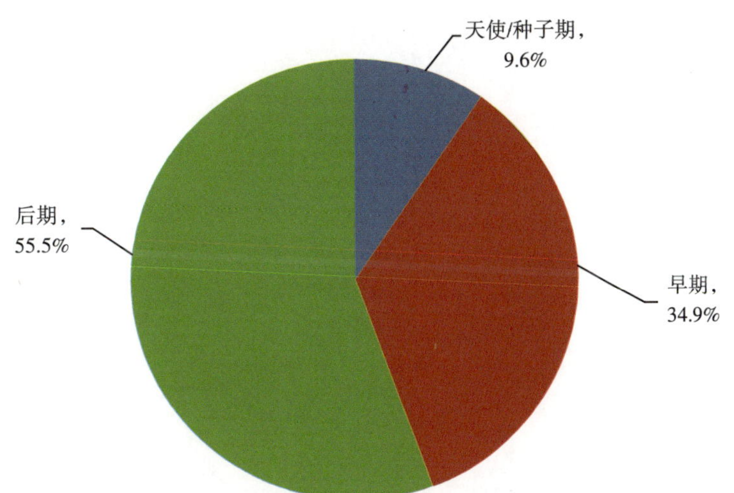

附图 1-3 创业投资基金的投资阶段（按资金占比）（2016）

资料来源：NVCA 2017 年鉴，PitchBook 提供数据。

（三）投资地区

2016 年，美国 50 个州和哥伦比亚特区，226 个大都市统计区，以及 435 个国会区中的 386 个地区分布了风险投资基金。其中，加利福尼亚州、马萨诸塞州和纽约州的创业公司吸引了最多的风险投资，占据了 2016 年美国风投投资资金的 75%；然而，三个地区的交易数总量的比例下降到了 52%（见附表 1–8）。

附表 1–8 美国风险资本投资前十大地区（2016）

地 区	企业数量（家）	交易数量（家）	投资额（百万美元）
加利福尼亚州	2658	2801	38060.29
纽约州	875	928	7361.49
马萨诸塞州	508	535	6099.65
得克萨斯州	439	456	1989.26
华盛顿州	292	311	1579.69
科罗拉多州	241	255	911.88
伊利诺伊州	239	247	1282.86
宾夕法尼亚州	228	235	1090.20
佛罗里达州	208	212	1678.32
北卡罗来纳州	143	148	764.86

除了国内的风险投资，美国以外的风险投资活动一直呈上升趋势。在 2015 年达到顶峰后，2016 年全球风险投资高达 1270 亿美元，这表明，各国看到了风险投资活动为其经济带来的价值，并推动国内创新。近年来，虽然全球风险投资总体有所增长，但美国的份额并没有以同样的速度增加。在 20 世纪 90 年代，美国占全球风险投资的 90%以上。而到 2016 年，美国创业公司投资 691 亿美元，相当于全球份额的 54%。

（四）投资轮次

从投资轮次分布来看，2016 年，美国风险创业投资中获得首轮投资的项目为 2340 项，金额 566 亿美元，分别占比 29.8%、47.5%（见附图 1–4、附图 1–5）。其中，软件行业获得了最大金额的首轮投资，达到 181 亿美元，其次是其他行业、生物医药行业等。

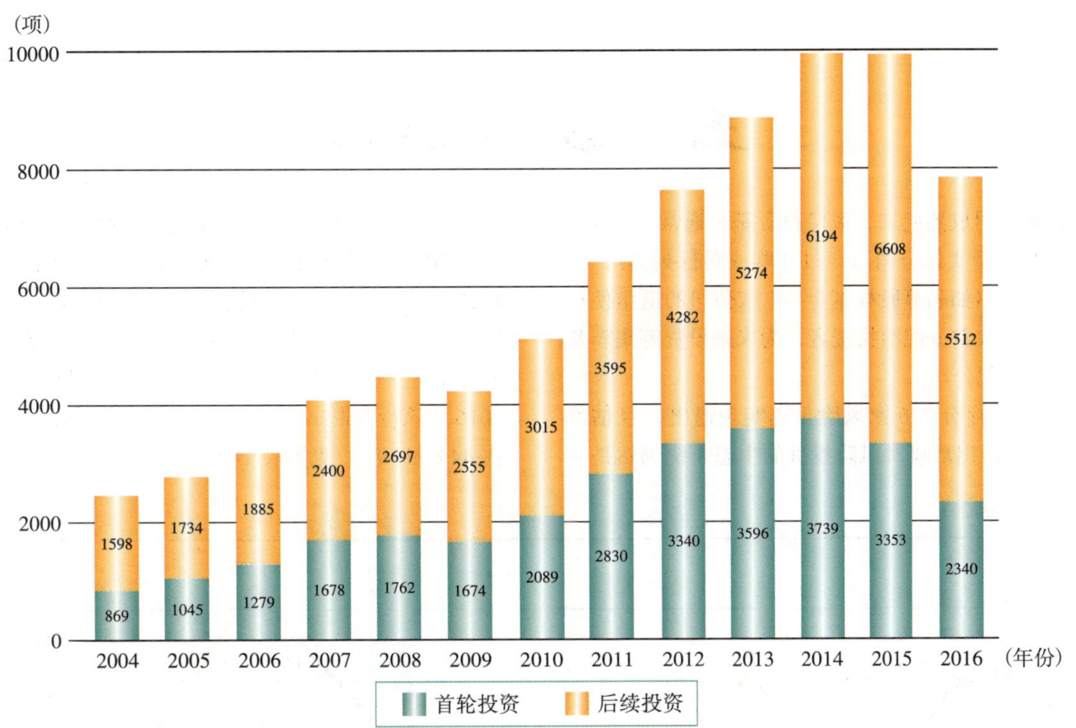

附图 1-4 美国风险投资的首轮投资与后续投资（2004~2016）（按交易量划分）

资料来源：NVCA 2017 年鉴，PitchBook 提供数据。

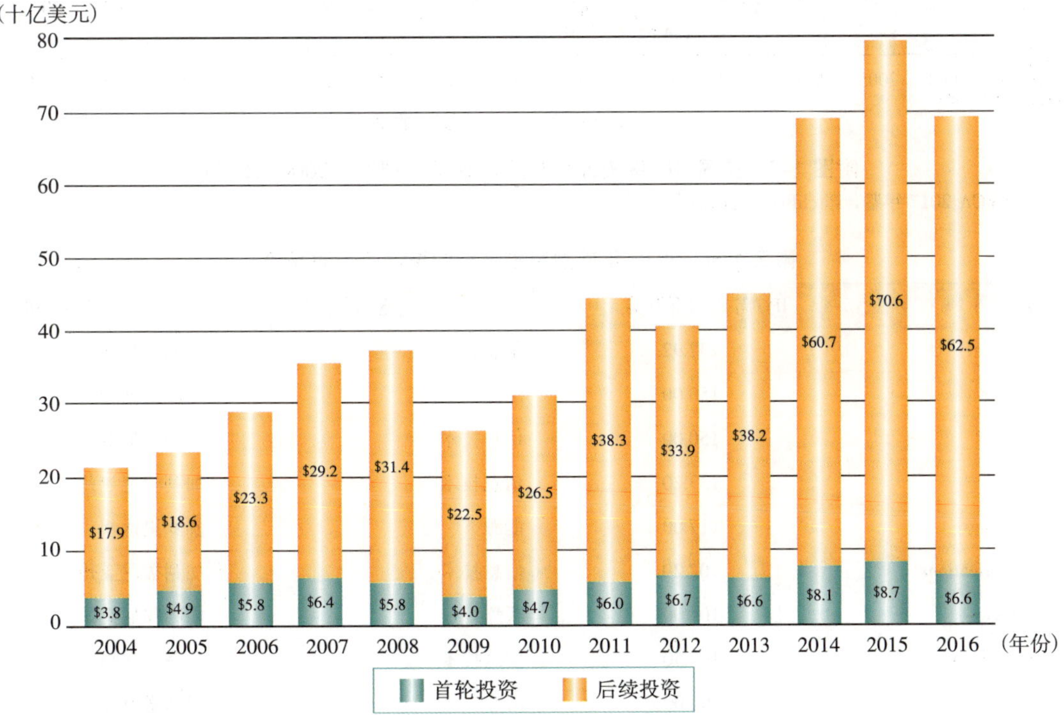

附图 1-5 美国风险投资的首轮投资与后续投资（2004~2016）（按交易金额划分）

资料来源：NVCA 2017 年鉴，PitchBook 提供数据。

五、投资退出

一旦创业公司成熟起来，风险投资基金通常通过 IPO 或将其出售给大型实体公司（通过并购或同行买卖），或出售给金融买家（如私募股权基金）。该公司的退出使得风险投资公司将收益分配给投资者，为未来投资筹集新基金，并投资下一代公司。

2016 年，尽管有 726 家风险投资实现退出，且估价 468 亿美元，但退出环境对风险投资的生态系统仍然是一个挑战。2016 年，共有 39 家美国风投支持的企业成功进行了 IPO，募集了 293 亿美元，产生了 161 亿美元的投后价值（见附图 1-6）。投资这些企业的风投基金从早期投资到 IPO 退出，平均时间为 8.3 年，最高达到 13 年之久。药品和生物技术行业连续四年在 IPO 退出中占比最高，2016 年该行业退出企业 17 家，IPO 募资 12 亿美元，分别占 44%和 39%（见附表 1-9）。

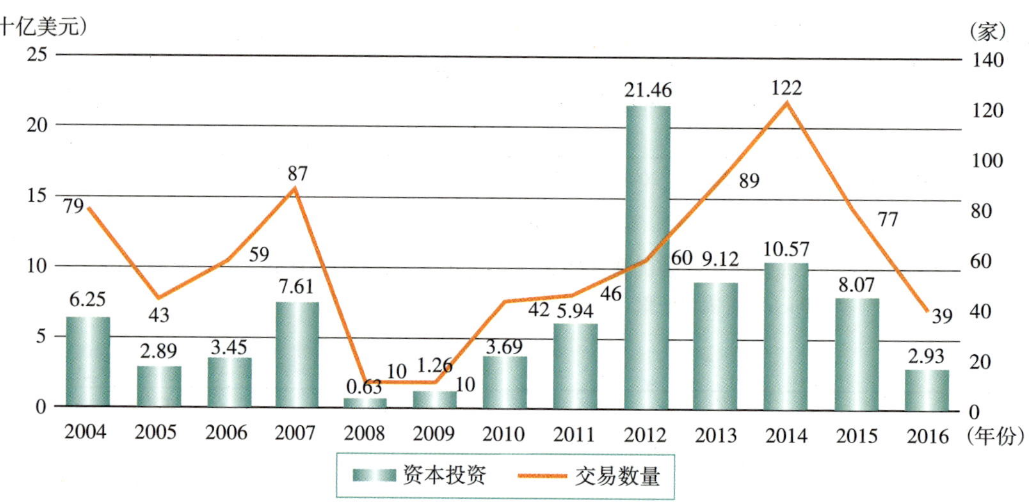

附图 1-6 美国风险投资公司支持企业 IPO 情况（2004~2016）

资料来源：NVCA 2017 年鉴，PitchBook 提供数据。

附表 1-9 2016 年美国风投支持的排行前十的 IPO

公 司	IPO 筹资（百万美元）	行业领域	地 区
Nutani	237.92	信息技术	加利福尼亚州
Intellia Therapeutics	150.00	医疗	马萨诸塞州
Twilio	150.00	信息技术	加利福尼亚州
Coupa Software	133.20	信息技术	加利福尼亚州
AquaVenture Holdings	117.00	能源	佛罗里达州
Quantenna Communications	107.20	信息技术	加利福尼亚州
iRhythm Technologies	107.00	医疗	加利福尼亚州
Acacia Communications	103.50	信息技术	马萨诸塞州
AveXis	96.00	医疗	伊利诺伊州
Apptio	96.00	信息技术	华盛顿州

资料来源：NVCA 2017 年鉴，PitchBook 提供数据。

尽管 39 家风险投资基金支持的企业 IPO 占去年所有 IPO 的 28%，与 2014 年和 2015 年相当，但是风险投资企业支持的 IPO 数量下滑仍然是一个大问题，NVCA 的政务团队正在积极地与政策制定者合作，向风投支持公司重新开放资本市场。不幸的是，数据显示，美国在 2000 年后的 IPO 平均数值低于 2000 年前的一半。同时，20 年来，上市公司总数下降了一半。场内市场在帮助创业公司成长和发展方面发挥关键作用，资本市场的健康对美国经济的发展至关重要。至少在短期内，2017 年 IPO 窗口保持相对较为活跃的乐观景象，大约 20 家风投支持公司目前在注册 IPO（见附表 1-10）。

附表 1-10　美国风投支持的 IPO 值及特征

年份	IPO	交易值（百万美元）	交易中值（百万美元）	交易均值（百万美元）	后期估值（百万美元）	后期中值（百万美元）	后期均值（百万美元）	首次风投至退出中期	首次风投至退出均期
2004	79	6250.6	49.8	84.5	41826.0	220.8	580.9	5.16	5.20
2005	43	2892.0	53.8	72.3	8628.8	199.3	227.1	4.77	4.52
2006	59	3452.9	55.5	63.9	13908.9	219.8	252.9	4.79	5.09
2007	87	7611.2	75.0	96.3	33492.2	333.8	418.7	5.17	5.54
2008	10	626.2	61.8	69.6	2773.4	237.0	396.2	2.82	4.61
2009	10	1255.0	86.6	125.5	4824.2	342.1	536.0	7.32	7.50
2010	42	3691.9	69.8	87.9	15903.4	278.7	378.7	6.90	7.38
2011	46	5938.9	87.7	138.1	45877.3	423.6	1092.3	5.88	6.87
2012	60	1457.5	81.0	390.1	114752.5	360.3	206.8	7.14	7.64
2013	89	9116.7	75.0	107.3	52808.8	319.5	628.7	6.77	7.30
2014	122	10565.5	65.6	88.0	52081.5	249.4	437.7	6.85	7.04
2015	77	8072.7	74.8	104.8	40814.5	289.5	551.5	6.94	6.75
2016	39	2928.5	70.5	75.1	16079.3	250.6	412.3	8.27	7.61

资料来源：NVCA 2017 年鉴，PitchBook 提供数据。

2016 年，687 家风险投资基金披露了并购情况，其中 177 家披露并购总值达 439 亿美元。披露的并购公司中值在 2016 年达到 9000 万美元，创下 12 年最高。据报告，软件行业约占并购数量的一半，其次是生命科学行业（包括制药和生物技术，以及医疗保健设备等），以及商业服务行业（见附图 1-7、附表 1-11）。

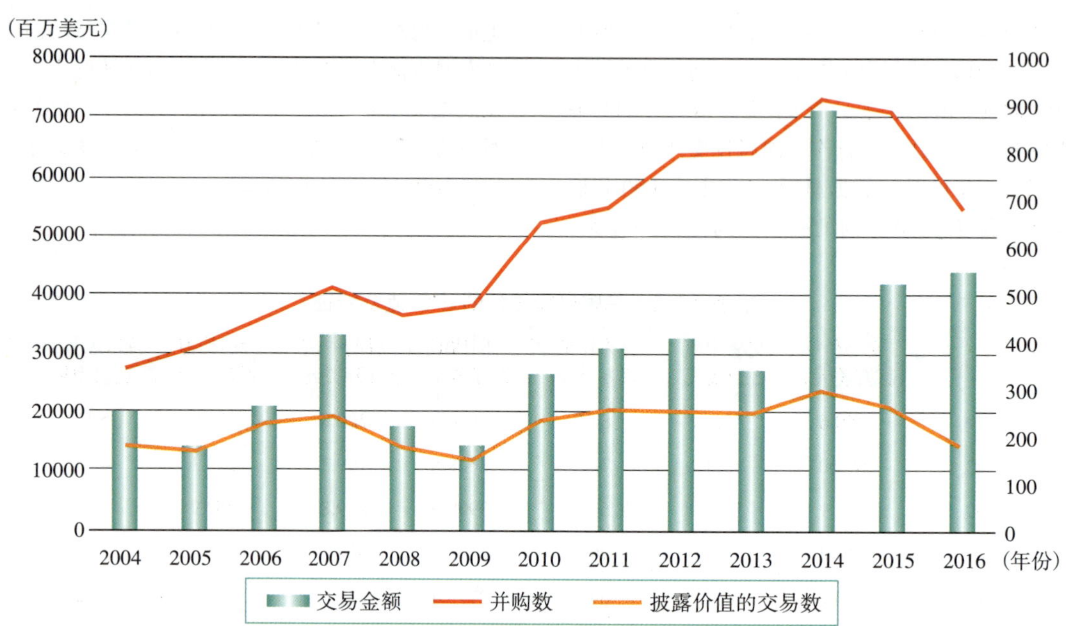

附图 1-7 美国风投支持的并购活动

资料来源：NVCA 2017 年鉴，PitchBook 提供数据。

附表 1-11 美国风投支持的并购交易及特征

年份	并购交易数（项）	披露并购数（项）	交易值（百万美元）	平均交易值（百万美元）	交易中值（百万美元）	从投资到退出时间的中位值（年）	平均投资时间（年）
2004	341	179	19745.0	110.3	43.7	3.90	4.07
2005	386	166	14086.9	84.9	38.1	4.74	4.59
2006	451	227	20666.5	91.0	44.7	4.70	4.72
2007	515	245	33180.1	135.4	50.0	4.57	4.82
2008	455	177	17523.4	99.0	36.0	4.75	4.89
2009	472	146	14437.0	98.9	25.0	4.34	4.86
2010	651	232	26583.8	114.6	36.5	4.36	5.00
2011	687	257	30956.5	120.5	50.0	4.21	4.89
2012	799	252	32478.5	128.9	48.5	4.51	4.99
2013	796	247	27124.0	109.8	37.3	4.08	5.05
2014	918	297	71176.4	239.7	52.0	4.44	5.29
2015	884	258	42299.5	164.0	50.0	4.31	5.42
2016	687	177	43894.6	248.0	90.0	4.67	5.83

附表 1-12　2016 年美国风投支持排名前十的并购公司

公司名称	交易规模（百万美元）	行业领域	地区
Stemcentrx	10000.00	医疗	加利福尼亚州
Jet	3300.00	消费产品和服务（B2C）	新泽西州
Jasper	1400.00	信息技术	加利福尼亚州
Afferent Pharmaceuticals	1250.00	医疗	加利福尼亚州
Cruise Automation	1000.00	信息技术	加利福尼亚州
Dollar Shave Club	1000.00	消费产品和服务（B2C）	加利福尼亚州
Chase Pharmaceuticals	1000.00	医疗	哥伦比亚特区
Telogis	900.00	信息技术	加利福尼亚州
Krux Digital	800.00	信息技术	加利福尼亚州
IronPlanet	758.50	消费产品和服务（B2C）	加利福尼亚州

资料来源：本文数据均由美国风险投资协会 National Venture Capital Association 提供。

附录 2　2016 年欧洲创业风险投资回顾

2016 年，欧洲私募股权基金超过 1200 多家，其中，88%的企业披露了管理资本，达到 6000 亿欧元。

一、资金募集

2016 年，欧洲整个私募股权市场总筹资达到 745 亿欧元，与 2015 年相比增加了 37%，是自 2008 年以来欧洲的最高水平，近 400 只基金获得了资本，较 2015 年下跌了 9%（见附表 2-1）。其中，养老基金所占比最大，占 34%，之后是母基金（18%），保险公司（12%）、主权财富基金（10%）和家族私人个体（9%），且来自欧洲之外的机构投资者占了 40%。

2016 年，欧洲风险投资基金上升至 64 亿欧元，达到了 2008 年以来的最高水平。这个趋势是由于较大规模风险投资基金增加所导致的（见附图 2-1）。45 只风险投资基金中有 13 只在最终交割时达到了 1 亿欧元以上，并占了总筹资金额的 80%。按资金来源分类，政府机构占了 25%，家族和私人个体占 20%，母基金和其他资产占 15%，企业投资者占 15%。欧洲以外的机构投资者占了 12%（见附图 2-2）。

附表 2-1　欧洲私募股权投资市场募集资金主要特征（2016）

2016	所有私募股权基金	风险投资	并购	成长资本
新募集基金额（亿欧元）	745	64	563	39
新募集基金数（只）	393	116	81	59

资料来源：投资欧洲/EDC。

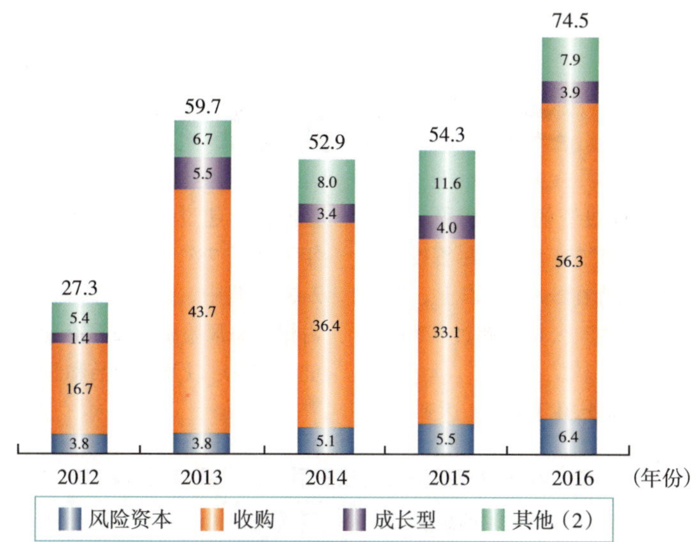

附图 2–1 欧洲私募股权基金募集情况（2012~2016）

注：其他（2）包括了夹层基金和通用基金。

资料来源：投资欧洲/ EDC。

按资金来源划分，2016 年，欧洲创业风险投资资金募集中，政府出资占主导，占比 25%，较 2015 年下降 6 个百分点（见附图 2–2）。

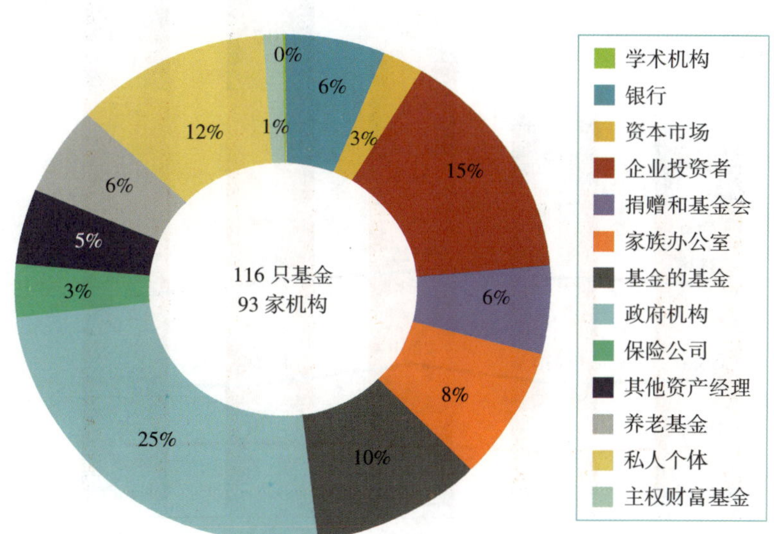

附图 2–2 欧洲创业风险投资募集基金来源（2016）

二、投资活动

与 2015 年相比，欧洲所有股权投资的总金额稳定在 537 亿欧元，这是自 2008 年以来的第二高水平。尽管投资公司的数量减少了 7%，但是仍保持在 5900 家以上，其中，83%的公司是中小型企业，且欧洲公司中超过 1/3 的投资金额来自跨国投资（见附表 2-2）。

与 2015 年相比，风险资本投资上升了 4%，达到 44 亿欧元，超过 3000 家公司获得了投资，这个数字较 2015 年下降了 7%，这说明有向较大规模融资的趋势（见附图 2-3）。其中，通信、计算机和电子部门获得的规模最大，占据了总风险资本投资金额的 45%，之后是生物技术和保健（27%）以及消费品和服务（9%）。

附表 2-2 欧洲股权投资市场投资活动的主要特征（2016）

2016 年市场统计	所有股权类基金	风险投资	并购	成长资本
投资金额（亿欧元）	537	44	373	99
投资项目数（家）	5942	3134	1025	1831
涉及的企业数（家）	1004	575	370	396
涉及的基金数（只）	2157	1113	649	945

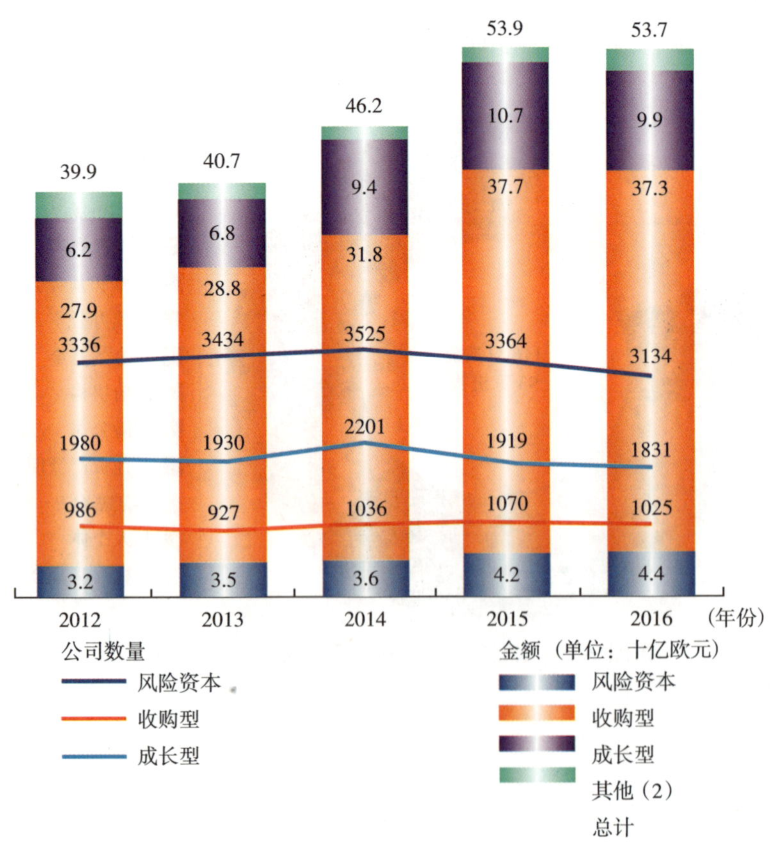

附图 2-3 欧洲股权投资趋势（2012~2016）

长期来看，2000 年至今，整个欧洲私募股权投资市场投资金额占 GDP 的比重为 0.2%~0.6%。2016 年，欧洲股权投资市场投资金额占 GDP 的比重为 0.34%，较 2015 年下降 0.01 个百分点。其中，创业风险投资的投资金额 GDP 的比重为 0.028%，丹麦创业风险投资占 GDP 的比重排在第一，达到 0.107%（见附图 2-4、附图 2-5）。

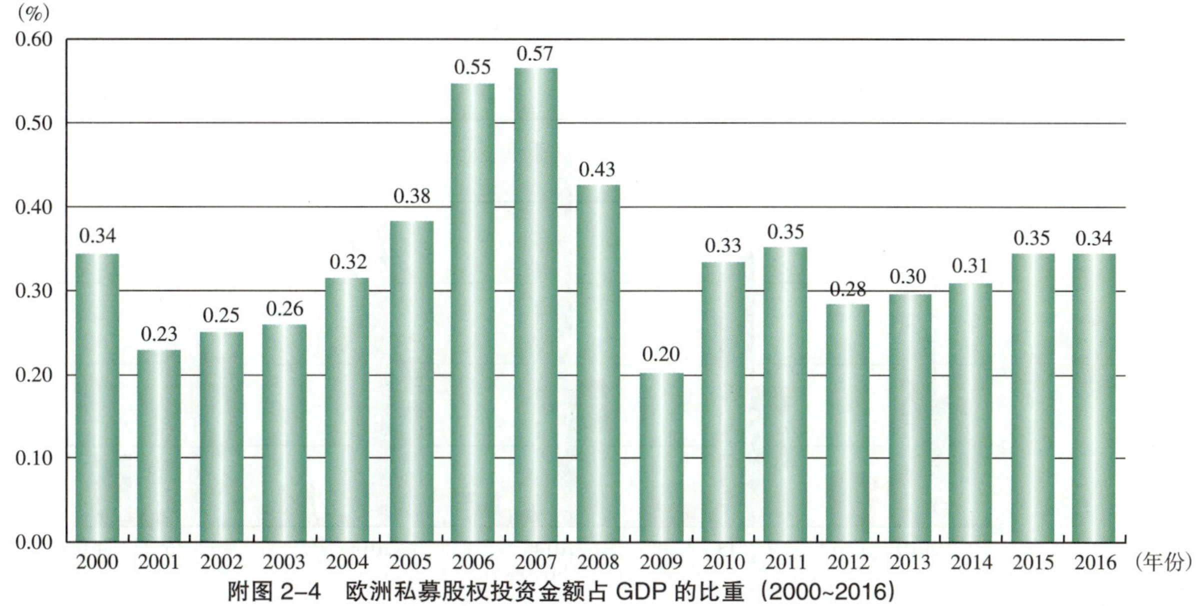

附图 2-4 欧洲私募股权投资金额占 GDP 的比重（2000~2016）

资料来源：国际货币基金组织，世界经济展望报告（GDP）/ 汤森路透（2000~2006）和投资欧洲/EDC（2007~2016）。

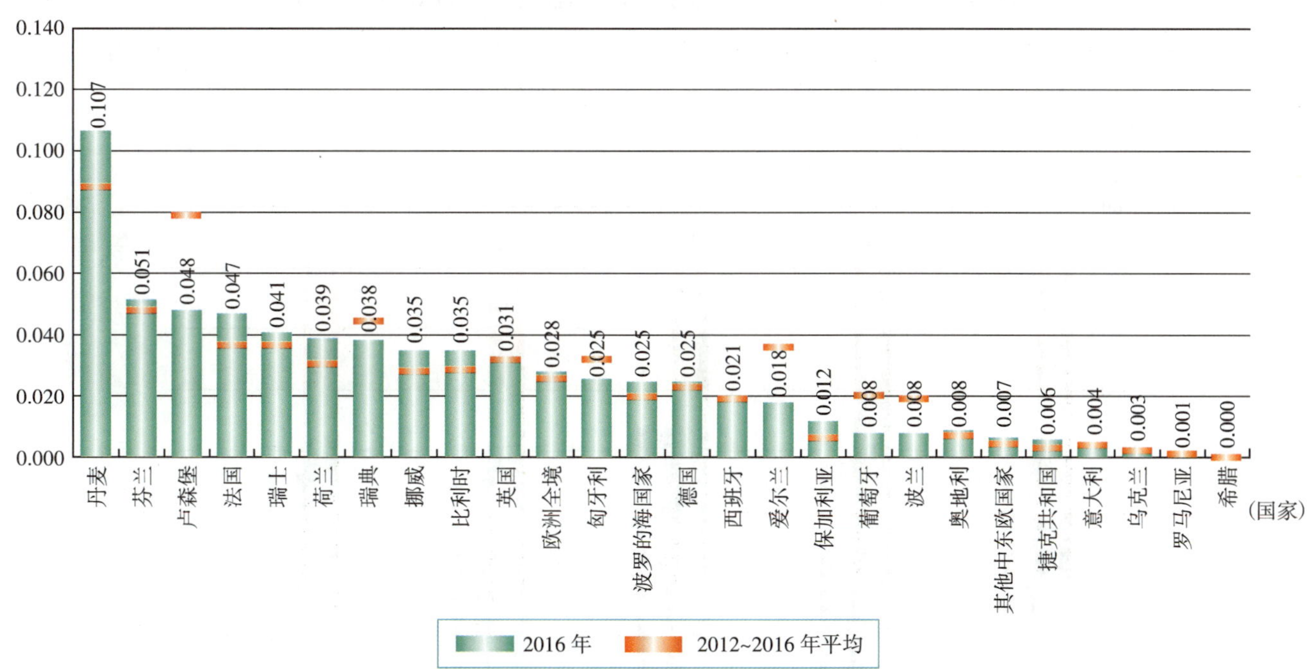

附图 2-5 欧洲主要国家风险投资占 GDP 的比重（2016）

注：* 其他中东欧国家包括前南斯拉夫和斯洛伐克。

资料来源：国际货币基金组织，世界经济展望报告（GDP）/ 投资欧洲/EDC。

(一) 投资阶段分布

2016 年，创业风险投资金额共计 44 亿欧元，较 2015 年增加 6 亿欧元，其中，种子期的投资金额 4 亿欧元，占比 9.0%；起步期的投资金额 21 亿欧元，占比 47.7%；合计占比 56.7%（见附图 2-6）。

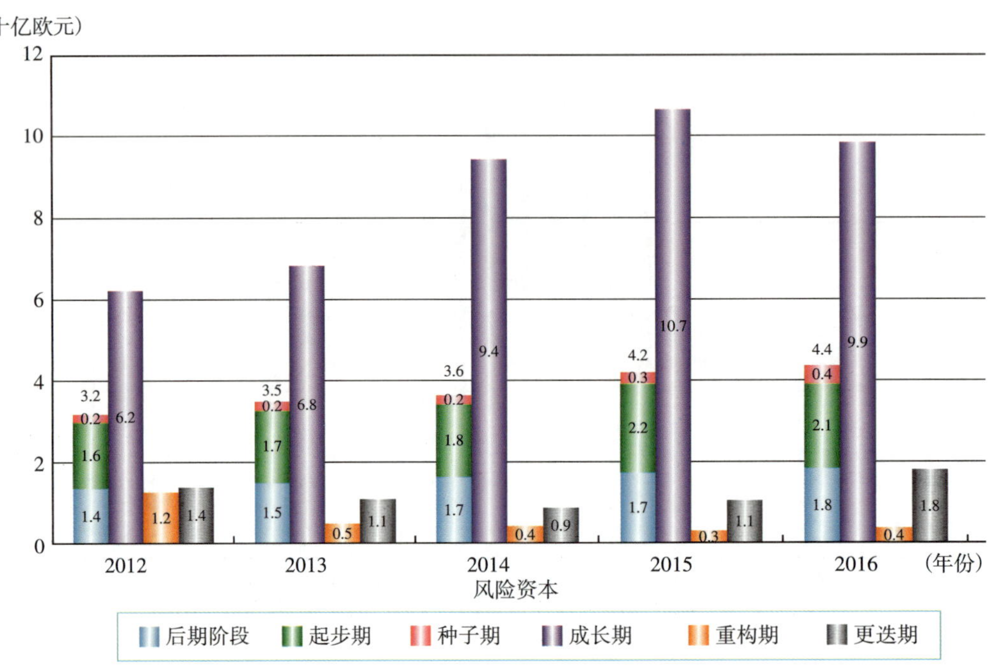

附图 2-6 欧洲创业风险投资基金投资阶段（按投资金额）(2012~2016)

按照投资项目数划分，2016 年欧洲创业风险投资行业全年投资项目数共计 3134 项，较 2015 年减少了 230 项。其中，投资于种子期的项目数为 827 项，占比 26.4%；投资起步期的项目数 1849 项，占比 59.0%；两者合计占比 85.4%（见附图 2-7）。

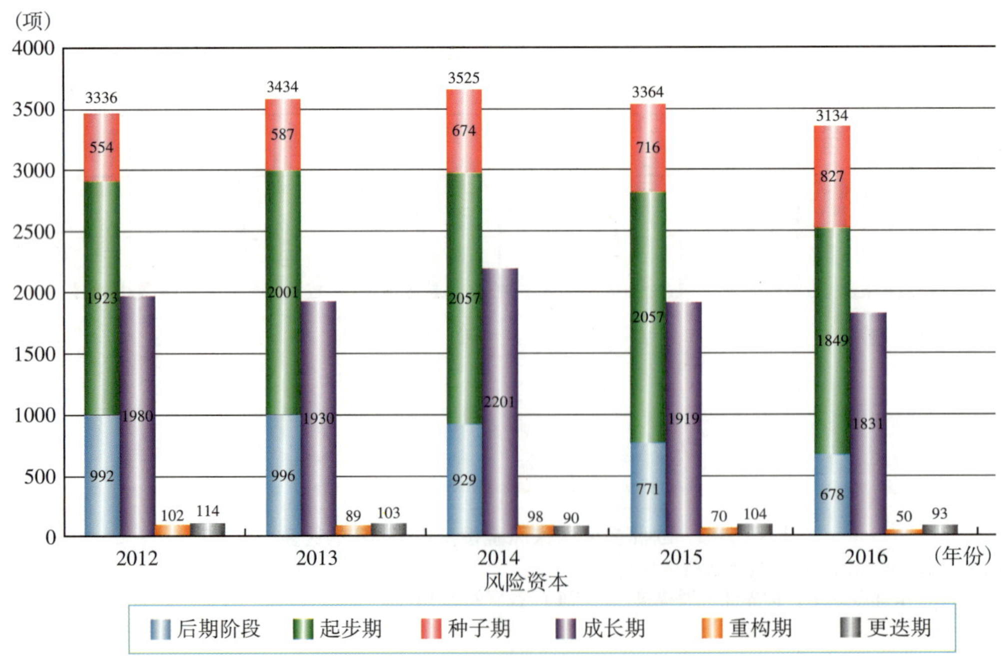

附图 2-7 欧洲创业风险投资基金投资阶段（按投资项目数）(2012~2016)

（二）投资行业分布

按创业风险投资的投资行业划分，无论从投资金额还是投资项目的角度，ICT、生命科学，以及消费品和服务业始终排在前三位（见附图 2-8、附图 2-9）。

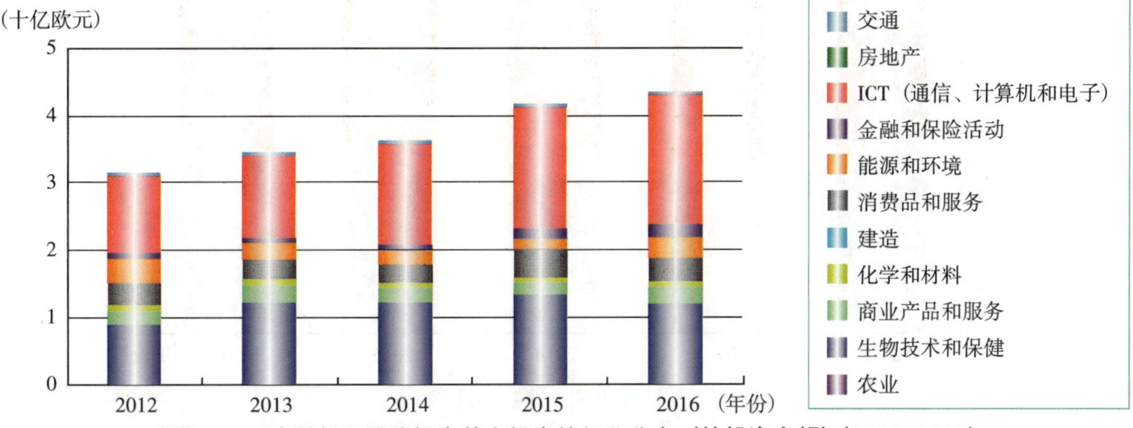

附图 2-8 欧洲创业风险投资基金投资的行业分布（按投资金额）（2012~2016）

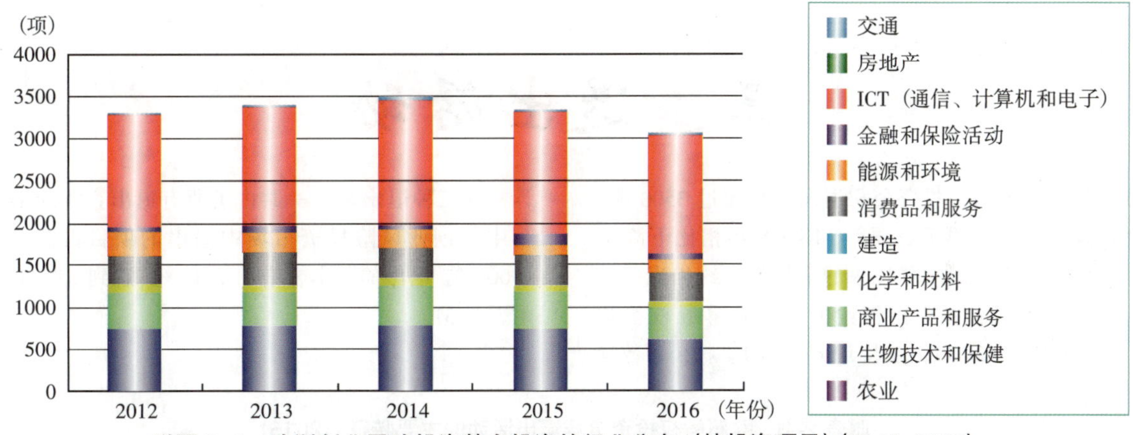

附图 2-9 欧洲创业风险投资基金投资的行业分布（按投资项目）（2012~2016）

（三）投资轮次分布

从投资轮次分布来看，欧洲股权投资市场的首轮投资与后续投资占比大致保持一致，首轮投资略少于后续投资。2016 年，首轮投资占 45%，后续投资占 55%，与 2015 年基本持平（见附图 2-10）。

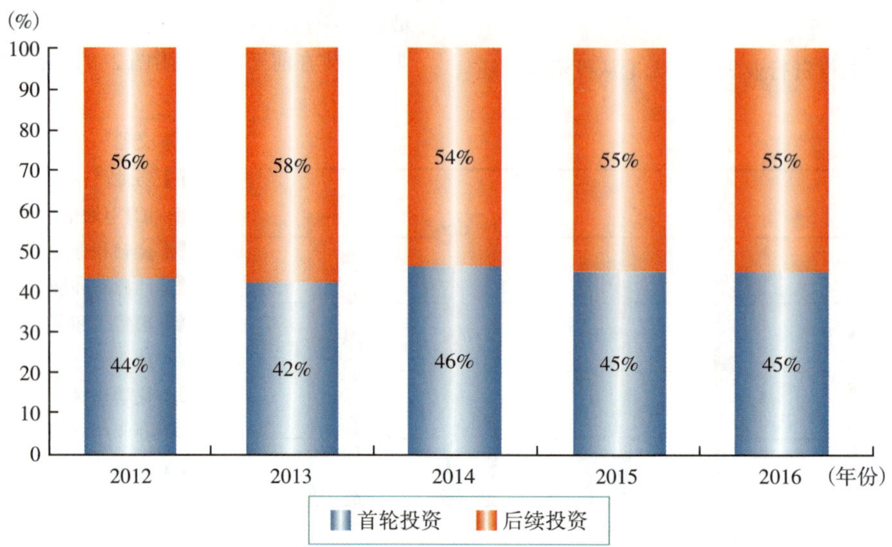

附图 2-10 欧洲股权投资的首轮投资与后续投资（2012~2016）

三、退出活动

2016 年，欧洲股权投资公司退出项目超过 3500 项，退出金额达到 389 亿欧元，虽然和 2015 年相比下降了 14%，但这个数字和 2012 年以来的平均值大约相当。其最主要的退出途径包括：出售给另一家私募股权机构（29%），贸易出售（27%），以及 IPO（17%）。按公司数量计，这三种退出途径一共占了所有退出企业的 1/3 以上。其中，创业风险投资市场中退出的项目占 35%，将近 1300 家。退出的股本金增加了 14%，达到 25 亿欧元（见附表 2-3）。

附表 2-3 欧洲股权投资市场退出活动的主要特征（2016）

2016	所有股权类基金	创业风险投资	并购	成长资本
退出金额（亿欧元）	389	25	284	60
退出项目数（家）	3508	1297	804	1401
涉及的企业数（家）	615	281	300	261
涉及的基金数（只）	1692	652	584	810

（一）退出方式

按退出金额划分，2016 年，欧洲创业风险投资的主要退出方式依次为贸易出售（占比 27%），较 2015 年大幅下滑了 23 个百分点；出售给管理层（占比 20%）；出售给金融机构（占比 15%）；清算（占比 11%）、出售给其他 PE 公司（占比 9%），全年通过 IPO 退出的企业占 7%，较 2015 年提高了 5 个百分点（见附图 2-11）。

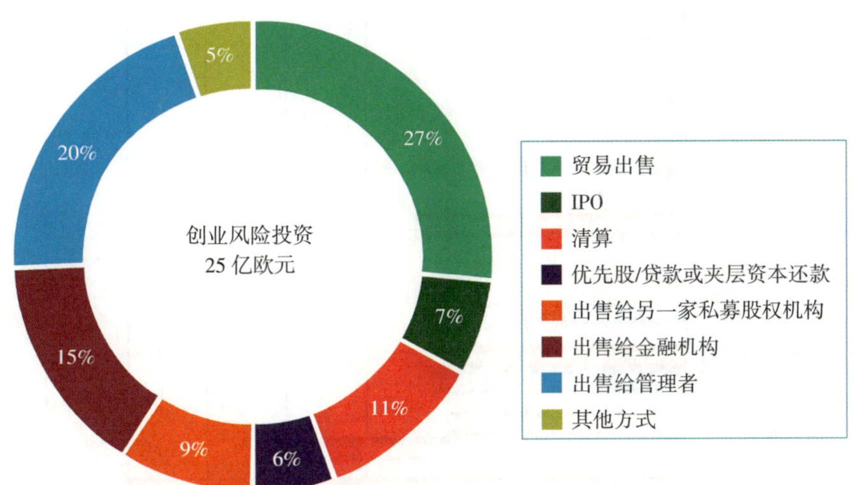

附图 2-11 欧洲创业风险投资的主要退出方式（按金额划分）(2016)

按退出项目划分，2016 年，欧洲创业风险投资的主要退出方式依次为优先股还款（占比 33%）、清算（占比 17%）、贸易出售（占比 16%）、出售给管理层（占比 11%）；全年通过 IPO 退出的占比 6%（见附图 2-12）。

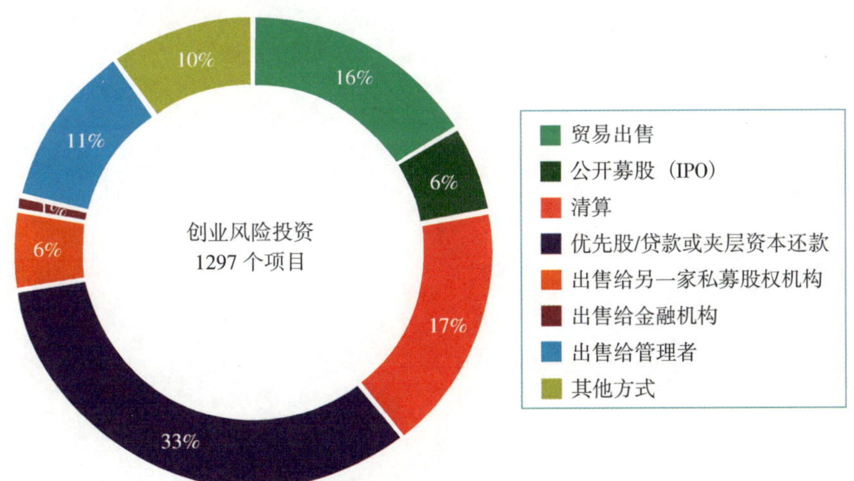

附图 2-12 欧洲创业风险投资的主要退出方式（按项目划分）(2016)

(二) 退出行业

按退出的行业划分，ICT（35%）、生物技术和保健（17%）、通信业（14%）、商业产品和服务（17%）、消费品和服务（15%）等；按退出金额划分，当年实现退出的金额依次为 ICT（40%）、消费品和服务（23%）、生物技术和保健（16%）、能源和环境（8%）等（见附图 2-13）。与 2015 年相比，ICT 退出的项目金额与数量均大幅增长。

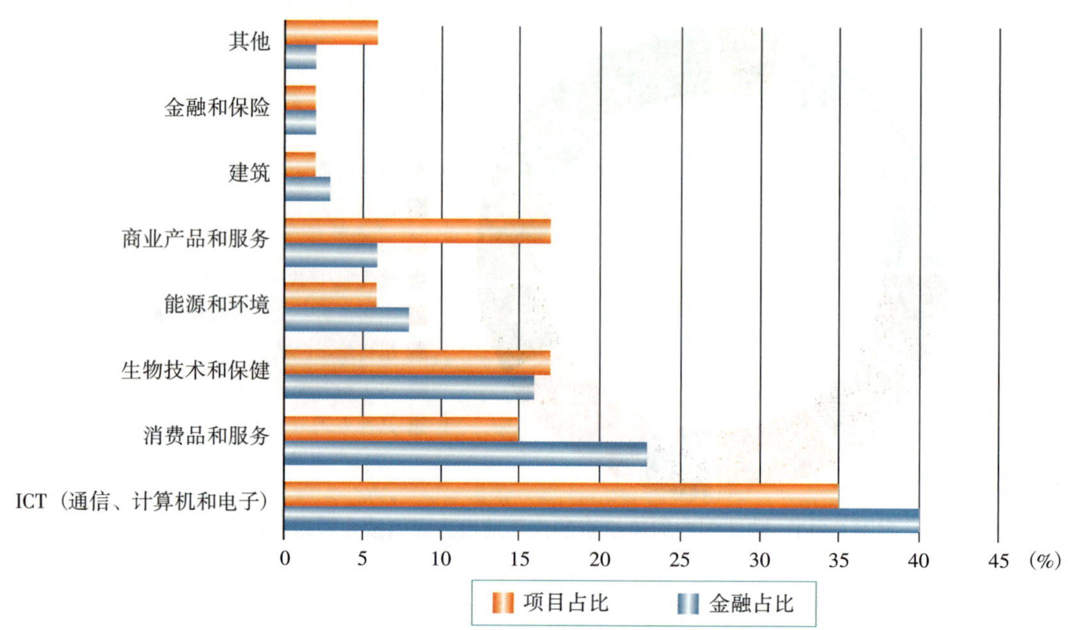

附图 2-13 欧洲风险投资退出的主要行业分布（2016）

资料来源：数据由欧洲私募股权和风险投资协会（European Private Equity and Venture Capital Association）提供。

附录 3 2016 年韩国创业风险投资回顾

一、韩国创业风险投资市场概况

2016 年，韩国政府继续开展创意经济和创新中心（CCEI）计划。在此计划鼓励下，2016 年韩国创业风险投资继续快速发展，新增创投机构 13 家，累计注册资本达 15026 亿韩元（见附表 3–1）。

附表 3–1 韩国创业风险投资公司概况（2005~2016）

指标 \ 年份	2005	2006	2007	2008	2009	2010	2011	2012	2013	2014	2015	2016
当年新注册数（注销数）	0（3）	13(11)	7(10)	5（9）	12（9）	13(10)	9（7）	6（6）	3（7）	6（4）	14（2）	13（8）
当年公司存量（家）	102	104	101	97	100	103	105	105	101	103	115	120
累计注册资本（十亿韩元）	1536.8	1553.7	1555.8	1457.8	1360.8	1383.8	1398.5	1445.5	1394.7	1418.5	1482.5	1502.6

截至 2016 年，共有 120 家风险投资企业管理着 610 只基金，其中当年新注册基金 120 只，继续延续增长态势；注销基金 43 只，较 2015 年有所上升；风险投资企业累计注册资本 167237 亿韩元（见附表 3–2、附图 3–1）。

附表 3–2 韩国创业风险投资基金概况（2005~2016）

指标 \ 年份	2005	2006	2007	2008	2009	2010	2011	2012	2013	2014	2015	2016
当年新注册数（只）	46	48	67	51	74	67	67	41	54	82	110	120
金额（十亿韩元）	945.4	861.7	1126.9	975.1	1421.4	1589.9	2277.8	821.3	1567.9	2584.2	2626.0	3199.8
当年注销（只）	69	98	90	49	54	53	45	46	31	37	26	43
金额（十亿韩元）	433.7	741.8	942.0	416.3	566.3	576.8	454.0	858.6	512.2	833.0	570.9	807.4
当年存量（只）	400	350	327	329	349	363	385	380	403	448	532	610
累计金额（十亿韩元）	4757.6	4877.5	5062.4	5621.2	6476.3	7489.4	9313.2	9275.9	10331.6	12082.8	14137.9	16723.7

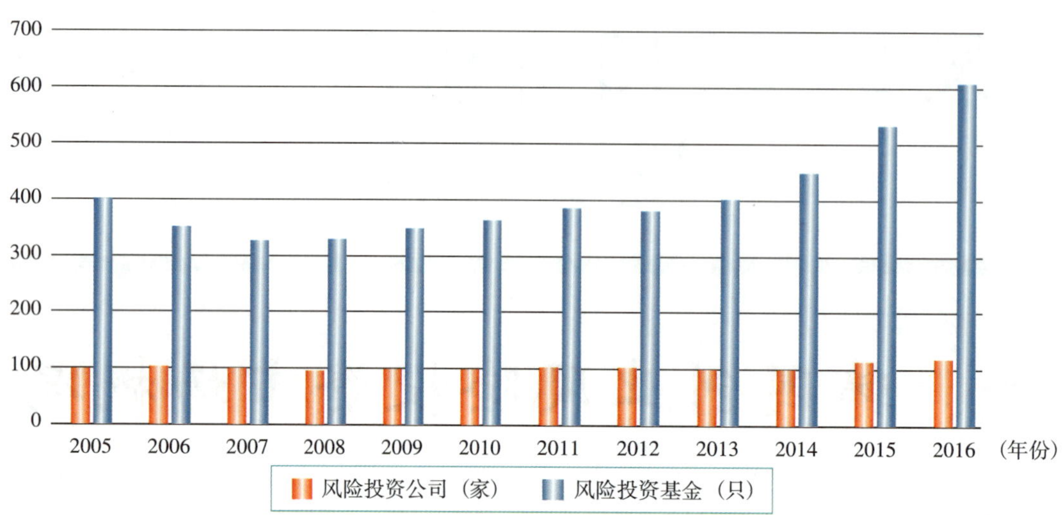

附图 3-1 韩国创业风险投资市场概况（2005~2016）

二、韩国风险投资活动

2016 年，韩国风险投资共投资项目 1191 项，投资金额为 21503 亿韩元，投资强度较 2015 年有所提升至 18.1 亿韩元/项（见附表 3-3）。

附表 3-3 韩国创业风险投资项目数及金额（2005~2016）

年份 指标	2005	2006	2007	2008	2009	2010	2011	2012	2013	2014	2015	2016
新投资项目数（项）	635	617	615	991.7	496	560	613	688	755	901	1045	1191
新投资金额数（十亿韩元）	757.3	733.3	991.7	724.7	867.1	1091.0	1260.8	1233.3	1384.5	1639.3	2085.8	2150.3
投资强度（十亿韩元/项）	1.19	1.19	1.61	1.46	1.65	1.95	2.06	1.79	1.83	1.82	1.44	1.81

三、韩国创业风险投资行业分布

2016 年，从投资金额看，ICT 服务、生物/医药两个行业仍然集中了大量资金，其中生物/医药行业投资金额较 2015 年增长了 47.82%。从投资项目看，排名占前三的分别是 ICT 服务、图像/性能/储存和生物/医药（见附表 3-4、附图 3-2）。

附表 3-4 韩国创业风险投资行业分布（2016）

指标＼行业	ICT 制造	ICT 服务	电子/机器/设备	化工/材料	生物/医药	图像/性能/存储	游戏	零售/服务	其他	总量
金额（十亿韩元）	95.9	406.2	212.5	150.2	468.6	267.8	142.7	249.4	157	2150.2
项目（项）	66	252	97	67	159	233	99	149	71	1191

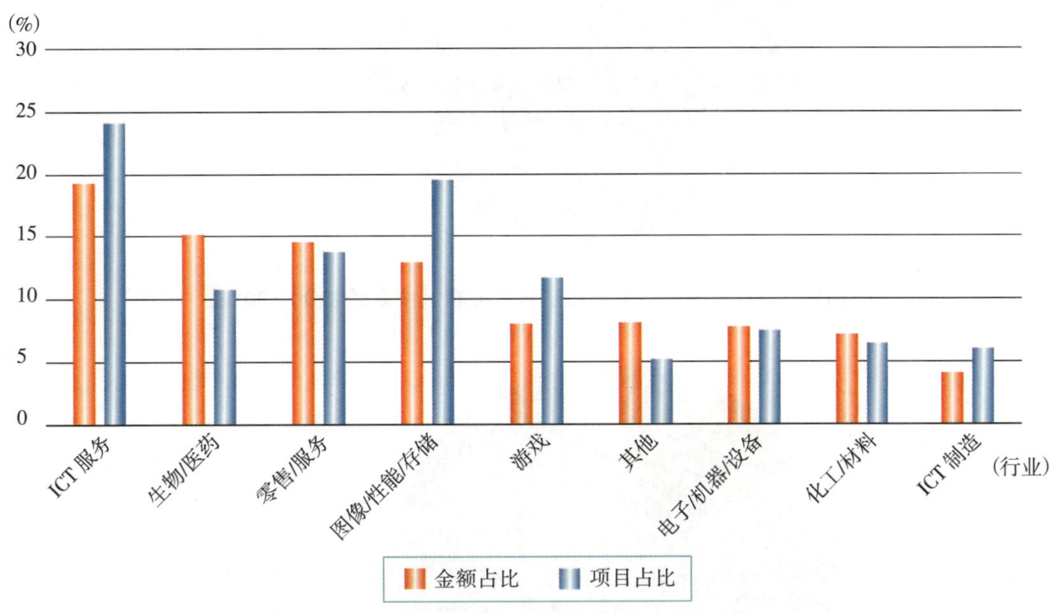

附图 3-2 韩国创业风险投资行业分布（2016）

四、韩国创业风险阶段分布

2016 年韩国风险投资项目仍然主要集中在早期阶段，与 2015 年韩国风险投资各阶段特征基本保持一致。从投资金额看，投资于早期、创建期和扩展期的差距较 2015 年有所缩小，分别占比 37%、29%和 34%；而投资项目则多集中于早期，占比 46%（见附表 3-5、附图 3-3、附图 3-4）。

附表 3-5 韩国创业风险投资阶段分布（2016）

阶段	早期	创建期	扩展期	总量
金额（十亿韩元）	790.9	615.6	743.8	2085.8
项目（项）	568	334	336	1191

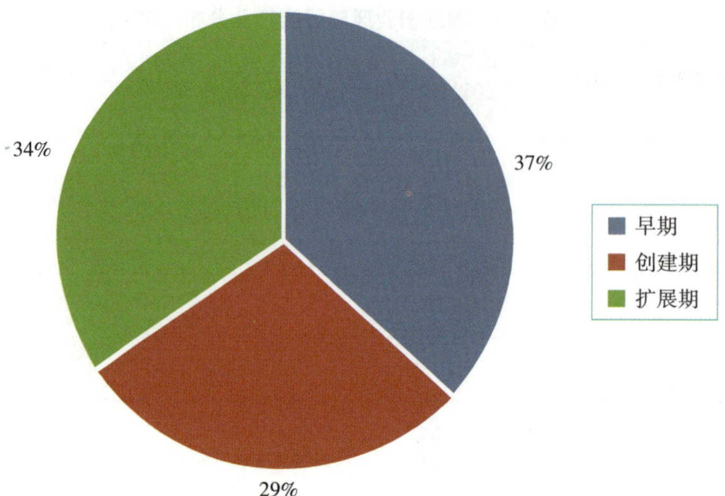

附图 3-3　韩国创业风险投资阶段分布（按金额划分）(2016)

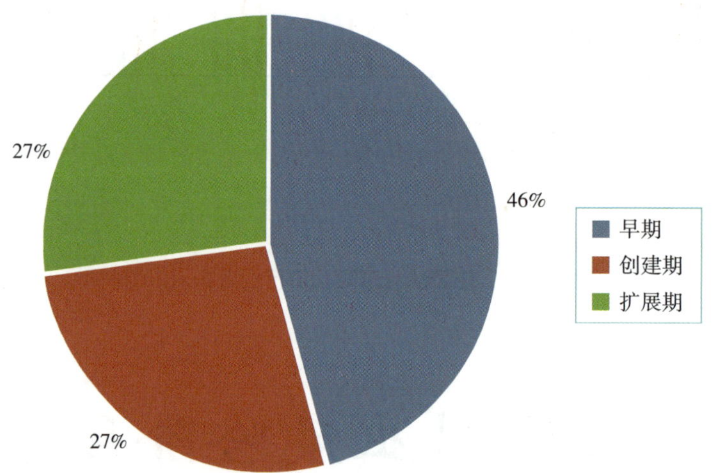

附图 3-4　韩国创业风险投资阶段分布（按项目划分）(2016)

资料来源：数据由韩国风险投资协会（Korean Venture Capital Association）提供。

附录 4 关于促进创业投资持续健康发展的若干意见

（国发〔2016〕53 号）

各省、自治区、直辖市人民政府，国务院各部委、各直属机构：

创业投资是实现技术、资本、人才、管理等创新要素与创业企业有效结合的投融资方式，是推动大众创业、万众创新的重要资本力量，是促进科技创新成果转化的助推器，是落实新发展理念、实施创新驱动发展战略、推进供给侧结构性改革、培育发展新动能和稳增长、扩就业的重要举措。近年来，我国创业投资快速发展，不仅拓宽了创业企业投融资渠道、促进了经济结构调整和产业转型升级，增强了经济发展新动能，也提高了直接融资比重、拉动了民间投资服务实体经济，激发了创业创新、促进了就业增长。但同时也面临着法律法规和政策环境不完善、监管体制和行业信用体系建设滞后等问题，存在一些投资“泡沫化”现象以及非法集资风险隐患。按照党中央、国务院的决策部署，为进一步促进创业投资持续健康发展，现提出以下意见。

一、总体要求

创业投资是指向处于创建或重建过程中的未上市成长性创业企业进行股权投资，以期所投资创业企业发育成熟或相对成熟后，主要通过股权转让获取资本增值收益的投资方式。天使投资是指除被投资企业职员及其家庭成员和直系亲属以外的个人以其自有资金直接开展的创业投资活动。发展包括天使投资在内的各类创业投资，应坚持以下总体要求：

（一）指导思想。

牢固树立和贯彻落实创新、协调、绿色、开放、共享的发展理念，着力推进供给侧结构性改革，深入实施创新驱动发展战略，大力推进大众创业万众创新，使市场在资源配置中起决定性作用和更好发挥政府作用，进一步深化简政放权、放管结合、优化服务改革，不断完善体制机制，健全政策措施，加强统筹协调和事中事后监管，构建促进创业投资发展的制度环境、市场环境和生态环境，加快形成有利于创业投资发展的良好氛围和“创业、创新+创投”的协同互动发展格局，进一步扩大创业投资规模，促进创业投资做大做强做优，培育一批具有国际影响力和竞争力的中国创业投资品牌，推动我国创业投资行业跻身世界先进行列。

（二）基本原则。

一是坚持服务实体。创业投资是改善投资结构、增加有效投资的重要手段。要进一步深化简政放权、放管结合、优化服务改革，创新监管方式，既要重视发挥大企业的骨干作用，也要通过创业投资激发广大中小企业的创造力和活力。以支持实体经济发展、助力创业企业发展为本，引导创业投资企业和创业投资管理企业秉承价值投资理念，鼓励长期投资和价值投资，防范和化解投资估值“泡沫化”可能引发的市场风险，积极应对新动能成长过程中对传统产业和行业可能造成的冲击，妥善处理好各种矛盾，加大对实体经济支持的力度，增强可持续性，构建“实体创投”投资环境。

二是坚持专业运作。以市场为导向，充分调动民间投资和市场主体的积极性，发挥市场规则作用，激发民间创新模式，防止同质化竞争。鼓励创业投资企业和创业投资管理企业从自身独特优势出发，强化专业化投资理念和投资策略，深化内部体制机制创新，加强对投资项目的投后管理和增值服务，不断提高创业投资行业专业化运作和管理水平，夯实“专业创投”运行基础。

三是坚持信用为本。以诚信为兴业之本、发展之基，加强创业投资行业信用体系建设，建立和完善守信联合激励和失信联合惩戒制度，促进创业投资企业和创业投资管理企业诚信守法，忠实履行对投资者的诚信义务，创建“信用创投”发展环境。

四是坚持社会责任。围绕推进创新型国家建设、支持大众创业万众创新、促进经济结构调整和产业转型升级的使命和社会责任，推动创业投资行业严格按照国家有关法律法规和相关产业政策开展投资运营活动，按照市场化、法治化原则，促进创业投资良性竞争和绿色发展，共同维护良好市场秩序，树立“责任创投”价值理念。

二、培育多元创业投资主体

（三）加快培育形成各具特色、充满活力的创业投资机构体系。鼓励各类机构投资者和个人依法设立公司型、合伙型创业投资企业。鼓励行业骨干企业、创业孵化器、产业（技术）创新中心、创业服务中心、保险资产管理机构等创业创新资源丰富的相关机构参与创业投资。鼓励具有资本实力和管理经验的个人通过依法设立一人公司从事创业投资活动。鼓励和规范发展市场化运作、专业化管理的创业投资母基金。（国家发展改革委、科技部、工业和信息化部、人力资源社会保障部、商务部、国务院国资委、工商总局、银监会、证监会、保监会按职责分工负责）

（四）积极鼓励包括天使投资人在内的各类个人从事创业投资活动。鼓励成立公益性天使投资人联盟等各类平台组织，培育和壮大天使投资人群体，促进天使投资人与创业企业及创业投资企业的信息交流与合作，营造良好的天使投资氛围，推动天使投资事业发展。规范发展互联网股权融资平台，为各类个人直接投资创业企业提供信息和技术服务。（国家发展改革委、科技部、证监会按职责分工负责）

三、多渠道拓宽创业投资资金来源

（五）大力培育和发展合格投资者。在风险可控、安全流动的前提下，支持中央企业、地方国有企业、保险公司、大学基金等各类机构投资者投资创业投资企业和创业投资母基金。鼓励信托公司遵循价值投资和长期投资理念，充分发挥既能进行创业投资又能发放贷款的优势，积极探索新产品、新模式，为创业企业提供综合化、个性化金融和投融资服务。培育合格个人投资者，支持具有风险识别和风险承受能力的个人参与投资创业投资企业。（国家发展改革委、财政部、国务院国资委、银监会、证监会、保监会按职责分工负责）

（六）建立股权债权等联动机制。按照依法合规、风险可控、商业可持续的原则，建立创业投资企业与各类金融机构长期性、市场化合作机制，进一步降低商业保险资金进入创业投资领域的门槛，推动发展投贷联动、投保联动、投债联动等新模式，不断加大对创业投资企业的投融资支持。加强“防火墙”相关制度建设，有效防范道德风险。支持银行业金融机构积极稳妥开展并购贷款业务，提高对创业企业兼并重组的金融服务水平。完善银行业金融机构投贷联动机制，稳妥有序推进投贷联动业务试点，推动投贷联动金融服务模式创新。支持创业投资企业及其股东依法依规发行企业债券和其他债务融资工具融资，增强投资能力。（国家发展改革委、科技部、人民银行、银监会、证监会、保监会按职责分工负责）

四、加强政府引导和政策扶持

（七）完善创业投资税收政策。按照税收中性、税收公平原则和税制改革方向与要求，统筹研究鼓励创业投资企业和天使投资人投资种子期、初创期等科技型企业的税收支持政策，进一步完善创业投资企业投资抵扣税收优惠政策，研究开展天使投资人个人所得税政策试点工作。（国家发展改革委、科技部、财政部、商务部、税务总局、证监会按职责分工负责）

（八）建立创业投资与政府项目对接机制。在全面创新改革试验区域、双创示范基地、国家高新区、国家自主创新示范区、产业（技术）创新中心、科技企业孵化器、众创空间等，开放项目（企业）资源，充分利用政府项目资源优势，搭建创业投资与企业信息共享平台，打通创业资本和项目之间的通道，引导创业投资企业投资于国家科技计划（专项、基金等）形成科技成果的转化。挖掘农业领域创业投资潜力，依托农村产业融合发展园区、农业产业化示范基地、农民工返乡创业园等，通过发展第二、三产业，改造提升第一产业。有关方面要配合做好项目对接和服务。（国家发展改革委、科技部、工业和信息化部、农业部、商务部按职责分工负责）

（九）研究鼓励长期投资的政策措施。倡导长期投资和价值投资理念，研究对专注于长期投资和价值投资的创业投资企业在企业债券发行、引导基金扶持、政府项目对接、市场化退出等方面给予必要的政策支持。研究建立所投资企业上市解禁期与上市前投资期限长短反向挂钩的制度安排。（国家发展改革委、科技部、财政部、人民银行、证监会按职责分工负责）

（十）发挥政府资金的引导作用。充分发挥政府设立的创业投资引导基金作用，加强规范管理，加大力度培育新的经济增长点，促进就业增长。充分发挥国家新兴产业创业投资引导基金、国家中小企业发展基金、国家科技成果转化引导基金等已设立基金的作用。对于已设立基金未覆盖且需要政府引导支持的领域，鼓励有条件的地方按照“政府引导、市场化运作”原则推动设立创业投资引导基金，发挥财政资金的引导和聚集放大作用，引导民间投资等社会资本投入。进一步提高创业投资引导基金市场化运作效率，促进政策目标实现，维护出资人权益。鼓励创业投资引导基金注资市场化母基金，由专业化创业投资管理机构受托管理引导基金。综合运用参股基金、联合投资、融资担保、政府出资适当让利于社会出资等多种方式，进一步发挥政府资金在引导民间投资、扩大直接融资、弥补市场失灵等方面的作用。建立并完善创业投资引导基金中政府出资的绩效评价制度。（国家发展改革委、科技部、工业和信息化部、财政部按职责分工负责）

五、完善创业投资相关法律法规

（十一）构建符合创业投资行业特点的法制环境。进一步完善促进创业投资发展相关法律法规，研究推动相关立法工作，推动完善公司法和合伙企业法。完善创业投资相关管理制度，推动私募投资基金管理暂行条例尽快出台，对创业投资企业和创业投资管理企业实行差异化监管和行业自律。完善外商投资创业投资企业管理制度。（国家发展改革委、商务部、证监会按职责分工负责）

（十二）落实和完善国有创业投资管理制度。鼓励国有企业集众智，开拓广阔市场空间，增强国有企业竞争力。支持有需求、有条件的国有企业依法依规、按照市场化方式设立或参股创业投资企业和创业投资母基金。强化国有创业投资企业对种子期、初创期等创业企业的支持，鼓励国有创业投资企业追求长期投资收益。健全符合创业投资行业特点和发展规律的国有创业投资管理体制，完善国有创业投资企业的监督考核、激励约束机制和股权转让方式，形成鼓励创业、宽容失败的国有创业投资生态环境。支持具备条件的国有创业投资企业开展混合所有制改革试点，探索国有创业投资企业和创业投资管理企业核心团队持股和跟投。探索地方政府融资平台公司转型升级为创业投资企业。依法依规豁免国有创业投资企业和国有创业投资引导基金国有股转持义务。（国家发展改革委、财政部、国务院国资委、证监会按职责分工负责）

六、进一步完善创业投资退出机制

（十三）拓宽创业投资市场化退出渠道。充分发挥主板、创业板、全国中小企业股份转让系统以及区域性股权市场功能，畅通创业投资市场化退出渠道。完善全国中小企业股份转让系统交易机制，改善市场流动性。支持机构间私募产品报价与服务系统、证券公司柜台市场开展直接融资业务。鼓励创业投资以并购重组等方式实现市场化退出，规范发展专业化并购基金。（证监会牵头负责）

七、优化创业投资市场环境

（十四）优化监管环境。实施更多的普惠性支持政策措施，营造公平竞争的发展环境，深化简政放权、放管结合、优化服务改革，搞好服务，激发活力。坚持适度监管、差异监管和统一功能监管，创新监管方式，有效防范系统性区域性风险。对创业投资企业在行业管理、备案登记等方面采取与其他私募基金区别对待的差异化监管政策，建立适应创业投资行业特点的宽市场准入、重事中事后监管的适度而有效的监管体制。加强信息披露和风险揭示，引导创业投资企业建立以实体投资、价值投资和长期投资为导向的合理的投资估值机制。对不进行实业投资、从事上市公司股票交易、助推投资泡沫及其他扰乱市场秩序的创业投资企业建立清查清退制度。建立行业规范，强化创业投资企业内控机制、合规管理和风险管理机制。加强投资者保护，特别是要进一步完善产权保护制度，依法保护产权和投资者合法经营、合法权益和合法财产。加强投资者教育，相关投资者应为具有风险识别和风险承受能力的合格投资者。建立并完善募集资金的托管制度，规范创业投资企业募集资金行为，打击违法违规募集资金行为。健全对创业投资企业募集资金、投资运作等与保护投资者权益相关的制度规范，加强日常监管。（国家发展改革委、科技部、国务院国资委、证监会按职责分工负责）

（十五）优化商事环境。各地区、各部门不得自行出台限制创业投资企业和创业投资管理企业市场准入和发展的有关政策。建立创业投资行业发展备案和监管备案互联互通机制，为创业投资企业备案提供便利，放宽创业投资企业的市场准入。持续深化商事制度改革，提高工商登记注册便利化水平。促进创业投资行业加强品牌建设。（国家发展改革委、工商总局、证监会会同各有关部门按职责分工负责）

（十六）优化信用环境。有关部门、行业组织和社会征信机构要进一步建立健全创业投资企业、创业投资管理企业及其从业人员信用记录，实现创业投资领域信用记录全覆盖。推动创业投资领域信用信息纳入全国信用信息共享平台，并与企业信用信息公示系统实现互联互通。依法依规在“信用中国”网站和企业信用信息公示系统公示相关信息。加快建立创业投资领域严重失信黑名单制度，鼓励有关社会组织探索建立守信红名单制度，依托全国信用信息共享平台，按照有关法律法规和政策规定实施守信联合激励和失信联合惩戒。建立健全创业投资行业信用服务机制，推广使用信用产品。（国家发展改革委、商务部、人民银行、工商总局、证监会按职责分工负责）

（十七）严格保护知识产权。完善知识产权保护相关法律法规和制度规定，加强对创业创新早期知识产权保护，在市场竞争中培育更多自主品牌，健全知识产权侵权查处机制，依法惩治侵犯知识产权的违法犯罪行为，将企业行政处罚、黑名单等信息纳入全国信用信息共享平台，对严重侵犯知识产权的责任主体实施联合惩戒，并通过“信用中国”网站、企业信用信息公示系统等进行公示，创造鼓励创业投资的良好知识产权保护环境。（国家发展改革委、人民银行、工商总局、知识产权局、证监会等按职责分工负责）

八、推动创业投资行业双向开放

（十八）有序扩大创业投资对外开放。发展创业投资要坚持走开放式发展道路，通过吸引境外投资，引进国际先进经验、技术和管理模式，提升我国创业投资企业的国际竞争力。按照对内外资一视同仁的原则，放宽外商投资准入，简化管理流程，鼓励外资扩大创业投资规模，加大对种子期、初创期创业企业支持力度。鼓励和支持境内外投资者在跨境创业投资及相关的投资贸易活动中使用人民币。允许外资创业投资企业按照实际投资规模将外汇资本金结汇所得的人民币划入被投资企业。（国家发展改革委、商务部、人民银行、国家外汇局按职责分工负责）

（十九）鼓励境内有实力的创业投资企业积极稳妥“走出去”。完善境外投资相关管理制度，引导和鼓励创业投资企业加大对境外及港、澳、台地区高端研发项目的投资，积极分享高端技术成果。（国家发展改革委、商务部、人民银行、国家外汇局按职责分工负责）

九、完善创业投资行业自律和服务体系

（二十）加强行业自律。加快推进依法设立全国性创业投资行业协会，鼓励具备条件的地区成立创业投资协会组织，搭建行业协会交流服务平台。充分发挥行业协会在行业自律管理和政府与市场沟通中的积极作用，加强行业协会在政策对接、会员服务、信息咨询、数据统计、行业发展报告、人才培养、国际交流合作等方面的能力建设，支持行业协会推动创业投资行业信用体系建设和社会责任建设，维护有利于行业持续健康发展的良好市场秩序。（国家发展改革委、科技部、民政部、证监会按职责分工负责）

（二十一）健全创业投资服务体系。加强与创业投资相关的会计、征信、信息、托管、法律、咨询、教育培训等各类中介服务体系建设。支持创业投资协会组织通过高等学校、科研院所、群团组织、创业投资企业、创业投资管理企业、天使投资人等多种渠道，以多种方式加强创业投资专业人才培养，加大教育培训力度，吸引更多的优秀人才从事创业投资，提高创业投资的精准度。（国家发展改革委、科技部、证监会按职责分工负责）

十、加强各方统筹协调

（二十二）加强政策顶层设计和统筹协调。国家发展改革委要会同有关部门加强促进创业投资发展的政策协调，建立部门之间、部门与地方之间政策协调联动机制，加强创业投资行业发展政策和监管政策的协同配合，增强政策针对性、连续性、协同性。建立相关政府部门促进创业投资行业发展的信息共享机制。（国家发展改革委、证监会会同有关部门按职责分工负责）

各地区、各部门要把促进创业投资持续健康发展作为深入实施创新驱动发展战略、推动大众创业万众创新、促进经济结构调整和产业转型升级的一项重要举措，按照职责分工抓紧制定相关配套措施，加强沟通协调，形成工作合力，确保各项政策及时落实到位，积极发展新经济、培育新动能、改造提升传统动能，推动中国经济保持中高速增长、迈向中高端水平。

国务院

2016 年 9 月 16 日

附录5 关于印发《中央引导地方科技发展专项资金管理办法》的通知

（财教〔2016〕81号）

各省、自治区、直辖市、计划单列市财政厅（局）、科技厅（局），新疆生产建设兵团财务局、科技局：

为深入实施创新驱动发展战略、落实科技体制改革部署，按照加强中央对地方专项转移支付管理有关要求，我们制定了《中央引导地方科技发展专项资金管理办法》。现印发给你们，请遵照执行。执行中如有问题，请及时向我们反映。

附件：中央引导地方科技发展专项资金管理办法

财政部　科技部

2016年5月16日

附件

中央引导地方科技发展专项资金管理办法

第一章　总　则

第一条　为规范中央引导地方科技发展专项资金（以下简称专项资金）管理，提高专项资金使用效益，根据《中华人民共和国预算法》、《中华人民共和国科技进步法》等国家有关法律法规，制定本办法。

第二条　本办法所称专项资金是指中央财政通过专项转移支付安排的，用于支持地方政府围绕国家科技发展战略和地方经济社会发展目标，改善地方科研基础条件，优化科技创新环境，支持基层科技工作，促进科技成果转移转化，提升区域科技创新能力的资金。

第三条　专项资金由财政部、科技部共同负责管理。财政部会同科技部制定专项资金管理制度，适时对专项资金进行评估，调整分配因素权重和支持方向。科技部会同财政部审定省级科技部门、财政部门上报的三年滚动规划，对专项资金管理使用开展绩效评价。

第四条　省级财政部门、科技部门应当结合本省实际制定专项资金管理细则，进一步明确资金使用重点方向和范围、支持方式和标准、三年滚动规划项目遴选标准和程序、资金支付方式、绩效管理及信息公开等。

第五条　专项资金管理遵循“中央引导、省级统筹，整合资源、完善体系，绩效导向、激励相容”的原则。

第二章　支持范围与方式

第六条　专项资金支持以下四个方面：

（一）地方科研基础条件和能力建设。主要指地市级以上地方政府所属科研单位（不含转为企业或其他事业单位的单位）的科研仪器设备购置和科研基础设施维修改造。

（二）地方专业性技术创新平台。主要指依托大学、科研院所、企业、转制科研机构建立的，通过产学研协同创新机制为区域发展提供研究开发支撑的专业性平台，包括产业技术研究院、技术创新中心（实验室、研究中心）、新型研发组织等。

（三）地方科技创新创业服务机构。主要指为中小微企业技术创新、基层科技创新活动提供技术转移、检验检测认证、创业孵化、知识产权、科技咨询、科技金融、科技资源共享等专业或综合性服务机构，包括科技园区、众创空间、科技企业孵化器、生产力促进中心、分析测试中心、技术转移机构、科技特派员工作站、科技金融服务中心等。

（四）地方科技创新项目示范。主要指围绕国家区域发展战略，结合科技惠民、县域科技、科技扶贫等任务，对政策目标明确、公益性属性明显、引导带动作用突出、惠及人民群众的科技成果进行转化应用的项目示范。

第七条 支持地方科研基础条件建设的资金一般采取直接补助的方式。支持地方专业性技术创新平台、地方科技创新创业服务机构和地方科技创新项目示范的资金，鼓励地方综合采用直接补助、后补助、以奖代补、贷款贴息、发放创新券等多种投入方式。

第八条 事业单位不得将专项资金用于支付各种罚款、捐款、赞助、投资、偿还债务等支出，不得用于编制内在职人员工资性支出和离退休人员离退休费，以及国家规定禁止列支的其他支出。

第三章 分配方法

第九条 专项资金采取因素法分配，分配因素主要有：

（一）体现地方科研综合能力的因素，主要包括：区域科研活动量和科技条件水平、科技资源开放共享水平等。

（二）体现地方创新综合能力的因素，主要包括：区域创新示范试点推进、科技创新服务平台作用、科技创新服务机构培育、科技金融创新实践、区域技术市场活跃程度等。

（三）绩效考评因素，主要根据上一年度绩效评价结果和财政部驻当地财政监察专员办事处（以下简称专员办）预算监管报告以及地方落实国家科技改革与发展重大政策等情况。

第十条 专项资金计算分配公式如下：

某省专项资金预算数=某省分配因素得分/∑各省分配因素得分×专项资金总额；

其中：某省分配因素得分=∑（某省分配因素值/全国该项分配因素总值×相应权重）×某省财政困难程度系数。

财政困难程度系数根据中央对地方均衡性转移支付办法确定。

第四章 下达与备案

第十一条 省级科技部门、财政部门每年根据本省科技创新规划和年度工作重点，编制专项资金三年滚动规划，报科技部、财政部审核，并抄送专员办。

三年滚动规划应当包括工作目标、重点任务及项目、组织管理、保障措施等。项目内容应包括实施主体、目标任务、绩效目标、资金规模及结构、支持方式、实施期限等信息。

第十二条 科技部会同财政部对各省份报送的三年滚动规划进行审核，并在 30 日内将审核意见反馈省级科技部门、财政部门。审核的依据有：与国家科技发展规划和科技创新政策的对接情况、设定的区域创新体系建设目标合理性、科技创新资源配置的效率、重大项目的示范引导作用等。省级科技部门、财政部门应当根据审核意见修改完善三年滚动规划。

第十三条 财政部、科技部按本办法规定，于每年 10 月 31 日前提前下达下年度专项资金预计数，全国人民代表大会审查批准中央预算后 90 日内正式下达专项资金预算。

第十四条 省级财政部门、科技部门应当在财政部、科技部下达预算数后 30 日内，将本省专项资金实施方案报财政部、科技部备案，并抄送专员办。实施方案应包括项目安排、支持内容、支持方式、项目绩效目标、组织实施能力与条件、预期社会经济效益等。

当年专项资金实施方案所安排的项目应当在经科技部、财政部审核后的三年滚动规划重点任务及项目范围内。

第十五条 对拟分配到企业的专项资金，省级财政部门、科技部门应当通过官方网站等媒介向社会公示，公示期一般不少于 7 日，公示无异议后方可上报备案并组织实施。

第十六条 专项资金实施方案备案后不得随意调整。如需调整，应当将调整情况及原因报财政部、科技部备案。

第十七条 专项资金支付按照国库集中支付有关规定执行。涉及政府采购的，应当按照政府采购有关法律执行。

第五章 监督与绩效

第十八条 获得专项资金的单位，应当按照国家财务、会计制度的有关规定进行账务处理，严格按规定使用资金，并自觉接受监督检查。

第十九条 省级财政部门、科技部门按照职责分工，加强对项目组织实施的监督检查。

第二十条 财政部、科技部根据专项资金的管理使用情况，适时开展监督检查。专员办按照工作职责和财政部要求，对专项资金预算执行情况进行全面监管，监管报告定期报送财政部。科技部会同财政部对上一年专项资金管理使用情况组织开展绩效评价。监督检查、绩效评价和监管报告所反映的情况是专项资金分配的重要参考。

第二十一条 凡有下列行为之一的，财政部将采取通报批评、停止拨款、收回专项资金等措施，并依照《财政违法行为处罚处分条例》规定处理。对严重违规、违纪、违法犯罪的相关责任主体，按程序纳入科研严重失信行为记录。

（一）编报虚假预算，套取专项资金的；

（二）挤占、截留、挪用专项资金的；

（三）未按照专项资金支持范围使用的；

（四）其他违反国家财经纪律的行为。

第六章 附 则

第二十二条 本办法由财政部、科技部负责解释。

第二十三条 本办法自印发之日起实施，《中央补助地方科技基础条件专项资金管理办法》（财教〔2012〕396号）同时废止。

附录 6 关于完善股权激励和技术入股有关所得税政策的通知

（财税〔2016〕101 号）

各省、自治区、直辖市、计划单列市财政厅（局）、国家税务局、地方税务局，新疆生产建设兵团财务局：

为支持国家大众创业、万众创新战略的实施，促进我国经济结构转型升级，经国务院批准，现就完善股权激励和技术入股有关所得税政策通知如下：

一、对符合条件的非上市公司股票期权、股权期权、限制性股票和股权奖励实行递延纳税政策

（一）非上市公司授予本公司员工的股票期权、股权期权、限制性股票和股权奖励，符合规定条件的，经向主管税务机关备案，可实行递延纳税政策，即员工在取得股权激励时可暂不纳税，递延至转让该股权时纳税；股权转让时，按照股权转让收入减除股权取得成本以及合理税费后的差额，适用“财产转让所得”项目，按照 20%的税率计算缴纳个人所得税。

股权转让时，股票（权）期权取得成本按行权价确定，限制性股票取得成本按实际出资额确定，股权奖励取得成本为零。

（二）享受递延纳税政策的非上市公司股权激励（包括股票期权、股权期权、限制性股票和股权奖励，下同）须同时满足以下条件：

1. 属于境内居民企业的股权激励计划。

2. 股权激励计划经公司董事会、股东（大）会审议通过。未设股东（大）会的国有单位，经上级主管部门审核批准。股权激励计划应列明激励目的、对象、标的、有效期、各类价格的确定方法、激励对象获取权益的条件、程序等。

3. 激励标的应为境内居民企业的本公司股权。股权奖励的标的可以是技术成果投资入股到其他境内居民企业所取得的股权。激励标的股票（权）包括通过增发、大股东直接让渡以及法律法规允许的其他合理方式授予激励对象的股票（权）。

4. 激励对象应为公司董事会或股东（大）会决定的技术骨干和高级管理人员，激励对象人数累计不得超过本公司最近 6 个月在职职工平均人数的 30%。

5. 股票（权）期权自授予日起应持有满 3 年，且自行权日起持有满 1 年；限制性股票自授予日起应持有满 3 年，且解禁后持有满 1 年；股权奖励自获得奖励之日起应持有满 3 年。上述时间条件须在股权激励计划中列明。

6. 股票（权）期权自授予日至行权日的时间不得超过 10 年。

7. 实施股权奖励的公司及其奖励股权标的公司所属行业均不属于《股权奖励税收优惠政策限制性行业目录》范围（见附件）。公司所属行业按公司上一纳税年度主营业务收入占比最高的行业确定。

（三）本通知所称股票（权）期权是指公司给予激励对象在一定期限内以事先约定的价格购买本公司股票（权）的权利；所称限制性股票是指公司按照预先确定的条件授予激励对象一定数量的本公司股权，激励对象只有工作年限或业绩目标符合股权激励计划规定条件的才可以处置该股权；所称股权奖励是指企业无偿授予激励对象一定份额的股权或一定数量的股份。

（四）股权激励计划所列内容不同时满足第一条第（二）款规定的全部条件，或递延纳税期间公司情况发生变化，不再符合第一条第（二）款第 4 至 6 项条件的，不得享受递延纳税优惠，应按规定计算缴纳个人所得税。

二、对上市公司股票期权、限制性股票和股权奖励适当延长纳税期限

（一）上市公司授予个人的股票期权、限制性股票和股权奖励，经向主管税务机关备案，个人可自股票期权行权、限制性股票解禁或取得股权奖励之日起，在不超过12个月的期限内缴纳个人所得税。《财政部　国家税务总局关于上市公司高管人员股票期权所得缴纳个人所得税有关问题的通知》（财税〔2009〕40号）自本通知施行之日起废止。

（二）上市公司股票期权、限制性股票应纳税款的计算，继续按照《财政部　国家税务总局关于个人股票期权所得征收个人所得税问题的通知》（财税〔2005〕35号）、《财政部　国家税务总局关于股票增值权所得和限制性股票所得征收个人所得税有关问题的通知》（财税〔2009〕5号）、《国家税务总局关于股权激励有关个人所得税问题的通知》（国税函〔2009〕461号）等相关规定执行。股权奖励应纳税款的计算比照上述规定执行。

三、对技术成果投资入股实施选择性税收优惠政策

（一）企业或个人以技术成果投资入股到境内居民企业，被投资企业支付的对价全部为股票（权）的，企业或个人可选择继续按现行有关税收政策执行，也可选择适用递延纳税优惠政策。

选择技术成果投资入股递延纳税政策的，经向主管税务机关备案，投资入股当期可暂不纳税，允许递延至转让股权时，按股权转让收入减去技术成果原值和合理税费后的差额计算缴纳所得税。

（二）企业或个人选择适用上述任一项政策，均允许被投资企业按技术成果投资入股时的评估值入账并在企业所得税前摊销扣除。

（三）技术成果是指专利技术（含国防专利）、计算机软件著作权、集成电路布图设计专有权、植物新品种权、生物医药新品种，以及科技部、财政部、国家税务总局确定的其他技术成果。

（四）技术成果投资入股，是指纳税人将技术成果所有权让渡给被投资企业、取得该企业股票（权）的行为。

四、相关政策

（一）个人从任职受雇企业以低于公平市场价格取得股票（权）的，凡不符合递延纳税条件，应在获得股票（权）时，对实际出资额低于公平市场价格的差额，按照“工资、薪金所得”项目，参照《财政部　国家税务总局关于个人股票期权所得征收个人所得税问题的通知》（财税〔2005〕35号）有关规定计算缴纳个人所得税。

（二）个人因股权激励、技术成果投资入股取得股权后，非上市公司在境内上市的，处置递延纳税的股权时，按照现行限售股有关征税规定执行。

（三）个人转让股权时，视同享受递延纳税优惠政策的股权优先转让。递延纳税的股权成本按照加权平均法计算，不与其他方式取得的股权成本合并计算。

（四）持有递延纳税的股权期间，因该股权产生的转增股本收入，以及以该递延纳税的股权再进行非货币性资产投资的，应在当期缴纳税款。

（五）全国中小企业股份转让系统挂牌公司按照本通知第一条规定执行。

适用本通知第二条规定的上市公司是指其股票在上海证券交易所、深圳证券交易所上市交易的股份有限公司。

五、配套管理措施

（一）对股权激励或技术成果投资入股选择适用递延纳税政策的，企业应在规定期限内到主管税务机关办理备案手续。未办理备案手续的，不得享受本通知规定的递延纳税优惠政策。

（二）企业实施股权激励或个人以技术成果投资入股，以实施股权激励或取得技术成果的企业为个人所得税扣缴义务人。递延纳税期间，扣缴义务人应在每个纳税年度终了后向主管税务机关报告递延纳税有关情况。

（三）工商部门应将企业股权变更信息及时与税务部门共享，暂不具备联网实时共享信息条件的，工商部门应在股权变更登记3个工作日内将信息与税务部门共享。

六、本通知自2016年9月1日起施行

中关村国家自主创新示范区2016年1月1日至8月31日之间发生的尚未纳税的股权奖励事项，符合本通知规定的相关条件的，可按本通知有关政策执行。

财政部　国家税务总局

2016年9月20日

附录 7 关于印发《政府出资产业投资基金管理暂行办法》的通知

（发改财金规〔2016〕2800 号）

中央和国家机关有关部委、直属机构，各省、自治区、直辖市及计划单列市、新疆生产建设兵团发展改革委：

为全面贯彻党的十八大和十八届三中、四中、五中全会精神，优化政府投资方式，发挥政府资金的引导作用和放大效应，提高政府资金使用效率，吸引社会资金投入政府支持领域和产业，根据《公司法》、《合伙企业法》、《中共中央国务院关于深化投融资体制改革的意见》（中发〔2016〕18 号）、《国务院关于促进创业投资持续健康发展的若干意见》（国发〔2016〕53 号）、《国务院关于创新重点领域投融资机制 鼓励社会投资的指导意见》（国发〔2014〕60 号）等法律法规和有关文件精神，我们制定了《政府出资产业投资基金管理暂行办法》。现印发给你们，请认真贯彻执行。

附件：政府出资产业投资基金管理暂行办法

国家发展改革委

2016 年 12 月 30 日

附件

政府出资产业投资基金管理暂行办法

第一章 总 则

第一条 为促进国民经济持续健康发展，优化政府投资方式，发挥政府资金的引导作用和放大效应，提高政府资金使用效率，吸引社会资金投入政府支持领域和产业，根据《公司法》、《合伙企业法》、《中共中央 国务院关于深化投融资体制改革的意见》（中发〔2016〕18 号）、《国务院关于促进创业投资持续健康发展的若干意见》（国发〔2016〕53 号）、《国务院关于创新重点领域投融资机制 鼓励社会投资的指导意见》（国发〔2014〕60 号）等法律法规和有关文件精神，制定本办法。

第二条 本办法所称政府出资产业投资基金，是指有政府出资，主要投资于非公开交易企业股权的股权投资基金和创业投资基金。

第三条 政府出资资金来源包括财政预算内投资、中央和地方各类专项建设基金及其它财政性资金。

第四条 政府出资产业投资基金可以采用公司制、合伙制、契约制等组织形式。

第五条 政府出资产业投资基金由基金管理人管理基金资产，由基金托管人托管基金资产。

第六条 政府出资产业投资基金应坚持市场化运作、专业化管理原则，政府出资人不得参与基金日常管理事务。

第七条 政府出资产业投资基金可以综合运用参股基金、联合投资、融资担保、政府出资适当让利等多种方式，充分发挥基金在贯彻产业政策、引导民间投资、稳定经济增长等方面的作用。

第八条 国家发展改革委会同地方发展改革部门对政府出资产业投资基金业务活动实施事中事后管理，负责推动政府出资产业投资基金行业信用体系建设，定期发布行业发展报告，维护有利于行业持续健康发展的良好市场秩序。

第二章 政府出资产业投资基金的募集和登记管理

第九条 政府向产业投资基金出资，可以采取全部由政府出资、与社会资本共同出资或向符合条件的已有产业投资基金投资等形式。

第十条 政府出资产业投资基金社会资金部分应当采取私募方式募集，募集行为应符合相关法律法规及国家有关部门规定。

第十一条 除政府外的其他基金投资者为具备一定风险识别和承受能力的合格机构投资者。

第十二条 国家发展改革委建立全国政府出资产业投资基金信用信息登记系统，并指导地方发展改革部门建立本区域政府出资产业投资基金信用信息登记子系统。中央各部门及其直属机构出资设立的产业投资基金募集完毕后二十个工作日内，应在全国政府出资产业投资基金信用信息登记系统登记。地方政府或所属部门、直属机构出资设立的产业投资基金募集完毕后二十个工作日内，应在本区域政府出资产业投资基金信用信息登记子系统登记。发展改革部门应于报送材料齐备后五个工作日内予以登记。

第十三条 政府出资产业投资基金的投资方向，应符合区域规划、区域政策、产业政策、投资政策及其他国家宏观管理政策，能够充分发挥政府资金在特定领域的引导作用和放大效应，有效提高政府资金使用效率。

第十四条 政府出资产业投资基金在信用信息登记系统登记后，由发展改革部门根据登记信息在三十个工作日内对基金投向进行产业政策符合性审查，并在信用信息登记系统予以公开。对于未通过产业政策符合性审查的政府出资产业投资基金，各级发展改革部门应及时出具整改建议书，并抄送相关政府或部门。

第十五条 国家发展改革委负责中央各部门及其直属机构政府出资设立的产业投资基金材料完备性和产业政策符合性审查。地方各级发展改革部门负责本级政府或所属部门、直属机构政府出资设立的产业投资基金材料完备性和产业政策符合性审查。以下情况除外：

（一）各级地方政府或所属部门、直属机构出资额50亿元人民币（或等值外币）及以上的，由国家发展改革委负责材料完备性和产业政策符合性审查；

（二）50亿元人民币（或等值外币）以下超过一定规模的县、市地方政府或所属部门、直属机构出资，由省级发展改革部门负责材料完备性和产业政策符合性审查，具体规模由各省（自治区、直辖市）发展改革部门确定。

第十六条 政府出资产业投资基金信用信息登记主要包括以下基本信息：

（一）相关批复和基金组建方案；

（二）基金章程、合伙协议或基金协议；

（三）基金管理协议（如适用）；

（四）基金托管协议；

（五）基金管理人的章程或合伙协议；

（六）基金管理人高级管理人员的简历和过往业绩；

（七）基金投资人向基金出资的资金证明文件；

（八）其他资料。

第十七条 新发起设立政府出资产业投资基金，基金组建方案应包括：

（一）拟设基金主要发起人、管理人和托管人基本情况；

（二）拟设基金治理结构和组织架构；

（三）主要发起人和政府资金来源、出资额度；

（四）拟在基金章程、合伙协议或基金协议中确定的投资产业领域、投资方式、风险防控措施、激励机制、基金存续期限等；

（五）政府出资退出条件和方式；

（六）其他资料。

第十八条 政府向已设立产业投资基金出资，基金组建方案应包括：

（一）基金主要发起人、管理人和托管人基本情况；

（二）基金前期运行情况；

（三）基金治理结构和组织架构；

（四）基金章程、合伙协议或基金协议中确定的投资产业领域、投资方式、风险防控措施、激励机制等；

（五）其他资料。

第十九条 政府出资产业投资基金管理人履行下列职责：

（一）制定投资方案，并对所投企业进行监督、管理；

（二）按基金公司章程规定向基金投资者披露基金投资运作、基金管理信息服务等信息。定期编制基金财务报告，经有资质的会计师事务所审计后，向基金董事会（持有人大会）报告；

（三）基金公司章程、基金管理协议中确定的其他职责。

第二十条 基金管理人应符合以下条件：

（一）在中国大陆依法设立的公司或合伙企业，实收资本不低于 1000 万元人民币；

（二）至少有 3 名具备 3 年以上资产管理工作经验的高级管理人员；

（三）产业投资基金管理人及其董事、监事、高级管理人员及其他从业人员在最近三年无重大违法行为；

（四）有符合要求的营业场所、安全防范设施和与基金管理业务有关的其他设施；

（五）有良好的内部治理结构和风险控制制度。

第二十一条 基金应将基金资产委托给在中国境内设立的商业银行进行托管。基金与托管人签订托管协议，托管人按照协议约定对基金托管专户进行管理。政府出资产业投资基金托管人履行下列职责：

（一）安全保管所托管基金的全部资产；

（二）执行基金管理人发出的投资指令，负责基金名下的资金往来；

（三）依据托管协议，发现基金管理人违反国家法律法规、基金公司章程或基金董事会（持有人大会）决议的，不予执行；

（四）出具基金托管报告，向基金董事会（持有人大会）报告并向主管部门提交年度报告；

（五）基金公司章程、基金托管协议中规定的其他职责。

第二十二条 已登记并通过产业政策符合性审查的各级地方政府或所属部门、直属机构出资设立的产业投资基金，可以按规定取得中央各部门及其直属机构设立的政府出资产业投资基金母基金支持。

第二十三条 已登记并通过产业政策符合性审查的政府出资产业投资基金除政府外的其他股东或有限合伙人可以按规定申请发行企业债券，扩大资本规模，增强投资能力。

第三章　政府出资产业投资基金的投资运作和终止

第二十四条 政府出资产业投资基金应主要投资于以下领域：

（一）非基本公共服务领域。着力解决非基本公共服务结构性供需不匹配，因缺乏竞争激励机制而制约质量效率，体制机制创新不足等问题，切实提高非基本公共服务共建能力和共享水平。

（二）基础设施领域。着力解决经济社会发展中偏远地区基础设施建设滞后，结构性供需不匹配等问题，提高公共产品供给质量和效率，切实推进城乡、区域、人群基本服务均等化。

（三）住房保障领域。着力解决城镇住房困难家庭及新市民住房问题，完善住房保障供应方式，加快推进棚户区改造，完善保障性安居工程配套基础设施，有序推进旧住宅小区综合整治、危旧住房和非成套住房改造，切实增强政府住房保障可持续提供能力。

（四）生态环境领域。着力解决生态环境保护中存在的污染物排放量大面广，环境污染严重，山水林田湖缺乏保护，生态损害大，生态环境脆弱、风险高等问题，切实推进生态环境质量改善。

（五）区域发展领域。着力解决区域发展差距特别是东西差距拉大，城镇化仍滞后于工业化，区域产业结构趋同化等问题，落实区域合作的资金保障机制，切实推进区域协调协同发展。

（六）战略性新兴产业和先进制造业领域。着力解决战略性新兴产业和先进制造业在经济社会发展中的产业政策环境不完善，供给体系质量和效率偏低，供给和需求衔接不紧密等问题，切实推进看得准、有机遇的重点技术和产业领域实现突破。

（七）创业创新领域。着力解决创业创新在经济社会发展中的市场环境亟待改善，创投市场资金供给不足，企业创新动能较弱等问题，切实推进大众创业、万众创新。

投资于基金章程、合伙协议或基金协议中约定产业领域的比例不得低于基金募集规模或承诺出资额的 60%。

国家发展改革委将根据区域规划、区域政策、产业政策、投资政策及其他国家宏观管理政策适时调整并不定期发布基金投资领域指导意见。

第二十五条 政府出资产业投资基金应投资于：

（一）未上市企业股权，包括以法人形式设立的基础设施项目、重大工程项目等未上市企业的股权；

（二）参与上市公司定向增发、并购重组和私有化等股权交易形成的股份；

（三）经基金章程、合伙协议或基金协议明确或约定的符合国家产业政策的其他投资形式。

基金闲置资金只能投资于银行存款、国债、地方政府债、政策性金融债和政府支持债券等安全性和流动性较好的固定收益类资产。

第二十六条 政府出资产业投资基金对单个企业的投资额不得超过基金资产总值的20%，且不得从事下列业务：

（一）名股实债等变相增加政府债务的行为；

（二）公开交易类股票投资，但以并购重组为目的的除外；

（三）直接或间接从事期货等衍生品交易；

（四）为企业提供担保，但为被投资企业提供担保的除外；

（五）承担无限责任的投资。

第二十七条 政府出资产业投资基金应在章程、委托管理协议等法律文件中，明确基金的分配方式、业绩报酬、管理费用和托管费用标准。

第二十八条 政府出资产业投资基金章程应当加强被投资企业的资金使用监管，防范财务风险。

第二十九条 基金一般应在存续期满后终止，确需延长存续期的，应报经政府基金设立批准部门同意后，与其他投资方按约定办理。

第四章 政府出资产业投资基金的绩效评价

第三十条 国家发展改革委建立并完善政府出资产业投资基金绩效评价指标体系。评价指标主要包括：

（一）基金实缴资本占认缴资本的比例；

（二）基金投向是否符合区域规划、区域政策、产业政策、投资政策及其他国家宏观管理政策，综合评估政府资金的引导作用和放大效应、资金使用效率及对所投产业的拉动效果等；

（三）基金投资是否存在名股实债等变相增加政府债务的行为；

（四）是否存在违反法律、行政法规等行为。

第三十一条 国家发展改革委每年根据评价指标对政府出资产业投资基金绩效进行系统性评分，并将评分结果适当予以公告。有关评价办法由国家发展改革委另行制定。金融机构可以根据评分结果对登记的政府出资产业投资基金给予差异化的信贷政策。

第三十二条 国家发展改革委建立并完善基金管理人绩效评价指标体系。评价指标主要包括：

（一）基金管理人实际管理的资产总规模；

（二）基金管理人过往投资业绩；

（三）基金管理人过往投资领域是否符合政府产业政策导向；

（四）基金管理人管理的基金运作是否存在公开宣传、向非合格机构投资者销售、违反职业道德底线等违规行为；

（五）基金管理人及其管理团队是否受到监管机构的行政处罚，是否被纳入全国信用信息共享平台失信名单；

（六）是否存在违反法律、行政法规等行为。

第三十三条 国家发展改革委每年根据评价指标对基金管理人绩效进行系统性评分，并将评分结果适当予以公告。有关评价办法由国家发展改革委另行制定。各级政府部门可以根据评分结果选择基金管理人。

第五章 政府出资产业投资基金行业信用建设

第三十四条 国家发展改革委会同有关部门加强政府出资产业投资基金行业信用体系建设，在政府出资产业投资基金信用信息登记系统建立基金、基金管理人和从业人员信用记录，并纳入全国信用信息共享平台。

第三十五条 地方发展改革部门会同地方有关部门负责区域内政府出资产业投资基金行业信用体系建设，并通过政府出资产业投资基金信用信息登记系统报送基金、基金管理人和从业人员有关信息。报送内容包括但不限于工商信息、行业信息、经营信息和风险信息等。

第三十六条 对有不良信用记录的基金、基金管理人和从业人员，国家发展改革委通过"信用中国"网站统一向社会公布。地方发展改革部门可以根据各地实际情况，将区域内失信基金、基金管理人和从业人员名单以适当方式予以公告。

发展改革部门会同有关部门依据所适用的法律法规及多部门签署的联合惩戒备忘录等对列入失信联合惩戒名单的基金、基金管理人和从业人员开展联合惩戒，惩戒措施包括但不限于市场禁入、限制作为供应商参加政府采购活动、限制财政补助补贴性资金支持、从严审核发行企业债券等。

第三十七条 国家发展改革委在"信用中国"网站设立政府出资产业投资基金行业信用建设专栏，公布失信基金、基金管理人和从业人员名单，及时更新名单目录及惩戒处罚等信息，并开展联合惩戒的跟踪、监测、统计和评估工作。

第六章　政府出资产业投资基金的监督管理

第三十八条　国家发展改革委会同地方发展改革部门严格履行基金的信用信息监管责任，建立健全政府出资产业投资基金信用信息登记系统，建立完善政府出资产业投资基金绩效评价制度，加快推进政府出资产业投资基金行业信用体系建设，加强对政府出资产业投资基金的监督管理。

第三十九条　对未登记的政府出资产业投资基金及其受托管理机构，发展改革部门应当督促其在二十个工作日内申请办理登记。逾期未登记的，将其作为"规避登记政府出资产业投资基金"、"规避登记受托管理机构"，并以适当方式予以公告。

第四十条　中央各部门及其直属机构出资设立的产业投资基金的基金管理人应当于每个会计年度结束后四个月内，向国家发展改革委提交基金及基金管理人的年度业务报告、经有资质的会计师事务所审计的年度财务报告和托管报告，并及时报告投资运作过程中的重大事项。

地方政府或所属部门、直属机构出资设立的产业投资基金的基金管理人应当于每个会计年度结束后四个月内，向本级发展改革部门提交基金及基金管理人的年度业务报告、经有资质的会计师事务所审计的年度财务报告和托管报告，并及时报告投资运作过程中的重大事项。

重大事项包括但不限于公司章程修订、资本增减、高级管理人员变更、合并、清算等。

第四十一条　发展改革部门通过现场和非现场"双随机"抽查，会同有关部门对政府出资产业投资基金进行业务指导，促进基金规范运作，有效防范风险。基金有关当事人应积极配合有关部门对政府出资产业投资基金合规性审查，提供有关文件、账簿及其他资料，不得以任何理由阻扰、拒绝检查。

第四十二条　对未按本办法规范运作的政府出资产业投资基金及其基金管理机构、托管机构，发展改革部门可以会同有关部门出具监管建议函，视情节轻重对其采取责令改正、监管谈话、出具警示函、取消登记等措施，并适当予以公告。

第四十三条　建立政府出资产业投资基金重大项目稽察制度，健全政府投资责任追究制度。完善社会监督机制，鼓励公众和媒体监督。

第四十四条　各级发展改革部门应当自觉接受审计、监察等部门依据职能分工进行的监督检查。各级发展改革部门工作人员有徇私舞弊、滥用职权、弄虚作假、玩忽职守、未依法履行职责的，依法给予处分；构成犯罪的，依法追究刑事责任。

第七章　附　则

第四十五条　本办法由国家发展改革委负责解释。

第四十六条　政府出资产业投资基金投资境外企业，按照境外投资有关规定办理。

第四十七条　本办法自 2017 年 4 月 1 日起施行，具体登记办法由国家发展改革委另行制定。本办法施行前设立的政府出资产业投资基金及其受托管理机构，应当在本办法施行后两个月内按照本办法有关规定到发展改革部门登记。

附录 8 中国创业风险投资机构名录

公司名称	成立时间	网址	传真
安徽安元投资基金有限公司	2015-07-17	—	—
安徽大学资产经营有限公司	2009-10-13	zcgs.ahu.cn	0551-65329875
安徽鼎信创业投资有限公司	2012-06-05	—	0551-65319112
安徽丰创生物技术产业创业投资有限公司	2013-04-02	—	0551-65182095
安徽高科创业投资有限公司	2010-01-28	www.ahgoco.com	0551-65319112
安徽高新金通安益二期创业投资基金（有限合伙）	2015-12-24	—	—
安徽高新金通安益股权投资基金（有限合伙）	2015-03-23	—	0551-66103790
安徽高新同华创业投资基金（有限合伙）	2015-03-25	—	—
安徽高新招商致远股权投资基金（有限合伙）	2015-03-23	—	—
安徽国安创业投资有限公司	2010-09-15	—	0551-65732844
安徽国耀创业投资有限公司	2013-11-28	—	—
安徽国元创投有限责任公司	2010-06-13	www.ahgyct.com	0551-63699700
安徽合信投资有限公司	2002-12-30	—	—
安徽恒兴创业投资管理有限公司	2002-04-26	—	—
安徽红土创业投资有限公司	2010-08-10	www.szvc.com.cn	0551-65666025
安徽华文创业投资管理有限公司	2003-06-04	—	0551-63533281
安徽徽商产业投资基金管理有限公司	2008-03-18	www.hygcapital.com	0551-5844598
安徽汇智富创业投资有限公司	2013-03-26	—	0551-65383158
安徽火花科技创业投资有限公司	2013-06-25	—	—
安徽昆冈创业股权投资合伙企业（有限合伙）	2010-08-17	—	0553-3887132
安徽联华盈创投资管理有限公司	2013-09-05	—	0551-65367321
安徽启光能源科技研究院有限公司	2012-10-31	www.qiguang.org	0553-3021991
安徽庆余投资管理有限公司	2012-07-23	—	—
安徽省安庆发展投资（集团）有限公司	2004-07-19	www.aqfztz.com	0556-5595212
安徽省创投资本基金有限公司	2010-07-27	—	0551-67131875

公司名称	成立时间	网址	传真
安徽省创业投资有限公司	2008-07-09	—	0551-63677211
安徽省高新创业投资有限责任公司	2009-12-23	—	0555-3116896
安徽省高新技术产业投资有限公司	2014-12-16	www.ahinv.com	0551-63677211
安徽省科创投资管理咨询有限责任公司	2000-10-31	—	0551-66195765
安徽省科技产业投资有限公司	1999-07	www.ahkjtz.com.cn	0551-66195708
安徽西格玛壹号投资合伙企业（有限合伙）	2013-05-24	—	—
安徽兴皖创业投资有限公司	2010-08-20	—	0551-65732843
安徽亿诚融资理财信息服务有限公司	2012-08-29	www.ahycrzlc.com	0556-5275508
安徽智鼎创业投资有限公司	2009-11	www.qyzyw.com	—
安庆百科实业有限公司	2004-02-09	—	0556-5323811
安庆发投创业投资有限公司	2012-09-28	—	—
蚌埠市科技创业投资有限公司	2008-06-26	—	0552-3186802
蚌埠市远大创新创业投资有限公司	2010-09-28	—	0551-63186678
蚌埠皖北金牛创业投资有限公司	2011-05-17	—	0552-4129773
蚌埠中城创业投资有限公司	2009-03-16	—	0552-3183880
池州中安创业投资基金合伙企业（有限合伙）	2016-06-01	—	—
滁州浚源创业投资中心（有限合伙）	2011-06	jycapital.cn	010-82661938
杭州海邦巨擎创业投资合伙企业（有限合伙）	2016-03-14	—	—
合肥高特佳创业投资有限责任公司	2010-04-19	www.szgig.com	0551-65310817
合肥高新产业投资有限公司	2016-07-12	—	0551-65326509
合肥高新创业投资管理合伙企业（有限合伙）	2015-08-21	www.hfgxt.com.cn	0551-65326509
合肥高新科技创业投资有限公司	2012-10-19	gxkt.hfgxjt.com	0551-65326509
合肥广电投资有限责任公司	2003-08-06	www.hfbtv.com	0551-63509205
合肥赛富合元创业投资中心（有限合伙）	2011-01-13	—	—
合肥世纪创新投资有限公司	2002-09-11	—	0551-66195765
合肥市创新科技风险投资有限公司	2000-08-28	www.hfgk.com	0551-62675471
合肥市高科技风险投资有限公司	2000-04-18	—	—
合肥同安创业投资基金行	2010-09-06	—	0551-63677135
合肥兴泰资本管理有限公司	1997-06-02	www.xtkg.com	0551-63758980
合和达投资管理有限公司	2011-11-04	—	—
华晟投资管理有限责任公司	2012-05-14	—	0551-63533681
淮南市创业风险投资有限公司	2011-11-26	—	0554-6679199
淮南市天使投资基金（有限合伙）	2016-07-26	—	—
黄山市天使投资基金	2016-07-25	—	0559-2528715
汇智创业投资有限公司	2009-04-29	—	0551-65321476

公司名称	成立时间	网址	传真
六安高科创业投资有限公司	2011-10-20	—	0564-3323933
鸟巢乐视体育文化产业基金	—	—	—
宁波市天使投资引导基金有限公司	2013-01-08	www.nbstf.org.cn	0574-27960368
苏州协立创业投资有限公司	2013-04-28	—	025-86816826
太湖县企业公有资产经营管理有限公司	2005-12-01	thzcgs5506@sina.com	0556-4162643
铜陵市中融大有天源创业投资有限合伙企业（有限合伙）	2016-08-23	—	—
铜陵天源股权投资集团有限公司	2007-02-01	—	0562-2885077
皖江产业转移投资基金（安徽）管理有限公司	2009-01-15	—	—
芜湖达成创业投资中心（有限合伙）	2010-04-28	—	—
芜湖富海浩研创业投资基金（有限合伙）	2012-12-27	—	0553-3850713
芜湖奇瑞科技有限公司	2001-11-21	www.mychery.com	0553-5922267
芜湖瑞建汽车产业创业投资有限公司	2010-07-01	—	0553-3812768
芜湖瑞业股权投资基金（有限合伙）	2009-12-21	—	021-64151936
芜湖市科创融资担保有限公司	2004-05-28	—	0553-5965868
芜湖市世纪江东创业投资中心（有限合伙）	2009-08-18	www.jd-capital.cn	0553-5772022
芜湖远大创业投资有限公司	2009-04-23	—	0553-5992133
浙江华睿火炬创业投资合伙企业（有限合伙）	—	—	—
浙江舟山如山汇盈创业投资合伙企业（合伙企业）	2016-04-28	www.chinadunan.com	0571-87896213
诸暨华睿庆丰创业投资合伙企业（有限合伙）	—	—	—
21 世纪天使资本	2011-06-01	www.21angel.cn	—
UC 移动游戏产业成长基金	2012-07-28	—	—
Vertical Oracle Ventures Fund	—	www.verticaloracle.com	—
爱康创业投资有限公司	2008-04-03	—	—
奥仁治创业投资管理（北京）有限公司	2008-09-26	—	—
北京安芙兰创业投资有限公司	2009-06-11	www.vcpe.hk	010-66416805
北京奥瑞吉创业投资有限公司	2007-12-11	—	—
北京白鲸创业投资有限公司	2010-02-23	—	—
北京宝盈银通创业投资有限公司	2009-11-02	—	—
北京北软汇智投资管理有限公司	2013-01-01	www.beiruanangel.com	010-82144889
北京北邮创业投资有限公司	2001-09-01	—	+86-10-85267699
北京滨复华耀资本投资管理中心（有限合伙）	2012-09-11	—	—
北京伯乐纵横投资管理中心（有限合伙）	—	—	—
北京铂运发投资基金管理有限公司	—	brainfunds.com.cn	+86-10-82525129
北京博瑞盛德创业投资有限公司	2009-11-09	—	—

公司名称	成立时间	网址	传真
北京博思辰光资产管理有限公司	2010-12-16	—	—
北京博星投资管理有限公司	2006-05-01	www.bestar.com.cn	+86-10-58561012
北京不等投资管理有限公司	2015-06	—	010-67767088
北京仓源投资基金管理有限公司	2010-06-01	www.cycap.com.cn	+86-10-84374537
北京长运兴安投资有限责任公司	2004-04-14	—	—
北京晨光创业投资有限公司	2000-12-25	www.chgvc.com	+86-10-69709488
北京晨光宏盛中小企业创业投资有限公司	2009-03-01	www.bjcghs.com	+86-10-89710922
北京崇德英盛投资管理有限公司	2015-05	—	010-59773801
北京初者之心投资管理有限公司	2015-04-22	www.chuxincapital.com	—
北京创动投资咨询有限公司	2011-03-24	—	—
北京创时信和创业投资有限公司	2009-08-06	—	—
北京达德厚鑫投资管理有限公司	2013-11-28	—	—
北京大河融科创业投资有限公司	2015-06-19	www.rivervc.com	010-62509768
北京大鹏财富创业投资中心（有限合伙）	2011-01-20	—	—
北京鼎晖时代创业投资有限公司	2007-10-11	—	—
北京鼎金翔辉创业投资有限责任公司	2009-01-01	www.dinkincapital.com	—
北京鼎元合创投资有限公司	2010-07-27	genesis-vc.com	+86-10-83528966-8016
北京东方博智创业投资中心（有限合伙）	2008-04-14	—	—
北京方圆天成投资管理有限公司	2010-09-07	—	—
北京芳晟投资管理中心（有限合伙）	2011-04-21	www.fangfund.com	+86-10-65035588
北京丰泽久源创业投资有限责任公司	2002-07-02	—	—
北京风云际会投资管理有限公司	2015-11-20	www.fengyun.vc	—
北京峰汇资本管理有限公司	2015-03-31	—	—
北京富坤中技投资管理有限公司	2010-05-01	—	+86-10-62679666
北京富智阳光投资管理有限公司	2010-07-16	—	—
北京高新技术创业投资有限公司	1998-10-27	www.bhti.com.cn	+86-10-62142499
北京工顺投资管理有限公司	2010-06-01	—	—
北京股权投资发展管理有限公司	2009-09-28	—	—
北京光大五道口投资基金管理有限公司	2015-03-24	—	—
北京国泰创业投资有限公司	2003-03-19	—	—
北京海富创业投资有限公司	2006-07-31	—	—
北京海纳百泉投资基金管理有限公司	2015-06-15	—	—
北京海豫祺创业投资管理有限公司	2012-02-22	—	—
北京合一科文投资管理有限公司	2013-05-06	—	—
北京和光嘉诚投资管理有限公司	2011-09-21	—	—

公司名称	成立时间	网址	传真
北京荷塘探索创业投资有限公司	2015-06-09	—	—
北京恒资时代创业投资股份有限公司	2011-02-01	www.bjhzsd.com	—
北京红日创业投资股份有限公司	2009-12-08	—	+86-10-85186396
北京宏泰中汇投资管理有限公司	2009-08-26	—	—
北京洪泰同创投资管理有限公司	2014-10-24	www.angelplus.cn	—
北京华创盛景投资管理有限公司	2010-01-26	—	—
北京华创智业投资有限公司	2010-05-01	hczycapital.com	+86-10-82525299-800
北京华汇通创业投资管理有限公司	2007-07-01	www.bjhhtvc.com	+86-10-82158841
北京华清博远创业投资有限公司	—	—	—
北京华商盈通投资有限公司	2008-03-07	—	—
北京华胜天成能源投资管理有限公司	2012-12	—	010-56907271-818
北京华信金石创业投资有限公司	2008-01-23	—	—
北京汇江华盛创业投资有限公司	2010-02-08	—	—
北京汇金立方投资管理中心（有限合伙）	2008-05-01	—	—
北京吉磊创业投资有限公司	2009-01-01	www.jileivc.com	+86-10-59604999
北京极客梦工场创业投资中心（有限合伙）	2011-02-28	—	—
北京加华伟业资本管理有限公司	2006-07-01	www.scharvestcap.com	+86-10-59897661
北京嘉华创业投资有限公司	2011-02-24	—	010-64685181
北京嘉木英实创业投资管理中心（有限合伙）	2012-05-02	—	—
北京金科同盛创业投资有限公司	2008-10-14	—	—
北京京富融源投资管理有限公司	2008-07-01	—	—
北京京国发投资管理有限公司	2011-12-19	—	—
北京晶创合创业投资有限公司	2009-05-21	—	—
北京晶世时代创业投资有限公司	2007-05-15	—	—
北京开物昌盛投资管理有限公司	2012-12	—	—
北京开物投资管理有限公司	2011-05-16	kaiwucapital.com	+86-21-34240559
北京科技风险投资股份有限公司	1998-10-28	www.bvcc.com.cn	+86-10-68943779
北京乐道兴创业投资有限公司	2001-12-25	—	—
北京乐视文创投资管理中心（有限合伙）	—	—	—
北京力帆科技创业投资有限公司	2006-11-07	—	—
北京龙磐投资管理咨询中心（普通合伙）	2010-08-23	—	—
北京梅花天使创业投资管理有限公司	2015-05	—	—
北京南车创业投资有限公司	2011-09	—	—
北京貔亿华丰投资管理中心（有限合伙）	2012-08-27	—	—
北京普凯瑞盛股权投资管理中心（有限合伙）	2011-09-06	—	—

公司名称	成立时间	网址	传真
北京奇伦天佑创业投资有限公司	2008-08-07	—	—
北京麒麟华夏创业投资中心（有限合伙）	2010-07-06	—	—
北京启赋投资咨询中心（有限合伙）	—	—	—
北京乾元盛创业投资有限责任公司	2007-05-23	—	—
北京乔戈里创业投资中心（有限合伙）	2009-11-12	—	—
北京青年创业投资有限公司	2000-04-29	—	—
北京青云创业投资管理有限公司	2001-07-13	www.cefund.com	+86-10- 56815788
北京清源德丰创业投资有限公司	2000-04-29	www.tsinghuavc.com	+86-10-62780287
北京瑞富时代投资有限公司	2000-09-04	—	—
北京瑞鑫安泰创业投资中心（有限合伙）	2008-02-02	—	—
北京神都天骄投资管理有限公司	2006-04-01	www.stutendril.com	+86-10-68169500
北京盛邦惠民创业投资有限责任公司	—	www.shbhm.com	+86-10-62151203
北京盛信开元投资管理有限公司	2011-09-23	—	—
北京盛元丰亨创业投资有限公司	2009-03-01	www.syfhct.cn	—
北京施拉特创业投资管理有限公司	—	—	—
北京世纪方舟资本管理中心（有限合伙）	2007-01-01	macapital.cn	+86-10-65666777
北京市富汇创业投资管理有限公司	2008-05	www.fuhocapital.com	010-8265666
北京市久盛立德创业投资管理中心（有限合伙）	2011-03-29	—	—
北京市元亨盈盛创业投资管理中心（有限合伙）	2011-03-29	—	—
北京首创创业投资有限公司	1998-07-24	www.capitalvc.com	+86-10-68964810
北京首业君立投资管理有限公司	2012-06-26	www.leadingcap.net	—
北京汤荣颐合风险投资有限公司	2006-06-20	—	—
北京天诚仕通投资有限公司	2008-01-01	—	—
北京天地融创创业投资有限公司	2006-02-21	—	—
北京天星四海投资管理有限公司	2015-06-29	—	—
北京通盈盛世投资基金管理有限公司	2010-01-01	—	—
北京同渡信成创业投资合伙企业（有限合伙）	2014	www.tenduuvc.com	—
北京拓世诺金投资有限公司	—	—	—
北京万丰创新投资有限公司	2009-08-03	—	+86-10-85297345
北京星河互联创业投资有限公司	2009-07-01	www.galaxyinternet.com	—
北京银富投资有限公司	—	www.yinfutz.com	+86-10-68413553
北京银河吉星创业投资有限责任公司	2010-06-09	—	—
北京银河金桥投资有限公司	2006-10-24	www.goldenbridge-inv.com	+86-10-62720225
北京引航创业投资有限公司	2007-11-08	www.pilotcapital.com	—
北京盈科创业投资管理有限公司	2007-01-24	—	—

公司名称	成立时间	网址	传真
北京用友幸福投资管理有限公司	2010-05-12	—	—
北京远望创业投资有限公司	2001-09-27	—	—
北京浙控金诚资产管理有限公司	2012-09-08	—	—
北京正润创业投资有限责任公司	2007-11-19	www.prope.com.cn	+86-10-88568883
北京正义合盈创业投资管理中心（有限合伙）	2008-03-03	—	—
北京致诚联合创业投资有限责任公司	2003-05-14	—	—
北京智谷创新管理公司（有限合伙）	—	—	—
北京中晨维金创业投资有限公司	2010-02-26	—	—
北京中富投资集团有限公司	2010-12-16	www.zfinvest.com	+86-10-65518503
北京中关村创业投资发展有限公司	1998-10-07	www.zgcvc.com	+86-10-82483075
北京中关村宏和投资咨询有限公司	—	—	+86-10-62793393
北京中关村青年科技创业投资有限公司	2000-01-05	www.bjcvc.com.cn	+86-10-62770009
北京中海创业投资有限公司	2003-04-09	www.zh-vc.com	+86-10-68947179-8118
北京中海投资管理公司	1993-01-01	www.zhtzgl.cn	+86-10-68947179-8123
北京中汇同信创业投资有限公司	2001-08-08	—	—
北京中技天博创业投资有限公司	2010-04-08	—	—
北京中经瑞益投资管理有限公司	2000-08-01	www.real-capital.cn	—
北京中联和众投资管理有限公司	—	—	—
北京中通和达创业投资管理有限公司	2008-02-03	—	—
北京中投新华投资管理有限公司	2014-11-14	—	—
北京中咨顺景创业投资有限公司	2009-07-24	—	—
北京子平创业投资有限公司	2001-12-26	—	—
崇德弘信（北京）投资管理有限公司	2012-12	—	—
德国 vk 风险投资有限公司	—	—	—
东方海辰创业投资	2005-01-01	sunupcapital.com	+86-10-52776866
东方元鼎（北京）投资咨询有限公司	—	www.oydcapital.com	+86-10-62668968
东海世纪投资管理有限公司	2011-11-23	www.donghaiziben.com	—
栋盛国际投资（北京）有限公司	—	—	—
多策投资管理合伙企业（有限合伙）	—	www.ducepital.com	—
二十一世纪天使创业投资有限公司	2011-06-01	www.21vc.com	—
福建劲达创业投资有限公司	—	www.jindavc.com	+86-10-68364631
富程（北京）投资基金管理有限公司	2012-01-01	www.foch-fund.com	+86-10-59196200
富汇创业投资管理有限公司	2008-05-01	www.fuhocapital.com	+86-10-82656666-666
歌石投资	2010-01-01	www.nextviewcapital.com	+86-10-63703935-8009
光大三山创业投资管理有限公司	2007-05-01	www.everbright165.com	+86-10-68943336

公司名称	成立时间	网址	传真
国开厚德（北京）投资基金有限公司	2012-11-20	—	—
国投高科技投资有限公司	—	—	+86-10-66579545
海风联投资顾问（北京）有限责任公司	2007-09-06	www.hflcapital.com	+86-10-59733465
和光股权投资管理合伙企业	2009-06-01	heguangcapital.com	+86-10-59718363
和润领航投资管理（北京）有限公司	2015-12-03	—	—
红土嘉智投资管理顾问（北京）有限公司	2009-04-02	—	—
洪范基金管理有限公司	2009-02-24	—	+86-10-59051120
华控汇金投资管理有限公司	2003-09-01	www.thcapital.com.cn	+86-10-59761180
华软资本管理集团股份有限公司	2010-09-21	www.chinasoftcapital.com	+86-10-65535560
华盛通宝（北京）股权投资基金管理有限公司	2011-10-25	—	—
华夏信诺创业投资管理（北京）有限公司	2006-09-12	—	—
华夏幸福创业投资有限公司	2010-11-26	—	—
汇力（北京）投资基金管理有限公司	2009-04-01	huilifund.com	+86-10-57611899
惠银东方（北京）投资管理有限公司	2010-08-24	www.sinoibg.com	+86-10-85615560
建银金辰创业投资有限公司	2011-01-07	—	—
经纬创投（北京）投资管理顾问有限公司	2008-01-28	www.matrixpartners.com.cn	+86-10-65000066
九州华伟创业投资有限公司	2010-05-10	www.chinagreat.cn	—
君联资本管理股份有限公司	2003-11-19	www.legendcapital.com.cn	+86-10-8913-9001
钧天创业投资有限公司	2009-04-28	—	—
开投基金	2007-03-01	—	+86-21-62950230
开信创业投资管理有限公司	2008-01-01	www.kaixininvestment.com	+86-10-58023996
凯旋创投	2008-04-01	www.keytonevc.com	+86-10-85192584
凯悦资本	2008-01-01	www.keyevents.com.cn	+86-10-85898667
乐耕资本	2010-01-01	www.elegantcapital.com.cn	+86-10-67136719
联想创投集团	2016-03-21	capital.lenovo.com	—
领航资本	2008-10-01	navicapital.com.cn	+86-10-85911565
龙渊云腾基金	2013-05-06	www.devfund.cn	—
马力创业投资有限公司	2000-11-06	—	+86-10-62791750
明石投资管理有限公司	1999-01-01	www.brightstone-fund.com	+86-10-60190322
摩根大通（中国）创业投资有限公司	2010-04-08	—	—
南山资产管理（天津）有限公司	2015-05-29	www.nanshancap.com	—
宁波梅花天使投资管理有限公司	2014-04-28	www.plumventures.cn	—
盘古创富（北京）创业投资管理有限公司	—	www.vangoocapital.com	—
启迪创业投资管理（北京）有限公司	2001-03-30	www.tsinghua-vc.com	+86-10-62705209
千乘资本	2016-01-01	—	—

公司名称	成立时间	网址	传真
青山同创投资有限公司	2013-01-01	www.hwazing.com	—
清华科技创业投资有限公司	2000-04-01	—	+86-10-62780287
清华兴业投资管理有限公司	1999-01-01	—	+86-10-62780159
清控创业投资有限公司	2011-06-14	—	+86-10-82150099
仁和金砂（北京）投资基金管理有限公司	2011-02-24	cpembj.com	+86-10-58672573
融鑫谷（北京）投资基金管理有限公司	2015-04	—	010-59773804
融银资本投资管理有限公司	—	ry-capital.com	+86-10-82871117
赛曼基金	—	—	—
上海常石投资管理有限公司	2014-10	longcapital.cn	—
尚心（北京）投资管理咨询有限公司	2007-08-31	—	—
深圳市前海青松创业投资基金管理企业（有限合伙）	2013-12-13	www1.qingsongfund.com	+86-55-33303333
盛世华韵	—	—	—
石景山互联网金融产业投资基金	2013-08-30	—	—
首一创业投资有限公司	2006-01-01	www.sonevc.com	010-64939855
天裕创业投资有限公司	2010-12-06	www.tyvc.com.cn	+86-10-88092065
通用技术创业投资有限公司	2012-03-19	www.gtimvc.com.cn	—
同冀华成创业投资（北京）有限公司	2010-10-27	—	—
完美世界风险投资基金	2011-12-31	—	—
万里锦程创业投资有限公司	2008-04-03	—	—
网易资本	—	—	—
旺家投资管理（北京）有限公司	2015-04-22	www.wjholding.com	86+010+84554986
维多利安创业投资管理有限公司	2012-04-27	—	—
沃美投资管理有限公司	2008-01-14	www.womei.com	—
一八九八创投基金	2015-10-18	—	—
一壹投资基金管理有限公司	2010-11-23	—	—
宜信新金融产业投资基金	2016-02-25	—	—
银港创业投资有限责任公司	2009-11-17	—	—
英诺天使基金	2013-04-01	www.innoangel.com	—
永威投资有限公司	1995-10-01	www.asiavest.com	+86-10-65687458
愉悦资本	2015-04-01	—	—
云天使基金	2012-08-20	www.cloudangelfunds.com	—
浙商万嘉（北京）创业投资管理有限公司	2010-12-22	www.entworks.com.cn	—
中发君盛（北京）投资管理有限公司	2009-12-12	—	—
中富创业投资（北京）有限公司	2007-09-21	www.zfinvest.com	010-65518503
中关村创业投资发展有限公司	1998-10	http:www.zgcvc.com	010-82483075

公司名称	成立时间	网址	传真
中国 LED 光电产业基金	2013-03-29	—	—
中国创业投资有限公司	—	www.chinavest.com	+86-21-63293951
中国高新投资集团公司	1989-04-19	www.gaoxin-china.com.cn	+86-10-63288606
中金创新（北京）国际投资管理顾问有限公司	—	—	—
中金创业国际投资管理有限公司	2005-12-01	cfim.com.cn	+86-10-84086012
中金高技术资产管理有限公司	2000-01-01	www.cicmc.cn	+86-10-66083532
中软科技创业投资有限公司	—	—	+86-10-62190210
中天利达风险投资有限公司	2001-11-15	—	—
中网百度创业基金	—	—	—
中英低碳创业投资公司	—	—	—
紫光创新投资有限公司	2000-04-19	www.thuvc.com	+86-10-68947226
福建北辰星投资管理有限公司	2014-12-12	wwwporitarcap.com	—
福建红桥创业投资管理有限公司	2007-08-29	hqcapital.com.cn	0592-2278628
福建华兴创业投资有限公司	2000-12-26	www.fjhxvc.com	0591-87858275
福建省乐助投资有限公司	2011-04-25	—	—
福建泽联股权投资管理有限公司	2013-06-04	—	0592-5793728
弘信创业工场投资集团股份有限公司	1996-10-30	—	0592-5627310
罗普特（厦门）投资管理有限公司	2013-05-30	—	0592-3662225
南安市红桥创业投资有限公司	2010-08-13	www.hqcapital.com.cn	0595-86392990
泉州市红桥创业投资有限公司	2010-02-22	www.hqcapital.com.cn	0595-28292990
泉州市红桥民间资本管理股份有限公司	2008-10-29	www.hqcapital.com.cn	0595-82032092
厦门保金股权投资基金管理有限公司	2012-12-24	—	0592-2239515
厦门冰与火创客投资管理有限公司	2015-08-04	www.future-pearl.com	—
厦门博芮投资股份有限公司	2012-05-29	www.xmbory.com	0592-5021184
厦门创翼创业投资有限公司	2008-06-20	—	0592-2360798
厦门创翼德晖股权投资合伙企业（有限合伙）	2011-02-11	www.divinecapital.com.cn	0592-2915616
厦门创兆地产投资管理有限公司	2012-03-26	—	—
厦门高新技术创业中心	1996-12-18	www.xmibi.com	0592-3923999
厦门高新技术风险投资有限公司	1998-12-09	—	—
厦门高新科创天使创业投资有限公司	2013-03-11	www.xmibi.com	0592-3923999
厦门国海坚果投资管理有限公司	2013-03-28	www.capitalnuts.com	0592-2577216
厦门海西创业投资有限公司	2015-06-09	www.hxvc.cn	0592-3929888
厦门红土创业投资有限公司	2010-06-08	—	0592-5778290
厦门红土投资管理有限公司	2010-06-12	—	0592-5770650
厦门华登创业投资有限公司	2008-08-13	www.xmerqing.com	0592-2219232

公司名称	成立时间	网址	传真
厦门火炬集团创业投资有限公司	2004-04-05	www.xmhjtz.com	0592-5711818
厦门吉比特股权投资有限公司	2016-08-24	—	0592-3180216
厦门嘉壹创业投资有限公司	2014-09-12	—	0592-5134308
厦门坚果投资管理有限公司	2012-08-07	www.capitalnuts.com	0592-2577216
厦门金拾股权投资基金管理有限公司	2015-06-05	—	0592-5311500
厦门科技创业投资有限公司	2011-04-06	—	0592-5711818
厦门隆领投资合伙企业（有限合伙）	2011-03-29	www.lognling.com	—
厦门铭源红桥投资管理有限公司	2011-08-31	—	0592-2278628
厦门七匹狼节能环保产业创业投资管理有限公司	2012-12-28	—	0592-5377752
厦门青瓦投资管理有限公司	2014-05-05	www.greytile.cn	0592-2387226
厦门软件产业投资发展有限公司	1998-12-02	www.xsoft.com.cn	0592-3929888
厦门松涛风险投资股份有限公司	2000-04-28	www.songtao.com.cn	0592-6093926
厦门携合创业投资合伙企业（有限合伙）	2013-08-01	—	0592-2278628
厦门永红创业投资有限公司	2006-12-19	—	0592-5058092
白银科键创新创业投资基金合伙企业（有限合伙）	2016-11-04	—	—
甘肃普高创业投资基金（有限合伙）	2016-09-14	—	—
甘肃省科技发展投资有限责任公司	2014-03-31	—	0931-8730629
甘肃省科技风险投资有限公司	2001-08	—	0931-8537887
甘肃现代农业产业创业投资基金有限公司	2012-12-25	—	0931-4890588
东莞市博源凯德创业投资合伙企业（有限合伙）	2011-01-24	—	0769-23022868
东莞市华科松湖创业投资有限公司	2009-12-23	—	0769-22899127
佛山市博古科技投资有限公司	2009-09-14	—	0757-87380711
佛山市科海创业投资有限公司	2002-05-15	—	0757-86683130
佛山市三水高新创业中心有限公司	2004-09-29	www.fscyzx.comcn	0757-87380711
广东博源创业投资有限公司	2009-09-24	—	0769-23022868
广东德运创业投资有限公司	2013-05-03	www.dmkjy.com	0757-22908821
广东广弘创业投资有限公司	2011-10-11	—	020-87228300
广东国科蓝海创业投资企业（有限合伙）	2015-06-17	—	—
广东合银投资管理咨询有限公司	2010-06-27	www.gdhyct.com	020-83983566
广东集成创业投资有限公司	2008-09-23	www.ipevc.cn	020-83206999
广东猎投创业投资基金合伙企业（有限合伙）	2014-10-28	—	020-81202990
广东南方星辰创业投资有限公司	2009-05-26	—	020-87329436
广东省科技创业投资有限公司	1992-11-05	www.gvcgc.com	—
广东省科技风险投资有限公司	1998-01-08	www.gvcgc.com	020-87684955
广东省粤科金融集团有限公司	2000-09-21	www.gvcgc.com	020-87682766

公司名称	成立时间	网址	传真
广州长策投资管理有限公司	2015-05-29	www.ccinv.cn	020-85235200
广州市杉华创业投资合伙企业（有限合伙）	2015-02-05	—	020-85601688
君盛投资管理有限公司	2003-01-13	www.junsancapital.com	0755-82571198
深圳国成世纪创业投资有限公司	2003-04-16	www.ciamvc.com	0755-82967097
深圳市分享投资合伙企业（有限合伙）	2007-08-27	www.sharecapital.cn	0755-86331909
深圳市天图创业投资有限公司	2002-04-11	www.tiantu.com.cn	0755-36909834
深圳市同威创业投资有限公司	2008-03-02	www.copowerpe.com	0755-26935161
银河粤科基金管理有限公司	2013-11-04	—	020-87682766
盈富泰克创业投资有限公司	2000-04-20	www.infovc.com	0755-82966479
招商局科技集团有限公司	1995-12-20	www.cmtech.net	0755-26888628
肇庆市粤科金瑞投资管理有限公司	2010-08-19	—	0758-2321528
肇庆市粤科金叶创业投资有限公司	2010-10-18	—	0758-2321528
珠海高新创业投资有限公司	2015-09-29	—	—
珠海红杉资本股权投资中心（有限合伙）	2010-03-26	—	010-84475669
珠海金控高新产业投资中心（有限合伙）	2014-04-23	—	—
珠海领先互联高新技术产业投资中心（有限合伙）	2014-09-03	—	0756-3333838
珠海清华科技园创业投资有限公司	2001-07	www.tspz.com	0756-3612000
珠海招商银科股权投资中心（有限合伙）	2012-01-21	—	0755-26677220
毕节市科技创业投资有限公司	2014-12-29	—	—
鼎信博成创业投资有限公司	2010-08-26	—	0851-85806514
贵阳博实火炬新兴产业创业投资企业（有限合伙）	2013-07-30	—	—
贵阳成创合力创业投资管理企业（有限合伙）	2011-03-25	—	0851-84757198
贵阳创新天使投资基金有限公司	2014-03-01	—	0851-85806514
贵阳工投生物医药产业创业投资有限公司	2013-02-19	—	0851-84757198
贵阳花溪科技创业投资有限公司	2011-07-19	—	0851-83863159
贵阳甲秀创业投资中心（有限合伙）	2011-04-08	—	0851-84757198
贵阳市创业投资有限公司	2010-12-28	www.gyvc.cn	0851-84757198
贵阳市服务外包及呼叫产业创业投资基金有限公司	2016-02-19	—	0851-84757198
贵阳市星火现代服务业创业投资有限公司	2014-05-13	—	—
贵阳市引凤高技术产业创业投资基金有限公司	2014-05-13	—	0851-84757198
贵州德欣禾悦创业投资管理有限公司	2014-04-08	—	—
贵州鼎信博成投资管理有限公司	2009-09-16	www.gztvc.net	0851-5806514
贵州鼎信卓越创业投资有限公司	2013-12-06	—	—
贵州红土创业投资有限公司	2014-08-22	—	—
贵州金通达投资有限公司	2012-10-22	www.jtd.cc	0592-5140333

公司名称	成立时间	网址	传真
贵州省科技风险投资有限公司	1998-12	www.gzstvc.net	0851-85806514
贵州中水建设管理股份有限公司	2004-02-17	www.gsgcgw.com	0851-85610887
贵州筑银资本管理有限公司	2012-03-02	—	0851-84757198
六盘水市科技创业投资有限公司	2011-04-14	—	—
铜仁梵净山科技创业投资有限公司	2013	—	—
遵义科技创业投资有限公司	2010-11-05	—	0851-28922337
海口市创新产业投资有限公司	2008-03-18	www.haikouvc.com	0898-66738612
海南海创众成股权投资基金合伙企业（有限合伙）	2015-12-01	—	—
海南青创投资管理有限公司	2014-03-17	www.cy110.cn	0898-65319797
保定市创元科技风险投资有限公司	2008-12-22	—	0312-3312105
保定市科锐特创业投资有限公司	2006-02-27	www.krtvc.com	0312-3371336
沧州渤海新区沿海发展投资基金合伙企业（有限合伙）	2015-10-29	—	0317-7558066
沧州市科技创业中心	—	—	—
河北科技投资集团有限公司	2001-02-15	www.hebvc.com	0311-85961613
河北科润杰创业投资有限公司	2013-07-25	—	0311-69053128
河北玛雅股权投资基金管理有限公司	2012-05-30	—	0311-67267294
河北天鑫创业投资有限公司	2011-07-04	—	—
河北天煜投资有限公司	2015-07-24	—	0311-89928602
河北燕郊燕胜创业投资有限公司	2011-05-27	—	0316-3357676
廊坊市高科创新创业投资有限公司	2006-10-19	—	0316-2235190
秦皇岛市科技投资公司	2000-02-18	www.qhdktgs.com	0335-3639739
秦皇岛燕大产业集团有限公司	1996-12-23	www.ysusp.com.cn	0335-8500962
荣盛创业投资有限公司	2007-09-08	—	010-59232688 转 804
石家庄方大投资有限公司	2011-11-14	—	0311-66685205
石家庄高新建设投资有限公司	2010-03-11	—	0311-66685155
石家庄高新区方亿投资有限公司	2009-08-06	—	0311-85384475
石家庄高新区科发投资有限公司	2010-03-23	—	0311-66699013
石家庄科创投资有限公司	2002-09-19	—	0311-66685160
石家庄石以创业投资管理有限公司	2009-11-30	—	0311-66699011
石家庄鑫汇金投资有限公司	2003-04-23	—	0311-87180977
唐山高新创业投资有限公司	2007-07-02	—	0315-3858385
唐山科技发展投资管理有限责任公司	2009-04-22	—	—
安阳惠通高创新材料创业投资合伙企业（有限合伙）	2012-07-25	—	0371-86615676
河南宝祥民营科技创业投资有限公司	2012-12-05	—	0371-55011760

公司名称	成立时间	网址	传真
河南创业投资股份有限公司	2002-08	www.hnvc.cn	0371-67897012
河南高科技创业投资股份有限公司	2001-04-29	www.hnvc.com.cn	0371-67895090
河南华祺节能环保创业投资有限公司	2013-06-20	www.haiyuqi.com	0371-86684801
河南华夏海纳创业投资集团有限公司	2009-06-18	www.huaxiahn.com	86-0371-86068196
河南睿达资产管理中心（有限合伙）	2012-12-06	www.henanruida.com	—
河南省国控基金管理有限公司	2010-10-31	—	0371-86556706
河南兴豫生物医药创业投资基金（有限合伙）	2014-05-29	—	0371-86661006
河南中证开元创业投资基金（有限合伙）	2013-09-17	—	0379-60662802
洛阳创业投资有限公司	2011-10-28	—	—
洛阳红土创新资本创业投资有限公司	2009-04-18	—	0379-64902650
洛阳宏科创新创业投资有限公司	2014-12-19	www.lyguohongtouzi.com	—
许昌市发展创业投资有限公司	2006-06-20	—	—
郑州百瑞创新资本创业投资有限公司	2007-07-30	www.szvc.com.cn	0371-69177638
郑州优埃富欧投资管理有限公司	2015-10-29	www.ufovc.com.cn	—
中鼎开源创业投资管理有限公司	2012-02-08	—	—
哈尔滨创新投资有限公司	2002-06-28	—	0451-84686552
哈尔滨创业投资集团有限公司	2009-02-26	www.hrbvc.com.cn	0451-84858002
哈尔滨东方汇富创业投资管理有限公司	2015-07-10	—	—
哈尔滨富德恒创业投资企业（有限合伙）	2014-01-24	—	—
哈尔滨哈以孵化器管理有限公司	2011-04-07	www.harbin-incubator.com	—
哈尔滨华滨光辉创业投资企业（有限合伙）	2014-12-29	—	—
哈尔滨君丰创业投资企业（有限合伙）	2015-01-29	—	0451-82336520
哈尔滨朗江创新股权投资企业（有限合伙）	2015-04-01	—	0451-84865258
哈尔滨联创创业投资企业（有限合伙）	2015-12-03	—	010-59393939
哈尔滨市阿里聚旺创业投资企业（有限合伙）	2015-11-30	—	0451-84013027
哈尔滨市科技风险投资中心	1998-05	—	0451-84686552
哈尔滨市天琪创业投资企业（有限合伙）	2014-07-30	—	0451-82287887
哈尔滨市天琪股权投资基金管理企业（有限合伙）	2014-07-30	tqtz.com.cn	0451-82287805
哈尔滨越榕阳光投资企业（有限合伙）	2014-12-25	—	—
哈尔滨云谷创业投资管理有限公司	2016-04-15	—	—
哈尔滨云谷创业投资企业（有限合伙）	2013-07-09	—	—
黑龙江辰能哈工大高科技风险投资有限公司	2001-08-28	www.hlj-cvc.com	0451-82285700
黑龙江红土科力创业投资有限公司	2011-07-11	—	0451-55553193
黑龙江凯致天使创业投资企业（有限合伙）	2015-11-04	—	—
黑龙江省大正赛富投资管理有限公司	2009-11-11	—	0451-58560601

公司名称	成立时间	网址	传真
黑龙江省科力高科技产业投资有限公司	2003-06-25	www.hljkl.com	—
黑龙江信泰投资有限公司	2014-09-03	—	0451-82336222
楚商领先（武汉）创业投资基金管理有限公司	2013-06-25	www.chushang-invest.cc	027-87750827
湖北当代高投创业投资基金合伙企业	2015-09-07	—	—
湖北高富信创业投资有限公司	2013-02-18	—	—
湖北高和创业投资企业	2009-12-08	—	027-86659549
湖北高金生物科技创业投资基金合伙企业（有限合伙）	2013-11-07	—	—
湖北高通投资基金管理有限公司	2016-05-19	—	—
湖北高宜产业投资管理有限公司	2015-11-03	—	0717-6276828
湖北国创高投产业投资基金管理有限公司	2016-09-13	—	027-87617400
湖北航天高投光电子投资基金管理有限公司	2016-07-01	—	—
湖北宏泰产业投资基金有限公司	2016-08-24	—	—
湖北交投资本投资管理有限公司	2014-04-21	—	027-87576561
湖北量科高投创业投资有限公司	2010-11-26	—	027-87440551
湖北珞珈梧桐创业投资有限公司	2014-04-23	www.luojiacapital.com	027-87115066
湖北省齐信达投资管理服务有限公司	2014-05-05	—	027-87571051
湖北盛世高金创业投资有限公司	2011-03-24	—	027-87440849
湖北同富创业投资管理有限公司	2012-08-13	www.ycgtjt.com	—
湖北新能源投资管理有限公司	2010-08-18	—	027-65796340
湖北政和基金投资管理有限公司	2016-04	www.hbzhjj.com	0712-2750900
科华银赛创业投资有限公司	2009-07-30	www.khysct.com	+86-27-59817377
武汉东湖创新科技投资有限公司	1999-12	www.whdhct.com	027-85613636
武汉斐然源通中以科技股权投资基金合伙企业（有限合伙）	2013-09-24	—	—
武汉高农生物创业投资有限公司	2010-08-04	—	027-87397896
武汉公牛创业投资有限公司	2011-11-12	—	—
武汉固德银赛创业投资管理有限公司	2009-04-21	www.gdysct.com	027-59817377
武汉光电工研院育成创业投资基金合伙企业（有限合伙）	2015-06-17	—	—
武汉光谷高新成长创业投资合伙企业（有限合伙）	2013-12-31	—	—
武汉光谷人才投资管理有限公司	2015-08-07	www.ggrctz.com	—
武汉光谷新三板股权投资基金合伙企业（有限合伙）	2013-01-25	www.cnhbgt.com	027-87440849
武汉华工创业投资有限责任公司	2000-09-11	www.hustvc.com.cn	027-81338733
武汉华工科技投资管理有限公司	2011-02-28	—	027-87180149
武汉华融天泽高投股权投资管理有限公司	2014-12-08	—	86-27-87440849

公司名称	成立时间	网址	传真
武汉惠人生物创业投资基金中心（有限合伙）	2013-02-28	—	—
武汉金科互联产业投资基金合伙企业（有限合伙）	2016-02-04	—	—
武汉零度创业投资管理有限公司	2015-05-22	www.lingducapital.com	—
武汉融和科技资本管理股份有限公司	2014-02-25	www.whrhcapital.com	027-87575508
武汉赛恩斯投资管理有限公司	2013-02-21	—	027-85680605
武汉武大创新投资有限公司	2002-02-09	—	—
武汉育成基金管理有限公司	2015-04-16	—	—
武汉誉达通创业投资基金合伙企业（有限合伙）	2016-08-22	—	—
宜昌悦和股权投资基金管理有限公司	2015-10-20	—	—
长沙高新技术创业投资管理有限公司	2000-09-09	www.cshvc.com	0731-88286898
长沙麓谷高新移动互联网产业投资有限公司	2014-03-25	—	—
长沙市科技风险投资管理有限公司	2000-05-18	www.csvcc.cn	0731-88286892
长沙先导产业投资有限公司	2009-05-15	www.cpih.cn	0731-88768823
长沙兴创投资管理合伙企业（有限合伙）	2007-11-13	—	0731-82953007
常德合金生物科技投资中心（有限合伙）	2015-12-31	—	—
常德新材料产业创业投资基金合伙企业（有限合伙）	2016-06-13	—	—
常德沅澧产业投资控股有限公司	2014-01-22	—	0736-7133995
常德中科芙蓉创业投资有限责任公司	2011-01-12	—	0736-7703079
衡阳高新南粤基金管理有限公司	2016-12-26	—	—
衡阳融达投资有限公司	2010-01-19	—	—
衡阳市银宏投资管理有限责任公司	2014-04-09	—	0734-8989020
衡阳岳涵新材料投资有限公司	2016-04-21	—	—
湖南财富同超创业投资管理股份有限公司	2010-07-19	—	0731-82567348
湖南财富同超创业投资有限公司	2010-10-10	—	0731-82567348
湖南达晨财鑫创业投资有限公司	2011-03-28	—	0736-7133995
湖南迪策创业投资有限公司	2002-12-05	—	0731-89952741
湖南鼎信泰和股权投资管理有限公司	2012-06-07	—	0731-85123296
湖南高科发创智能制造装备创业投资有限公司	2013-02-05	—	0731-28861596
湖南高新创业投资管理有限公司	2011-03-10	www.hhtvcm.com	0731-85165395
湖南国微集成电路创业投资基金合伙企业（有限合伙）	2015-12-24	—	0731-89952611
湖南国微投资管理合伙企业（有限合伙）	2015-11-27	—	0731-89952611
湖南海捷投资有限公司	2010-04-09	www.hiyield.cn	0731-88780198
湖南海捷先进装备创业投资有限公司	2013-05-08	www.hiyield.cn	0731-88780198
湖南汉坤股权投资管理有限公司	2012-02-17	—	0731-89917899

公司名称	成立时间	网址	传真
湖南弘高高技术服务创业投资有限公司	2015-07-07	—	0731-28861551
湖南湖大海捷津杉创业投资有限公司	2011-04-29	www.hiyield.cn	0731-88780100
湖南华鸿景开投资管理有限公司	2010-06-08	—	0731-88186795
湖南金科投资担保有限公司	2003-11-27	—	0731-85810466
湖南浚源鼎立创业投资管理有限公司	2015-06-25	—	—
湖南浚源鼎立股权投资私募基金合伙企业（有限合伙）	2015-07-08	—	0731-82263898
湖南麓晨创业投资有限公司	2016-02-18	—	—
湖南美雅资本管理有限公司	2008-08-21	—	0781-82226297
湖南三泽生物医药创业投资企业（有限合伙）	2012-07-23	www.sunzfund.com	0731-82768320
湖南省广信创业投资基金有限公司	2012-06-05	—	0731-88737722
湖南省中小微企业产业投资基金管理有限公司	2014-08-11	—	—
湖南同超投资股份有限公司	2008-01-23	www.hntctz.com	0731-82567348
湖南文正投资集团有限公司	2012-01-05	www.wzjt.net	0734-8856728
湖南湘投高科技创业投资有限公司	2000-02-23	www.hnhvc.com	0731-85188649
湖南新能源创业投资基金企业（有限合伙）	2010-05-14	—	0731-82768320
湖南永创伟业投资管理有限公司	2015-07-07	—	—
湖南兆富投资控股（集团）有限公司	2009-08-24	www.zaffer.cn	0731-88737722
湖南浙商嘉立创业投资有限公司	2010-08-06	—	0731-85696977
湖南臻泰股权投资管理合伙企业（有限合伙）	2012-12-27	—	0731-88705906
湖南中大联合创业咨询有限公司	2013-08-09	www.zdlhcy.com	—
湖南中大融港投资管理有限公司	2015-12-28	www.zhongdafund.com	—
三泽创业投资管理有限公司	2008-02-28	www.sunzfund.com	0731-82768320
湘潭火炬创业投资有限公司	2012-04-20	—	0731-55567188
湘潭智造谷产业投资管理有限责任公司	2016-03-15	—	—
中创投天使二号（湖南）创业投资股份有限公司	2014-08-08	—	—
株洲高新天诚先进装备制造创业投资合伙企业（有限合伙）	2016-08-31	—	—
株洲广信兆富投资管理有限公司	2012-02-28	—	0731-88737722
株洲科创创业投资管理有限公司	2015-04-26	—	—
株洲科聚创业投资企业（有限合伙）	2016-11-21	—	—
株洲市国投创新创业投资有限公司	2015-11-27	www.zzgtct.com	0731-28688892
株洲市世富投资有限公司	2009-12-14	www.zzsafer.com	0731-22727013
株洲兆富成长企业创业投资有限公司	2010-10-13	—	0731-88737722
株洲中车时代高新投资有限公司	2003-05-12	www.timesinvest.cn	0731-22877368
3icity 众创空间	2007-05-28	www.3icity.com	—

公司名称	成立时间	网址	传真
吉林省摆渡创新工场有限公司	2014-05-23	www.baiduworks.com	0431-81940765
博辰创业投资管理（苏州）有限公司	2007-11-26	—	0512-66969661
长汉共同合作基金	2007-09-18	—	025-85529900
常创（常州）创业投资合伙企业（有限合伙）	2013-09-03	—	0512-85228057
常创天使（常州）创业投资中心（有限合伙）	2014-03-04	—	0512-85228057
常熟博瀚创业投资有限公司	2009-11-23	—	0512-52351556
常熟博融创业投资有限公司	2016-08-12	—	0512-52351556
常熟金茂创业投资管理有限公司	2010-11	www.jolmo.com	025-84730375
常熟经济开发区高新技术创业投资有限公司	2009-06	—	0512-52292926
常熟市国发创业投资有限公司	2010-11-25	—	0512-52876487
常州常金创业投资有限公司	2014-12-12	—	—
常州常荣创业投资有限公司	2009-09-08	www.ndinvest.cn	0519-89816672
常州常以创业投资管理有限公司	2009-12-31	—	0519-89629972
常州常以创业投资中心（有限合伙）	2010-01-12	—	0519-89629972
常州大智创业投资中心（有限合伙）	2015-03-11	—	0519-85300255
常州德丰杰清洁技术创业投资中心（有限合伙）	2009-12	www.dfjcompass.com	0519-89182227
常州德丰杰投资管理有限公司	2009-12	www.dfjcompass.com	0519-89182227
常州德丰杰正道创业投资中心（有限合伙）	2012-03	www.dfjcompass.com	0519-89182227
常州德丰杰正道投资管理有限公司	2012-02-20	www.dfjcompass.com	0519-89182227
常州蜂鸟创业投资合伙企业（有限合伙）	2012-06-21	—	0519-81231818
常州高睿创业投资管理有限公司	2007-09-24	—	0519-85150557
常州高投创业投资有限公司	2008-07-22	—	0519-85150557
常州高新创业投资有限公司	2012-01-18	—	0519-81235008
常州高新技术风险投资有限公司	2000-12-22	www.cz-vc.com	0519-85150557
常州高新区印刷电子产业基金创业投资有限公司	2013-09-05	—	0519-69885597
常州和泰股权投资有限公司	2001-10-29	—	0519-85176186
常州和裕创业投资有限公司	2011-04	—	0519-85176186
常州华软投资管理有限公司	2010-07-07	—	—
常州金陵华软创业投资合伙企业（有限合伙）	2010-08-05	—	—
常州金码创业投资管理合伙企业（有限合伙）	2011-11-30	www.jolmo.net	025-84730211
常州金茂经信创业投资管理企业（有限合伙）	2013-12-31	www.jolmo.net	025-84730211
常州金茂新兴产业创业投资合伙企业（有限合伙）	2011-09	www.jolmo.net	025-84730375
常州力合创业投资有限公司	2008-10-10	http:www.leaguercapital.com	0519-86220138
常州力合投资管理有限公司	2008-08	www.leaguercapital.com	0519-86220138
常州牡丹江南创业投资有限责任公司	2010-03-15	—	0519-68866908

公司名称	成立时间	网址	传真
常州青年创业投资中心（有限合伙）	2012-12-20	—	0519-85228057
常州青企联合创业投资合伙企业（有限合伙）	2013-01-05	—	0519-85228057
常州睿泰创业投资中心（有限合伙）	2012	—	—
常州赛富高新创业投资中心（有限合伙）	2009-12	www.sbaif.com	0519-89606122
常州市久益股权投资中心（有限合伙）	2010-07-30	www.nd-invest.cn	0519-89816672
常州市民生投资中心（有限合伙）	2007-11-15	—	0519-85164197
常州武进红土创业投资有限公司	2008-08-19	www.szvc.com.cn	0519-86318682
常州武岳峰创业投资管理有限公司	2011-03-03	www.summitviewcapital.com	0519-86620218
常州武岳峰创业投资合伙企业（有限合伙）	2011-03-23	www.summitviewcapital.com	0519-86220218
常州信辉创业投资有限公司	2007-05-11	—	0519-88137096
常州钟楼红土创业投资有限公司	2013-08-23	www.szvc.com.cn	0519-86318682
丹阳市高新技术创业投资有限公司	2010-12-31	—	0511-86922610
斐然创业投资管理（苏州）有限公司	2011-01-05	—	—
福斯特创业投资海安有限公司	2016-09-23	—	0513-88823778
高投名力成长创业投资有限公司	2007-04-29	www.mcgf.com.cn	021-62889166
高瞻（无锡）创业投资有限公司	2011-04	www.tallwoodvc.com	0510-85228386
高瞻（无锡）企业管理有限公司	2011-05	www.tallwoodvc.com	0510-81814997
国本创业投资江苏有限公司	2012-11-09	—	0516-8268995
国润创业投资（苏州）管理有限公司	2008-05	www.guorun.com	0512-62998663
海安达志创业投资有限公司	2016-09-18	www.dzct.cn	0513-88856600
海安得一创业投资有限公司	2015-12-14	—	021-64178726
海安东阳创业投资有限公司	2015-03-31	—	—
海安丰睿创业投资有限公司	2015-08-20	—	—
海安峰融创业投资有限公司	2014-12-18	—	—
海安峰融投资管理有限公司	2014-10-15	—	—
海安海高创业投资有限公司	2016-03-28	—	—
海安海开创业投资有限公司	2016-03-28	—	—
海安晗泰创业投资有限公司	2016-06-29	—	0513-88651598
海安恒益创业投资有限公司	2016-06-23	—	—
海安金鑫创业投资有限公司	—	—	—
海安开泰创业投资有限公司	2016-03-28	—	—
海安昆鹏投资有限公司	2016-09-12	—	—
海安蓝天创业投资有限公司	2016-11-15	—	0513-88869873
海安青蓝创业投资有限公司	2015-03-26	—	—
海安申海创业投资有限公司	2016-11-03	—	—

公司名称	成立时间	网址	传真
海安圣义创业投资有限公司	2015-06	—	—
海安双惠创业投资有限公司	2015-03-25	—	0513-88765006
海安泰港创业投资有限公司	2015-06-24	—	—
海安信拓创业投资有限公司	2016-06-30	—	0513-88833885
海安知己基石创业投资有限公司	2014-09-05	—	—
海门时代伯乐股权投资合伙企业（有限合伙）	2014-09-26	—	0513-82197321
红塔创新（昆山）创业投资有限公司	2008-07-09	—	010-58555666
鸿海创业投资发展海安有限公司	2015-03-31	—	—
华穗食品创业投资企业	2009-04-13	—	021-2898817
建湖县建科创业投资有限公司	2010-12	4408499.czvv.com	0515-86233503
江苏艾利克斯投资有限公司	2006-01-19	—	0511-86900801
江苏博硕高新技术产业投资发展有限公司	2011-09-18	—	—
江苏昌盛阜创业投资有限公司	2008-08-22	—	0512-69560268
江苏诚行投资管理有限公司	2011-03-16	—	—
江苏大丰众成科技创业投资有限公司	2010-04	—	0515-83855826
江苏鼎信资本管理有限公司	2009-06-25	—	025-86586898
江苏多良创业投资有限公司	2008-03-31	—	0519-83872660
江苏高弘投资管理有限公司	2006-09	—	025-52313062
江苏高晋创业投资有限公司	2008-06-12	—	0519-85150557
江苏高科技投资集团有限公司	1992-07-30	www.js-vc.com	025-85529999
江苏高投邦盛创业投资合伙企业（有限合伙）	2014-05-09	—	—
江苏高投成长创业投资有限公司	2008-01	—	025-85529900
江苏高投成长价值股权投资合伙企业（有限合伙）	2011-05	—	025-85529999
江苏高投创新价值创业投资合伙企业（有限合伙）	2011-05-19	—	025-85529900
江苏高投创新科技创业投资合伙企业（有限合伙）	2011-04	—	025-85529900
江苏高投创新中小发展创业投资合伙企业（有限合伙）	2012-12-25	—	025-85529900
江苏高投创业投资管理有限公司	1999-01-29	—	025-85529999
江苏高投发展创业投资有限公司	2010-07-16	—	025-85529999
江苏高投科贷创业投资合伙企业（有限合伙）	2013-12-31	—	025-85529900
江苏高投宁泰创业投资合伙企业（有限合伙）	2012-01-30	—	025-85529900
江苏高投中小企业创业投资有限公司	2009-05	—	025-85529900
江苏高新创业投资管理有限公司	2005-01-14	www.js-vc.com	025-85529900
江苏高新创业投资有限公司	2005-08-15	www.js-vc.com	—
江苏格瑞石墨烯创业投资有限公司	2012-04-10	—	0519-81090019

公司名称	成立时间	网址	传真
江苏昊海投资发展集团有限公司	2012-11-26	www.hhco.cc	0518-85917545
江苏弘瑞科技创业投资有限公司	2002-09	—	025-52313062
江苏红黄蓝创业投资有限公司	2014-02-19	—	025-88869883
江苏华成华利创业投资有限公司	2009-10-21	—	0512-67161932
江苏华创医药研发平台管理有限公司	2007-06	—	—
江苏华控创业投资有限公司	2008-07-10	www.huakongpe.com	025-87716620-801
江苏华控投资管理有限公司	2008-01-15	—	025-87716220-801
江苏华全创业投资有限公司	2013-01-05	—	0523-80959672
江苏华睿投资管理有限公司	2010-06-12	—	—
江苏汇鸿创业投资有限公司	2004-07-06	—	025-86770714
江苏火炬创业投资有限公司	2010-10-19	www.huojujijin.com	0510-81813907
江苏嘉睿创业投资有限公司	2008-03-28	—	—
江苏金炻创业投资有限公司	2012-05-25	—	0515-82342000
江苏津通创业投资有限公司	2007-06-25	www.jinton.com	0519-86226016
江苏九洲投资集团创业投资有限公司	2007-09-19	www.jiuzhouinvest.com	0519-85228057
江苏巨能投资集团有限公司	2010-08-23	—	025-86716841
江苏聚融创业投资有限公司	2011-11-16	—	0511-87899196
江苏科泉高新创业投资有限公司	2012-10-31	www.kequanvc.com	025-85589174
江苏旷达创业投资有限公司	2007-06	—	0519-86546893
江苏联发创业投资有限公司	2011-12-13	—	0513-88869069
江苏隆鑫创业投资有限公司	2006-05	—	025-84401201
江苏盟邦创业投资有限责任公司	2015-08-24	—	—
江苏乾融集团有限公司	2008-06-05	www.jsqr.com.cn	0512-62998656
江苏乾融资本管理有限公司	2011-06-02	—	0512-62998656
江苏人才创新创业投资二期基金（有限合伙）	2015-05-19	—	025-85529900
江苏如东高新创业投资有限公司	2014-05-05	—	0513-88158132
江苏瑞明创业投资管理有限公司	2009-12-30	jsrm2009@yeah.net	025-83172132
江苏省高科技产业投资股份有限公司	1997-04-08	www.jsvc.com.cn	025-86639999
江苏省高新技术创业服务中心	1996-10	www.jsbi.cn	025-83232021
江苏省苏高新风险投资股份有限公司	2000-03-31	www.sz-vc.com	0512-68243439
江苏省无锡江大大学科技园有限公司	2001-12-30	www.j-park.jiangnan.edu.cn	0510-85189107
江苏省现代服务业发展创业投资基金（有限合伙）	2015-05-29	—	025-85529900
江苏晟华创业投资有限公司	2009-04-09	www.shct1688.com	0516-83897897
江苏盛泉创业投资有限公司	2007-06	www.vc-century.com	025-58071508
江苏盛宇丹昇创业投资有限公司	2008-10-28	—	0511-86929333

公司名称	成立时间	网址	传真
江苏苏大天宫创业投资管理有限公司	2010-10-08	sdkjy.suda.edu.cn	86-512-62925790
江苏苏大投资有限公司	2001-02	—	0512-67504016
江苏苏豪投资集团有限公司	1999-05-06	—	—
江苏腾海创业投资有限公司	2015-03-27	—	—
江苏天氏创业投资有限公司	2005	—	0512-87752270
江苏通顺创业投资有限公司	2009-08-25	—	0512-69560268
江苏同兴财富投资管理有限公司	2008-05	—	0512-69560268
江苏威望创业投资有限公司	2009-10-14	—	—
江苏新材料产业创业投资企业（有限合伙）	2013-11-13	www.jolomo.net	025-84730375
江苏新创投资有限公司	2007-10-17	—	0523-84623002
江苏新顶旭科技创业投资有限公司	2010-04-27	—	—
江苏信泉创业投资管理有限公司	2006-12-30	—	025-58071508
江苏兴科创业投资有限公司	2007-08-20	www.jsxinkect.com	0519-86302628
江苏毅达并购成长股权投资基金（有限合伙）	2014-11-26	—	025-85529900
江苏毅达成果创新创业投资基金（有限合伙）	2015-05-19	—	—
江苏毅达股权投资基金管理有限公司	2014-02-18	—	025-85529900
江苏鹰能创业投资有限公司	2007-08-28	—	025-85529900
江苏中关村科技产业园创业投资有限公司	2016-04-26	—	—
江苏中科华艺创业投资有限公司	2007-03-30	—	0513-88869883
江苏中科物联网科技创业投资有限公司	2010-07-14	www.casiot.com	0510-85380859
江苏紫金文化产业发展基金（有限合伙）	2010-03-15	—	025-85529900
江苏紫金文化创业投资合伙企业（有限合伙）	2011-08-04	—	025-85529900
江阴滨江科技创业投资有限公司	2016-06-20	—	0510-86869513
江阴市高新技术创业投资有限公司	2007-02-06	—	0510-81602090
江阴银杏谷股权投资合伙企业（有限合伙）	2014-12-08	—	—
姜堰市高新实业投资有限公司	2010-12-23	—	0523-88117969
靖江市高新技术创业投资有限公司	2010-03	—	0523-89181480
凯风创业投资有限公司	2006-10-30	—	0512-66969533
昆山市国科创业投资有限公司	2001-08-31	—	0512-57367277
昆山银桥投资中心（有限合伙）	2016-11-24	—	—
连云港金海创业投资有限公司	2006-07-19	www.lygjhvc.com	0518-85523512
连云港市润财创业投资发展有限公司	2010-10-22	—	0518-85520303
连云港中科黄海创业投资有限公司	2010-03-22	www.csm-inv.com	0518-85807928
麦克逊创业投资海安有限公司	2016-09-28	—	0513-88856583
明石创业投资江苏有限公司	2015-01-13	—	—

公司名称	成立时间	网址	传真
南京创业投资管理有限公司	2008-11-26	www.nj-vc.com	025-86579660
南京高达资本管理有限公司	2011-09-22	www.goodvc.cn	025-83153546
南京高新创业投资有限公司	2012-06-01	—	025-58696594
南京红土创业投资有限公司	2010-05-31	www.szvc.com.cn	025-58867560
南京市高新技术风险投资股份有限公司	2001-02-24	www.nj-vc.com	025-86599660
南京市栖霞区科技创业投资有限公司	2009-07-31	—	025-85566570
南京市栖霞区科技发展投资有限公司	2012-03-16	—	025-85578993
南京外滩明珠创业投资有限公司	2011-03-17	—	025-89669155
南京文化创业投资有限公司	2011-02	—	025-86579660
南京协立创业投资有限公司	2009-05-11	—	025-86816826
南京中成创业投资有限公司	2009-08	—	025-86579660
南京中原创业投资有限公司	2010-12-17	—	025-86579660
南京紫金创投基金管理有限责任公司	2011-09-02	—	025-86579655
南京紫金科技创业投资有限公司	2011-08-08	www.njzjkc.com	025-86579616
南通东凯科技创业基金中心（有限合伙）	2016-12-20	—	—
南通高胜成长创业投资有限公司	2008-09-10	www.js-vc.com	025-85529900
南通高特佳汇金投资合伙企业（有限合伙）	2013-05-24	—	0513-81288026
南通瀚信股权投资合伙企业（有限合伙）	2016-03-21	—	0513-82190309
南通恒富创业投资合伙企业（有限合伙）	2013-12-16	—	0513-86126133
南通红土创新资本创业投资有限公司	2007-09	—	0513-83562508
南通红土伟达创业投资管理有限公司	2014-04-21	www.szvc.com.cn	0513-83562508
南通红土伟达创业投资有限公司	2014-04-21	www.szvc.com.cn	0513-83562508
南通康成亨重点成长型企业股权投资合伙企业（有限合伙）	2012-10-25	—	0513-80770310
南通康融创业投资有限公司	2016-04-08	—	0513-88355999
南通科创创业投资管理有限公司	2013-04-23	—	0513-85728713
南通科技创业投资有限公司	2011-04-22	—	—
南通磊泽投资有限公司	2011-09-07	—	0513-80113579
南通平衡创业投资基金中心（有限合伙）	2015-06-11	—	025-51889757
南通七龙景华投资中心（有限合伙）	2015-07-07	—	0513-80787002
南通如意物联网产业投资基金管理中心（有限合伙）	2010-09-09	—	0513-87300528-815
南通杉创创业投资中心（有限合伙）	2015-06-04	—	—
南通杉杉创业投资中心（有限合伙）	2012-06-08	—	021-51561587
南通松禾创业投资合伙企业（有限合伙）	2009-01	—	0513-85507237
南通松禾创业投资中心（有限合伙）	2011-08-01	—	0513-85517915

公司名称	成立时间	网址	传真
南通松禾资本管理有限公司	2009-01-05	—	0513-85507237
南通苏海投资管理中心（有限合伙）	2013-11-26	—	0513-88782028
南通通光投资中心（有限合伙）	2012-10-23	—	0513-82867666
南通五水投资发展有限公司	2013-06-17	—	0513-85609598
南通兴华投资有限公司	2016-09-27	—	0513-88826382
南通迅通投资有限公司	2016-03-28	—	0513-88765006
南通晔司创业投资有限公司	2015-02-31	—	0513-88809966
邳州市高新区科创园投资发展有限公司	2014-07-18	—	—
软库博辰创业投资企业	2008-03-03	—	0512-66969661
苏州安固创业投资有限公司	2007-09-30	—	0512-67414881
苏州创东方富诚投资企业（有限合伙）	2010-09-20	—	0512-68322281
苏州创禾创业投资管理有限公司	2014-10-21	—	0512-63493186
苏州荻溪文化创意产业投资中心（有限合伙）	2012-04-28	—	0512-65808803
苏州鼎融投资管理有限公司	2009-12-10	www.jsqr.com.cn	0512-62998656
苏州东方汇富创业投资企业（有限合伙）	2012-12-06	—	—
苏州方广创业投资管理合伙企业（有限合伙）	2012-05-28	www.fgventure.com	021-54245723
苏州方广创业投资合伙企业（有限合伙）	2012-09-25	www.fgventure.com	021-54245723
苏州斐然向风创业投资中心（有限合伙）	2011	—	—
苏州富丽东方能源股权投资企业（有限合伙）	2011-07-28	—	0512-68322281
苏州富丽高新投资企业（有限合伙）	2010-11-10	—	0512-68322281
苏州富丽明康投资企业（有限合伙）	2011-07-26	—	0512-68322281
苏州富丽启康投资企业（有限合伙）	2011-07-25	—	0512-68322281
苏州富丽泰泓投资企业（有限合伙）	2010-12-24	—	0512-68322281
苏州富丽投资有限公司	2010-07-29	www.fuli-capital.com	0512-68322281
苏州高创天使三号投资合伙企业（有限合伙）	2016-12-21	—	—
苏州高创天使一号投资合伙企业（有限合伙）	2015-11-09	—	—
苏州高锦创业投资有限公司	2009-03-27	—	0512-68243439
苏州高新创业投资集团融联管理有限公司	2012-02-08	—	0512-68081156
苏州高新创业投资集团新麟管理有限公司	2008-12-04	—	0512-68762955
苏州高新创业投资集团有限公司	2008-07-30	www.sndvc.com	0512-68311200
苏州高新创业投资集团中小企业发展管理有限公司	2013-12-05	—	—
苏州高新创业投资集团中小企业天使投资有限公司	2015-09-09	—	—
苏州高新风投创业投资管理有限公司	2009-02-23	—	0512-68243439
苏州高新国发创业投资有限公司	2009-05-22	—	0512-65126380
苏州高新启源创业投资有限公司	2011-05	www.sndvc.com	—

公司名称	成立时间	网址	传真
苏州高新区创业科技投资管理有限公司	2003-03-03	—	—
苏州高铖创业投资管理有限公司	2011	—	0512-68243439
苏州工业园区辰融创业投资有限公司	2008-05-14	www.jsqr.com.cn	0512-62998656
苏州工业园区弘丰创业投资有限公司	2010-04	—	0512-69560268
苏州工业园区华穗创业投资管理有限公司	2008-07	—	021-62898817
苏州工业园区领军创业投资有限公司	2012-12-20	—	0512-67068099
苏州工业园区领军天使创业投资中心（有限合伙）	2015-10-08	—	0512-69560268
苏州工业园区南凯创业投资有限公司	2011-03	—	0512-69560268
苏州工业园区元禾原点创业投资管理有限公司	2013-09-24	—	—
苏州工业园区原点创业投资有限公司	2008-03-26	—	0512-66969998
苏州工业园区原点正则壹号创业投资企业（有限合伙）	2013-11-19	—	0512-66969533
苏州国发创富创业投资企业（有限合伙）	2010-07-14	—	0512-65126380
苏州国发创业投资控股有限公司	2008-05-08	www.sidvc.com	0512-65126380
苏州国发东方创业投资管理有限公司	2008-11-14	—	0512-65126380
苏州国发服务业创业投资企业（有限合伙）	2012-04-23	—	0512-65126380
苏州国发高铁文化创业投资管理有限公司	2013-08-19	—	—
苏州国发高铁文化创业投资中心（有限合伙）	2013-09-29	—	—
苏州国发高新创业投资管理有限公司	2008-12-17	—	0512-65126380
苏州国发宏富创业投资企业（有限合伙）	2011-04	—	0512-65126380
苏州国发建富创业投资企业（有限合伙）	2010-06-30	—	0512-65126380
苏州国发聚富创业投资有限公司	2010-03-25	—	0512-65126380
苏州国发黎曼创业投资有限公司	2010-05-19	—	0512-65126380
苏州国发融富创业投资管理企业（有限合伙）	2009-12-28	—	0512-65126380
苏州国发融富创业投资企业（有限合伙）	2010-01-20	—	0512-65126380
苏州国发天使创业投资企业（有限合伙）	2011-06	—	0512-65126380
苏州国发添富创业投资企业（有限合伙）	2012-05-09	—	0512-65126380
苏州国发文化产业创业投资企业（有限合伙）	2012-12-17	—	—
苏州国发涌富创业投资企业（有限合伙）	2011-06	—	0512-65126380
苏州国发源富创业投资企业（有限合伙）	2011-01	—	0512-65126380
苏州国发智富创业投资企业（有限合伙）	2010-03	—	0512-65126380
苏州国润创业投资发展有限公司	2008-07	www.guorunpe.com	0512-62998661
苏州国润瑞祺创业投资企业（有限合伙）	2011-07	www.guorunpe.com	0512-62998663
苏州海达通科技创业投资有限公司	2015-04-21	—	0512-63010366
苏州合融创新资本管理有限公司	2007-11	www.jsqr.com.cn	0512-62998656

公司名称	成立时间	网址	传真
苏州合盈创业投资管理有限公司	2010	—	0512-67060338
苏州恒融创业投资有限公司	2007-12	www.jsqr.com.cn	0512-62998656
苏州华创赢达创业投资基金企业（有限合伙）	2012	—	0512-63936955
苏州纪源科星股权投资合伙企业（有限合伙）	2011-06-14	—	021-54503060
苏州聚新中小科技创业投资企业（有限合伙）	2015-04-21	—	0512-68311200
苏州君实协立创业投资有限公司	2014-01-06	—	025-86816823
苏州君玄创业投资中心（有限合伙）	2011	—	025-86816826
苏州科技城创业投资有限公司	2007-12-24	—	—
苏州科技创业投资公司	1993-07	—	0512-69330076
苏州坤融创业投资有限公司	2010-03-15	—	0512-62998656
苏州蓝贰创业投资有限公司	2010-01	—	0512-62725933
苏州蓝壹创业投资有限公司	2008-03	—	0512-62725933
苏州龙瑞创业投资管理有限公司	2009-12	—	0512-66969306
苏州龙跃投资中心（有限合伙）	2010-01	—	0512-66969306
苏州清商成长创业投资企业（有限合伙）	2011-09	—	0512-68075806
苏州清研汽车产业创业投资企业（有限合伙）	2014-10-18	—	0512-63936955
苏州清研资本管理企业（有限合伙）	2014-03-07	—	0512-63936955
苏州仁华创业投资有限公司	2010-04	—	0512-67060338
苏州融联创业投资企业（有限合伙）	2012-03-15	—	0512-68081156
苏州瑞华投资合伙企业（有限合伙）	2015-07-06	—	025-83172132
苏州瑞璟创业投资企业（有限合伙）	2010-11-17	—	0512-68326637
苏州深蓝创业投资有限公司	2007-09-04	www.deepblues.cn	0512-69211368
苏州盛泉百涛创业投资管理有限公司	2010-12-15	—	025-58071508
苏州盛泉海成创业投资合伙企业（有限合伙）	2014-10-23	—	025-58071508
苏州盛泉万泽创业投资合伙企业（有限合伙）	2011-03-03	—	025-58071508
苏州市吴江创迅创业投资有限公司	2014-12-04	—	0512-63493186
苏州市吴江创业投资有限公司	2008-09-16	—	0512-63493186
苏州市吴中创业投资有限公司	2007-01-12	—	0512-66356670
苏州市吴中科技创业园管理有限公司	2004-06	www.wzcy.cn	0512-65270617
苏州市相城创业投资管理有限责任公司	2009-01-16	—	0512-65808803
苏州市相城创业投资有限责任公司	2008	—	0512-65808803
苏州市相城埭溪创业投资有限责任公司	2016-06-17	—	0512-65808803
苏州市相城高新创业投资有限责任公司	2009-03-12	—	0512-65808803
苏州顺融创业投资管理合伙企业（有限合伙）	2014-09-10	www.shunrongvc.com	—
苏州顺融天使三期创业投资合伙企业（有限合伙）	2015-10-16	www.shunrongvc.com	—

公司名称	成立时间	网址	传真
苏州天宫号投资管理有限公司	2016-07-21	www.sudatiangong.com	86-512-62925790
苏州天宫一号投资中心（有限合伙）	2016-01-14	www.sudatiangong.com	86-512-62925790
苏州蔚蓝投资管理有限公司	2008-03-07	—	0512-62725933
苏州吴中国发创业投资管理有限公司	2008-08-28	—	0512-65126380
苏州吴中国发创业投资有限公司	2008-08-28	—	0512-65126380
苏州吴中科技创业投资有限公司	2012-10-26	—	0512-65855966
苏州羲融创业投资有限公司	2010-02-01	—	0512-62998656
苏州相渭汽车产业投资中心（有限合伙）	2015-12-08	—	0512-65808803
苏州香塘创业投资有限责任公司	2007	—	0512-53560126
苏州协立投资管理有限公司	2011-03	—	025-86816826
苏州协睿创业投资管理有限公司	2011-08-15	—	025-86816826
苏州新麟创业投资有限公司	2009-01-22	—	0512-68762955
苏州新麟二期创业投资企业（有限合伙）	2011-11	—	0512-68762955
苏州新协创业投资有限公司	2006-05	—	0512-62620019
苏州信慧成创业投资管理有限公司	2014-07-28	—	025-58071508
苏州衍盈投资管理有限公司	2015-10-16	—	—
苏州亿和创业投资有限公司	2009-12-29	—	0512-65214770
苏州亿文创新资本管理有限公司	2007-12-03	—	0512-65214770
苏州亿文投资有限公司	2007-12-17	—	0512-65214770
苏州亿新熠合投资企业（有限合伙）	2012-09-28	—	0512-65214770
苏州银基创业投资有限公司	2006-05-10	—	0512-67156968
苏州银基美林创业投资管理有限公司	2012-09-03	—	0512-36830119
苏州银基美林创业投资合伙企业（有限合伙）	2012-10-23	—	0512-67156968
苏州元风创业投资有限公司	2007-04	—	0512-66969998
苏州元禾控股股份有限公司	2007-09-11	www.oriza.com.cn	0512-66969998
苏州兆戎空天创业投资合伙企业（有限合伙）	2015-02-26	—	025-58071508
苏州钟鼎创业二号投资中心（有限合伙）	2011-12-02	www.easternbellvc.com	021-61652669
苏州钟鼎创业投资中心（有限合伙）	2010-01-14	www.easternbellvc.com	021-61652669
苏州钟鼎汇元创业投资管理中心（有限合伙）	2011-09-14	www.ebvc.com.cn	021-61652669
宿迁国发创业投资企业（有限合伙）	2011-07-22	—	0527-87031252
宿迁科技创业投资有限公司	2012-03-23	—	0527-87031252
宿迁市开创创业投资有限公司	2010-09-07	—	0527-88859628
睢宁县天使创业投资有限责任公司	2013-03-06	—	0516-88037115
太仓衍盈壹号投资管理中心（有限合伙）	2015-12-09	—	0512-53290273
泰兴市高新投资有限公司	2010-12-27	—	0523-87627940

公司名称	成立时间	网址	传真
泰州华诚高新技术投资发展有限公司	2005	www.tzibi.com	0523-86196007
泰州华健创业投资有限公司	2007-06-08	—	—
泰州健鑫创业投资有限公司	2012-12-14	—	0523-82216000
泰州市创业风险投资有限公司	2001-08	—	0523-86196199
泰州市高港高新区开发投资有限责任公司	2010-08	—	0523-86118800
泰州市高科创业投资有限公司	2010-08-25	—	0523-86966047
泰州市环晟创业投资有限公司	2011-11	—	—
泰州中国医药城融健达创业投资有限公司	2013-03-19	—	0523-82216000
无锡 TCL 创业投资合伙企业（有限合伙）	2010-07	—	—
无锡滨湖科技创业投资有限责任公司	2006-07-18	—	0510-85898528
无锡创业投资集团有限公司	2000-10-26	www.wxvcg.com	0510-82700936
无锡高新技术风险投资股份有限公司	2000-08	www.wxvc.com.cn	0510-85226431
无锡国联浚源创业投资中心（有限合伙）	2010-04-16	www.jycapital.cn	0510-82700340
无锡航天国华物联网投资企业（有限合伙）	2012-06-11	—	0510-85386420
无锡江南大学国家大学科技园有限公司	2009-04-03	www.j-park.jiangnan.edu.cn	0510-85189107
无锡均衡创业投资有限公司	2007-11-14	—	0510-86216651
无锡力合创业投资有限公司	2008-11	www.leaguercapital.com	0510-83590286
无锡力合清源创业投资合伙企业（有限合伙）	2011-09-09	www.leaguercapital.com	0510-83590296
无锡力合投资管理咨询有限公司	2009-04-17	www.leaguercapital.com	0510-83590296
无锡领峰创业投资有限公司	2009-12-11	—	0510-85213378
无锡清研投资有限公司	2009-08-14	—	0510-83591879
无锡瑞明博创业投资有限公司	2010-12-15	—	025-83172132
无锡市金惠创业投资有限责任公司	2006-11	—	0510-83590163
无锡市锡山创业投资有限公司	2007-08	—	0510-88705868
无锡新区领航创业投资有限公司	2009-08-03	www.wxvc.com.cn	0510-85226431
无锡源清创业投资有限公司	2012-06-28	—	0510-81801998
无锡源清盛华创业投资有限公司	2013-04-28	—	0510-81801998
无锡耘杉创业投资中心（有限合伙）	2013-07-12	—	—
无锡正海联云投资企业（有限合伙）	2012-12-04	—	—
无锡中科汇盈创业投资有限责任公司	2008-03-07	—	0510-85383122
无锡中科汇盈二期创业投资有限责任公司	2010-04-07	—	0510-85383122
吴江东方创富创业投资企业（有限合伙）	2012-10-29	—	—
吴江东方国发创业投资有限公司	2008-11-11	—	0512-65126380
吴江东方融富创业投资管理企业（有限合伙）	2012-10-12	—	—
吴江东运创业投资有限公司	2008-06-24	www.dyvc.net	0512-63960764

公司名称	成立时间	网址	传真
吴江海博科技创业投资有限公司	2010-08-20	www.haiboinvestment.net	0512-63010566
吴江华业创业投资管理中心（有限合伙）	2011-12-21	—	0512-63936955
兴化市高新投资有限公司	2010-07-16	—	0523-83242633
徐州博灏创业投资管理有限公司	2014-01-06	www.bohoasset.com	—
徐州风彩创业投资有限公司	2016-12-26	—	—
徐州高新创业投资有限公司	2010-02-24	—	0516-85906737
徐州国盛鸿运创业投资有限公司	2014-01-21	—	—
徐州淮海红土创业投资有限公司	2014-01-14	www.szvc.com.cn	—
徐州环晟创业投资有限公司	2016-02-17	—	—
徐州汇尔康创业投资有限公司	2016-12-26	www.xzhek.com	0516-85777288
徐州启迪泽陆创业投资管理中心（有限合伙）	2016-12-30	—	+86-10-82151307
徐州勤智创业投资企业（有限合伙）	2017-01-12	—	—
徐州市凯亚东峰创业投资有限公司	2016-12-22	—	—
徐州天福创业投资有限公司	2016-12-26	—	0516-82166216
扬州长晟创业投资有限公司	2014-11-25	—	0514-82058968
扬州平衡宜创创业投资基金中心（有限合伙）	2014-12-22	—	025-51889757
扬州市创业投资有限公司	2007-05-21	—	—
扬州英飞尼迪创业投资管理有限公司	2010-11-08	—	0514-87785512
张家港市金茂创业投资有限公司	2008-04-15	www.zjgsjmgs.com zjgjmtz	0520-58157063
镇江高科创业投资有限公司	2012-03-16	—	0511-87056055
镇江高投创业投资有限公司	2008-08	—	025-85529900
镇江高新创业投资有限公司	2010-06-11	—	0511-83179317
镇江国投创业投资有限公司	2011-10-19	—	0511-85606910
镇江红土创业投资有限公司	2011-04-22	www.szvc.com.cn	0511-85988773
镇江京口高新技术创业服务中心	2006-09	—	0511-88793155
镇江君鼎协立创业投资有限公司	2013-02-04	—	025-86816826
镇江君舜协立创业投资中心（有限合伙）	2016-09-08	—	025-86816826
镇江康成亨创业投资管理有限公司	2013-07-23	—	—
镇江康成亨创业投资合伙企业（有限合伙）	2013-08-12	—	—
镇江力合天使创业投资企业（有限合伙）	2012-12-13	—	0511-88884035
镇江乾鹏创业投资基金企业（有限合伙）	2012-11-20	—	0511-80896166
镇江亿致能源科技孵化器有限公司	2010-10-18	—	0511-85630166
镇江银河创业投资有限公司	2012-06-11	—	010-66568253
镇江中科金山创业投资企业（有限合伙）	2011-08-24	www.csm-inv.com	0510-85383122
镇江中以景润创业投资管理有限公司	2013-10-12	—	0511-81882260

公司名称	成立时间	网址	传真
中节能南通合同环境管理投资基金中心（有限合伙）	2013-04-03	—	0513-81288030
中新苏州工业园区创业投资有限公司	2001-11-28	—	0512-66969998
大连北方科技企业孵化基地	2003-06-12	www.bffhjd.cn	0411-87505839
大连创业工坊科技服务有限公司	2002-08-07	chuangyegongfang.com	—
大连德泰投资有限公司	2004-02-27	www.detainvestment.com	0411-87612476
大连港航产业基金管理有限公司	2011-07-01	www.chnpsf.com	0411-86768576
大连海融高新创业投资管理有限公司	2008-02-18	—	—
大连海融高新创业投资基金有限公司	2007-12-29	—	—
大连嘉创投资集团有限公司	2003-09-24	—	0411-88120533
大连精石文化产业投资有限公司	2014-04-28	—	0411-83792186
大连科技风险投资基金有限公司	2000-02	www.dstvc.com.cn	0411-82781352-11
大连赛伯乐创业投资中心（有限合伙）	2013-09-13	—	4006761188-1037
大连天使创业投资有限公司	2006-04-14	—	0411-84753186
大连万融天使投资有限公司	2010-11-30	—	—
大连网信创业投资管理有限公司	1999-06-28	—	0411-82859969
大连知你小巢科技服务有限公司	2016-04-18	—	—
大连中以英飞投资管理有限公司	2014-03-04	www.zhongyifund.com	0411-39576019
大连众创空间企业管理有限公司	2015-07-10	—	—
德晟创业投资有限公司	2011-03-09	—	0411-82779477
联合创业集团有限公司	2005-07-07	—	0411-88009300
辽宁科技创业投资有限责任公司	2000-02-28	www.lnvc.com.cn	024-23244922
盘锦中以英飞投资管理有限公司	2016-06-29	—	0427-2680603
沈阳科技风险开发事业中心	1992-06-02	—	024-22790094
沈阳科技风险投资有限公司	1998-11-04	—	024-22790094
特地世界（大连）科技股份有限公司	2015-03-17	www.tediword.com	0411-82740076
泽星投资管理（大连）有限公司	2015-11-09	—	0411-88079959
内蒙古自治区科技风险基金管理办公室	1998	www.fengxianjijin.com	0471-6280827
宁夏穆坤投资基金管理有限公司	2014-03-19	www.mukunpe.com	0951-6852601
宁夏中财高新投资管理有限公司	2013-04-17	www.nxzcgx.com	0951-8507997
银川市产业基金管理有限公司	2014-08-26	www.ycfof.com	0951-6981990
青海国科创业投资基金（有限合伙）	2013-10-23	—	0971-5115081
青海汇富科技成果转化投资基金（有限合伙）	2015-12-21	—	0971-5115081
青海科技创新投资基金（有限合伙）	2013-12-25	—	010-88555416
滨州高新技术创业投资有限公司	2010-05-07	—	0543-8191177
东营经济开发区斯博特创业投资有限公司	2012-06-04	—	0546-8300909

公司名称	成立时间	网址	传真
东营市金凯高新投资有限公司	2009-02-16	—	0546-8300909
黄河三角洲投资管理有限公司	2009-04-03	—	0546-7768881
黄蓝创业投资有限公司	2012-08-06	—	0543-5164888
济南华科创业投资合伙企业（有限合伙）	2013-11-12	—	0531-88887576
济南科技风险投资有限公司	2001-04	www.jnvc.com.cn	0531-88879277
济南科信创业投资有限公司	2011-10	—	0531-88879277
济南云海创业投资有限公司	2013-05-24	—	0531-85106246
济宁共创投资有限公司	2013-09-29	—	—
济宁英飞尼迪创业投资管理有限公司	2010-12-22	www.infinity-equity.com	0537-3281510
济宁英飞尼迪创业投资中心（有限合伙）	2011-04-21	www.infinity-equity.com	0537-3281505
巨野汇通创业投资有限公司	2008-11-05	—	0530-8310399
莱芜创业投资有限公司	2009-12-28	—	0634-8891182
莱芜瑞德投资有限公司	2012-02-23	—	0531-67803781
美世联合创业投资股份有限公司	2007-04-04	www.usbcc.cn	0543-5164777
青岛高创澳海股权投资管理有限公司	2016-07-21	—	—
青岛高创投资管理有限公司	2009-12-25	—	0543-88727626
青岛海尔赛富智慧家庭创业投资中心（有限合伙）	2014-09-01	—	010-65630251
青岛厚土创业投资有限公司	2005-08	—	0532-66715788
青岛里程碑创业投资管理有限公司	2011-05-20	—	0532-80931757
青岛连科股权投资基金合伙企业（有限合伙）	2014-10-29	www.qdlchk.com	—
青岛市科技风险投资有限公司	2000-08-17	huatongvc.com	0532-85063780
日照华和科技创业投资有限责任公司	2010-05-28	—	0633-8339288
山东昌润创业投资股份有限公司	2008-08-22	www.crtz.com	0635-2119616
山东德泰创业投资有限公司	2010-03-29	www.sddetai.cn	0535-3942685
山东多盈节能环保产业创业投资有限公司	2014-01-07	—	—
山东红桥创业投资有限公司	2011-12-22	—	0531-67803781
山东红桥股权投资管理有限公司	2011-11-30	—	0531-67803781
山东江诣创业投资有限公司	2010-08-12	—	0535-6719638
山东京德创业投资有限公司	2012-12-13	www.sdjdct.com	0633-8332328
山东君联创业投资有限公司	2015-11-27	—	—
山东科创投资有限公司	2010-10-22	—	0537-3292806
山东科融天使创业投资合伙企业（有限合伙）	2015-02-06	—	0531-67803781
山东利泰投资有限公司	2009-03-24	—	—
山东齐星创业投资有限公司	2007-01-30	—	0543-4309019
山东旗城科技创业投资股份有限公司	2009-08-19	—	0536-2139207

公司名称	成立时间	网址	传真
山东泰山创业投资股份有限公司	2008-08-27	—	0538-8261790
山东中泰天使创业投资基金企业（有限合伙）	2015-12-17	—	—
潍坊鲁信厚源创业投资中心（有限合伙）	2014-06-13	—	—
潍坊万通创业投资有限公司	2009-09-28	—	—
烟台安芙兰创业投资中心（有限合伙）	2015-12-11	—	—
烟台鼎亿创业投资管理有限公司	2012-03-14	—	—
烟台海源投资咨询有限公司	2014-09-24	www.haiyuanvc.com	0535-6267189
烟台建信蓝色经济创业投资有限公司	2011-12-15	—	021-62967868
烟台鲁创恒富创业投资中心（有限合伙）	2012-06-06	—	—
烟台瑞卿创业投资有限公司	2015-10-13	sdxy.gov.cn	—
烟台市蓝海创业投资有限公司	2011-12	—	0535-6891612
烟台市双兴创业投资有限公司	2010-08-04	—	0535-6662956
烟台泰达创业投资管理有限公司	2014-01-23	—	—
烟台盈智创业投资有限公司	2014-03-11	—	0535-6291105
烟台源创科技投资中心（有限合伙）	2014-07-17	—	010-58143806
淄博高新技术风险投资股份有限公司	2003-07- 10	www.zbvc.net	0533-3586969
淄博齐鲁创业投资有限责任公司	2002-12-06	www.zbqlct.com	0533-6206621
山西省科技基金发展总公司	1993-06	www.sxstf.com	0351-2026370
陕西高端装备高技术创业投资基金（有限合伙）	2013-06-28	—	0917-3322919
陕西科控投资管理有限责任公司	2016-02-04	—	—
陕西天健君合投资管理有限公司	2008-07-11	www.shxtjjh.com	029-88785306
陕西源丰投资发展有限公司	2009-03-24	—	029-68255896
西安高新技术产业风险投资有限公司	1999-02-01	www.capitech.com.cn	029-65690878
西安高新技术产业风险投资有限责任公司	1999-02-01	www.capitech.com.cn	029-65690878
西安迈朴投资发展有限公司	2002-01-08	—	029-81113288
西安润丰投资有限责任公司	2002-03	—	029-88250444
西安同泽投资有限公司	1995-05-05	—	029-88312715
西安西交科创股权投资合伙企业（有限合伙）	2016-02-04	—	029-83395811
杨凌东方富海现代农业生物产业股权投资企业（有限合伙）	2011-06-17	—	—
海硅（上海）创业投资合伙企业（有限合伙）	2011-08-05	—	021-65650817
上海晨晖创业投资管理有限公司	2013-10-23	www.chvc.com.cn	—
上海复旦创业投资有限公司	2000-11-09	—	021-65642533
上海国盛古贤创业投资管理有限公司	2012-12-12	www.gsgx-capital.com	021-58303168
上海国盛古贤创业投资合伙企业（有限合伙）	2013-04	www.gsgx-capital.com	021-58303168

公司名称	成立时间	网址	传真
上海慧立创业投资有限公司	2000-06-19	www.sjtu-vc.com	021-52989041
上海科技创业投资股份有限公司	1993-06-30	www.sstic.com.cn	021-64330776
上海浦东创业投资有限公司	1997-01-09	www.pdvc.com	021-50801728
上海浦东科技投资有限公司	1999-06	www.pdsti.com	021-50276385
上海浦软晨汇创业投资中心（有限合伙）	2014-08-27	—	—
上海浦软创业投资有限公司	2010-12-08	—	—
上海浦软汇智创业投资合伙企业（有限合伙）	2013-11-21	—	—
上海千骥创业投资管理有限公司	2010-01-07	www.cenova.com	021-64375623
上海千骥创业投资中心（有限合伙）	2012-07-12	www.cenova.com	—
上海千骥诺格医药创业投资管理有限公司	2012-05-30	www.cenova.com	—
上海千骥生物医药创业投资有限公司	2010-04-29	www.cenova.com	—
上海荣顾创业投资有限公司	2015-12-17	—	021-61273919
上海瑞经达创业投资有限公司	2010-02-10	—	025-83172132
上海时空五星创业投资管理有限公司	2009-11-18	—	021-61218707
上海时空五星创业投资合伙企业（有限合伙）	2009-12-31	—	021-61218709
上海新进创业投资管理有限公司	2013-04-09	www.newgenvc.com	—
上海徐汇科技创业投资有限公司	1998-12-02	www.xhvc.net	021-33680013
上海寅福创业投资有限公司	2010-05-06	—	021-65650817
上海寅嘉创业投资管理有限公司	2010-06-22	www.incufortune.com	021-65650817
上海张江创业投资有限公司	2000-07-12	www.zj-vc.com	021-50801918
上海正海聚弘创业投资中心（有限合伙）	2014-08-21	—	021-50937905
上海正海资产管理有限公司	2008-01-31	www.royalsea-capital.com	021-50937905
上海正赛联创业投资管理有限公司	2011-01-31	www.cacfund.com	021-64275106
上海正赛联创业投资有限公司	2010-10-22	www.cacfund.com	021-64275106
上海正淄资产管理有限公司	2015-09-06	www.shzamc.com	021-58301102
上海中嘉兴华创业投资管理有限公司	2012-10-17	—	—
上海中嘉兴华创业投资合伙企业（有限合伙）	2012-12-31	—	—
天翼科技创业投资有限公司	2012-07-23	www.189chuangyi.com	021-20989590
原子（上海）投资股份有限公司	2012-04-01	www.atomvc.com	021-65055235
成都成创创业投资有限公司	2015-07-13	—	—
成都成创汇智创业投资有限公司	2009-12-16	—	028-85337115
成都创新风险投资有限公司	2001-06-08	www.cd-vc.com.cn	028-85337115
成都德同银科创业投资合伙企业（有限合伙）	2010-03-03	www.dtcap.com	028-85231897
成都电科鹰熊创业投资中心（有限合伙）	2015-11-26	—	—
成都高特佳银科创业投资合伙企业（有限合伙）	2011-07-01	—	028-86586808

公司名称	成立时间	网址	传真
成都高投创业投资有限公司	2004-05-17	www.cdhtivc.com	028-85335111
成都硅谷天堂通威银科创业投资有限公司	2010-12-22	—	028-83202890
成都合力蓉信股权投资基金管理有限公司	2015-12-16	—	—
成都宏泰银科创业投资合伙企业（有限合伙）	2011-07-18	www.honorink.net	—
成都激创投资管理有限公司	2015-07-06	www.suhehui.com	028-83334288
成都阶梯创业投资合伙企业（有限合伙）	2016-03-09	—	028-65471211
成都阶梯创业投资有限公司	2015-04-15	—	028-65471211
成都凯晟投资管理中心（有限合伙）	2010-11-19	—	—
成都昆仑投资有限责任公司	2012-09-10	—	028-69591966
成都老鹰易真创业投资有限公司	2015-06-05	—	—
成都生产力促进中心	1997-07	www.cdppc.cn	028-65575920
成都晟唐银科创业投资企业（有限合伙）	2011-01-30	—	028-85987150
成都双流聚源创业投资有限公司	2009-10-28	—	028-85810763
成都银科九鼎投资中心（有限合伙）	2011-09-06	—	—
成都盈创德弘创业投资合伙企业（有限合伙）	2015-09-23	—	028-85335111
成都盈创德弘股权投资基金管理有限公司	2015-09-08	—	—
成都盈创泰富股权投资基金管理有限公司	2015-06-11	—	—
成都盈创兴科创业投资合伙企业（有限合伙）	2014-09-26	—	028-85988444
成都盈创兴科股权投资基金管理有限公司	2014-09-23	—	028-85988444
成都招商局银科创业投资有限公司	2010-12-31	—	—
成都真然股权投资基金管理有限公司	2015-01-30	www.zhenranziben.com	—
德阳阳光天使投资有限公司	2015-07-03	http:sc.gsxt.gov.cn	—
德阳盈创阳光天使创业投资管理有限公司	2015-09-14	—	0838-6939393
广元市广发创业投资有限公司	2013-03-15	www.gygfct.com	0839-3289981
合之力蓉盛成都创业投资中心（有限合伙）	2015-12-31	—	—
绵阳金慧通股权投资基金管理有限公司	2014-12-02	—	—
绵阳久盛科技创业投资有限公司	2004-03-05	—	—
绵阳思迈创业投资管理中心（有限合伙）	2013-07-02	—	—
攀枝花市金源创业投资有限公司	2008-08-15	www.jinyuanvc.com	0812-3373896
四川鼎祥股权投资基金有限公司	2014-07-17	www.dinxcapital.com	—
四川雅惠新材料创业投资基金有限公司	2015-09-22	—	0831-2400925
四川中物创业投资有限公司	2007-02-08	www.caep-vc.com	028-85311576
北方国际集团控股（天津）有限公司	2011-12-22	—	022-58367529
鸿丰鼎翊（天津）投资管理有限公司	2014-01-13	www.dyifund.cn	—
日亚（天津）创业投资管理有限公司	2011-06-13	www.jaic-vc.co.jpcnindex.html	—

公司名称	成立时间	网址	传真
日亚（天津）创业投资企业	2011-08-01	—	—
天创博盛（天津）股权投资基金合伙企业（有限合伙）	2011-10-18	—	022-86259326
天津滨海北辰镒泰股权投资基金有限公司	2009-11-03	—	022-28301133
天津滨海财富股权投资基金有限公司	2007-08-21	www.behycapital.com	022-23374077
天津滨海创投投资管理有限公司	2007-09-18	www.binhaicapital.com	022-58909361
天津滨海高新技术产业开发区科鑫创业投资有限公司	2012-01-12	—	022-58785820
天津滨海天创众鑫股权投资基金有限公司	2010-02-04	—	022-86259326
天津滨海天使创业投资有限公司	2006-09-11	—	022-58909386
天津滨海新区创业风险投资引导基金有限公司	2008-02-04	www.bhsf.com.cn	022-65831777
天津琛瑛投资有限公司	2010-12-20	—	022-23374055
天津创业投资管理有限公司	2003-03-28	www.tjvcm.com	022-86259326
天津迪恩投资管理有限公司	2012-06-13	—	022-59385952
天津东虹科技创业投资发展有限公司	2011-04-28	—	022-58785820
天津阜通乾元股权投资基金管理有限公司	2015-09-09	—	022-87455108
天津海达创业投资管理有限公司	2007-11-29	www.hideavc.com	022-59852168
天津海泰滨海创业投资有限公司	2008-04-16	—	—
天津海泰戈壁创业投资管理有限公司	2008-02-21	www.htgvc.com	—
天津海泰红土创新投资有限公司	2008-05-28	—	—
天津和悦谷雨股权投资基金合伙企业（有限合伙）	2011-04-20	www.grainsvalley.com	010-85910113
天津虹联创业投资有限公司	2009-12-28	—	022-26530257
天津火石信息服务业创业投资合伙企业（有限合伙）	2013-02-06	—	022-59385952
天津开明创业投资发展有限公司	2004-04-16	www.ttkama.com	022-58792370
天津科创天使投资有限公司	2006-06-19	www.tjacco.com	022-87893289
天津科技融资控股集团有限公司	2010-11-24	www.tjstgroup.com	022-58785820
天津科技投资集团有限公司	1997-12	www.stic.com.cn	022-86430531-804
天津锟桥创业投资有限公司	2003-08-07	www.kqvc.com	022-87893441
天津联想之星创业投资有限公司	2012-01-09	—	022-82982400
天津南开区苑鑫创业投资有限公司	2012-10-12	—	022-58785820
天津市武清区信邦科技创业投资发展有限公司	2011-05-23	—	022-58785820
天津水星创业投资有限责任公司	2010-05-10	—	022-59852168
天津泰达科技投资股份有限公司	2000-10-13	www.tedavc.com.cn	022-66297288
天津天宝创业投资有限公司	2004-08-09	www.tjtianbao.com	022-23133080
天津天保成长资产管理有限公司	2007-03-06	—	022-86259326

公司名称	成立时间	网址	传真
天津天创华鑫现代服务产业创业投资合伙企业（有限合伙）	2012-12-04	—	022-86259326
天津天创盈讯创业投资合伙企业（有限合伙）	2011-09-26	—	022-86259326
天津天地酬勤创业投资合伙企业（有限合伙）	2016-05-19	—	022-23708158
天津天地酬勤股权投资管理有限公司	2015-11-16	www.tianjinvc.net	022-23708158
天津天地酬勤天使创业投资有限公司	2016-05-24	—	022-23708158
天津天富创业投资有限公司	2007-12-04	—	022-86259326
天津天以生物医药股权投资基金有限公司	2010-11-25	—	022-86259326
天津天英创业投资管理有限公司	2010-06-22	—	022-86259326
天津信石基业投资咨询有限公司	2011-04-13	—	022-87820130
天津浔渡创业投资合伙企业（有限合伙）	2011-04-08	—	0510-87822121
天津沅渡创业投资合伙企业（有限合伙）	2010-08-11	—	0510-87822121
天津中科达创业投资管理有限公司	2015-10-28	—	—
中投财富辛卯（天津）创业投资合伙企业（有限合伙）)	2011-07-18	—	010-85325935
霍尔果斯嘉泽创业投资有限公司	2012-11-28	—	—
喀什新昆创业投资有限公司	2012-07-24	—	—
乌鲁木齐市科技投资经营中心	2001-07-25	—	0991-4538283
新疆创投资本管理有限责任公司	2010-07-15	www.xjvc.net	0991-3682873
新疆大藏资产管理股份有限公司	2015-04-17	treasure_capital@163.com	0991-3821497
新疆火炬创业投资有限公司	2012-08-09	www.tvcxj.com	0991-3678085
新疆江之源股权投资合伙企业（有限合伙）	2010-12-02	—	0991-7864660
新疆融汇鑫创业投资管理有限公司	2011-11-30	—	0991-6990026
新疆赛科森投资咨询有限责任公司	2002-04	—	0991-6611966
新疆天裕华盛股权投资管理有限公司	2011-10-27	—	0991-2612357
新疆维吾尔自治区国有资产投资经营有限责任公司	1998-04-23	—	0991-2810861
新疆新科源科技风险投资管理有限公司	2004-08	—	0991-3680756
新疆兴华富疆股权投资管理有限公司	2015-08-06	—	0991-3778323
新疆益通投资有限合伙企业	2011-03-01	—	0571-63431799
新疆浙新股权投资有限合伙企业	2011-11-02	—	—
新疆中科援疆创新创业私募基金管理有限公司	2015-10-09	—	0991-3820157
新疆中小企业创业投资股份有限公司	2010-01-26	www.xjvc.cn	0991-4583310
红塔创新投资股份有限公司	2000-06-15	—	010-58555666
云南惠众股权投资基金管理有限公司	2011-07-06	—	0871-63620252
云南宁祥股权投资基金管理有限公司	2012-10-19	—	—

公司名称	成立时间	网址	传真
云南省现代农林投资有限公司	2009-05-27	www.cnynfi.com	0871-68338757
云南银河之星金融服务有限公司	2014-10-22	—	0871-68358445
安丰创业投资有限公司	2008-02-28	—	0571-87633580
伯乐遇马天使投资有限公司	2012-03-09	www.boleyuma.com	0574-27956851
长兴惠宏投资合伙企业（有限合伙）	2012-05-28	—	—
长兴科创投资管理合伙企业（有限合伙）	2015-10-19	—	0571-89939766
长兴科商创业投资合伙企业（有限合伙）	2015-06-15	—	0571-88869317
长兴科威创业投资合伙企业（有限合伙）	2014-12-30	—	—
长兴天使投资管理合伙企业（有限合伙）	2015-10-22	—	0571-89939766
海宁力合天使创业投资合伙企业（有限合伙）	2014-09-30	—	—
海宁普华友创股权投资管理合伙企业（有限合伙）	2015-09-15	—	—
海宁三仁腾兴股权投资合伙企业（有限合伙）	2015-06-02	—	—
海宁三仁望岳股权投资合伙企业（有限合伙）	2015-06-02	—	—
杭州安丰宸元创业投资合伙企业（有限合伙）	2016-01-21	—	0571-87633580
杭州安丰慧元创业投资合伙企业（有限合伙）	2016-03-15	—	0571-87633580
杭州安丰玖号创业投资合伙企业（有限合伙）	2015-09-28	—	0571-87633580
杭州安丰上盈创业投资合伙企业（有限合伙）	2015-01-09	—	0571-87633580
杭州葆光投资管理有限公司	2012-10-18	—	0571-85455412
杭州长江创业投资有限公司	1996-01-06	—	0571-86624323
杭州诚和创业投资有限公司	2006-06-01	—	0571-88219849
杭州创客加速投资管理有限公司	2014-12-02	www.makeraccel.com	0571-87981960
杭州德同创业投资合伙企业（有限合伙）	2010-07-08	—	0571-86690981
杭州德同投资管理有限公司	2010-04-21	—	0571-86690981
杭州鼎聚芥园创业投资合伙企业（有限合伙）	2011-05-28	—	—
杭州鼎聚景远创业投资合伙企业（有限合伙）	2016-05-23	—	—
杭州鼎聚坤华创业投资合伙企业（有限合伙）	2011-12-21	—	—
杭州鼎聚茂华创业投资合伙企业（有限合伙）	2013-01-07	—	—
杭州鼎聚投资管理有限公司	2011-04-06	—	—
杭州东方星空创业投资有限公司	2008-10-29	—	0571-85058016
杭州敦和创业投资有限公司	2011-04-11	www.dunhevc.com	0571-87789050
杭州福生创业投资管理有限公司	2016-04-27	—	0571-86166991
杭州复朴共进投资合伙企业（有限合伙）	2015-03-31	—	0571-86690981
杭州复朴投资管理有限公司	2014-09-17	—	0571-86690981
杭州高特佳股权投资管理有限公司	2010-12	—	—
杭州高特佳龙之海脉投资管理合伙企业（有限合伙）	2011-06-15	—	—

公司名称	成立时间	网址	传真
杭州高新风险投资有限公司	2005-12-29	—	0571-88212247
杭州高盈创业投资合伙企业（有限合伙）	2009-06-18	—	0571-87960022
杭州高盈蓝驰投资有限公司	2009-08-25	—	0571-87960022
杭州广润创业投资有限公司	2007-11-28	—	0571-86951902
杭州贵诚投资合伙企业（有限合伙）	2016-02-06	—	—
杭州贵巨创业投资合伙企业（有限合伙）	2015-09-23	—	0571-86951902
杭州海邦投资管理有限公司	2010-12-10	www.hbvc.com.cn	0571-81022997
杭州海邦新湖人才创业投资合伙企业（有限合伙）	2013-08-02	www.hbvc.com.cn	0571-81022997
杭州海邦药谷从正创业投资合伙企业（有限合伙）	2015-06-05	—	0571-81022997
杭州海邦引智投资管理有限公司	2012-06-01	www.hbvc.com.cn	0571-81022997
杭州汉洋友创投资合伙企业（有限合伙）	2015-01-29	—	0571-87397929
杭州杭商宝石创业投资合伙企业（有限合伙）	2011-02-21	—	0571-86586927
杭州好望角启航投资合伙企业（有限合伙）	2011-07-28	httpgsxt.zjaic.gov.cn	0571-28239066
杭州好望角投资管理有限公司	2007-08-22	httpgsxt.zjaic.gov.cn	0571-88236955
杭州浩盈投资合伙企业（有限合伙）	2010-11-12	—	—
杭州宏桥爱富投资合伙企业（有限合伙）	2015-08-14	—	0571-87031727
杭州宏桥锦上添花投资合伙企业（有限合伙）	2015-08-13	—	0571-87031727
杭州宏桥精彩未来投资合伙企业（有限合伙）	2015-08-10	—	0571-87031727
杭州宏桥熠熠生辉投资合伙企业（有限合伙）	2015-08-07	—	0571-87031727
杭州厚初创业投资合伙企业（有限合伙）	2014-05-22	—	0571-87988858
杭州戒和投资管理合伙企业（有限合伙）	2015-12-22	—	—
杭州金永信创业投资合伙企业（有限合伙）	2009-12-21	—	0571-85279925
杭州金永信润禾创业投资合伙企业（有限合伙）	2010-05-04	—	0571-85279925
杭州金永信天时创业投资合伙企业	2010-04-07	—	0571-85279925
杭州经济技术开发区创业投资有限公司	2008-10-09	—	0571-88062089
杭州科发创业投资合伙企业（有限合伙）	2013-01-09	www.zdkfcapital.com	0571-88250427
杭州科发天使投资合伙企业（有限合伙）	2015-02-12	zdkfcapital.com	0571-88250427
杭州浪淘沙势弘投资合伙企业（有限合伙）	2016-06-14	—	0571-88771697
杭州浪淘沙投资管理有限公司	2014-09-19	www.ltsvc.com	0571-88771697
杭州浪淘沙智选创业投资合伙企业（有限合伙）	2014-11-06	—	0571-88771697
杭州立元创业投资股份有限公司	2006-12-08	www.cnlyjt.com	0571-87769018
杭州灵瑛投资合伙企业（有限合伙）	2013-06-03	—	0571-85455412
杭州睦和投资管理合伙企业（普通合伙）	2010-05-28	—	—
杭州普华博帆投资合伙企业（有限合伙）	2016-01-21	—	—
杭州钱江浙商创业投资合伙企业（有限合伙）	2009-06-03	—	0571-89922221

公司名称	成立时间	网址	传真
杭州庆诚投资合伙企业（有限合伙）	—	—	—
杭州如山创业投资有限公司	2007-08	—	0571-87896213
杭州润琰投资合伙企业（有限合伙）	2013-04-08	—	0571-85455412
杭州市高科技投资有限公司	2000-08	—	0571-86699729
杭州泰恒投资管理有限公司	2010-06-03	—	—
杭州天赋投资管理合伙企业（有限合伙）	2016-04-29	—	—
杭州天联投资管理合伙企业（有限合伙）	2014-03-14	—	—
杭州天璞创业投资合伙企业（有限合伙）	2013-07-05	—	—
杭州万豪碧扬投资合伙企业（有限合伙）	2012-03-15	—	—
杭州万豪绵汐投资合伙企业（有限合伙）	2012-03-15	—	—
杭州万豪培汕投资合伙企业（有限合伙）	2012-03-15	—	—
杭州万豪投资管理有限公司	2006-01-09	—	0571-88129640
杭州文诚创业投资有限公司	2012-07-09	—	—
杭州文广创业投资有限公司	2010-12-29	—	0571-89870615
杭州文广股权投资管理有限公司	2010-11-10	—	0571-89870615
杭州西牛投资管理有限公司	2016-04-18	—	—
杭州盈开投资管理有限公司	2009-06-23	www.incapital.cn	0571-87960022
杭州盈翔创业投资合伙企业（有限合伙）	2011-03-04	—	—
杭州友创天使投资合伙企业（有限合伙）	2016-07-20	—	0571-87397929
杭州云祥创新投资合伙企业（有限合伙）	2011-09-23	—	0571-87960022
杭州云卓投资合伙企业（有限合伙）	2016-04-22	—	0571-87960022
杭州浙科汇福创业投资合伙企业（有限合伙）	2016-10-12	—	0571-88869550
杭州浙科汇庆创业投资合伙企业（有限合伙）	2013-04-10	—	—
杭州浙科友业投资管理有限公司	2011-11	—	0571-88869550
湖州市创业投资有限责任公司	2008-09	—	0572-2212918
嘉兴禾焕投资合伙企业（有限合伙）	2016-10-25	—	—
嘉兴华睿布谷鸟创业投资合伙企业（有限合伙）	2014-08-14	—	—
嘉兴天禀投资合伙企业（有限合伙）	2014-05-16	—	—
嘉兴天玑创业投资合伙企业（有限合伙）	2014-04-04	—	—
嘉兴天爵投资合伙企业（有限合伙）	2016-09-29	—	—
嘉兴天澜投资合伙企业（有限合伙）	2014-11-17	—	—
嘉兴天禄投资合伙企业（有限合伙）	2014-12-22	—	—
嘉兴天叶投资合伙企业（有限合伙）	2016-06-24	—	—
金华市普华百川股权投资合伙企业（有限合伙）	2015-07-27	—	—
金华中呼股权投资管理有限公司	2011-08-17	—	0579-82056869

公司名称	成立时间	网址	传真
宁波安丰和众创业投资合伙企业（有限合伙）	2011-03-10	—	0571-87633580
宁波安丰汇群创业投资合伙企业（有限合伙）	2011-08-12	—	0571-87633580
宁波安丰汇盈创业投资合伙企业（有限合伙）	2011-08-12	—	0571-87633580
宁波安丰领先创业投资合伙企业（有限合伙）	2011-04-26	—	0571-87633580
宁波安丰添富创业投资合伙企业（有限合伙）	2012-07-13	—	0571-87633580
宁波安丰众盈创业投资合伙企业（有限合伙）	2010-04-27	—	0571-87633580
宁波北岸智谷海邦创业投资合伙企业（有限合伙）	2016-07-07	—	0574-83088686
宁波北远创业投资中心（有限合伙）	2010-08-27	—	0574-27706565
宁波创业风险投资有限公司	1999-05-06	—	0574-86881546
宁波东元创业投资有限公司	2005-05-16	www.nbvc.com.cn	+86-0574-87294001
宁波海邦人才创业投资合伙企业（有限合伙）	2011-09-29	—	0574-83088686
宁波海达睿盈股权投资管理有限公司	2017-01-08	—	022-59852168
宁波华桐创业投资管理有限公司	2016-02-24	—	0574-87294001
宁波开云融汇创业投资合伙企业（有限合伙）	2015-05-18	—	0574-88182007
宁波科发宝鼎创业投资合伙企业（有限合伙）	2016-11-16	www.zjkfcapital.com	0571-88250328
宁波科发海鼎创业投资合伙企业（有限合伙）	2014-05-30	www.zdkfcapital.com	0571-88250427
宁波民和风险投资有限公司	2010-06-03	—	0574-55001908
宁波欧迅创业投资有限公司	2010-09-28	—	0574-83887737
宁波赛伯乐甬科股权投资合伙企业（有限合伙）	2011-11-28	—	—
宁波杉杉望新科技创业投资有限公司	2009-12-14	—	0574-56801577
宁波市伯乐开图创业投资合伙企业（有限合伙）	2013-06-19	—	0574-88182007
宁波市科发二号股权投资基金合伙企业（有限合伙）	2012-09-18	www.zdkfcapital.com	0571-88250427
宁波市科发股权投资基金合伙企业（有限合伙）	2012-03-01	www.zdkfcapital.com	0571-88250427
宁波天骥赢和股权投资管理有限公司	2016-04-18	—	0574-87359666
宁波天堂硅谷合众股权投资合伙企业（有限合伙）	2012-02-16	—	0571-86483535
宁波天堂硅谷融创股权投资合伙企业（有限合伙）	2014-01	—	—
宁波天堂硅谷融正股权投资合伙企业（有限合伙）	2014-01-08	—	0571-87089718
宁波天堂硅谷新象股权投资合伙企业（有限合伙）	2015	—	—
宁波新以创业投资管理有限公司	2010-01-13	www.infinty-equity.com	0574-87993884
宁波新以创业投资合伙企业（有限合伙）	2010-01-29	www.infinity-equity.com	0574-87993884
宁波英飞伯乐创业投资管理有限公司	2015-06-25	www.infinity-equity.com	0574-8799384
宁波英飞伯乐创业投资合伙企业（有限合伙）	2015-09-10	—	0574-87993884
宁波浙科汇聚创业投资合伙企业（有限合伙）	2014-07-16	—	—
宁波浙科永强创业投资合伙企业（有限合伙）	2015-12-09	—	0571-88869350
绍兴天堂硅谷恒煜股权投资合伙企业	2016-09-27	—	

公司名称	成立时间	网址	传真
台州科金创业投资合伙企业（有限合伙）	2014-11-12	—	0571-89939766
万向创业投资股份有限公司	2000-12	—	0571-87153792
温州市科技创业投资有限公司	2012-07-27	—	0577-88287875
义乌科发创业投资合伙企业（有限合伙）	2016-01-21	www.zjkfcapital.com	0571-88250328
义乌浙科汇富创业投资合伙企业（有限合伙）	2016-01-25	—	0571-88869550
鹰潭联浙商投创业投资合伙企业（有限合伙）	2016-01-14	—	0571-88771697
浙江爱杭股权投资基金管理有限公司	2015-07-21	www.ihangcapital.com	0571-82565965
浙江安丰进取创业投资有限公司	2009-03-25	—	0571-87633580
浙江博通创业投资有限公司	2007-07	—	0571-87087810
浙江春晖创业投资有限公司	2007-10-17	—	0575-82150888
浙江大学创新技术研究院有限公司	2012-09-29	www.zjuiti.com	0571-58122629
浙江大学科技创业投资有限公司	2008-10-29	zdkc.zju.edu.cn	0571-87397929
浙江东翰高投长三角股权投资合伙企业（有限合伙）	2010-09-20	—	025-85529900
浙江富国创新投资有限公司	2010-08-12	—	0571-88068369
浙江富国创业投资有限公司	2007-04-29	—	0571-88068369
浙江富鑫创业投资有限公司	2008-02-03	www.zfinvest.com	0571-88352033
浙江国信创业投资有限公司	2003-03	—	0571-85069200
浙江海邦人才创业投资合伙企业（有限合伙）	2011-12	www.hbvc.com.cn	0571-81022997
浙江海宁天玑创业投资管理合伙企业（有限合伙）	2015-06-19	—	—
浙江海宁天擎创业投资管理合伙企业（有限合伙）	2015-07-06	—	—
浙江海洋经济创业投资有限公司	2010-01-19	—	0580-2036865
浙江浩誉创业投资有限公司	2011-01-14	—	0571-85814767
浙江合力创业投资有限公司	2011-03-09	—	0571-87988858
浙江红石创业投资有限公司	2007-11-27	—	—
浙江红土创业投资有限公司	2010-04-21	—	0573-83710180
浙江华瓯创业投资有限公司	2007-11-16	www.hovc.cn	0571-87988858
浙江华瓯股权投资管理有限公司	2011-05-17	—	0571-87988858
浙江华睿北信源数据信息产业投资合伙企业（有限合伙）	2015-08-19	—	—
浙江华睿布谷鸟创业投资合伙企业（有限合伙）	2015-06-03	—	—
浙江华睿产业互联网股权投资合伙企业（有限合伙）	2015-04-13	—	—
浙江华睿德银创业投资有限公司	2010-05-04	—	0571-88163180
浙江华睿点金创业投资有限公司	2009-08-10	—	—
浙江华睿点石投资管理有限公司	2007-11-14	—	0571-88163180
浙江华睿富华创业投资合伙企业（有限合伙）	2012-07-03	—	—

公司名称	成立时间	网址	传真
浙江华睿海越光电产业创业投资有限公司	2009-12-23	—	—
浙江华睿海越现代服务业创业投资有限公司	2010-01-28	—	0571-88163180
浙江华睿弘源智能产业创业投资有限公司	2010-03-22	—	0571-88163180
浙江华睿互联投资有限公司	2010-10-20	—	0571-88163180
浙江华睿控股有限公司	2002-08	www.sinowisdom.cn	0571-88163180
浙江华睿蓝石创业投资有限公司	2014-09-02	—	—
浙江华睿庆余创业投资有限公司	2013-12-30	—	—
浙江华睿如山创业投资有限公司	2010-12-07	—	0571-88163180
浙江华睿如山装备投资有限公司	2009-10-13	—	—
浙江华睿睿银创业投资有限公司	2007-03-28	—	—
浙江华睿盛银创业投资有限公司	2009-08-11	—	—
浙江华睿泰信创业投资有限公司	2008-07-21	—	—
浙江华睿泰银投资有限公司	2009-07-20	—	—
浙江华睿祥生环境产业创业投资有限公司	2010-11-15	—	0571-88163180
浙江华睿兴华股权投资合伙企业（有限合伙）	2012-12-24	—	—
浙江华睿医疗创业投资有限公司	2011-01-24	—	0571-88163180
浙江华睿中科创业投资有限公司	2010-07-05	—	0571-88163180
浙江嘉海创业投资有限公司	2010-01-13	—	0571-89922221
浙江嘉庆投资有限公司	2010-06-29	—	0571-86821212
浙江嘉银投资有限公司	2006-05-24	—	0571-88163180
浙江金桥创业投资有限公司	2007-08-14	www.jinqiaojituan.com	0571-89283995
浙江金永信投资管理有限公司	2005-03-24	—	0571-85279925
浙江君亚创业投资合伙企业（有限合伙）	2012-05-21	—	0571-86751630
浙江科发资本管理有限公司	2003-11-11	www.zdkfcapital.com	0571-88250427
浙江科金天使启航股权投资合伙企业（有限合伙）	2011-11-14	—	0571-89939766
浙江莱沃东辰创业投资有限公司	2009-07-08	www.uslever.com	0574-82815775
浙江蓝石创业投资有限公司	2008-05-15	—	—
浙江蓝源投资管理有限公司	2011-10-21	www.bluesource.hk	0574-89019226
浙江美林创业投资有限公司	2008-07-11	www.merrillcapital.cn	0571-85455412
浙江瓯联创业投资有限公司	2009-05-12	—	0571-87988858
浙江瓯盛创业投资有限公司	2008-06-03	—	0571-87988858
浙江瓯信创业投资有限公司	2009-04-02	—	0571-87988858
浙江普华天勤股权投资管理有限公司	2011-06-20	www.puhuacapital.comindex.aspx	0571-87755559
浙江如山成长创业投资有限公司	2008-08-18	www.chinadunan.com	0571-87896213
浙江如山高新创业投资有限公司	2010-11-10	www.chinadunan.com	0571-87896213

公司名称	成立时间	网址	传真
浙江如山汇金资本管理有限公司	2010-09-26	www.chinadunan.com	0571-87896213
浙江如山汇鑫创业投资合伙企业（有限合伙）	2015-11-05	www.chinadunan.com	0571-87896213
浙江如山新兴创业投资有限公司	2012-09-11	—	0751-87896213
浙江若溪投资合伙企业（有限合伙）	2014-08-14	—	—
浙江赛伯乐科创股权投资管理有限公司	2011-08-09	www.cybernautvc.com	0571-88085123
浙江绍兴普华兰亭文化投资合伙企业（有限合伙）	2015-12-07	—	—
浙江省创业投资集团有限公司	2000-09-30	www.zjvc.cn	0571-88259222
浙江省科技风险投资有限公司	1993-06	www.zvc-zj.com	0571-88869550
浙江省浙创启元创业投资有限公司	2012-12-31	—	0571-88259222
浙江泰银创业投资有限公司	2007-10-26	—	—
浙江天使湾创业投资有限公司	2010-09-29	tisiwi.com	0571-89715708
浙江天堂硅谷长泰股权投资合伙企业（有限合伙）	2011-07-15	—	0571-86483535
浙江天堂硅谷朝阳创业投资有限公司	2007-04-16	—	0571-86483535
浙江天堂硅谷晨曦创业投资有限公司	2007-10-16	—	0571-86483535
浙江天堂硅谷大康股权投资合伙企业（有限合伙）	2012-08-21	—	0571-86483535
浙江天堂硅谷海天汇缘创业投资合伙企业（有限合伙）	2013-03-04	—	0571-86483535
浙江天堂硅谷合丰创业投资有限公司	2009-10-13	—	0571-86483535
浙江天堂硅谷合胜创业投资有限公司	2009-10-20	—	0571-87089718
浙江天堂硅谷合众创业投资有限公司	2007-10-24	—	0571-86483523
浙江天堂硅谷恒通创业投资有限公司	2008-05-26	—	0571-86483535
浙江天堂硅谷恒裕创业投资有限公司	2008-01-03	—	0571-86483535
浙江天堂硅谷久和股权投资合伙企业（有限合伙）	2012-03-01	—	0571-86483535
浙江天堂硅谷久鸿股权投资合伙企业（有限合伙）	2013	—	0571-86483535
浙江天堂硅谷久晟股权投资合伙企业（有限合伙）	2011	—	0571-87089718
浙江天堂硅谷鲲诚创业投资有限公司	2006-12-01	—	0571-86483535
浙江天堂硅谷鲲鹏创业投资有限公司	2009-06-26	—	0571-86483535
浙江天堂硅谷七弦股权投资合伙企业（有限合伙）	2011	—	0571-86483535
浙江天堂硅谷融源股权投资合伙企业（有限合伙）	2014-01	—	—
浙江天堂硅谷时顺股权投资合伙企业（有限合伙）	—	—	—
浙江天堂硅谷台州合盈股权投资有限公司	2011	—	0571-86483535
浙江天堂硅谷阳光创业投资有限公司	2006-06-20	—	0571-86483535
浙江天堂硅谷银嘉股权投资合伙企业（有限合伙）	2010-11-16	—	0571-86483523
浙江天堂硅谷银泽股权投资合伙企业（有限合伙）	2010-10-19	—	0571-86483523
浙江天堂硅谷盈丰股权投资合伙企业（有限合伙）	2010-07-30	—	0571-87089718

公司名称	成立时间	网址	传真
浙江天堂硅谷盈通创业投资有限公司	2010-06-01	—	0571-86483535
浙江天堂硅谷资产管理集团有限公司	2000-11-11	www.ttgg.com.cn	0571-86483535
浙江维科创业投资有限公司	2008-02-28	—	0571-87207613
浙江新安创业投资有限公司	2011	—	0571-88050547
浙江新锐浙商科技投资管理有限公司	2013-06-14	—	0571-87203404
浙江信德丰创业投资有限公司	2010-05-27	—	0571-87225400
浙江以琳创业投资有限公司	2014-08-08	—	—
浙江亿都创业投资有限公司	2007-11	—	0571-85310058
浙江盈瓯创业投资有限公司	2010-11-05	—	0571-87988858
浙江浙大大晶创业投资有限公司	2001-01-03	—	0571-87382889
浙江浙大友创投资管理有限公司	2001-01-21	—	0571-87397929
浙江浙科汇丰创业投资有限公司	2010-09	—	—
浙江浙科汇利创业投资有限公司	2010-05	—	—
浙江浙科汇涛创业投资合伙企业（有限合伙）	2011-05-09	—	—
浙江浙科汇盈创业投资有限公司	2009-08	—	—
浙江浙科美林创业投资有限公司	2011-04	—	—
浙江浙科升华创业投资有限公司	2010-10	—	—
浙江浙科银江创业投资有限公司	2010-10-14	—	—
浙江浙商长海创业投资合伙企业（有限合伙）	2010-12-14	—	0571-89922221
浙江浙商创业投资股份有限公司	2007-11	www.zsvc.com.cn	0571-89922221
浙江浙商海鹏创业投资合伙企业（有限合伙）	2008-06-03	—	0571-89922221
浙江浙商诸海创业投资合伙企业（有限合伙）	2010-04-14	—	0571-89922221
浙江中新力合科技金融服务股份有限公司	2011-09-29	—	0571-89939766
浙江诸暨惠风创业投资有限公司	2008-08-06	—	0575-87026018
诸暨鼎信创业投资有限公司	2008-07-29	—	0571-87896213
诸暨贵银创业投资有限公司	2014-05-14	—	—
诸暨华睿嘉银创业投资合伙企业（有限合伙）	2014-11-21	—	—
诸暨华睿文华股权投资合伙企业（有限合伙）	2015-06-10	—	—
诸暨华睿新锐投资合伙企业（有限合伙）	2015-06-01	—	—
杭州兰德润广投资管理有限公司	2010-12-20	—	0571-86963977
杭州兰德优势创业投资合伙企业（有限合伙）	2011-07-07	—	—
昊云（重庆）股权投资基金管理有限公司	2012-11-23	www.howinfund.com	023-67511558
民商（重庆）股权投资基金管理有限公司	2014-02-26	—	—
西证重庆股权投资基金管理有限公司	2013-07-18	—	023-63786322
圆基（重庆）股权投资基金管理有限公司	2010-02-05	—	023-63329022

公司名称	成立时间	网址	传真
重庆贝信投资有限公司	2014-02-21	—	023-86713575
重庆博永投资管理有限公司	—	www.boyond.cn	—
重庆渤溢股权投资基金管理有限公司	2014-09-30	—	023-67468572
重庆辰龙股权投资基金管理有限公司	2012-03-05	—	023-63218290
重庆宸西股权投资基金管理有限公司	2014-05-19	—	023-63080193
重庆川鼎股权投资基金管理有限公司	2015-01-13	—	023-88727111
重庆达达股权投资基金管理有限公司	2015-09-09	www.ddafund.com	023-61914181
重庆大乘股权投资基金管理有限公司	2014-05-23	—	023-63507862
重庆大石投资管理有限公司	2013-09-17	www.upcubator.com	—
重庆德同创业投资中心（有限合伙）	2010-04-01	—	023-67889905
重庆德同领航创业投资中心（有限合伙）	2014-04-30	—	023-67889905
重庆德同投资管理有限公司	2009-12-29	—	023-67889905
重庆峰瑞卓越一期股权投资基金合伙企业（有限合伙）	2016-04-19	—	023-65308717
重庆富坤创业投资中心（有限合伙）	2009-09-22	www.rlequities.com	023-67030600
重庆富坤新智能交通投资合伙企业（有限合伙）	2014-04-08	www.rlequities.com	023-67030700
重庆高新创投红马资本管理有限公司	2014-04-14	www.cqrhcapital.com	023-67990972
重庆高新创投两江品牌汽车产业投资中心（有限合伙）	2014-04-14	www.cqrhcapital.com	023-67990972
重庆高新创业投资有限公司	2007-08	—	023-67308830
重庆汉能科技创业投资中心（有限合伙）	2011-08-30	www.hinagroup.com.cn	010-85889001
重庆瀚曦股权投资基金管理有限公司	2010-09-13	www.aktiscapital.com	023-63103106
重庆皓顺股权投资基金管理有限公司	2013-07-01	www.cqhsjj.com	023-63519299
重庆和信融智股权投资基金管理有限公司	2014-12-02	—	023-67305590
重庆和亚化医投资管理有限公司	2014-03-10	—	023-63428005
重庆恒锐源股权投资基金管理有限公司	2009-12-23	www.chinahry.com	023-86798500
重庆弘远渝富股权投资基金管理有限公司	2010-01-13	—	023-88505110
重庆鸿曜股权投资基金管理有限公司	2014-12-29	—	—
重庆华犇创业投资管理有限公司	2010-04-16	www.chinarunvc.com	023-63318955
重庆华犇电子信息创业投资中心（有限合伙）	2010-11-16	www.chinarunvc.com	023-63318955
重庆环保产业股权投资基金管理有限公司	2015-10-12	—	—
重庆洹杉股权投资基金管理有限公司	2015-01-15	—	—
重庆桓泰投资有限公司	2011-08-05	—	023-67995507
重庆皇极股权投资基金管理有限公司	2014-08-05	www.ff2020.com	023-60369188
重庆开创高新技术创业投资有限公司	2005-03-25	—	023-68601100
重庆科技风险投资有限公司	1993-01-16	www.cqskjvc.com	023-67516883

公司名称	成立时间	网址	传真
重庆科兴乾健创业投资有限公司	2011-12-01	—	—
重庆两江新区创新创业投资发展有限公司	2011-09-26	www.chinaljcapital.com	023-88283537
重庆临空开发投资集团有限公司	2014-11-24	—	023-61962565
重庆临云股权投资基金管理有限公司	2014-08-22	www.linyunziben.com	023-88796706
重庆诺鼎资产管理有限公司	2015-01-13	—	023-62388929
重庆勤晟股权投资基金管理有限公司	2013-06-14	—	—
重庆青商聚丰股权投资基金管理有限公司	2013-08-14	—	023-67100005
重庆清研股权投资基金管理中心（有限合伙）	2016-03-15	—	—
重庆润鑫股权投资基金管理有限公司	2014-11-12	—	—
重庆三屋领行投资有限公司	2014-02-18	—	—
重庆三屋领秀创业投资有限公司	2012-11-22	—	023-62611660
重庆三屋投资有限公司	2009-12-02	www.cqswtz.com	023-62611660
重庆深渝创新投资管理有限公司	2007-06-26	—	023-88609961
重庆盛美股权投资基金管理有限公司	2015-10-22	—	—
重庆市大渡口区科技产业创业投资有限公司	2013-01-21	—	023-67516108
重庆市虹陶投资股份有限公司	2015-01-15	www.httz818.com	023-67733366
重庆泰豪渝晟股权投资基金中心（有限合伙）	2011-08-05	—	023-63022990
重庆天使科技创业投资有限公司	2010-01-25	—	023-67516883
重庆天使投资引导基金有限公司	2009-07-17	www.cqvcgf.com	023-67516108
重庆天毅伟业医药投资管理中心（有限合伙）	2014-02-18	—	023-88537630
重庆同禾股权投资基金管理有限公司	2014-11-10	—	—
重庆同弘股权投资基金管理有限公司	2014-08-26	—	—
重庆拓景股权投资基金管理有限公司	2014-12-01	—	—
重庆万业美科股权投资基金管理有限公司	2011-01-30	www.wanyec.com	023-67741365
重庆文化股权投资基金管理有限责任公司	2012-10-22	—	—
重庆西证渝富股权投资基金管理有限公司	2012-05-10	—	023-67760963
重庆先石投资管理有限公司	2013-10-30	www.firststonegroup.com	—
重庆信展股权投资基金管理有限公司	2011-12-16	—	023-86879520
重庆兴农股权投资基金管理有限公司	2014-05-07	www.cqxnjj.com	—
重庆星耀辉腾股权投资基金管理有限公司	2016-02-01	—	023-88658889
重庆扬子创投股权投资基金管理有限公司	2014-11-04	www.yangtzefund.cn	023-81699090
重庆易一天使投资有限公司	2013-06-08	www.yiyitianshi.com	023-86788098
重庆英飞恒信投资管理有限公司	2013-08-13	—	023-62968915
重庆英飞尼迪创业投资中心（有限合伙）	2011-08-16	www.infinity-equity.com	023-63051585
重庆英飞尼迪投资管理有限公司	2011-11-11	www.infinity-equity.com	023-63051585

公司名称	成立时间	网址	传真
重庆圆基新能源创业投资基金合伙企业（有限合伙）	2011-01-27	—	023-63329022
重庆正银广惠股权投资基金管理有限公司	2011-08-15	www.cqzygh.com	023-63107199
重庆中福创新股权投资基金管理有限公司	2014-03-17	www.cftfund.com	023-63420250
重庆众利商贸流通产业股权投资基金管理有限公司	2014-12-17	—	023-63656929